D1615127

KING ALFRED'S COLLEGE
WINCHESTER

To be returned on or before the day marked
below :—

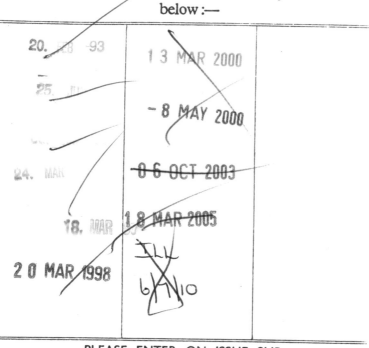

20. FEB 93

25. JU

24. MAR

18. MAR

2 0 MAR 1998

1 3 MAR 2000

- 8 MAY 2000

0 6 OCT 2003

1 8 MAR 2005

ILL

6/X/10

PLEASE ENTER ON ISSUE SLIP:

AUTHOR VAUGHAN

TITLE John the Fearless

ACCESSION No. 77353

John the Fearless

THE GROWTH OF BURGUNDIAN POWER

RICHARD VAUGHAN

LONGMAN
London and New York

Longman Group Limited London

*Associated companies, branches and representatives
throughout the world*

*Published in the United States of America
by Longman Inc., New York*

© Richard Vaughan 1966, 1979

First published 1966
First published in paperback 1979

British Library Cataloguing in Publication Data
Vaughan, Richard, b.1927
    John the Fearless.
    1. Burgundy – History
    944'.4'026   DC611.B78   78–40803
    ISBN 0–582–49047–2

Printed in Great Britain by
Richard Clay (The Chaucer Press) Ltd.
Bungay, Suffolk

Contents

List of Maps

Abbreviations

AB	*Annales de Bourgogne*
ABSHF	*Annuaire-bulletin de la Société de l'histoire de France*
ACFF	*Annales du Comité flamand de France*
ACO	Archives départementales de la Côte-d'Or, Dijon
AD	Archives communales, Dijon
ADN	Archives départementales du Nord, Lille
AGR	Archives générales du royaume, Brussels
AHAL	*Archives historiques, artistiques et littéraires*
AHVN	*Annalen des Historischen Vereins für den Niederrhein*
AM	*Annales du Midi*
AMSL	*Archives des missions scientifiques et littéraires*
AN	Archives nationales, Paris
AOG	*Archiv für österreichische Geschichte*
ASEB	*Annales de la Société d'émulation de Bruges*
ASHAG	*Annales de la Société d'histoire et d'archéologie de Gand*
ASRAB	*Annales de la Société royale d'archéologie de Bruxelles*
AUL	*Annales de l'Université de Lyon*
BA	Bibliothèque de l'Arsenal
BAAB	*Bulletin de l'Académie royale d'archéologie de Belgique*
BARB	*Bulletin de l'Académie royale de Belgique*
BCHDN	*Bulletin de la Commission historique du département du Nord*
BCRH	*Bulletin de la Commission royale d'histoire*
BD	Bibliothèque publique, Dijon
BEC	*Bibliothèque de l'École des chartes*
BEFAR	Bibliothèque des Écoles françaises d'Athènes et de Rome
BIHBR	*Bulletin de l'Institut historique belge de Rome*
BJR	*Bulletin of the John Rylands Library*
BM	British Museum
BM	*Bulletin monumental*
BN	Bibliothèque nationale, Paris
BSASH	*Bulletin de la Société d'agriculture, science, commerce et arts du département de la Haute-Saône*

viii

BSHAG	*Bulletin de la Société d'histoire et d'archéologie de Gand*
BSHF	*Bulletin de la Société de l'histoire de France*
BSHP	*Bulletin de la Société de l'histoire de Paris*
BSVAH	*Bulletin de la Société verviétoise d'archéologie et d'histoire*
BSY	*Bulletin de la Société des sciences historiques et naturelles de l'Yonne*
BV	Vatican Library
CDIHF	Collection de documents inédits sur l'histoire de France
CH	*Le Cabinet historique*
CHCLG	*Cahiers d'histoire publiés par les universités de Clermont, Lyon, Grenoble*
CRH	Commission royale d'histoire
DAEM	*Deutsches Archiv für Erforschung des Mittelalters*
DRA	*Deutsche Reichstagsakten*
EHR	*English historical review*
GBA	*Gazette des beaux-arts*
GSJ	*Galpin Society journal*
GWU	*Geschichte in Wissenschaft und Unterricht*
IAB, etc.	Printed inventories of archives, see below, pp. 297-8
IG	*L'Intermédiaire des généalogistes*
JS	*Journal des savants*
MA	*Le Moyen Âge*
MAA	*Mémoires de l'Académie d'Arras*
MAD	*Mémoires le l'Académie des sciences, arts et belles-lettres de Dijon*
MAH	*Mélanges d'archéologie et d'histoire. École française de Rome*
MARBL	Mémoires de l'Académie royale de Belgique, Lettres
MCACO	*Mémoires de la Commission des antiquités du département de la Côte-d'Or*
MSAF	*Mémoires de la Société nationale des antiquaires de France*
MSBGH	*Mémoires de la Société bourguignonne de géographie et d'histoire*
MSE	*Mémoires de la Société éduenne*
MSED	*Mémoires de la Société d'émulation du Doubs*
MSEJ	*Mémoires de la Société d'émulation du Jura*
MSHA Beaune	*Mémoires de la Société d'histoire, d'archéologie et de littérature de Beaune*
MSHDB	*Mémoires de la Société pour l'histoire du droit et des institutions des anciens pays bourguignons, comtois et romands*
MSHP	*Mémoires de la Société de l'histoire de Paris et de l'Île-de-France*
OED	*Oxford English Dictionary*
OW	*Ostdeutsche Wissenschaft. Jahrbuch des Ostdeutschen Kulturrates*

PRO	Public Record Office
PSHIL	Publications de la section historique de l'Institut grand-ducal de Luxembourg
PTSEC	*Positions des thèses soutenues à l'École des chartes*
RAAM	*Revue de l'art ancien et moderne*
RB	*Revue bourguignonne*
RBN	*Revue belge de numismatique*
RBPH	*Revue belge de philologie et d'histoire*
RCC	*Revue des cours et conférences*
RH	*Revue historique*
RHD	*Revue d'histoire diplomatique*
RHDFE	*Revue historique de droit français et étranger*
RHE	*Revue d'histoire ecclésiastique*
RHS	Royal Historical Society
RIHM	*Revue internationale d'histoire militaire*
RN	*Revue du Nord*
RQH	*Revue des questions historiques*
RS	Rolls Series
RUB	*Revue de l'Université de Bruxelles*
RV	*Rheinische Vierteljahrsblätter*
SHAWP	*Sitzungsberichte der Heidelberger Akademie der Wissenschaften. Philosophisch-historische Klasse*
SHF	Société de l'histoire de France
VKVAL	Verhandelingen van der Koninklijke Vlaamse Academie. Letteren
WG	*Die Welt als Geschichte*
WZ	*Westdeutsche Zeitschrift*
ZK	*Zeitschrift für Kirchengeschichte*

Introduction

This book, though it bears for title the name of one man, is not meant as a biography of John the Fearless. It is the second of a projected series of four volumes on the history of Burgundy under the Valois dukes. Not that I wish to belittle the dukes themselves, as persons. Far from it. I merely seek to warn the reader that my book has no hero. Its subject is not the life of a man, but the history of the Burgundian state from 1404 to 1419, when John the Fearless was its ruler.

Although it is always invidious to single out a few from among many, I cannot forbear here to salute the genius and industry of a handful of scholars whose studies of John the Fearless have alone made possible this contribution of mine, slender as it is compared to theirs. Those to whom I must primarily acknowledge my indebtedness are Alfred Coville, Léon Mirot and B. A. Pocquet du Haut-Jussé. The bibliography at the end of this book contains the names of many others whose works I have used and whose labours have facilitated my own.

I wish to thank all those who have helped me to write this book. Professor Bruce Dickins has kindly read the whole text through in typescript. Professor C. R. Cheney and Mr. C. A. J. Armstrong have given me advice and help on many occasions. Dr. P. King has assisted me with some difficulties of medieval Flemish; Mr. K. D. Simpkin with financial calculations. At Dijon, M. P. Quarré and Professor J. Richard have put their knowledge at my disposal; Professor F. Petri and Herr G. Hövelmann have given me copies of their papers; and I would like to thank Mrs. Stabel-Stasino and Mrs. Milis-Proost for lending me copies of their theses and permitting me to make use of them. At Lille, Professor F. Crouzet has been of great assistance to me, and I wish to thank, too, the authorities of the Centre Régional d'Études Historiques there for allowing me to make use of

xi

several theses mentioned in the notes. Finally, I extend my grateful thanks to the authorities of the libraries and archive repositories where I have been permitted to work.

RICHARD VAUGHAN

January 1965

Author's note to the paperback reprint

The only changes from the original edition made in this reprint are the omission of the nine illustrations and the references to them, and the correction of minor errors. Important corrections and revisions, in particular critical, and rightly so, of the figures on pp. 110–11 below, which have not been incorporated into the text of the reprint, will be found in W. Prevenier's review of *John the Fearless* in *RBPH* xlviii (1970), 510–12. He shows that my figures from Flanders need to be completely revised in the light of A. Zoete's unpublished Ghent University thesis of 1967 entitled 'De beden in het graafschap Vlaanderen onder Jan zonder Vrees, 1405–1419'.

One major collection of source material has appeared since *John the Fearless*: *Comptes généraux de l'Etat bourguignon entre 1416 et 1420*, ed. M. Mollat and others, 3 vols. Recueil des historiens de la France. Documents financiers. Paris, 1965–9.

Other relevant works published since 1966 or not noted in *John the Fearless* are:

Blockmans, W. P. 'La participation des sujets flamands à la politique monétaire des ducs de Bourgogne, 1384–1500'. *RBN* xix (1973), 103–34.

Buntinx, W. 'De enquête van Oudenburg. Hervorming van de repartitie van de beden in het graafschap Vlaanderen, 1408'. *BCRH* cxxxiv (1968), 75–137.

Cockshaw, P. 'Comptes généraux de l'état Bourguignon. A propos d'un livre récent'. *RBPH* xlv (1967), 490–3.

Cockshaw, P. 'Les premières monnaies de Jean sans Peur: l'émission de 1407'. *Cercle d'études numismatiques. Bulletin trimestriel* viii (1971), 41–52.

Cockshaw, P., 'Un Compte de la recette générale de Jean sans Peur retrouvé à Dijon'. *AB* xlix (1977), 24–30.

Grandeau, Y. 'Le dauphin Jean, duc de Touraine, fils de Charles VI (1338–1417). *Bulletin historique et philologique du Comité des travaux historiques* (1968), 665–728.

Lesur, S. 'La tour de Jean sans Peur'. *Document Archeologia* 1973 (3), 71–88.

Van der Wee, H. 'L'échec de la réforme monétaire de 1407 en Flandre vu par les marchands Italiens de Bruges'. *Studi in onore di A. Fanfani* iii. 579–89, Milan, 1962.

Willard, C. C. 'The manuscripts of Jean Petit's Justification. Some Burgundian propaganda methods of the early fifteenth century'. *Studi francesi* xiii (1969), 271–80.

RICHARD VAUGHAN

University of Hull

September 1978

CHAPTER ONE

John the Fearless and his Inheritance: 1404–9

The funeral of Philip the Bold

When Philip the Bold died in the Stag Inn at Hal, near Brussels, on 27 April 1404, his eldest son and successor John the Fearless and his second son Anthony were both with him. His funeral exhibited all the bizarre and extravagant pomp which was customary on such occasions, and which the Valois dukes of Burgundy were so adept at deploying. The day after Philip's death his receiver-general, Jehan Chousat, opened a special account of the funeral expenses, which were entered in meticulous detail on a parchment roll eight feet long and one foot wide, still preserved in the archives at Dijon.[1]

First, the traditional opening and embalming of the corpse was performed. The entrails were buried on the spot, in the church of Our Lady at Hal; the heart was despatched to the abbey of St. Denis, outside Paris, to be placed alongside the mortal remains of Philip the Bold's royal ancestors, kings of France. His body, clothed in the habit of a Carthusian monk, was wrapped in thirty-two ells of waxed cloth and three cowhides, and placed in a leaden coffin weighing 700 lb. While the morticians were at their grim work, over 2,000 ells of black cloth were ordered from Brussels; steps were taken to pay for the immediate expenses of the funeral by pawning up to 6,000-gold-crowns-worth of the late duke's plate and jewellery;[2] and word was sent to Dino Rapondi at Bruges to supply urgently a number of cloths of Lucca, to present to the twelve churches where the duke's body would rest on its 300-mile journey from Hal to Dijon.

The cortège left Hal on 1 May and, avoiding the direct route across

---

[1] ACO B310; see *Itinéraires*, 574–9 and Plancher, iii. 200–2.
[2] The crown or *écu à la couronne* was a gold coin first minted by Charles VI in 1385 with the value of one *livre* of Tours, weighing 4·079 gm.

Hainault, travelled through Philip the Bold's own territories, via Courtrai, Oudenaarde and Lille, to Douai. The hearse was draped with a magnificent pall of cloth-of-gold edged with black, adorned, in the centre, with a crimson velvet cross. At each corner fluttered a blue banner emblazoned with the arms of Philip the Bold. It was drawn by six horses caparisoned in black, and followed by sixty mourners or *pleurants* dressed in black gowns with ample hoods. The procession was accompanied as far as Douai by John and Anthony with their personal attendants; by the counts of Richemont and Ostrevant; by sixteen chaplains of the dead duke's chapel; by leading members of his household and administration; and by six principal representatives of the Flemish nobility. All were attired in a solemn livery of black. At Douai, on the borders of Philip the Bold's northern territories, his body rested for ten days, while John the Fearless and Anthony left with their personal followings for Arras, where their widowed mother, Duchess Margaret of Male, was awaiting them.

When the funeral procession continued on its way across the 150 miles of French territory which separated Flanders from the northern frontier of the duchy of Burgundy, it was much reduced in size, and was now led no longer by men, but by boys, for the place of John and Anthony was taken now by their thirteen-year-old brother, Philip, later count of Nevers, and the ten-year-old Arthur, count of Richemont. At the abbey of St. Seine in Burgundy, where it arrived on 28 May, the cortège was halted for nearly three weeks while John the Fearless transacted certain pressing affairs in Paris, including the disbanding of the dead duke's household staff, amounting to some 180 persons.[1] Meanwhile, the municipality of Dijon, the capital of Burgundy, had resolved to honour the deceased duke. At Val-Suzon, ten miles north-east of the city, the funeral cortège was to be met and augmented by the mayor and aldermen of Dijon, 100 burgesses and 100 poor men arrayed in black; while from the outskirts of the city to the Charterhouse of Champmol, all the clergy of Dijon were to take part in the procession. Here, in the church which he himself had founded, Philip the Bold was finally interred, on 16 June 1404, in the centre of the choir.

John the Fearless before 1404

The childhood of John the Fearless, eldest son of Philip the Bold and Margaret of Male, was spent in the duchy of Burgundy, mostly in the ducal château at Rouvres, where he was born on 28 May 1371. The

---

[1] Mirot, *AB* xi (1939), 132–5.

few scraps of information that have survived from this period are of a domestic and trivial nature, and it was not until 1384 that John began to play a part in the affairs of state. Until his father-in-law Louis of Male's death on 30 January 1384, Philip the Bold possessed only the duchy of Burgundy; but then the five counties of Flanders, Artois, Rethel, Nevers and Burgundy were added to the duchy, and almost at once, on 16 March 1384, provision was made for John by the gift to him of the county of Nevers.[1] On his thirteenth birthday, 28 May 1384, he joined his father in Paris for a first brief visit to the French capital. A year later, on 12 April 1385, he was married in Cambrai cathedral to Margaret of Bavaria.

Little is known for certain of John's activities in the eleven years between his wedding in 1385, when he was thirteen, and his departure on crusade in April 1396, aged twenty-four. He did not have a household of his own and his apanage of Nevers existed only on paper, for he neither administered it nor enjoyed its revenues. He received a modest allowance from his father, and he and his wife were normally attached either to Philip the Bold's or to Margaret of Male's household. Although he was given no responsibilities of his own, apart from a brief period as his father's lieutenant in Burgundy in 1385, John was thoroughly initiated, during these years, into the arts of government and even of warfare. He accompanied his father on the French campaign against the duke of Guelders in autumn 1388, and was with him in Paris and Burgundy during much of 1388 and 1389 and again in the autumn and winter of 1392 and the early part of 1395. When he was not in France with his father, John was usually in Burgundy, and it seems that it was not until the summer of 1394 that he paid his first visit to the Low Countries and Artois. But this must have been a peculiarly instructive occasion, for not only did he visit the capitals of Artois and French-speaking Flanders, Arras and Lille, and lay the foundation-stone of the tour de Bourgogne at Sluis, he also participated, with his mother, in some difficult negotiations with the delegates of the powerful Flemish towns.[2] The detailed reports which he sent to his father on this occasion show that John the Fearless had

---

[1] Plancher, iii. no. 77.
[2] *Handelingen*, no. 291. For the next sentence, see ADN B18822, fos. 153, 164, 168, 171, 270 and 284; partly printed and analysed in *Docs. pour servir à l'histoire de la Maison de Bourgogne en Brabant et en Limbourg*, nos. 19, 22, 26 and 29. For this and the preceding paragraph, see *Itinéraires* and Vaughan, *P. the Bold*, 66-7, 86-7, and 110 and n. 1. For the next two paragraphs, see Vaughan, *P. the Bold*, 59-78 and Mirot, *ABSHF* (1938), 129-245.

already acquired a considerable knowledge of the complex affairs of the county of Flanders.

The crusade which John led on his father's behalf in 1396 to Hungary against the Ottoman Turks ended in defeat and disaster. John himself and a handful of companions survived the bloody field of Nicopolis, but were captured, and remained for some time prisoners of Sultan Bayazid before the 200,000-ducat ransom demanded for them could be paid or pledged. Eventually, John the Fearless reached Dijon on 22 February 1398, nearly two years after he had left; and on 22 March he joined his father at Ghent for a joint tour of the principal towns of Flanders and Brabant. Subsequent military history shows conclusively that John had not failed, at Nicopolis, to learn some important lessons on the art of warfare from the fatal errors and vain, uncalculating precipitation of the military advisers his father had appointed over his head: he became the only one of the four Valois dukes of Burgundy who really knew how to use an army.

In the six years between his return from Nicopolis in 1398 and his father's death in April 1404, John the Fearless spent rather more than half his time with Philip the Bold in Paris, at the centre of both French and Burgundian affairs, but he was by no means entirely dependent on his father. He had been provided, in 1398, with a separate household of his own and, though he still received no income from the county of Nevers, adequate funds were made available by his father to his *maître de la chambre aux deniers*, Jehan de Velery, for his own and his household's use. Besides his prolonged stays in Paris and elsewhere in France with his father, John, who was evidently very fond of his mother,[1] stayed with her at Arras at least annually. But, though he visited Lille, the administrative capital of the northern territories, in these years, he never once, after the summer of 1398, went as far as Flemish-speaking Flanders. On the other hand he renewed his acquaintance with the duchy of Burgundy, enjoying three lengthy stays there with his wife and children in 1399–1400 and 1403. In fact, John was the only member of the ducal family who did visit the duchy in these years and, when he was there, he acted as his father's representative, presiding over meetings of the ducal council at Dijon and of the three Estates of the duchy, and receiving ambassadors.

Before 1404 then, although John the Fearless had lived very much in the shadow of his father, he had certainly not been deprived of all political responsibilities. He had become familiar with the royal court and government at Paris and with all parts of the Burgundian terri-

[1] See his letter of 30 June 1394 to her, ADN B18822, f. 164.

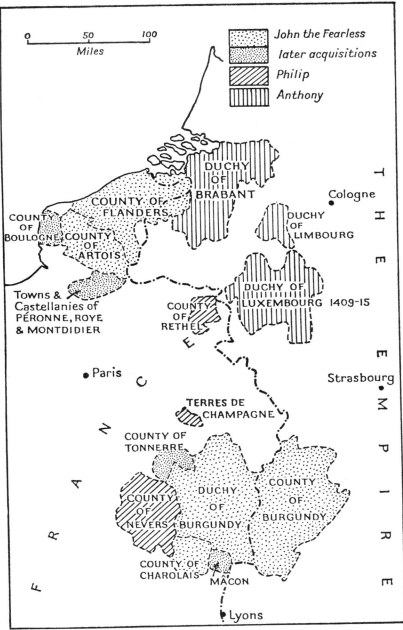

Map labels:

0 50 100
Miles

John the Fearless
later acquisitions
Philip
Anthony

DUCHY OF BRABANT

Cologne

THE

COUNTY OF FLANDERS

DUCHY OF LIMBOURG

COUNTY OF BOULOGNE

COUNTY OF ARTOIS

EMPIRE

Towns & Castellanies of PÉRONNE, ROYE & MONTDIDIER

COUNTY OF RETHEL

DUCHY OF LUXEMBOURG 1409-15

Paris

Strasbourg

TERRES DE CHAMPAGNE

COUNTY OF TONNERRE

FRANCE

COUNTY OF NEVERS

DUCHY OF BURGUNDY

COUNTY OF BURGUNDY

COUNTY OF CHAROLAIS

MÂCON

Lyons

I. The division of Burgundian territories between John the Fearless and his brothers, and territories later acquired by John the Fearless

tories;[1] and he had led a crusade. Now, at the age of thirty-three he became a ruler.

The inheritance

The essence of Philip the Bold's plan for the future of his territories, which was defined in detail in the partition act of 1401 and only slightly modified after his death, was the transference of a more or less unified Burgundian state to his eldest son John. How exactly was this transference effected?

When Philip the Bold died on 27 April 1404 his widow, Margaret of Male, became sole ruler of the three major constituent pieces of the superb inheritance which she had brought to him on her father's death twenty years before: the counties of Flanders, Artois and Burgundy. The other sections of her inheritance, consisting of the counties of Nevers and Rethel, were retained by John and Anthony respectively, while John now succeeded his father as duke of Burgundy. Of the Burgundian lands in Champagne, those which formed part of Margaret of Male's inheritance—Isle-Aumont, Villemaur, Chaource—returned to her and later passed to John and Anthony's younger brother Philip, while those which had been ceded temporarily to Philip the Bold by Charles VI—Beaufort, Nogent-l'Artaud, Lassicourt, Soulaines—returned to the French crown and were thence transferred to the king of Navarre.[2] Of Philip the Bold's other territorial acquisitions, the county of Charolais in the south formed part of the duchy of Burgundy and passed with it to John on his father's death, while the duchy of Limbourg, in the north, returned on Philip's death to his aunt, the eighty-two-year-old Duchess Joan of Brabant, from whom he had acquired it in 1396. Philip the Bold had tried, but failed, to annex the duchy of Brabant to the Burgundian state; instead, he had had to rest content with the designation, and acceptance by those concerned, of his second son Anthony as heir to Brabant. It was while engaged in negotiations in April 1404, with the

[1] He had not, as Calmette states (*Grands ducs*, 104), 'surtout vécu en Flandre'. Indeed he knew Flanders much less well than any other Burgundian territory, and had only twice, in 1394 and 1398, visited Flemish-speaking Flanders. We may well question in what sense it is true to say that 'he spoke Flemish' (Calmette, *Grands ducs*. 104 and *Algemene geschiedenis*, iii. 218); probably not at all, except for his own Flemish motto *ich houd* = 'I hold', and a few words of greeting.
[2] For the former, see Plancher, iii. 212–13, *IADNB* i (2), 75, and BN Coll. de Bourg. 72, f. 326; for the latter, Relig. de St. Denys, iii. 150–6. See, too, Vaughan, *P. the Bold*, 102 and Boutiot, *Troyes*, ii. 304–5 and 330.

aged Duchess Joan, about the future of Brabant, that Philip had con-
tracted his fatal illness. These negotiations, which concerned nothing
less than the abdication of Joan in favour of Anthony, were implemented immediately after Philip's death. On 7 May 1404 Joan transferred her duchy to his widow, Margaret of Male, and, on 19 May,
Margaret appointed Anthony governor or *ruwaert* of Brabant. A few
months later, on 2 September 1404, the title of duke of Limbourg was
granted by Joan to Anthony.[1]

To a superficial observer, the division of the Burgundian state in
1404 between Margaret of Male, ruling the three counties of Flanders,
Artois and Burgundy; John duke of Burgundy and count of Nevers;
and Anthony, heir to Brabant and Limbourg, might be taken for
dismemberment. But this was not the case, for Brabant never had
formed part of the Burgundian state, and John and his mother worked
so closely together, and the administrative structure of the state was
modified by them in such a palpably temporary manner, that there
was no question of its permanent division between them. By and
large, things went on as before, and Margaret of Male remained at
Arras, as she had done in the last few years of Philip's reign, to keep
an eye on the northern group of territories while he was occupied in
Paris; remained, that is, until 21 March 1405, when she died suddenly
in her hôtel at Arras.

The skill, unanimity and decision with which the surviving members of Philip the Bold's family coped with the complex situation
brought about by his death, was repeated a year later on that of his
widow.[2] Again, Philip the Bold's plans were, in the main, respected.
His three sons assembled at Lille to bury their mother in St. Peter's
Church next to her father Louis of Male on 25 March 1405, and they
remained together in conference at Arras until 11 April, when a
detailed and definitive partition treaty made between them was published. Philip the Bold had intended his youngest son, Philip, to be
given the county of Nevers as soon as his eldest son, John, inherited
Flanders from his mother: this intention was now honoured, and
Philip duly signed the partition treaty as count of Nevers. Philip the

---

[1] These and related documents are printed in *Brabantsche Yeesten*, ii. nos.
167-71 and 176. For this paragraph in general, see de Lichtervelde, *Grand
commis*, 113-15 and Vaughan, *P. the Bold*, 101-2, and, for the next, Mirot,
ABSHF (1938), 209-19 and Pocquet, *MSHDB* iv (1937), 54-5.
[2] For this and the next paragraph see de Lichtervelde, *Grand Commis*,
125-30, 142-3 and 146-7. The text of the treaty of 11 April 1405 is in ADN
B1600, fos. 26-7b; see, too, ACO B1543, f. 62b and B1547, f. 145b.

Bold had also intended that Anthony should not only retain Rethel, but receive Artois as well, until such time as, after the death of Duchess Joan, he became duke of Brabant. This intention was modified: to avoid unnecessary changes of ruler and to promote good relations between the brothers, it was John who now inherited the county of Artois from his mother; though only on condition that Anthony did obtain possession of Brabant, and in return for an annual payment until that event of 32,800 crowns—a sum which represented the annual revenues of Artois.

Duchess Joan had not ceded Brabant to the house of Burgundy without financial considerations. Indeed, the word 'sale' would perhaps be more accurate in this connection than 'cession', for Margaret of Male had promised Joan repayment of her numerous debts, as well as an annual pension for life of 28,000 crowns. In the treaty of 11 April detailed provision was made for the allocation of these heavy financial commitments between all three brothers, though it was agreed that the contributions of John and Philip to the repayment of Joan's debts would cease as soon as Anthony took possession of Brabant. When, in the same treaty, arrangements were made for the sale of part of the family jewellery, the three brothers agreed that the 'debts of Brabant' should have priority to the extent of the first 25,000 crowns realized from the proceeds, and this was stated to be for the benefit of all three brothers, and to ensure the Burgundian succession to Brabant.

The transference of the duchy of Brabant to a junior branch of the Burgundian ducal house was at last achieved in December 1406, when, after Joan's death, and after the Estates of Brabant had demanded and obtained from John a repetition of the formal renunciation of his claims to Brabant which he had already made to his brothers, Anthony was proclaimed duke. But the final event in the complex story of the transference of the Burgundian heritage to John and his brothers took place on 27 January 1407, when Anthony ceded the county of Rethel to his younger brother Philip. No further changes between the three brothers took place after this: John retained Flanders, Artois and the two Burgundies; Anthony kept the duchies of Brabant and Limbourg; and Philip remained count of Nevers and of Rethel. Again, there was no question of a division of the Burgundian state, of the power which had been created and maintained by Philip the Bold: it was ruled by John the Fearless.

The two Burgundies to 1409

John the Fearless visited Burgundy on six occasions during his reign as duke, and three of these visits, averaging two months each in duration, took place in his first three years: in June–July 1404, in winter 1404-5, and in July–September 1406. After this initial period of sporadic contact between the duchy and its ruler, it seems that John resolved to groom his eldest son Philip, count of Charolais, who succeeded him in 1419 as Philip the Good, to fulfil the rôle of his lieutenant in the duchy, for the eleven-year-old boy was sent to Burgundy with his four unmarried sisters in the summer of 1407,[1] 'to enjoy better air and nourishment, which they would not have in Flanders, and also to enable our aforesaid son to get to know the nobles of Burgundy'.

The youthful count of Charolais remained in Burgundy throughout 1408 and the first half of 1409 and, in the intervals between hunting and learning to play the harp, he began to act politically on behalf of his father. He attended a meeting of the Beaune *Parlement* on 8 October 1407; he was occupied in June 1408 with a disputed mayoral election at Beaune; above all, he received the lordship of Besançon for his father on 2 October 1408. Yet, for some reason, John's plans were changed, for in May 1409 he installed his duchess Margaret of Bavaria in the duchy of Burgundy, while Philip was transferred to Ghent. Her rule in the duchy will be the subject of a later chapter: here we are concerned only with the two Burgundies in the first five years of John's reign, up to the summer of 1409.

For the most part, this was a time of peace in both the Burgundies, and we hear of no military or even quasi-military officers, either governors or captains-general, being appointed during these years in the duchy, though the marshal of Burgundy, Jehan III de Vergy, lord of Fouvent, continued in his office of governor of the county. The occasional alarms caused by rumours of troops near the frontiers normally came to nothing, but the usual precautions were taken. In March 1406 the proceeds from judicial fines, confiscations, pardons, legitimations and ennoblements were allocated to the repair and upkeep of the ducal castles, as they had been under Philip the Bold; on 17 July 1407 this allocation was confirmed and one of the ducal *maîtres*

---

[1] He was there in October 1407, Plancher, iii. 249, but at Douai in March 1407, BN Coll. de Bourg. 54, f. 130. The quotation following is from ACO B1551, f. 3. For the rest of the paragraph, see *Itinéraires*, especially 589 and 594; Plancher, iii. 249, 256-7 and 243-4; and Bazin, *MSHA Beaune* (1897), 65-6.

des comptes at Dijon, Nicolas le Vaillant, was specially commissioned to visit the castles and other buildings and see that these funds were properly used for their repair.[1] Moreover, the circumstances and manner in which the castles might be used as places of retreat by the inhabitants were defined in detail in the important ducal defence *ordonnance* of 31 August 1408, a document which was much used in the fifteenth century and reprinted in the sixteenth and seventeenth centuries. On the same day, ducal officers were warned not to hinder the inhabitants from carrying arms.

The tranquillity of the two Burgundies during the opening years of John's reign is reflected in the absence of serious quarrels between the ducal administration and the towns, and in the ease with which John was able to raise finance from the inhabitants. The most serious dispute with any town was a trivial one with Dijon over the liability of the duke's *gens des comptes* there to contribute towards the present of gilt plate made by the town to the duke on his state entry in June 1404. It was resolved by the duke in January 1405 in favour of his officers.[2] As to finance, the subvention or *aide* of 36,000 francs voted by the duchy on 6 December 1405 was levied in 1406 and 1407, and *aides* were also voted by the county of Burgundy in 1406 and 1408, the latter of 9,000 *livres* of Tours. At the same time, money was raised in both the duchy and county by means of forced loans: in the county, 6,000 francs were collected in this way in September 1405 and sent off in barrels to Paris; in the duchy, over 10,000 francs was borrowed in 1405 and a further 16,000 *livres* of Tours in 1407. Even the turbulent nobility of the county of Burgundy remained tolerably quiescent in these years, and many of them obeyed the summons to support Duke John in arms in Paris in autumn 1405. One serious incident, however, had repercussions throughout John's reign.

Some time during the winter of 1406–7, while John's wife the duchess Margaret of Bavaria was holding court at Douai, a young noble from the county of Burgundy, Louis de Chalon, who had become count of Tonnerre in 1398 and who was a brother of Jehan de Chalon, prince of Orange, fell in love with an Aragonese lady-in-

[1] BN. Coll. de Bourg. 54, f. 132; Plancher, iii. 245 and 318–19 and Coll. de Bourg. 54, fos. 176–7. For the next sentence, see *Ords. franc-comtoises*, no. 17 and Coll. de Bourg. 54, f. 217.
[2] Plancher, iii. 216–17, and no. 233. For what follows, see BN Coll. de Bourg. 54, fos. 102–4; Plancher, iii. 225–6, 231–3 and 252; Billioud, *États de Bourgogne*, 382; Clerc, *Franche-comté*, ii. 290; and Humbert, *Finances de Dijon*, 216.

waiting of Margaret of Bavaria called Juana de Perellos.[1] Her charms proved irresistible, and his passion drove Louis de Chalon to an unpardonable indiscretion: he broke into the duchess's apartments at night; carried off his paramour by force of arms; and installed her as his mistress in the castle of Maulne in his county of Tonnerre, which lay on the north-west frontier of the duchy of Burgundy. Not that this sort of thing was particularly unusual, but Louis had insulted the duchess of Burgundy. Moreover, he happened to be married to Marie de la Trémoille. John the Fearless was bound to take action. After three summonses against him had failed to produce the culprit, the duke, on 13 March 1407, ordered the confiscation of all his lands in the duchy of Burgundy and, that same summer, he was banished from the county of Burgundy and his lands there seized. Louis de Chalon's reaction to these measures was to apply to the papal court for the annulment of his marriage with Marie de la Trémoille; to raise funds by the sale of his lands, including the county of Tonnerre, which John the Fearless ordered his *gens des comptes* at Dijon to bid for when it came up for auction in August 1407; and finally, in 1408, he appeared in arms in the county of Burgundy. Although he was pardoned by John the Fearless in 1410, Louis de Chalon had been thoroughly alienated and, as we shall see in a later chapter, he became from then on one of the leading supporters of the Armagnacs in the two Burgundies.

In the two Burgundies, John the Fearless inherited from his father an effective administration run by experienced personnel; centralized in the loosely combined *chambre des comptes* and council at Dijon; and regulated or modified by ducal *ordonnances*, which often applied to both duchy and county.[2] The system seems to have been working well, but John the Fearless was determined to improve it, and his reforming zeal found expression in a series of projects and *ordonnances* some of which, like his *ordonnance* separating the Dijon council from the *chambre des comptes*, were in practice ignored; while others, like his application of the duchy castellanies and provostships, which had hitherto been farmed out, to the domain, and his reorganization of the *tabellionages*,[3] had to be repealed because they were found to be

[1] For this paragraph, see Petit, *BSY* xlv (1891), 247-315.
[2] See Vaughan, *P. the Bold*, 114-26 and, for the next sentence, Plancher, iii. no. 235, *ord.* of 4 August 1404; Plancher, iii. no. 241 and p. 245; *Ords. des ducs*, no. 15; BN Coll. de Bourg. 54, f. 174; and Simonnet, *Docs. inédits*, Book I and Appendix.
[3] *Tabellionage*, or office of tabellion, an 'official scribe having some of the functions of a notary' (*O.E.D.*).

wholly impracticable; while still others, like the defence *ordonnance* of 31 August 1408 and the reforms of the Dijon *chambre des comptes*, proved of permanent value. These last constituted a remarkable and not wholly unsuccessful attempt to modernize the *chambre des comptes* and speed up its auditing procedure by dividing it into several *bureaux* or offices; by appointing a new official, the *auditeur*; and by some drastic measures to persuade the receivers to make up their accounts and submit them to the *chambre des comptes* for audit as soon as possible after the end of the financial year.[1] Measures against lethargic accounting officers became particularly severe at the end of the period under review here when, in March 1409, John the Fearless ordered all the Burgundian receivers and other accounting officers who had accounts from the period before 1 January 1408 still not audited, to be suspended from their offices until they had made up their accounts and had them audited and passed by the *chambre des comptes*. As a result, at least twenty-two officers were ordered to be suspended—a figure which comprised the great majority of the ducal financial officers in the duchy.

The judicial as well as the financial administration of the two Burgundies received attention early in John's reign as duke. On 15 June 1405, following a precedent set by his father Philip the Bold in 1381,[2] he appointed a special commission of *réformateurs généraux*, under the presidency of Antoine Chuffaing, bailiff of Dijon, to supplement the ordinary judicial administration. This reforming commission, which seems to have been mainly a device for raising funds, was given sweeping powers to 'gather information and enquire into the truth concerning all crimes and excesses perpetrated by our officers in the duchy and county of Burgundy; to cause all malefactors against our officers and subjects generally to be arrested; to ascertain without any ceremony or form of process the truth about all excesses, abuses, crimes, outrages and injuries; to carefully punish and correct all malefactors and delinquents, either in criminal or civil law; to deprive or suspend from their offices any officers charged under the terms of this reformation . . . until we provide otherwise. . . .' In the year after its installation, this reforming commission lost its president,

[1] *Ordonnances* of 14 August 1404, 21 February 1406 and 26 February 1407: see Plancher, iii. 239–40 and no. 252; Lameere, *Grand conseil*, xii–xiii; Andt, *Chambre des comptes*, 160–2. For the *auditeur*, first appointed on 17 May 1406, see ACO B15, f. 71b and d'Arbaumont, *Armorial*, 313. For what follows, see ACO B15, f. 83a–b.

[2] Vignier, *MSHDB* xix (1957), 117. For the reforming commission, see *Ords. des ducs*, no. 16.

who died on 6 July 1406, but it gained a *procureur général*, elected by the commission itself on 5 May.[1] Its subsequent history is so far shrouded in obscurity.

One administrative project put forward in these years was far more ambitious than any of those so far mentioned: this was nothing less than a scheme to set up a new and separate administrative capital for the county of Burgundy at Besançon, complete with its own *Parlement* and *chambre des comptes*.[2] This radical plan was not entirely due to Duke John's inventive genius. It happened like this.

The lordship of Besançon, an imperial city which was not part of the county of Burgundy though it was its natural capital, had for long been shared and disputed by city and archbishop. On 28 July 1405 John the Fearless renewed his father's close relations with the city of Besançon by agreeing to retain its *garde*, that is, agreeing to protect it, in return for a continuance of the 500 francs per annum it had paid for this service to Philip the Bold. A year later the new archbishop, the obstinate and opinionated Thibaud de Rougemont, had fallen foul of the city. A juridical dispute led to his flight to the archiepiscopal fortress of Gy; to the confiscation of his share of the lordship, or regalian rights, by the magistrates; and to their consequent excommunication by the archbishop. While the city of Besançon lay under interdict, a ducal councillor living there, Guy Armenier, persuaded the magistrates to offer the lordship of the city to Duke John, provided he agreed to set up a *Parlement* and *chambre des comptes* there for the county of Burgundy. John the Fearless signed a treaty to this effect with the Besançon magistrates on 12 October 1407 which was confirmed at John's request on 28 February 1408 by Wenzel, one of the rival German rulers who had been crowned king of the Romans and aspired at that time to the imperial throne and title. On 19 July 1408 a detailed *ordonnance* was promulgated, setting up at Besançon all the governmental organs necessary to establish the county as a quite separate entity from the duchy: a supreme court of justice or *Parlement* (to meet shortly under the presidency of Guy Armenier); a council (president, Armenier); a chancery (governor, the ubiquitous Armenier); and a *chambre des comptes*. Thus was the higher administration of the duchy to be duplicated in the county: Besançon to

[1] *Mémoires*, ii. 98 n.b. and Lameere, *Grand conseil*, xi–xii.
[2] Plancher, iii. 257, 271–5 and nos. 259 and 266; Clerc, *Franche-Comté*, ii. 287 and n. 1, 290–3, 296–307; *Ords. franc-comtoises*, nos. 16 and 20; Piquard, *MSED* (10) i (1931), 86–101 and idem *PTSEC* (1929), 193–200; Blondeau, *MSEJ* (11) 4 (1926), 185–203 and *MSED* (10) viii (1938), 56–76.

become the equivalent of Dijon, and the county to lose its hitherto subordinate status.

While John's son and heir, Philip, count of Charolais, formally took possession of the city on 2 October 1408, Jehan Bonost, newly-appointed *maître* of the Besançon *chambre des comptes*, was busy inventorying all the documents and registers at Dijon which concerned the county. On 6 January 1409 he moved house to Besançon with his wife and children.[1] But opposition to the project was gathering force in all quarters, and on 24 April 1409 eight of the leading ducal councillors and officers in the two Burgundies submitted a memorandum to John the Fearless protesting against it and criticizing in detail the terms of his treaty with Besançon. A month later, the duke gave way; Bonost was recalled; the *ordonnance* of 19 July 1408 was repealed; a treaty was negotiated with Thibaud de Rougemont which had the effect of dividing the lordship of Besançon between archbishop and duke; and the magistrates and inhabitants of Besançon were left in the lurch. In spite of this failure, the scheme was mooted again shortly afterwards, but the subsequent history of this affair must be left till Chapter Seven.

Flanders: 1405–9

In the last two centuries of the middle ages the Flemish were politically organized in the so-called Four Members of Flanders: Ghent, Bruges, Ypres and the Franc or castellany of Bruges. Assemblies or *parlementen* of these Four Members met at frequent intervals to discuss their own affairs and those of their ruler. They had become the accepted representative organ in Flanders. They spoke and voted taxes for the whole populace. It was they who, within days of the news of his mother's death, sent a deputation to John the Fearless at Arras at the end of March 1405, asking him to come to Flanders, to conclude a treaty with the English, and to abolish or reform the ducal council at Lille.[2] By the time he reached Ghent at Easter for his state entry there, the Four Members had elaborated and added to these demands, and they then insisted on their engrossment, together with John's replies, in a formal written instrument. This remarkable document, which sets the tone for John the Fearless's subsequent relations with the Four Members, may be summarized in part as follows:[3]

1. *Request:* That the duke resides with the duchess in some Flemish

---

[1] ACO B1559, f. 64.   [2] *Précis analytique*, (2) i. 84 and *IAB* iii. 506.
[3] *Verzameling van XXIV origineele charters*, no. 7; Blommaert, *Belgisch museum*, i (1837), 83–98; *IAB* iii. 509–15.

town of his choice and that, if he has to be absent, she be empowered to rule in his place with the help of councillors who are familiar with Flanders.

Reply: That the duke has always been extremely fond of Flanders and has had great pleasure in visiting it, all the more so now that he has become its lord and prince. He fully intends to reside in Flanders. When he must be absent, he will leave his wife there with full powers and councillors familiar with the country; and if, when he is away, he should find it necessary, whether for the wedding of one of his children or for some other reason, to have his wife with him, he will leave some of his councillors to look after things in Flanders.

2. *Request:* That the duke maintains the privileges, rights, laws and customs of the Flemish, and that the council of Flanders be transferred across the Lys into Flemish Flanders and that its proceedings be held in Flemish.

Reply: That the duke intends to maintain the privileges, rights, laws and customs of the Flemish and, when he has wound up affairs in the council at Lille, to install it in Flemish Flanders.

3. *Request:* That the duke carry into effect without delay the treaty now under negotiation between Flanders and England for the protection of the maritime trade on which the prosperity of Flanders depends.

Reply: That, directly after the death of his mother, the duke did his best, both at Paris with the king and with the English ambassadors, to further the treaty; and that because he wishes to support the commerce and industry of his land and thus to increase its wealth and the wealth of his subjects, he will continue to do all in his power to bring the negotiations for a treaty to a successful conclusion.

4. *Request:* That all requests made either to the duke, the duchess or the council of Flanders by the Four Members of Flanders or any one of them, be answered in Flemish.

Reply: Agreed.

Thus, with evasive but affirmative replies, John parried the thrusts which had been made, in similar terms and on many occasions, at his father, Philip the Bold. But, while Philip had invariably ignored the Flemish demands, his son tried to meet them. During the whole of the last four years of his reign, Philip the Bold had spent only about a week in Flanders, and nobody was appointed to deputize for him there; but John, during the first four years of his reign, was in Flanders for a total of nearly a year, and his wife resided at Ghent on his behalf for almost two years. Between the reigns of the two dukes was the short, single-year reign of Duchess Margaret of Male, who, though she was pestered with Flemish requests to reside in Flanders,[1] remained firmly in her hôtel at Arras, the capital of Artois.

The residence in Flanders of John the Fearless and Margaret of Bavaria in the period under review in the present chapter, that is, between his accession in March 1405 and the summer of 1409, may conveniently be tabulated as follows:

Year	John	Margaret
1405	April–June	
	July–August	
	(9 weeks)	
1406	October[2]	
	(1 week)	
1407	February–April	April–December
	May–August	
	December–January '08	
	(total of *c.* 6 months)	
1408	July–September	Whole year
	October–November	
	(11 weeks)	
1409		January–February

The fact is, that in spite of continued Flemish protests against absentee rulers, a marked change occurred with the accession of John the Fearless. Before then, Flemish complaints were abundantly justified. After 1405, however, irregular, but often quite prolonged, personal contacts were maintained between the rulers and their Flemish subjects. Moreover, Duchess Margaret of Bavaria did not stay in Ghent doing nothing: she actually ruled. The bailiffs' and other Flemish accounts make this abundantly clear,[3] though the following surviving fragment of her correspondence with the bailiff of Bruges perhaps illustrates the more frivolous side of her government of Flanders in these years:

The duchess of Burgundy, countess of Flanders, to Robert de Capples, bailiff of Bruges. Ghent, 4 November 1407.

Dear and well-beloved, we have received the parrot you sent us, which arrived in good fettle, and we are grateful for the trouble you have taken. But we pray you earnestly, as soon as you've seen these letters, to pur-

---

[1] Prevenier, *Leden en Staten*, 204–6. For her movements, see e.g., *IADNB* vii. 218–25 and viii. 1–2.

[2] *IAB* iv. 5–6; otherwise, *Itinéraires*.

[3] Especially the account of the receiver of fines of the council of Flanders for April 1407–December 1408, AGR CC21788. The letter which follows is AGR Trésor de Flandre, (1) 2514.

chase at Bruges or elsewhere . . . the smallest monkey you can find and send it to us as soon as possible, letting us know what it cost so that we can refund you. God keep you.   J. de Maroilles

The government of Flanders was at this time based on two central institutions which exercised jurisdiction in judicial, administrative and financial matters over Flanders proper or *Flandre flamigante*; Lille, Douai and Orchies or *Flandre gallicante*; the county of Artois; and Malines. These institutions were the *chambre du conseil* or council of Flanders, the special judicial sessions of which, called the *audience*, became infrequent early in John the Fearless's reign and ceased altogether in 1409, and the *chambre des comptes*. In Philip the Bold's reign, both council and *comptes* were at Lille, and both conducted their business in French, but in August 1405 John the Fearless, in keeping with his earlier promise to the Flemish and in the interests, no doubt, of administrative convenience, transferred the council of Flanders from Lille to Oudenaarde, and at Oudenaarde it sat, in the house of Jan van de Walle, from 18 August 1405 until 21 May 1407.[1]

The everyday work of the council at Oudenaarde is revealed in all its complex detail by the receiver of its judicial fines, Guiot de Boeye, who, fortunately for us, took the trouble to record in his accounts the dates and summarized contents of all the council's outgoing correspondence. Much of its work concerned the Four Members of Flanders. It received their complaints and spied on their activities, and reported on both to the duke in Paris. It intervened in a dispute between two of the Four Members, Bruges and the Franc of Bruges; kept an eye on the movements of the English fleet in the autumn of 1406; and dealt with complaints by the Hanseatic League of the molestation of their merchants by Flemish pirates. Left by itself at Lille, the *chambre des comptes* was much less involved in the turbulent political life of Flanders and its powerful municipalities. It continued to look after the duke's finances, domain and administrative personnel, and its incoming correspondence, the bulk of it from the bailiffs, receivers and other ducal officers, has survived to illustrate its activities. Here is a representative example:[2]

From the receiver-general of Flanders, André de Douay, to the *gens des comptes* at Lille. Ypres, 27 August 1406.
Honoured sirs, I commend myself to you with all my heart, and I pray

---

[1] Buntinx, *Audientie*; Lameere, *Grand conseil*, xxix; van der Meersch, *Belgisch museum*, ii (1838), 40-3; *IAGRCC* i. 6; and de Lichtervelde, *Grand commis*, 188 n. 11. For the next paragraph, see AGR CC21787.
[2] ADN B17608-17610. This letter is from 17609.

you to forgive me for not having been to see you since I left Lille. In truth the cause is that, not long ago when on the way to Oudenaarde, I caught a cold, which has occasioned such indisposition in my limbs that I have been unable to ride. At present I am so occupied with the wedding of my daughter, who, if it please God, will be married next Sunday, that I really cannot leave this town. Do please let me know if any receivers have arrived with their accounts, which ones, and what their balance. Honoured sirs, I am always ready, as I am bound by reason to be, to execute anything which you may be pleased to command. May Jesus Christ grant you a good life and a long one.

It was not long before a further change was made in the administrative arrangements of Flanders, for Oudenaarde soon proved unsuitable and unpopular as a seat for the council and in May 1407 it was transferred to the natural capital and largest town of Flanders, Ghent.[1] Finally, on 17 August 1409, one of the most interesting and elaborate of all John the Fearless's administrative acts was published: a council *ordonnance* which was clearly inspired by, and indeed some clauses were repeated verbatim from, Philip the Bold's similar *ordonnance* of 1386 setting up the council of Flanders at Lille. It consisted of forty-four separate articles, regulating the membership and procedure of the council of Flanders in minute detail.

Instructions for the councillors of the duke of Burgundy, count of Flanders, ordered by him to reside continually at Ghent.

1. First, certain councillors—notable knights, clerks and others—are made members of the council . . . at Ghent, who are obliged to reside continually at Ghent; and one of them shall be president. . . .

2. Item, in documents issued by them they shall call themselves 'the members of the council of my lord the duke of Burgundy, count of Flanders, of Artois and of Burgundy, appointed in Flanders', and they shall seal [these documents] with their [own individual] seals, as has been customary.

3. Item, there shall be a *greffier*, who may have one or more clerks; one or two ushers; and a *procureur général*. . . .

11. Item, the councillors shall take cognizance of cases concerning the rights of the duke . . . such as those touching the foundation of churches and injuries done to ecclesiastics in violation of the ducal safeguard; those concerning the ducal domain; and anything touching the ducal officers by virtue of their office. [They shall also

---

[1] De Lichtervelde, *Grand commis*, 188 n. 11; *IAGRCC* i. 6–7; van der Meersch, *Belgisch museum*, ii (1838), 47. For the *ordonnance*, see *Placcaerten van Vlaanderen*, 237–44.

take cognizance of] . . . crimes committed by the inhabitants of Flanders; [of cases arising out] of the peace settlement of Tournai [1385]; of disputes between the Flemish towns and castellanies . . .; [of matters arising out] of the privileges granted to foreign merchants like the Scots, the Italians and the Hansards; and, in general, they shall take cognizance of all cases over which the council, when at Lille, had jurisdiction.

26. Item, interrogations made by the councillors or by their commissioners shall be made in Flemish, when the written statements of the parties are in Flemish.

31. Item, the councillors shall inform the duke and his chancellor of all important events happening in Flanders. . . .

33. Item, the councillors shall meet every working day in the morning, and sit till dinner. . . . And they shall hear cases on Monday, Tuesday and Thursday and hold council on the other days.

36. Item, the duke has ordered that, behind closed doors, French will be spoken in the council chamber; but, in open court, he has agreed that each party may speak his own language, and that Flemish speakers will be answered in Flemish. . . .

The administrative reforms of John the Fearless in Flanders were very much in line with the aspirations of his subjects there: he had installed the council at Ghent and made detailed provisions for the use of Flemish in its proceedings. But what of their desire for a firm commercial treaty with England? It is not possible here to enter in detail into the complex story of the Anglo-Flemish negotiations of the years 1404-9. They formed part of a wider whole, a long series of conferences, which constituted a sort of standing institution for the settlement of differences and the allotment of reparations for damages done. They took place in Calais or Gravelines, or somewhere between the two along the frontiers of Flanders, France and the English territory of Calais, and they were three-sided, comprising normally deputies of the king of England, the duke of Burgundy in his capacity of count of Flanders, and the Four Members of Flanders. These negotiations continued without interruption, regardless of war and piracy and regardless even of truces and treaties between the interested parties, from 1401 onwards throughout the whole of John the Fearless's reign.

It is against this background of perpetual negotiation and unceasing exchanges of correspondence between ambassadors that John's relations with England in 1404-9 must be placed. As to the motives and real intentions of the parties concerned, these can only be surmised. Violence and duplicity were resorted to on all sides, and the pacific intentions of each party were vitiated or interrupted by uncontrollable elements in their own ranks. The Four Members of Flanders certainly wanted peace, but Flemish, as well as French, pirates and freebooters continued their predatory activities on English merchant shipping. John the Fearless was, on the whole, in favour of a commercial treaty between England and Flanders, and if, in the years 1405–7, his French connections caused him to entertain hostile projects against England and to promote anti-English projects in France, he took care to ensure that the Anglo-Flemish negotiations for a commercial treaty were not affected.[1]

In supporting the Flemish request for a peace treaty with England, John was pursuing the policy laid down by his father who, in 1403, had obtained leave from the French king Charles VI to negotiate a separate Anglo-Flemish trade treaty. His mother, Margaret of Male, had pursued the same policy and did her best to support the negotiations in spite of the mutual reprisals which took place in 1404: on 14 August 1404 an English party landed on an island near Sluis, burnt down a church and some farms, and carried off some cattle; and on 10 September 1404 the Flemish retaliated by capturing the king of England's confessor, Robert Mascall, bishop of Hereford, at sea, and imprisoning him at Dunkirk. The death of the duchess in March 1405 caused no break in the negotiations, nor were they seriously interrupted by Waléran de Luxembourg's unsuccessful attempt to besiege and capture the English outpost of Marck, near Calais, on 12 May 1405,[2] and his arrest at Gravelines, at this very moment, of another

---

[1] For these negotiations, see the narratives of Champion and de Thoisy, *Bourgogne-France-Angleterre*, 28–45; de Coussemaker, *ACFF* xxvi (1901–2), 290–336; Huguet, *Aspects de la guerre de Cent Ans en Picardie Maritime*, i. 1–125; Kuhnast, *Guerre de course*, 112–16 and 119–27; Nordberg, *Ducs et la royauté*, 131–49; Owen, *Connection between England and Burgundy*, 20–3; idem, *EHR* xxviii (1913), 13–23 and 26; and Wylie, *England under Henry IV*, i. 441–2, 464–8, 471–2; ii. 76, 78, 80, 83, 89, 96, 106; and iv. 1, 4 and 6. The relevant inventories and printed documents are: *Actes concernant les rapports entre les Pays-Bas et la Grande-Bretagne*, nos. 4, 5 and 6; *Cal. Close Rolls. H. IV.*, iii. 222–3, 261 and 324–5; *Docs. pour servir à l'histoire des relations entre l'Angleterre et la Flandre*, nos. 35–123; *Foedera*, iv (1), 72–155; Huguet, *Aspects*, ii. nos. 3–20; *IAB* iii. 525–34; *IADNB* i (1), 220, 361–70 and iv. 47–8; *IAY* viii, no. 2316; Pot, *R. Pot*, 317–18; *Procs. and Ords. of the P.C.*, i. 256–7 (other docs. here are printed in *Docs. pour servir . . .*); *Royal and historical letters of Henry IV.*, i; Varenbergh, *Relations diplomatiques*, 546–72. See, too, ADN B1600, fos. 55b–58, 62a–b, 78–79b and 80–81.

[2] For the battle of Marck, besides the sources mentioned in the preceding

English prelate, this time Richard Young, the newly-appointed bishop of Rochester. Although, as count of St. Pol, Waléran was his vassal, John the Fearless firmly disavowed the siege of Marck, maintaining that it had nothing to do with him. But he justified the arrest of the bishop by claiming that he was travelling without a safeguard and in disguise.

For once John the Fearless was telling the truth, at least about the attack on Marck, for this had been undertaken by the count of St. Pol acting in his capacity as captain-general of Picardy for the French king, and on the orders of the French government, then dominated by Louis, duke of Orleans. But the English evidently thought otherwise; and they thought, too, that an armed demonstration against the Flemish would speed up the protracted peace negotiations. Accordingly a fleet, which for some time had been poised at Sandwich with the intention of making reprisals against Flemish shipping, was despatched under the command of Henry IV's sixteen-year-old son, Thomas, to raid and perhaps capture the Flemish port of Sluis.[1] Soon after they arrived in the estuary of the Zwin on 22 May, the English sent pillaging expeditions ashore in various places and concentrated their troops for an assault on Sluis itself which took place on 24 or 25 May and which was repulsed. Meanwhile John the Fearless, as he advanced from Ypres to Sluis between 23 and 26 May, sent an urgent call for help to his brother Anthony, governor of Brabant, and, at the same time, summoned the Flemish militia to defend their own shores against the invader. Some historians have pretended that the Flemish burghers, especially those of Bruges, were unwilling to fight on this occasion because of their hostility to

---

note, see *Chronographia regum Francorum*, iii. 249–54; Monstrelet, *Chronique*, i. 100–6; Otterbourne, *Chron. reg. Angliae*, 252; Relig. de St. Denys, iii. 258–62; de Coussemaker, *ACFF* xxvi (1901–2), 379–81; Kirby, *RN* xxxvii (1955), 24–5; Mirot, *RQH* xcv (1914), 341.

[1] This history of this expedition may be pieced together from the following: *Hansisches Urkundenbuch*, v. no. 667 and Varenbergh, *Relations diplomatiques*, 493–5 (documents); *Annales Ric. II et Henrici IV*, 401; *Chron. comitum Flandrensium*, 249–50; *Chronographia regum Francorum*, iii. 256–7; O. van Dixmude, *Merkwaerdige geb.*, 24–7; *Eulogium hist.*, iii. 401; *Memorieboek der stad Ghent*, i. 144; Monstrelet, *Chronique*, i. 107; and Otterbourne, *Chron. reg. Angliae*, 253 (chronicles); de Lichtervelde, *Grand commis*, 130–1; Mirot, *ABSHF* (1938), 222; Pocquet, *MSHDB* vi (1939), 141; Wylie, *England under Henry IV*, ii. 100–5; and Zuylen van Nyevelt, *Épisodes*, 194–9 (modern accounts). There is no evidence, as Zuylen van Nyevelt supposes (*Épisodes*, 194), that this raid was occasioned by the intrigues of Louis of Orleans.

John the Fearless and his alleged anti-English policies.[1] Actually, the men of the Franc of Bruges had already successfully engaged the enemy by 25 May, and Ypres, too, sent a contingent of militia. At Ghent the facts are revealed by the well-kept accounts of the ducal bailiff, Danckaert d'Ogierlande.

25 May. Jehan de Gand, the bailiff's usual messenger, sent to the duke and his chancellor at Male with letters from Clais Utenhove and the bailiff reporting their interview with the city council of Ghent, at which they had explained the duke's need for 20,000 men to resist the invaders, and were promised a reply next day.

26 May. Another messenger sent to the duke reporting that Ghent had agreed to serve the duke in arms and that her troops would leave the city on the following day.

27 May. Another messenger sent to the duke, reporting that the militia of Ghent, some 5,000 to 6,000 strong, had already set out.

In point of fact, the magistrates of Bruges had at first refused the ducal summons for military aid, but the well-informed contemporary chronicler Oliver van Dixmude makes it clear that this was because they were involved in a dispute with Sluis at that time, and had no desire to rush to their rival's assistance. They even refused, for the same reason, to admit the militia of the Franc of Bruges, in which Sluis was situated, within their walls.[2] Moreover, it is also clear that not everyone at Bruges, not even all the magistrates, supported this policy, and that the original decision was reversed in time for a Bruges contingent to join the general muster at Aardenburg. In the face of this gathering and formidable opposition, the English withdrew; Anthony and his knights, arriving at Bruges on 30 May, were disappointed of a fight; and the men of Ghent were home again by 1 June.

The English raid on Sluis was, of course, a flagrant violation of the Anglo-Flemish trade truce, the prolongation of which was being negotiated at the very time it was launched; and John the Fearless's first reaction was to suggest to the two Baltic powers which also suffered from English piracy and English aggression, the Grand Master of the Order of Teutonic Knights and the Hanseatic League,

[1] E.g., Kervyn, *Flandre*, iv. 133–4 and Varenbergh, *Relations diplomatiques*, 495. The extracts which follow are from AGR CC14109, account for 11 May 1405–21 September 1405, f. 17a–b.

[2] O. van Dixmude, *Merkwaerdige geb.*, 25 and Zuylen van Nyevelt, *ASEB* lxvi (1923), 118.

a policy of armed intervention against their common enemy. His letter to the Hanse runs in part as follows:[1]

John, duke of Burgundy, etc. to the consuls of the German Hanse towns . . ., greetings. . . . Dearest friends, we have heard that the incorrigible English, who have neither loyalty nor honour, have repeatedly attacked your citizens and merchants. . . . And now, that is, less than a month ago, these infamous people have dared to enter my port of Sluis stealthily with a numerous fleet, in spite of the treaty between the English and my Flemish subjects, while I was visiting my land [of Flanders] for the first time and making my state entry into it, expecting no affront of any kind. . . . And when they failed to implement their damnable project because of the resistance of the people of Sluis, they set fire to some houses and other buildings near the sea. Wherefore, since you and our predecessors and subjects have always willingly collaborated in the past, we invoke your friendship, and we hope that you may be persuaded to join with us and likewise lend effective aid towards their downfall: for we really do intend to attack the English and their friends with God's help and all our power. You should not listen to what the English ambassadors who, it is said, have now been sent to you, have to say, for they certainly lack all truth and fidelity, and are rather spreading abroad deceit, treachery and poisonous counterfeiting. . . . Dearest friends, may the Most High give you happiness and longevity.

Ghent   8 June 1405

Both the Hanseatic League and the Teutonic Knights preferred conferences to war, and the continuance of the negotiations for an Anglo-Flemish trade treaty shows that John the Fearless's aggressive aspirations must not be taken too seriously. On 18 June 1405 Richard Aston, the English royal lieutenant in Calais, wrote to the captain of Gravelines, Thomas de Bauffremez, expressing his astonishment that there had been no sign of ambassadors from either Duke John or the Four Members of Flanders, though the truce had only been extended, from 25 May, for ten days. But no break in the negotiations occurred, and sporadic conferences and interminable exchanges of correspondence continued throughout the rest of 1405 and subsequent years, regardless alike of the commercial truce or treaty for one year which was drawn up on 30 November 1406 and ratified by John the Fearless on 10 January 1407, and of the hostile activities of the English fleet, which had been cruising off Flanders for some

[1] *Hanserecesse*, v. nos. 255-7, 271, 272, 276 and 277. This letter is no. 256.

months and had even dared, on 19 July 1406, to land twelve men and a dog at Ostend to reconnoitre the Flemish coastal defences there.[1] Moreover, during the whole of the first half of November 1406, John the Fearless was at St. Omer assembling troops for an attack on Calais on behalf of the French government which, in the event, was never made.

This situation was repeated in the following spring. On 10 March 1407 the king of England ratified the one-year Anglo-Flemish treaty of 10 January 1407 which, incidentally, was to hold good even in the event of a Franco-English war. Yet at this very time John had reverted to his earlier scheme of trying to persuade the Baltic powers into warlike activities against England. On 11 March 1407 he had sent word to the Hansards at Bruges, under the strictest secrecy, offering to join the Hanse in an attack on the English. The Hansards referred him to their next diet at Lübeck in May, where John's ambassadors offered an alliance with himself and France against the English; but the diet eventually resolved to try to get favourable terms from the English first, before they risked the use of force in the dubious company of John the Fearless.[2]

Although duplicity and deception were extensively and almost continually practised on each side, Anglo-Flemish commerce was protected, at least on paper, by the truce which, having been renewed for one year in June 1407, was extended for a further three years in June 1408. Here then was the treaty which, John freely admitted, had been made by him at the request of his Flemish subjects; a treaty which was supported and strengthened in August 1408 by a separate but parallel treaty, likewise to run for three years, of a rather novel type, for it established and guaranteed general security at sea north and east of a line between Winchelsea and St. Valéry. Nevertheless, after this, as before, the patient ambassadors were fully and continuously engaged: if there was no further treaty to negotiate in the near future, the pirates on both sides of the Channel ensured that there were infringements of existing treaties to be investigated and reparations to be settled.

During his first four years as count of Flanders, John the Fearless had accepted and even implemented the main demands of his subjects as expressed by the Four Members. But what sort of *quid pro quo*

---

[1] AGR CC21787, fos. 19 and 23b–24. See, too, *Précis analytique*, (2) i. 93–4.
[2] *Hanserecesse*, v. nos. 364, 372, 374, 390, 391, 392, 402–4, 420, 449 and 459 and ibid., viii. nos. 1055 and 1056.

did he obtain from them? The wealthy and populous Flemish cities could be useful in two ways: by providing military aid in the form of infantry or militia; and by voting, from time to time, a financial subvention or *aide*. The evidence about both these is incomplete, but it is clear that the Flemish were extremely recalcitrant. True, they called out the militia in May 1405 in the face of an English invasion, but they evidently refused outright John's requests for troops to operate in France, whether against Louis of Orleans in 1405 or to defend the duke and duchess in Paris in spring 1408. The only major military expedition undertaken by John in these years was in autumn 1408 against Liège, but the Four Members were only asked for 6,000 men, and Ghent's refusal to contribute to this contingent caused John to desist from his request.[1] Financially, too, the Flemish were reluctant to help their ruler; it was two years before they could be persuaded to vote the substantial sum which John the Fearless first demanded in 1405 for his state entry into Flanders, and three years before detailed and final agreement was reached with the Four Members concerning the allotment and payment of this sum, which had eventually been settled at 108,000 double crowns.[2]

Although the attitude of the Four Members towards their ruler, in the early years of John's reign, was at times menacing and usually uncooperative, there was no serious or concerted opposition to him. This was partly because the three urban Members, Ghent, Bruges and Ypres, were each involved in bitter disputes with the smaller towns and countryside surrounding them—disputes caused, in the main, by their attempts to enforce a virtual monopoly for themselves in the manufacture of cloth—and partly because of the menace, which was still a very real one, within each of these towns, of artisan revolts

[1] O. van Dixmude, *Merkwaerdige geb.*, 44: 'ende bad hemlieden omme zes duust serianten, omme met hem to trecken, twelke die van Ghent hem ontseid zouden hebben, also men besief, omme twelke myn heere van zinen versouke achter bleef. . . .' Yet some modern historians claim that Ghent did send troops to Othée: *Algemene geschiedenis*, iii. 221; *Geschiedenis van Vlaanderen*, iii. 76 and *IAB* iv. 33–4. For the 1405 and 1408 requests, mentioned above, see AGR CC14109, account of 11 May 1405–21 September 1405, f. 17b and *Précis analytique*, (2) i. 109.

[2] AGR CC14109, account for 11 May 1405–21 September 1405, f. 17a–b; *Précis analytique*, (1) i. 57; (2) i. 107 and (2) vi. 139–47 and 176–82; *IAB* iv. 19–30; van der Meersch, *Belgisch museum*, ii (1838), 271–6. The Four Members were at the same time permitted by John to recoup 20,000 double crowns from the rest of Flanders. The *double écu* or *dubbel schild* was a gold coin minted by John in Flanders in 1407 with the value of 48 Flemish groats.

against the ruling urban patriciate. This situation, already favourable to the duke, was skilfully exploited by him. His policy, in these early years, was consistent and successful: to cultivate and maintain, within each urban Member, a party favourable to himself.

In all three of the urban Members of Flanders, Ghent, Bruges and Ypres, John the Fearless had, by 1407, either ensured the rise to power in the magistrature of his own partisans, or persuaded the existing magistrature to support him. At Ghent popular risings against the magistrates in July and December 1406 were by themselves sufficient to win Jacob Sneevoet and his supporters in power over to the duke; and this understanding between the magistrature of Ghent and John the Fearless was further improved when, in May 1407, John transferred the council of Flanders from Oudenaarde to their city. The degree to which the magistrates of Ghent at this time supported the duke and his policies is shown by their refusal to support Bruges when John bullied that town into submission in the spring of 1407, and by their failure, in the same year, to give whole-hearted support to the attempt of Oudenaarde to remove its quarrel with Aalst from the cognizance of the council of Flanders.[1]

At Bruges, instead of currying favour with the magistrates in office, John the Fearless first undermined their position by adding to their number some partisans of his who had formerly been exiled from Bruges for embezzlement. Then, in April 1407, when they proved reluctant to accept his settlement of the dispute between Bruges and the Franc of Bruges over the cloth-manufacturing monopoly of the former, he visited Bruges in person, expelled the offending magistrates from office, confiscated all their belongings, and had them banished for one hundred years and a day. On 24 April 1407 a new pro-ducal bench of magistrates was sworn in, and on the next day a crushing blow at the communal liberties of Bruges was delivered

[1] Van der Meersch, *Belgisch museum*, ii (1838), 289–303. For this and the following paragraphs, the main chronicle source is O. van Dixmude, *Merkwaerdige geb.*, 30–40. See, too, in general, *Algemene geschiedenis*, iii. 218–20; *Geschiedenis van Vlaanderen*, iii. 74–6 and 275–7; Kervyn, *Flandre*, iv. 140–5. For Bruges and the Franc, especially, see Fris, *BAAB* (1911), 183–274; Zuylen van Nyevelt, *ASEB* lxvi (1923), 114–46 and idem, *Épisodes*, 180–208; *IAB* iii. 534–40 and iv. 1–19; de Lichtervelde, *Grand commis*, 162–4; and AGR Trésor de Flandre, (1) 2514. For Ghent, see AGR CC21787, f. 18b (riot in July 1406); and, for Ypres, see AGR CC14544, accounts for 5 May 1404–22 September 1404 and 10 January 1406/7–9 May 1407.

under the guise of a concession to the craft-gilds, who were permitted
to have their own banners, but on draconian conditions:[1]

Bruges   25 April 1407
John, duke of Burgundy, etc. . . . At the humble request of the
burgomasters, aldermen, council and good people of our town of
Bruges . . . we . . . have granted and given and do grant and give by
these presents to the craft gilds of our town of Bruges authority to have
banners to be used reasonably according to the conditions, restrictions
and obligations hereinafter declared. That is to say, if in future the
members of the craft gilds or any one of them or their successors make
or cause to be made—which God forbid—any disturbance or armed
riot, popular revolt or alliance of any kind against us or our heirs and
successors . . . or . . . cause any banner or banners to be carried in any
place or places in Bruges . . . except by our special command . . . and
also not before our own banner . . . has been unfurled in the market-
place, then the person or persons charged and convicted with these
misdeeds . . . shall be decapitated in the market-place at Bruges . . .
and their goods shall be forfeit and confiscated to the profit of us and
our heirs and successors; and if they cannot be found, they shall be
banished from Flanders for one hundred years and a day. . . .

Once he was in firm control, John the Fearless inflicted further
indignities on Bruges. He forced the new magistrates to accept
a financial arrangement whereby, in place of the annual tax hitherto
paid to the duke, the city was to pay him one-seventh of all its
revenues. Finally, the humiliation of Bruges was consummated and
engrossed in two remarkable documents of 24 May 1407, in which
the magistrates and the craft gilds humbly accepted and confirmed
these ducal 'reforms'.

The third urban Member, Ypres, was handled just as successfully,
though less ruthlessly, by John the Fearless. Here, opposition to the
bailiff and other ducal officers had made itself felt from 1404 onwards.
In December 1406 a manifesto supporting the town's privileges was
drawn up by a general assembly of citizens and ratified by the magistrates and craft gilds, in spite of the bailiff's prohibition of these
proceedings. But John's treatment of Bruges in April 1407 destroyed
the confidence of the anti-ducal party at Ypres, and on 30 April 1407
the duke went there in person to receive the formal submission and
apologies of her magistrates and citizens. No more was heard of the
manifesto, and it seems that only two of the offending magistrates
were banished.

[1] *IAB* iv. 14-16.

Thus Ypres followed the example, and fate, of Ghent and Bruges. All three were won over, within two years of John the Fearless's accession as count of Flanders, to his interests and support, not so much by playing one Member off against another, still less by supporting Ghent against the others, but rather by the exploitation of circumstances already favourable to the duke and by a cunningly devised and cleverly executed policy of intervention in the internal affairs of the individual Members.

CHAPTER TWO

Louis of Orleans:
1404–7

On his death-bed, Philip the Bold made his sons, John and Anthony, swear to be loyal and obedient to King Charles VI of France—an assurance which they doubtless readily gave.[1] But how exactly should one interpret this exhortation? A ducal *ordonnance* of 1408 claimed that John the Fearless had to reside a good deal in France 'because of the important affairs of the king, whom we wish to support with all our power, as we are bound to do by virtue both of lineage and homage, among other things. . . .' It seems scarcely credible that political realists and opportunists of the calibre of Philip the Bold and John the Fearless should have intervened in French affairs through motives of mere altruism. On the contrary, it was self-interest which dictated their policies. The words 'among other things' in this extract conceal the true motives of the duke. In France, John simply followed the policy of his father: to try to maintain influence and control in order to protect his own interests and exploit French resources and the French connection for his own advancement. The secret of success was, of course, control of the person of the king. 'Obedience and loyalty' to Charles VI meant dominating and making use of this weak and periodically insane ruler. Some of the chroniclers evidently knew what they were talking about: Cousinot suggests that John wanted power in France because of his own lands, and Juvenel des Ursins tells us that the French princes were pursuing their own advantages, instead of the common good.[2]

[1] Monstrelet, *Chronique*, i. 88, is confirmed by Jehan Chousat's letter of 21 August 1405 in Gachard, *Rapport . . . Dijon*, 104. See, too, *Livre des Trahisons*, 14. The quotation which follows is from *Ords. franc-comtoises*, no. 16.
[2] Cousinot, *Geste des nobles*, 110 and Juv. des Ursins, *Hist. de Charles VI*, 430. See below, pp. 228–9.

In the internal history of France, Philip the Bold's death marked a change of government. Hitherto Philip, relying on the support of his brother John, duke of Berry, and some other princes, had been in firm control of French affairs. Now his death gave Louis, duke of Orleans and brother of Charles VI, the opportunity he had long awaited of seizing the reins of power. This he did, with the help, in particular, of Queen Isabel, who was suspected by many of being his mistress as well as ally; but also with the support of John of Berry and the other princes of the blood. There is abundant evidence of the dominating position in the French government which Louis of Orleans achieved within a month or two of Philip the Bold's death at the end of April. On 5 June 1404 he was able to arrange a very advantageous marriage for his son Charles to Charles VI's daughter Isabel, the widow of King Richard II of England, and Charles VI promised, with her, the enormous dowry of 300,000 francs; on 6 June he became royal captain-general and lieutenant in Picardy and Normandy; and on 7 June it was he, together with the grand master of the royal household, Jehan de Montagu, who was responsible for the royal grant of all *aides* in the county of Artois to the dowager duchess of Burgundy, Margaret of Male.[1] Even if the sceptical reader of the loquacious chronicler who goes under the name of 'the monk of St. Denis' declines to attach much credence to his statement that Louis was at this time virtual ruler of France,[2] he must surely accept the evidence of the reliable and strictly contemporary writer, Nicolas de Baye, the clerk of the court at the Paris *Parlement*. He says that the royal decree of 27 July 1404, ordering the 'most rigorous punishment of those who write, distribute or fix defamatory pamphlets to gates, doors or houses', was occasioned by the appearance in public places of some libellous attacks on the duke of Orleans. From which we may deduce that he was not only powerful but also unpopular, at least in some quarters. But for the moment John the Fearless made no attempt to intervene in French affairs. Indeed, he was not yet in a position to do so effectively, and had to content himself, in the spring of 1404, with a lavish distribution of Burgundian wine among his potential supporters in Paris: prominent prelates, merchants and royal officials, among them, Nicolas de Baye.[3]

The duke of Orleans was not only firmly in power in France within

---

[1] Jarry, *Louis d'Orléans*, 310 and 308; ADN B1280/23573.
[2] 'Regni rectorem precipuum', Relig. de St. Denys, iii. 188, and, for what follows, de Baye, *Journal*, ii. 288.
[3] ACO B1538, f. 200a–b.

months of Philip the Bold's death; he was also using that power throughout 1404 and 1405 to feather his own nest. A shower of royal gifts and grants of *aides* descended on him at this time, and it has been conjectured that, of his annual revenues in 1404-5 of 454,158 *livres* of Tours, nearly 159,000 *l.* came from royal *aides* ceded to him, some 45,000 *l.* was income from his own lands, and the rest consisted of royal gifts.[1] Meanwhile Louis of Orleans was adding to the extensive nexus of territories and alliances which he had built up, mainly since 1400, in north-eastern France and in the area of the Rhine and Moselle. Luxembourg was already his; now, in 1404, he persuaded or bribed Waléran de Luxembourg, count of St. Pol, Édouard de Bar, marquis du Pont, and the cities of Toul and Liège, to become his vassals or allies. All this in an area which lay next to, and indeed partly encircled, the northern territories of the Burgundian state, ruled at this time from Arras by the dowager duchess of Burgundy.

The entry of John the Fearless on the French political stage seems to have been contrived with some skill, for it appears to have been purposely delayed until an opportunity arose for John to play the rôle of leader of the opposition to the unpopular government of Louis of Orleans and, more important, to the taxes which Louis found it necessary to raise. This opportunity occurred in mid-February 1405, when John, not content with protesting, at a meeting of the royal council, against Louis's proposed *aide*, followed this up by summoning his own private assembly of leading French officials —the two first presidents of the Paris *Parlement*, three of the *maîtres des comptes*, and the provost of the merchants—to which he repeated this protest. Soon after John the Fearless left Paris on 16 February 1405 Louis of Orleans and the duke of Berry interviewed these same officials to discover exactly what John the Fearless had said to them and what they thought of his remarks: ' . . . to which they replied that it seemed to them that my lord [the duke of Burgundy] . . . was indeed moved with sympathy and pity for the people, and that his way of thinking was sound and laudable. And at once, without delay, they were told to go. . . .'[2]

---

[1] Coville, *Petit*, 374. See, too, Nordberg, *Ducs et la royauté*, 17-23. For this paragraph in general see Jarry, *Louis d'Orléans*, 308-13; Mirot, *RQH* xcv (1914), 330-4; Pocquet, *RUB* vii (1954-5), 394-6; and Schoos, *Machtkampf zwischen Burgund und Orleans*. For Orleans and Liège, see Minder, *BSVAH* xli (1954), 139.
[2] ADN B554/23923.

John the Fearless's pose as an anti-taxer may have irritated Orleans and Berry, but it certainly won him popular support. In the spring of 1405 he was already regarded in France as a desirable alternative to the unpopular Louis of Orleans as unofficial regent of France. His programme was at first limited to the specious promise to abolish or much diminish the *aides*, but by May 1405 he was evidently offering an alternative and more acceptable religious policy. There were two rival pretenders to the papal throne at this time, Benedict XIII and Innocent VII, and Louis of Orleans supported the former, in spite of his unpopularity in France. The growing opposition to Louis's government on these religious grounds found expression in May 1405 in a deputation sent by Paris University to John the Fearless with certain requests:[1]

1. That he would write to the king asking him to send an embassy to [Innocent VII at] Rome.

2. That, in order to further the cause of the Union of the Church, he would see to it that the papal bulls sent to the University by 'him of Rome' were published.

3. That he would inform the papal agents in Paris and elsewhere that the members of the University had been excused payment of the tenth recently imposed by [Pope Benedict XIII].

4. That, finally, he himself would come to Paris.

While John the Fearless was thus establishing claims to popular esteem in France, he by no means neglected the support of those princes who could be counted among his relatives or friends. Alliances were cemented with Amadeus VIII, count of Savoy, in December 1404, and with Queen Isabel of France in February. Then, on 21 July 1405, a tripartite treaty of alliance was made at Le Quesnoy between the three principal rulers of the Netherlands: John the Fearless, count of Flanders; his brother Anthony, then governor of Brabant; and his brother-in-law William of Bavaria, count of Holland, Hainault and Zeeland.[2] At the very time of this alliance, John was engaged in concerting plans for a forceful intervention in French affairs, in company with his brothers Anthony and Philip; with John of Bavaria, the bishop-elect of Liège; William, count of Namur;

---

[1] De Coussemaker, *ACFF* xxvi (1901–2), 380.
[2] Plancher, iii. 216. For the texts of these three treaties, see, respectively, ACO B11928; Plancher, iii. no. 234 (ACO B11892); and ibid., no. 247 (see de Lichtervelde, *Grand commis*, 133 and n. 74 and below, p. 242).

Adolf, count of Cleves, and other partisans and relatives.[1] Indeed, he must have been about to execute this project when a royal summons to attend the council in Paris reached him at Douai on 26 July. This invitation, which was apparently due to Charles VI's desire, during one of his few lucid moments, to strengthen his council with a representative gathering of French princes, furnished John with a useful pretext for his visit to Paris. Another was his obligation to do homage to Charles VI for his county of Flanders.

It was 14 August when John finally left Arras for Paris, accompanied by a thousand or so knights and squires, secretly armed. Louis of Orleans promptly withdrew from Paris on 17 August to Melun, taking Queen Isabel with him, and at once began assembling troops and despatching urgent messengers to his numerous allies. At the same time arrangements were made for the ten-year-old dauphin, Louis, duke of Guienne, to be brought from Paris to Melun on the following day. He set out on 18 August but on 19 August occurred the famous incident of his interception and return to Paris by John the Fearless. The substantial accuracy of Monstrelet's account is borne out by other contemporary chroniclers and by the documents.[2]

> When the duke of Burgundy had concluded his business at Arras, he set out . . . towards Paris, accompanied by a body of men, amounting to some 800 combatants, secretly armed. He stopped some days at the town of Louvres en Parisis, where letters were brought to him from Paris reporting that the king had recovered from his illness and that the queen and the duke of Orleans had left Paris for Melun and Chartres, and had arranged for the duke of Guienne, dauphin of Vienne, to go with them. After he had considered the contents of these letters and slept for a short time, he left the town very early the next morning at the sound of the trumpet, and hastened with all his men to Paris, to try to find the dauphin. But on his arrival there he was told that he had already left to go to Melun, following after his mother, which was true. Upon which the duke, without dismounting or delaying at all, rode hard through Paris with his troops as fast as he could in pursuit of the dauphin. He overtook him near Corbeil, where the queen and the duke of Orleans were waiting dinner for him. With the dauphin were his uncle on his mother's side, Louis of Bavaria, [Édouard de Bar], the

---

[1] For what follows, see de Lichtervelde, *Grand commis*, 133–6, and, especially, Mirot, *RQH* xcv (1914), 329–55 and *RQH* xcvi (1914), 47–68 and 369–419, and the references given there. See, too, Nordberg, *Ducs et la royauté*, 185–207.

[2] Monstrelet, *Chronique*, i. 108–13.

marquis du Pont, son of the duke of Bar, the count of Dammartin, [Jehan de] Montagu, grand master of the king's household, with many other lords. . . . When the duke of Burgundy approached the dauphin, he made him the most respectful obeisances, and implored him to return to and remain in Paris where, he said, he would be better off than in any other part of France; adding that he wanted to discuss certain matters with him which touched him personally. After this conversation, Louis of Bavaria, seeing that the dauphin was inclined to comply with the request of the duke, said: 'My lord duke of Burgundy, permit my nephew the dauphin to go with the queen his mother and his uncle the duke of Orleans, since he has had the consent of his father for so doing. . . .' Notwithstanding this delay, and other conversation which, for the sake of brevity I omit, the duke of Burgundy had the dauphin's litter turned about and brought him and all his attendants back to Paris, excepting the marquis du Pont, the count of Dammartin, and several other members of the duke of Orleans's household. These last galloped off toward Corbeil, where they told the queen and the duke of Orleans how the duke of Burgundy had made the dauphin return against his will to Paris. . . . The duke of Burgundy . . . accompanied the dauphin to Paris; and the king of Navarre, the dukes of Berry and of Bourbon, the count of la Marche, with many other nobles and an immense crowd of the citizens of Paris, came out to meet him, and escorted him most honourably into the city. . . . The next day the rector and a large part of the University of Paris came to pay their respects to the duke of Burgundy, and to thank him publicly, with all humility, for his great love and affection towards the king, the royal family, and the whole realm. They [said they] were convinced of his good intentions concerning the reform and restoration of the kingdom, and asked him to persevere in these endeavours, notwithstanding any obstacles that he might meet with.

John the Fearless had certainly won the first round, having gained possession of the person of the dauphin with the connivance and support of the dukes of Berry and Bourbon and the king of Navarre; for these three, the leading French princes apart from the dukes of Burgundy and Orleans themselves, had evidently been annoyed by Louis of Orleans's attempt to remove the dauphin from Paris. By 25 August, however, John had handed him over to the duke of Berry, and now deadlock ensued. Both John and Louis soon assembled an army. John's, based on Paris, was joined on 20 August by Anthony and on 11 September by John of Bavaria, each with an 800-strong contingent, not to mention others; while Louis's army was assembled at Melun. Civil war seemed about to follow John's unsuccessful *coup d'état.* A kind of reforming petition or manifesto, consisting of a series of complaints against the government of Louis of Orleans and the queen, was drawn up jointly by John and his two brothers and presented verbally at the Louvre on 21 August by Jehan de Nieles to an assembly of notables including the princes of the blood, the royal council, the *Parlement*, University and *chambre des comptes*. But this led only to a sterile pamphlet war in which Louis's counter-accusations against John and John's defence of his actions were circulated round France to no purpose. This situation of stalemate is well illustrated by the letter of a Burgundian official in Paris to his Dijon colleagues, written more than a month after the beginning of the crisis.[1]

Jehan Chousat to the *gens des comptes* at Dijon.
Paris   27 September 1405

Dear sirs . . . my lord [the duke of Burgundy] has here at the moment 4,560 lances or men-at-arms, knights and squires, at what cost and expense it is frightful to think. But still, nothing is done, because my lords of France, that is to say the king of Navarre, my lords of Berry and of Bourbon and all the other royal councillors, keep putting him off with delays. They hold out to him hopes of their doing something about the demands made by him and his brothers for the good of the king and the kingdom [on 21 August]; but no action is taken. However, my lord [the duke] has asked them several times, in particular last Saturday, because of his and his brothers' sympathy for the wretched country people . . . who are much oppressed by the troops now stationed in the countryside and living off it (something which their own men are not doing and about whom, thanks be to God, not a single complaint has yet been made, nor will be), to agree that they should all disband a large part of their armies. . . . This on condition that the king of Navarre, the dukes of Berry, Orleans and Bourbon, the count of la Marche, the constable, and all members of the king's council, the *Parlement*, the *chambre des comptes,* the provost of Paris and the provost of the merchants, swear on the Holy Gospels that, once the king has recovered his health, they will . . . do all in their power to persuade him, for his own and his kingdom's sake, to acknowledge and deal with the complaints made by my lord [the duke of Burgundy] and his brothers. . . .

On which my lords of France, always temporizing with the duke, asked for time to take advice and reply, and to put this matter to the hostile party [i.e., the duke of Orleans and his supporters]; because the council never does anything except with their advice and consent. And today, news has come to my lord that the queen, who has been continuously at Melun since the middle of August with the duke of Orleans,

---

[1] Gachard, *Rapport . . . Dijon,* 106-7.

has left Melun and is due to arrive tomorrow at the Bois de Vincennes. My lord [the duke] has decided to go out to meet her in arms with all his power, to accompany her as far as the Bois de Vincennes. I wish to God that one or two of you could see the army and assembly, to tell the others about it. In my lord's council, at which delegates from the University are present daily, there are many and diverse views, for some believe in requests, petitions and declarations; while others, in their different ways, suggest various other methods which cannot be committed to writing because one never knows into whose hands letters may fall. Indeed, it is said here that ducal messengers going to [Burgundy] have had all their letters seized. . . .

By the time peace was at last formally made in mid-October and the rival armies disbanded, it was clear that John's attempt on the French government had failed. The demand for reforms, first submitted by John and his brothers in the manifesto of 21 August, was still being pressed by him in December, doubtless with the aim of maintaining or increasing his already considerable popularity and then extracting from the princes, in exchange for the abandonment of these proposals, some *quid pro quo* in the shape of a definite share in the French government. Jehan Chousat, writing again at length about the Paris situation in early December, reports a certain hardening of the princely opposition to John, which took the form of an alliance between Berry and Orleans that had actually been made on 1 December, and to which Queen Isabel was also a party.[1]

Jehan Chousat to the bailiff of Dijon.
Paris   [9 or 10 December 1405]

Dear sir, as to news from here, last Saturday my lord [the duke of Burgundy] sent for the constable [of France] and the royal chamberlains to remonstrate with them about the business which had brought him here [to Paris] and the promises and oaths which were made by my lords [the French princes] and himself. They held council together from the morning until one o'clock in the afternoon and, when the council was over, my lord made them promise that they would dine with him next day in his hôtel, so that he could talk to them again about this. . . .

On the very same Saturday, my lords of Berry, Orleans, Bourbon and Tancarville, with my lord the grand master of the king's household . . . and several others, held council in the Bastille St. Antoine, and are said to have discussed the question of the [royal] finances in the

[1] Text of this alliance in *Choix de pièces inédites*, i. no. 120 and *Quelques pièces*, no. 128. The letter which follows is from ACO B11942, no. 13. Although 9 December fell on a Thursday in 1406, internal evidence shows that this letter dates from 1405.

last two months to their hearts' content without any reference to my lord [the duke of Burgundy]; but at dinner-time they sent him an invitation to dine with them, which he flatly refused. . . . When my lords of Berry and Orleans discovered that the constable and chamberlains had promised to dine next day with my lord [the duke of Burgundy] they sent for them and prohibited them on any account from going, on the grounds that [if they did] the people would think that my lord [the duke of Burgundy] obviously had a perfect right to undertake the reformation of this kingdom, and that these chamberlains were about to join his party. . . . This prohibition made my lord [the duke] very angry. The aforesaid chamberlains did not come to dinner with him, but sent their excuses; though he had everything ready for their entertainment. He spoke about this in such a way that my lords of Berry and Orleans—who are allied and leagued together by oath and pledge, and have been exchanging gifts of expensive jewellery with each other—had guards posted in their hôtels and kept their people there in arms throughout the Sunday night. It is said that this alliance was brought about by my lords the bishops of Chartres and Poitiers, and my lord the grand master of the king's household . . . and several others.

On the Monday following, my lords of Berry and Orleans, with all their people, went with covered arms to the [royal] council in the hôtel de St. Pol, and my lord [the duke of Burgundy] also, with a very fine company almost entirely unarmed. At the council, only the queen and the princes of the blood royal were present, and I do not know what was done there, except only that, as rumour has it, the business [of the duke of Burgundy's proposed reforms] seems to be going badly. . . .

Written at Paris, on Thursday, 9 December, very late.

It was apparently not till the end of January 1406 that the situation was clarified by an ill-defined agreement among the princes which admitted John to a share of power only, and shelved his reforming proposals. This arrangement found documentary expression on 27 January, when John was substituted for his dead father in the council of regency which had been set up, some years before, to rule France during Charles VI's 'absences', and in the guardianship of the royal children in case of Charles VI's death.[1] In future, France was to be governed, when the king suffered his periodic fits of insanity, by Queen Isabel and the four dukes of Berry, Burgundy, Orleans and Bourbon, with a council which, though it contained some devoted followers of John the Fearless, was constituted in July 1406 so that the supporters of Louis of Orleans predominated. John had achieved something; but was this enough?

[1] Plancher, iii. nos. 243 and 244. For the council, see Valois, *Conseil*, 113-15 and Nordberg, *Ducs et la royauté*, 215-24.

The period between January 1406 and the murder of the duke of Orleans by John the Fearless's hired assassins in November 1407, was one of uneasy truce in France. At times in 1406 he and Louis of Orleans appeared to be collaborating more or less harmoniously. In June the weddings of a son of Charles VI to a granddaughter of John the Fearless, and a daughter, Isabel, to Louis of Orleans's son, were celebrated at Compiègne by John and Louis with extravagant protestations of friendship. They even wore each other's emblems, for John the Fearless turned out on the first day of the accompanying tournament in a surcoat of alternate or and argent bands decorated with his favourite device, the plane; while, on the next day, he did honour to Louis by wearing a black surcoat embroidered with Orleanist cudgels.[1] In July John agreed to share the lordship of Pisa, which had been ceded to him on 31 May, with Louis of Orleans. His banner was unfurled on the walls of Pisa on 7 July, and the two dukes made a concerted but unsuccessful attempt to save that city from conquest by Florence. It fell on 9 October 1406, but John and Louis continued their collaboration after this event by the futile gesture of arresting the ambassadors who had been sent to France by Florence to explain and justify her policy towards Pisa.

In the summer of 1406 the French government resolved on a more striking plan for the cooperation, at a convenient distance from each other, of John the Fearless and Louis of Orleans. A grand attack was planned on the two great English continental bastions, Calais and Bordeaux, on the lines of the twin offensive which had been projected first in 1403. While John attacked Calais, Louis was to besiege Bordeaux; their expenses to be paid out of a special *aide* to be equally divided between them. By mid-October King Henry IV's spies had reported Louis's departure from Paris for Guienne on 16 September, and John's intention to be under the walls of Calais by 25 November.[2] Each took his mission in deadly earnest, but in

[1] De Laborde, *Ducs de Bourgogne*, i. 21–2; Jarry, *Louis d'Orléans*, 335–6; and Monstrelet, *Chronique*, i. 129–30. For what follows, see especially Mirot, *BEC* xcv (1934), 74–115 and de Boüard, *France et Italie*, 298–337. Tits-Dieuaide, *BIHBR* xxx (1957), 97–112 re-edits John the Fearless's letter to Boucicaut of 15 July 1406, apparently unaware of its previous edition from the same MS. by de la Roncière, *MAH* xv (1895), 231–44.
[2] *Cal. Close Rolls. H. IV.*, iii. 222–3. For what follows, see Jarry, *Louis d'Orléans*, 346–7. For the next paragraph, see Plancher, iii. no. 254; BN Coll. de Bourg. 57, f. 295a–b; ACO B1543, f. 108b; ibid., fos. 75b, 76b and 89b; and ACO B1547, f. 72b. Chousat's letters are from BN Coll. de Bourg. 57, f. 26a–b. For the offensive projecte d in 1403, see de la Roncière, *Marine française*, ii. 176 and n. 2.

January 1407 Orleans was forced to abandon his attempts to capture
the castle of Bourg-sur-Gironde, without having achieved the
slightest military advantage; while John the Fearless never even set
out from his headquarters at St. Omer.

The reasons for the cancellation of his expedition remain obscure.
Ordered and empowered by King Charles VI on 23 September 1406
to assemble an army at royal expense and lead it against the English
in Picardy, John was promised a personal salary of 6,000 francs per
month from 1 September onwards. On 25 October, at Hesdin, he
issued his letters convoking the army, and troops were being reviewed
at St. Omer, where he himself arrived on 30 October, on 2 and
3 November. On 3 November a ducal secretary, Guillaume Vignier,
was given twenty crowns to buy himself a basinet and other armour
at St. Omer, so that he could serve the duke in arms against the
English. Meanwhile repeated efforts by John the Fearless to obtain
the promised royal funds to pay his troops and other expenses were
proving unsuccessful. On 7 November, that indefatigable correspond-
ent, Jehan Chousat, wrote from St. Omer to the *gens des comptes* at
Dijon:

> [The duke of Burgundy has sent word] to the king and to my lords
> [the French princes] that he has now been here for a long time; that his
> funds are exhausted; and that he cannot very well maintain his large
> army in being any longer. . . .
> He has had magnificent equipment prepared, as fine as has ever been
> seen in the kingdom of France: for instance a fortress and a redoubt of
> wood, which can be placed wherever they are needed for a siege, to be
> manned and held against all comers. He has 120 cannons, 20 casks of
> powder, 200,000 quarrels, 1,000 battle-axes, 20,000 caltrops,[1] 1,200
> shields . . . [etc. etc. He has assembled] boats . . . and a vast number of
> transport wagons from the neighbourhood, which are already prepared
> and loaded for departure tomorrow. . . . And I can assure you that for
> this . . . [campaign] my lord [the duke] has today lodged with him in
> this town and the surroundings, 3,800 knights and squires . . ., 1,800
> crossbow-men, about 1,000 pikemen and 3,500 pioneers, [etc] . . .
> all ready to set out tomorrow with my lord as soon as he has heard
> Mass. . . .

However, the expedition did not leave St. Omer on 8 November.
Instead, by the middle of the month, it had been called off altogether.

---

[1] A caltrop is 'an iron ball armed with four sharp prongs, placed so that,
when thrown on the ground, it has always one projecting upwards. Used to
impede cavalry' (*O.E.D.*). A quarrel is a crossbow bolt.

Jehan Chousat did not fail to keep his Dijon colleagues informed of the course of events:

Hesdin   [About 20 November 1406]

Dear sirs, may it please you to know that after my lord [the duke] had payed his troops their wages for fifteen days and all was ready for an attack on Guines, which is a fine castle and the strongest the English possess hereabouts, the royal chamberlains, who are with the duke, in number about eight, together with the lord of Calleville, commissioned by the king for this purpose, produced royal letters patent prohibiting the duke and his men . . . from leaving St. Omer, for fear of the damage which might ensue to his army and the kingdom. My lord has been and is as saddened and angered by this as it is possible to be in all the world, and no one can placate him. He himself has offered to pay the expenses of 2,000 combatants for two or three months, but nothing has prevented the whole expedition from being cancelled, and all the equipment which my lord had got ready for the campaign has been stored away in case he returns another time. . . .

On 17 November John the Fearless was back at Hesdin, whence he sent Jehan, lord of Croy and Renty, and Jehan de Chalon, lord of Arlay, to Paris, 'to report . . . to the king and certain princes of the blood how, because of lack of finance and through other just causes [the duke] has disbanded the . . . troops which he had assembled at St. Omer in October and November to advance towards Calais'. Thus the clerk, who wrote up the ducal accounts; perhaps not so well informed as Jehan Chousat.[1] We may take it that Monstrelet and others are right in stating that the expedition was called off from Paris at the last moment and that this cancellation infuriated John the Fearless, but there is insufficient evidence to implicate Louis of Orleans, who had left Paris for Guienne some time before. John himself is said to have later protested to the king that he had received neither men nor money from the government; that Louis, duke of Anjou, had refused to permit the *aide* for John's Calais campaign to be levied in Anjou and Maine; and that all the money that had been raised had been sent to Louis of Orleans in Guienne.

If the exact truth about the cancellation of this expedition seems unattainable, there can be no doubt about its French nature. John the Fearless, who had been appointed royal lieutenant and captain-

[1] ACO B1554, f. 213. For Monstrelet's account, see *Chronique*, i. 135–6; see, too, *Chron. comitum Flandrensium*, 250–1, and, for what follows, Juv. des Ursins, *Hist. de Charles VI*, 436 and Plancher, iii. 237.

general of Picardy and West Flanders by Charles VI on 21 April 1406, was acting on this occasion as a French prince, for the French government and under its orders. But, at the very moment of his arrival at St. Omer under royal instructions to attack the English at Calais, he was engaged, as count of Flanders, in negotiating a truce with the English. Indeed on 1 November 1406 he instructed his ambassadors Renier Pot and Jaques de Courtiambles to guarantee, as part of the proposed treaty, that 'no act of war against Calais or other English castles in Picardy would be made by the garrisons of Gravelines, Bourbourg, Dunkirk and the other fortresses in West Flanders. . . .' [1] That is to say, he guaranteed the neutrality of his own Flemish frontier fortresses in the event of a French attack on Calais led by himself. In fact, throughout the first half of November, when John the Fearless was at St. Omer, his Flemish ambassadors were in contact with the English, though they could not agree whether to hold the next Anglo-Flemish conference at Calais or Bourbourg. There is no need to invoke duplicity here; merely a distinction between the royal captain-general of Picardy and the count of Flanders; between France and Burgundy.

John the Fearless must evidently have found episodes like the countermanding of his attack on Calais both embarrassing and frustrating. But the weakness, or inadequacy, of the position accorded to him by his rivals in France in 1406-7 is nowhere better displayed than in the sphere of finance. Under Philip the Bold the principal value of the French connection was financial: nearly half Philip's revenues, to the tune of some 235,000 francs per annum, came from the French royal treasury.[2] But after 1404 the duke of Burgundy received no pension from the crown and practically no gifts. He continued to receive a regular income from the royal *aides* voted in Artois, but he no longer enjoyed those of Nevers and Rethel. The most he could hope for was occasional compensation for real or invented expenses incurred in France or on behalf of the French government, and an annual allowance of 12,000 francs for the upkeep and garrisoning of Sluis castle. Even these sums were more often promised than actually paid.

It is instructive to compare the degree of financial exploitation of the French crown achieved by these two dukes in the period 1402-1407, as revealed in the accounts of their receipt-general of all

[1] Pot, *R. Pot*, 317-18 and, for what follows, de Coussemaker, *ACFF* xxvi (1901-2), 313-15. Cf. Nordberg, *Ducs et la royauté*, 144-6.
[2] Vaughan, *P. the Bold*, 231.

Years	Account no.	Total receipts in gifts and pensions from crown
	PHILIP THE BOLD	
1402–3	ACO B1532	198,941[1]
1403–4	ACO B1538	188,600[1]
	JOHN THE FEARLESS	
1405–6	ACO B1543	37,000
1406–7	ACO B1547	2,000

finances. The figures demonstrate well enough the striking contrast between the two, but they include both cash receipts and receipts in the form of assignments.[2] To ascertain what was actually paid *in cash*, and what was owing, to John the Fearless, we must have recourse to another document. In the winter of 1406–7, John made a determined effort to persuade the French government to pay its debts to him and, in April 1407, royal letters were issued ordering the sum of 347,591 francs to be paid in annual instalments from the royal *aides* in the dioceses of Amiens, Beauvais, Chalons and Troyes. In these royal letters, Charles VI's debts to John are set out in interesting detail:

Analysis of Royal Letters of 15 April 1407 listing Charles VI's debts to John the Fearless (figures in francs)

Date	Nature	Total amount	Amount not paid
27.4.04–30.9.05	Pension of 36,000 f. p.a. granted to John on his father's death, terminating 30.9.05	45,300	45,300
27.4.04–30.4.07	Allowance for the defence of Sluis castle, of 12,000 f. p.a.	36,000	25,000
17.6.06	Grant towards cost of Compiègne wedding festivities	15,000	15,000
15.4.07	Military expenses incurred against the English, 1405 and 1406	72,625	72,625
15.4.07	Crown debts owed to Philip the Bold	189,666	189,666
GRAND TOTAL OWING TO JOHN, 15 APRIL 1407			347,591

Besides the sums mentioned in these letters, a handful of other

[1] Figures from van Nieuwenhuysen, *Recette générale*; others direct from the accounts. In this and what follows I have worked over the same ground as Pocquet, *MSHDB* vi (1939), 113–44 and ibid., vii (1940–1), 95–129 and Nordberg, *Ducs et la royauté*, 30–4.
[2] An assignment was an order, addressed to a receiver or accounting officer, instructing him to pay a stated sum to the bearer.

royal grants or gifts made to or on behalf of John the Fearless in these years are traceable:

Date	Nature of grant	Amount	Comment	Source
23.1.06	Grant towards repairing Sluis castle	18,000 francs	Probably at least partly paid	ACO B1543, f. 51 a–b and Pocquet *MSHDB*, vi (1939), 140–1.
16.7.06	Grant towards cost of a hôtel in Paris for Philip of Nevers	10,000 francs	Probably paid direct to Philip	Coville, *Petit*, 363.
1406	Gift from proceeds of royal salt-tax	20,000 crowns	Probably never paid	ibid.

Since there is no sign whatsoever, in the ducal accounts, that the sum of 347,591 francs, mentioned in the royal letters just analysed, ever was paid to John the Fearless, we may safely conclude that he was obtaining next to nothing from French sources in 1405–7.

John the Fearless's failure to maintain the flow of wealth from France to Burgundy which his father had engineered, threatened to undermine the whole financial situation of the Burgundian state. Moreover, the funds once enjoyed by Burgundy were now being diverted to Orleans, whose annual income from the French crown in 1405–17, excluding that from royal *aides* granted to him, must have exceeded 200,000 francs.[1] Clearly, among the many motives which impelled John the Fearless to assassinate his rival Louis of Orleans, was the need for funds from France, combined with the bitter knowledge that Louis was obtaining them.

In almost every direction, in every field of political activity, the two dukes were at cross purposes. While John supported the University of Paris in demanding extreme measures against the intransigent Benedict XIII, Louis was much more favourably inclined towards the Avignon pope. In the Low Countries, Louis was allied with several enemies of the Burgundian house, notably with the city of Liège, which was in open revolt, after September 1406, against its bishop-elect, who was John the Fearless's brother-in-law and ally, John of Bavaria, and with Reinald IV, duke of Guelders. The alliance of these two, Liège and Guelders, against John of Bavaria, which was

---

[1] Coville, *Petit*, 361–2 and 365–6; Mirot, *RQH* xcv (1914), 333–4 and Pocquet, *RUB* vii (1954–5), 394–5. For what follows, see Valois, *Schisme*, iii. 419–20, 426, 430–1, etc. and Minder, *BSVAH* xli (1954), 121–90.

signed on 1 October 1407, may well have been brought about by
Louis of Orleans. Nor were his activities in this area limited to
alliances and the proferring of fief-rents. Within a month of the final
accession to the duchy of Brabant in December 1406 of John's
brother Anthony, Louis of Orleans, acting as ruler of the duchy of
Luxembourg, had informed the captains of the castles of Millen,
Waldfeucht, Gangelt and Fauquemont, all of which were on Duke
Anthony's territories, that he proposed to take possession of them,
on the grounds that they really belonged to Luxembourg. Louis had
been ruler of that duchy since 1402, and John the Fearless must have
been well aware that he was the only serious obstacle to the further
progress of the Burgundian dynasty in the Netherlands, north-east
France, and the valley of the Rhine.[1]

Although it would be wrong to exclude personal considerations
altogether from the murder of Louis of Orleans by John the Fearless,
it was, primarily, a political assassination. Yet contemporaries, and
many subsequent writers, have preferred a purely personal or even
romantic explanation. Basin, the fifteenth-century Norman chronicler,
describes how Louis of Orleans, who lusted after almost every beautiful woman he met, took a fancy to John's wife, the fair Margaret of
Bavaria (Plate 2), pursued her during a ball into a corner of the
royal palace and, having failed to persuade her to commit adultery
with him, actually tried to take her by force. According to Basin, John
swore to avenge this indignity by killing Louis.[2] Others record how
John the Fearless, happening one day to enter a private portrait
gallery of Louis of Orleans's, in which were hung paintings of all
the women whose favours he had enjoyed, found his own wife among
them.

Be this as it may, the murder committed on 23 November 1407
was certainly premeditated and carefully planned in advance. As
early as June 1407 enquiries were being made among the Paris
property-agents for a suitable house near the royal hôtel de St. Pol
which could be rented and used as a base by the gang of assassins
which John had got together under a Norman knight, Raoul

---

[1] Pirenne, *Hist. de Belgique*, ii. 226.
[2] Basin, *Charles VII*, i. 12–13. For what follows, see Collas, *Valentine de
Milan*, Celier, *Mélanges . . . L. Halphen*, 119–23, Cartellieri, *SHAWP* iii
(1912), no. 11, 3–9, Sellier, *Quartier Barbette* and Nordberg, *Ducs et la
royauté*, 225–30. The main sources are Raymond, *BEC* xxvi (1865), 215–49
(the extract below is from pp. 227–8), de Baye, *Journal*, i. 206–7 (whence the
extract which follows), and Monstrelet, *Chronique*, i. 154–64.

d'Anquetonville. The murder itself was thus described by Nicolas de Baye, clerk of the court at the Paris *Parlement*.

Wednesday, 23 November.

This evening, at about eight o'clock, Messire Louis, son of King Charles V and brother of the King Charles now ruling, duke of Orleans, count of Valois, of Blois, of Beaumont, of Soissons, of Angoulême, of Dreux, of Porcien, of Périgord, of Luxembourg and of Vertus; lord of Coucy, of Montargis, of Château-Thierry, of Épernay and of Sedan in Champagne and many other lands; married to Madame [Valentina], daughter of the late duke of Milan, Giangaleazzo [Visconti], by whom he had three sons and a daughter, as he was returning from the queen's hôtel, which is near the Porte Barbette, towards the church of the Blancs-Manteaux, accompanied, modestly enough for someone of his rank, by three mounted men and two on foot, with one or two torches . . . aged about thirty-six years, was struck down and killed by eight or nine armed men who had been hidden in a [neighbouring] house . . . for a week or two. They cleaved his head in two with a halberd so that he was knocked from his horse and his brains strewn on the pavement. One of his hands was cut clean off and, with him, they killed one of his valets, who had thrown himself on him to protect him. . . . Thus he, who was such a great and powerful lord, and to whom naturally, whenever there was no effective ruler, the government of this realm belonged, in so brief a moment ended his days, hideously and shamefully.

The inquest, which was opened next day by the provost of Paris, revealed the details, though only one witness saw the actual murder:

Jaquette, wife of Jehan Griffart, shoemaker, living in rented rooms in the hôtel of the marshal of Rieux in the Vieille rue du Temple, aged about thirty-four years, sworn in and examined by me, Guillaume Marescot, *examinateur* [of the Châtelet], on Thursday, 24 November 1407, made this statement on oath:

Yesterday evening between seven and eight o'clock, having gone to her window overlooking the street to see if her husband was coming, and also to take in some of her child's bedclothes which she had put out to dry on a pole, she saw a nobleman on horseback accompanied by five or six mounted men and three or four on foot, with two or three torches carried in front, who were coming from the direction of the queen's hôtel, that is to say, from the Porte Barbette. The nobleman was bareheaded and was playing with a glove or a muffle and, it seemed to her, singing. After she had watched for a moment, she left the window to put her child to bed. But, almost at once, she heard someone shout 'Kill him! Kill him!' She returned hurriedly to the window, still holding her child, and saw the nobleman on his knees in the middle of the street in front of the entrance to the hôtel of the marshal of Rieux, still bare-headed . . . with seven or eight masked men around him, who were armed with swords and axes. She did not see any horses. These men were striking the nobleman, whom she saw once or twice ward off a blow with his arm, exclaiming 'What's this? Who does it come from?' To which nobody replied. Then she saw him fall, all stretched out in the middle of the street, while the men continued to lay about him with all their might . . . as if they were beating a mattress. While they were doing this, she yelled 'Murder!' as loud as she could; on which one of the men in the street . . . whom she could not actually see, called out 'Shut up, you damned woman! Shut up!'

While all this was going on, two or three torches were being held up to provide illumination for the nobleman's attackers. When they had struck him [down] in this way, she noticed coming out of the house 'at the sign of Our Lady', which was and is opposite the scene described, a big man wearing a large red hood which concealed his face. He approached the aforesaid attackers and said to them, 'Put out the lights! Let's go! He's dead! Take heart!' And immediately they left the nobleman, who was no longer moving at all, with a burning torch lying on the ground near him, and fled at once, accompanied by the big man with the red hood, into the rue des Blancs-Manteaux, at the entrance to which she saw them extinguish the other torches they had in the roadside mud. . . .

When the culprits had gone, she noticed that someone was lying on the ground near the nobleman. This man, as soon as they had gone, raised his head and cried 'Haro! My master!' or 'My lord!' she was not sure which. Meanwhile she repeatedly called out 'Murder!' and so did another woman, whose name she did not know, who lived in the rue des Rosiers and who happened to come along. On this, several people arrived on the spot and she heard them say that the dead man was my lord of Orleans, and that the other person on the ground with him was his valet. . . .

On Thursday, 24 November, while the provost of Paris began taking down the depositions of witnesses, members of Louis's household staff found the severed hand and scattered brains of their murdered master, and placed them in a lead box in his coffin. The mutilated remains were then interred in the church of the Celestins, accompanied there by the dukes of Anjou, Berry, Bourbon and, in solemn mourning like the rest of them, John the Fearless, perpetrator of the ghastly deed.

Suspicion at first fell on a Picard knight, Albert de Chauny, for it was public knowledge that his wife, Mariette d'Enghien, had been seduced by Louis of Orleans. Indeed later scandal-mongers claimed that de Chauny had had to suffer a worse affront even than this at the hands of the dead duke, for it was said that, on one occasion, Louis had shown him his wife, quite naked, though with her face covered, and asked him to judge her beauty. But it was soon ascertained that de Chauny had been away from Paris for more than a year and, almost at once, a much more promising line of enquiry was started: the interrogation of the Parisian water-carriers. This revealed that one of them, who had supplied water to the occupants of the house 'at the sign of Our Lady', was staying in John the Fearless's hôtel d'Artois, where he could not legally be arrested without leave of the owner. Word was immediately sent to John, asking permission to question the individual concerned. The messenger found him at the duke of Berry's hôtel de Nesle, in council with the other princes. At this juncture it seems that John's face must have betrayed his real feelings and, when the duke of Anjou drew him aside to ask him if he knew anything of this affair, he confessed that he was the cause of his cousin's death. But, while John of Berry broke down in tears, John the Fearless kept his nerve and abruptly left the room. Brushing aside a puzzled duke of Bourbon, whom he met as he hurriedly descended the stairs and informed that he was only going to the lavatory, John took horse at once and fled from Paris with a handful of companions, on Saturday, 26 November. It seems that he covered the hundred-odd miles to Bapaume, on the frontiers of his own territory of Artois, in one day, stopping only to break down behind him the bridge over the Oise at Pont Ste. Maxence. Legend has it that, galloping finally into Bapaume at one o'clock in the morning, John ordered the church bells to be rung in future on that night and at that hour, in memory of his narrow escape from mortal peril; and this annual midnight peal of bells was for long afterwards known as the duke of Burgundy's angelus.[1]

What happened to the murderers of Louis of Orleans? Léon Mirot, who devoted a lifetime of scholarship to the reign of Charles VI, discovered a great deal about Raoul d'Anquetonville, the ringleader. His motives for undertaking the crime were evidently financial: he was always in debt. But John the Fearless promised to make him solvent for the rest of his life and, on 12 August 1408, he was granted the handsome annual pension or allowance of 1,200 francs 'in consideration of the notable services which . . . [he] had

---

[1] De Barante, *Histoire des ducs*, i. 226. For the next paragraph, see Mirot, *BEC* lxxii (1911), 445–58 and ADN B17611 and 17614, letters of Raoul of 14 May 1409 and 29 June 1412, and ibid., 17615, letter from Jehan le Bossu, reporting Raoul's death, of 14 July 1413.

rendered to the king and [the duke of Burgundy] . . . for the special
and evident advantage of my lord the king and the royal family . . . ,
of us and ours, and of the whole kingdom, in preventing my lord
[the king] from being bereft . . . of his crown and we ourselves from
suffering a cruel death. . . .' After this, Mirot found no further trace
of the assassin, a failure which, in the circumstances, is hardly surprising, for he and his accomplices were in fact exiled to Bruges, and
remained there, isolated and, it seems, unhappy, during the succeeding years. Among the correspondence of the Lille *chambre des comptes*
are two letters from Raoul, one of which, dated 14 May 1409, from
Bruges, shows that he was again in financial trouble.

I have heard that the allowances of my poor companions and myself
have been stopped by ducal command, since when you have ordered the
receivers to cease paying us. . . . I know that you have heard about our
situation and that [you realize that] we shall have nothing to live on if
our allowances are stopped. . . . I apologize for not coming to the
chambre des comptes in person, but we are not like other people, because
we cannot go wherever we please. However [one day], when it pleases
my lord [the duke], we shall go where we like, for he is certainly powerful
enough [to arrange this]. . . .

But Raoul never could go wherever he pleased. He may have been
paid, but he remained immured at Bruges until death overtook him
on 24 May 1413.

CHAPTER THREE

Liège

Each of the Valois dukes of Burgundy found himself opposed, at one time or another, by the artisans of the great cities of the Netherlands. In 1382 Philip the Bold crushed the citizen-militia of Ghent on the field of Roosebeke; in 1408 it was the turn of Liège to be vanquished at Othée by John the Fearless. Each of these battles marked a further step in the subjection of the Low Countries to Burgundian influence and control; each was a capital event in the military annals of Burgundy; and each furnished subjects for a special commission of tapestry by the duke. In a sense, John the Fearless's expedition to Liège was something special and separate from the rest of his reign as duke, something which, although relevant and related to other events and activities, nevertheless demands a chapter apart.[1]

Liège, in the later middle ages, was an imperial prince-bishopric whose extensive territories along the river Meuse embraced numerous towns, some of them, like Liège itself, Huy and Dinant, Walloon; while others, like Tongres and St. Trond, were Flemish-speaking. Lying for the most part between the duchies of Brabant and Limbourg, it formed a vast enclave in the territories which, after 1406, were ruled by Duke Anthony of Brabant, brother of John the Fearless. Eighteen miles below Liège, on the Meuse, the flourishing city of Maastricht was ruled jointly by the bishop of Liège and the duke of Brabant.

[1] For the tapestries, see Plancher, iii. 289; de Laborde, *Ducs de Bourgogne*, ii. 270; Michelant, *BCRH* (3) xiii (1872), 245–6; and Bauyn, *BSHF* (1847–8), 232 and 242. For this chapter in general, see Daris, *Histoire de Liège*; Kurth, *Cité de Liège*; Lallemand, *Lutte de Liège contre Bourgogne*; Schneider, *Johann von Baiern*; Pirenne, *Hist. de Belgique*, ii; Tourneur, *BIHBR* xxvii (1952), 293–316; Minder, *BSVAH* xli (1954), 121–90; *Algemene geschiedenis*, iii. 299–303, and the works cited by them. On the battle of Othée itself, few have improved on or read Wille's thesis, *Die Schlacht von Othée*.

During the fourteenth century the principality of Liège, like much of the rest of the Netherlands, had been the scene of prolonged and bitter class warfare. From 1316, the prince-bishop had been forced to share power with the clergy, nobles and towns. In 1373, in the so-called Peace of the Twenty-Two, he made further important concessions. Finally, in 1384, when the weavers and other artisans of Ghent were in open though unsuccessful revolt against their ruler the count of Flanders, the craft gilds of Liège virtually seized control of the city. But successive prince-bishops were not easily content with the mere shadow of power: they took every opportunity to reassert themselves, and none tried harder to restore episcopal authority than John of Bavaria, brother of John the Fearless's wife Margaret, who in 1390, at the age of seventeen, became bishop-elect of Liège. Since he had taken only sub-deacon's orders, he could not be enthroned as bishop: he had to be content with the title 'elect of Liège'. Certain naïve or ill-informed chroniclers claimed that the inhabitants of Liège rebelled against John of Bavaria because he refused to take higher orders. In fact, the open revolt against him which first broke out in 1394 and which was renewed in 1402 and the succeeding years, was entirely due to his vigorous if rash attempts to establish and maintain his own authority. Indeed his aims, or dreams, seem to have been the complete overthrow of the civic constitution of Liège, and the transformation of the principality into an hereditary state.[1]

The issues at stake at Liège were not simply internal to that city or principality. In the first place, personal relationships were involved, for John of Bavaria was closely related to the three most powerful rulers in the Low Countries: the count of Flanders was his brother-in-law John the Fearless; John's brother, Anthony, duke of Brabant, was likewise his brother-in-law; while the ruler of the united counties of Hainault, Holland and Zeeland was his brother William, whose ducal status was based on a rather shadowy claim to use the title duke of Bavaria. Furthermore, religious loyalties were involved, for John of Bavaria had been recognized as bishop-elect of Liège by the 'Roman' pope, Boniface IX and, though he withdrew his allegiance or obedience from the 'Roman' pope soon after Charles VI of France withdrew his obedience from the 'Avignon' pope in 1398, he returned to the obedience of Innocent VII in 1404, a year after France had returned to that of Benedict XIII. Because of John of Bavaria's allegiance to the 'Roman' pope, the opposition to him in Liège was supported, from 1406 on, by the 'Avignon' pope, Benedict XIII. A third pheno-

[1] Mirot, *AB* iii (1931), 316.

menon was bound up with John of Bavaria's struggle against his own subjects: the rivalry of John the Fearless and Louis of Orleans. Louis was a partisan of Benedict XIII; he helped to persuade Benedict to support the citizens of Liège against John of Bavaria; he had entered into an alliance with Liège in December 1404 and, above all, Liège, lying on the northern frontier of his duchy of Luxembourg and surrounded on the east and north by his allies or vassals, was an obvious target for his territorial ambitions.

The intrigues and evident ambitions of Louis of Orleans, combined perhaps with an element of family solidarity, would probably have been sufficient inducement for John the Fearless to intervene in favour of his brother-in-law, but there was a further important motive. At the very moment, in 1406–7, when John of Bavaria turned to John the Fearless for help against the artisans of Liège, the Flemish weavers were manifesting their discontent in Ghent, Bruges and Ypres. What could be more natural and desirable, in these circumstances, than for John the Fearless to plan and deliver a blow which would strike simultaneously at the aspirations of the communes and the ambitions of Louis of Orleans? In fact, however, Louis was murdered almost a year before the citizens of Liège were crushed at Othée. But we must turn now to look at the course of events.

In 1406, the intermittent revolts of Liège against its bishop were taken a stage further by the election, in September, of a regent or *mambour* and a new bishop, or rather anti-bishop, to replace John of Bavaria, who was formally deposed. The regent, Henry, lord of Perwez, now set about the systematic conquest of the principality from John of Bavaria, and had soon reduced the whole of it apart from the fortress of Bouillon and the town of Maastricht. Meanwhile, his nephew Thierry de Perwez, the newly-elected anti-bishop, sent an embassy to the 'Avignon' pope Benedict XIII to ask for his recognition and support. It was at this juncture that John of Bavaria, who had on two recent and critical occasions, in 1401 and 1405, led a contingent of troops to Paris on the duke of Burgundy's behalf, turned for help to John the Fearless. On 5 November 1406, John the Fearless ordered the payment of 4,000 crowns to John of Bavaria; and this was followed, in January 1407, by the despatch to Bouillon of a contingent of 235 knights, squires and archers under the command of Girart de Bourbon,[1] which, however, failed to save the castle from falling into the hands of the lord of Perwez on 28 January 1407.

---

[1] ACO B1543, f. 111 and B1547, fos. 162a–b and 215a–b. For the next paragraph, see *Chron. de J. de Bavière*, 167–8 and Valois, *Schisme*, iii. 66–7.

John the Fearless's help was by no means limited to financial and military aid. In November 1406, for instance, at the request of the canons of St. Lambert's, Liège, then in exile at St. Trond, he wrote to the aged Duchess Joan of Brabant and his brother Anthony, asking them to grant asylum in Louvain and Brabant generally to the canons of St. Lambert's and other political refugees who had fled from the rebels or been banished by them. In 1407, moreover, it was evidently John the Fearless who was responsible for arresting at Langres the ambassador from Liège who was returning from Benedict XIII with papal bulls recognizing the eighteen-year-old Thierry de Perwez as bishop of Liège and permitting him to take all the ecclesiastical orders in one day. This ambassador, Jaques Badus, a quondam road-mender who has achieved a certain dubious fame through citation by some over-romantic historians as an example of the democratic character of the revolutionary government at Liège, was later released from prison at the instigation of Louis of Orleans.

John of Bavaria's situation grew more precarious during 1407. The chronicler Jehan de Stavelot claims that, had it not been for his pre-occupation with Louis of Orleans in the summer and autumn of 1407, John the Fearless would have led an army to his brother-in-law's aid in the autumn of that year.[1] In actual fact, a general mobilization was ordered by John the Fearless on 13 August 1407, the marshal of Burgundy, Jehan de Vergy, being instructed to assemble all available troops at La Capelle-en-Thiérache on 25 September, to go to the aid of John of Bavaria. But these plans were altered, not because of John the Fearless's preoccupation with Louis of Orleans, but because of the request of Duke Anthony of Brabant for military help in his war against Reinald IV, duke of Guelders—the Red Duke, as he was known to contemporaries—who was allied with the revolutionary government at Liège. Thus John's troops were diverted from Liège to join Anthony and his brother Philip of Nevers in their attack on Guelders in October 1407.[2] John of Bavaria, who had hoped to reconquer his principality with the aid of Burgundian and other forces in the last week of September 1407, was disappointed, and found himself, from 24 November onwards, besieged by Henry, lord of Perwez, in Maastricht. This time, John the Fearless's failure to help him *was* due to his rivalry with the duke of Orleans, for he was fully

[1] De Stavelot, *Chronique*, 126–7. For what follows, see *Itinéraires*, 586.
[2] *Geschiedenis van Vlaanderen*, iii. 88–90; de la Chauvelays, *Armées*, 165–7 and ACO B1547, f. 215a–b; ACO B1554, f. 213b; *Chron. de J. de Bavière*, 170–1 and 177. The next paragraph is based on this chronicle.

occupied with French affairs for some months after the murder of
Louis on 23 November—the day before the start of the siege of
Maastricht. Actually it was the extremely cold winter which saved
John of Bavaria, by interfering with military operations to such an
extent that the lord of Perwez was forced to raise the siege on
7 January 1408.

He was back again within a few months. On 31 May 1408 he once
more led out the militia of Liège to besiege Maastricht, which still
held out for John of Bavaria. But the town was well defended, and
John himself arrived in June from Holland with substantial reinforcements, which easily broke through the besiegers' lines. At first,
John of Bavaria tried to make peace with his attackers by sending out
letters inviting them to overthrow the extremist elements among them
and return to their homes; but the only reply he obtained was a
diploma made out of the bark of a tree and 'sealed' with a lump of
cow-dung. He retaliated in the time-honoured manner by hanging
some prisoners in full view of the besieging army, and returning a
party of them with their eyes gouged out, led by one of their number
with one eye left. In July the city of Maastricht was subjected to a
fearsome artillery bombardment, which permitted the anonymous
chronicler of the reign of John of Bavaria to colour his work with an
impossible series of miraculous escapes.

During the whole of the early part of the siege of Maastricht, until
5 July in fact, John the Fearless was in Paris with Duke Anthony of
Brabant. The latter must have been somewhat embarrassed by his
brother-in-law's requests for help, because Henry of Perwez was his
loyal vassal and ally. He at first resolved on cautious neutrality, while
William of Bavaria, count of Hainault-Holland, signed an alliance
with his brother John of Bavaria on 17 July 1408, which must have
embodied a firm promise of immediate military aid. By 4 August, the
chronicler tells us, 'the good news concerning the lord dukes of
Burgundy and Hainault was known at Maastricht',[1] and it must have
been at about this time that John the Fearless and the other allies
sent their challenges or ultimatums to Henry of Perwez, inviting him
to raise the siege or fight. The chronicler describes the desperate
attempts made by the leaders of the Liège rebels somehow to frustrate
or delay this threatened combination against them. Forged royal
letters were sent to John the Fearless, ordering him to desist from his
attack on Liège; forged letters of John of Bavaria were distributed to

[1] *Chron. de J. de Bavière*, 192, and, for the rest of the paragraph, de Stavelot,
Chronique, 116; ACO B1560, f. 82 and *Chron. de J. de Bavière*, 192-3.

the allies; and bogus pilgrims were despatched to spread the false news of the surrender of Maastricht and the flight of John of Bavaria. Other sham pilgrims, calculated to demoralize the defenders, were infiltrated into Maastricht to assure the townspeople that, though they had travelled through France, Burgundy, Picardy and Flanders, they had seen no sign of any troops coming to their and John of Bavaria's aid.

John the Fearless and his brother-in-law William of Bavaria were not to be so easily put off. They organized a preliminary attack on Liège in August, while their main forces were being assembled. John's contribution to this pillaging expedition, which failed to cause Henry of Perwez to raise the siege of Maastricht, is recorded in the accounts of his receiver-general of all finances, Jehan de Pressy:[1]

> To the aforesaid Pressy, the sum of 3,818 francs, 16/3d. of Tours, royal money, which he has paid and handed over for the following purposes, that is to say:
>
> For the payment of four knights-banneret, 33 other knights-bachelor, 284 squires, in all 366 men, whom our lord [the duke of Burgundy] sent . . . in the month of August 1408 to the country of Liège, in the company of my lord of Hainault, to try to raise the siege which the Liègeois had laid to Maastricht and to devastate the said country with fire; these troops to be paid for fifteen days . . .   2,745 f.
>
> Item, for the wages of 267 archers who took part in this expedition . . .
>
> Item, for the purchase of arrows at Arras and St. Quentin . . .
>
> Item, for pennons to fix on the ends of lances   10 crowns
>
> Item, to two carters, for the transport of viretons[2] from St. Omer to Beaumetz-lèz-Cambrai   6 crowns
>
> Item, for the trumpeter who accompanied these troops, by way of gift   6 crowns
>
> Item, to two heralds   12 crowns
>
> [Total] for this, paid by order dated 4.9.1408   3,818 francs, 16/3d.

Meanwhile, John the Fearless's preparations for the main expedition went on apace. The marshal was on active service from 17 August

---

[1] ACO B1554, f. 225b; see Relig. de St. Denys, iv. 144–8 and *Chron. de J. de Bavière*, 194, on this expedition.
[2] A vireton is a 'crossbow bolt so constructed as to rotate on its axis while flying' (*O.E.D*).

onwards; from 5 September on, the ducal financier Dino Rapondi was engaged in raising the necessary funds; on 8 September the duke ordered 25 barrels of oats from Malines, because supplies were short in Flanders;[1] and, on 9 September, we find him instructing the bailiff of Bruges to make urgent arrangements for the payment of a Scottish contingent, the leader of which, Alexander Stewart, earl of Mar, who had agreed to serve in the Burgundian army against Liège, was returning to Scotland from a pilgrimage to the Holy Land. This letter has a postscript written by John the Fearless in his own hand—the only surviving example, apart from signatures, of his autograph.

From the duke of Burgundy, count of Flanders, of Artois, and of Burgundy.

Dear and well-beloved bailiff, God willing, we have decided on our departure for the Liège campaign. We must have men-at-arms and bowmen where we can best find them and, for this reason, we are sending for the earl of Mar, who comes from Scotland and is at the moment in our town of Bruges with a number of excellent soldiers and, especially, bowmen, in his company. Neither the earl nor his troops can enter our service without ready money, with which, at the moment, as you may have heard, we are not very plentifully supplied. We therefore pray and require you, on all the loyalty and service which you owe to us as dearly as you love our person and our honour, and on pain of incurring our eternal indignation, to send us at once the sum of 500 gold crowns and pay and hand over these 500 gold crowns to our beloved and faithful secretary, Master Johannes de le Keythulle, who has been instructed and ordered by us to deliver them to the aforesaid earl of Mar so that he can come to us with his company. If by any chance you have not got the aforesaid sum, you must borrow it regardless of the difficulties and cost, and we shall wholly return and refund to you the expenses and loss which you incur in doing this. And also we want you to recoup this sum of 500 gold crowns from the first [available] judicial revenues of your bailiwick, [entering it] on the account which you are due to render next January, and we shall send you letters patent for this.

You had better not mean in any way to let us down over this, because in truth, if there is any defaulting, it will displease us more than anything else could, and we shall certainly remember it in the future. Dear and well-beloved friend, may God keep you. Written at Tournai, the

---

[1] ACO B1556, f. 177a–b and B1558, f. 191a–b; de Lichtervelde, *Grand commis*, 155 n. 148. The letter which follows is said to be in AGR Acquits de Lille, but I have not found it there, though the authorities kindly supplied me with the photograph reproduced here. See, too, *Chron. de J. de Bavière*, 197 and Monstrelet, *Chronique*, i. 351.

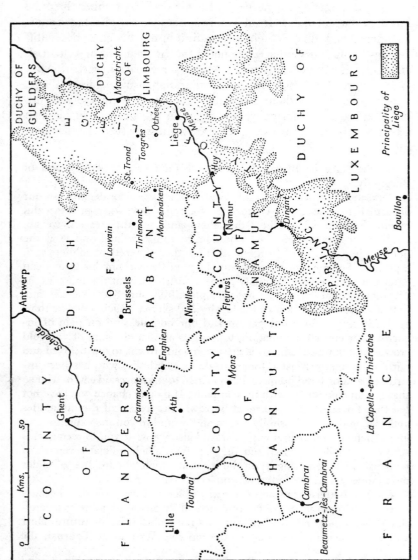

2. Map illustrating the campaign of Othée, 1408

ninth day of September. And, so that you recognize that this comes from our own initiative and wishes, we have written what follows with our own hand:

Bailiff, accomplish what I have written to you about or, if not, I shall show you how displeased I am.

Jehan   Fortier

John's main army was concentrating at or near Tournai, then a French city, in the last week of August and early September, under his personal supervision. Attempts on the part of the French government to delay or cancel his campaign were as unsuccessful as those of the people of Liège. Royal letters had been sent on 29 August 1408 prohibiting the citizens of Tournai from permitting any troops whatsoever, even those of princes of the blood royal, to enter their city; but, by the time these letters were read out to the consuls or magistrates of Tournai on 9 September, it was a fortnight too late. John the Fearless himself had been there since 27 August and was only too glad to offer to withdraw, for by then he was all set to march. He left the city on 11 September, promising not to return the same way, and taking with him, apparently, Tournai's very modest contribution to his army—twenty-five crossbow-men. Some time after John the Fearless's departure from Tournai, eighteen cartloads of wine rumbled out of the city and followed in the wake of the Burgundian army towards Liège: refreshments for the combatants.[1]

Such was the hurry to start on campaign, that there had been no time for the Burgundian troops to be properly reviewed, but this was done at Nivelles, in Brabant, on 15 and 16 September, by the marshal of Burgundy, Jehan de Vergy, and by David de Brimeu, councillor and chamberlain of the duke. Some guide to the way in which the Burgundian contingent on the Liège campaign was made up, and perhaps to its total size, is provided by the records of these reviews surviving at Dijon and printed by de la Chauvelays, and by the payments entered in the accounts of the receipt-general of all finances. This information is set out on the following page. To these troops must be added certain other contingents: an unspecified number (perhaps 20 or 30) of crossbow-men from Cambrai and Termonde; 80 crossbow-men and 37 archers sent by the towns of Picardy; a group of 72 men-at-arms and 24 archers which arrived only two days before the battle; and a 600-strong contingent led by

---

[1] Houtart, *Les Tournaisiens et le roi de Bourges*, 43-4; *Lettres closes*, 66-7; *Itinéraires*, and ACO B1558, f. 70b.

	Men-at-arms, i.e., knights and squires	Bowmen, i.e., archers and arbalestriers	Trumpets, minstrels, etc.	TOTALS
The two Burgundies, etc.	1,241	150	20	1,411
Flanders, Artois, etc.	1,367	967	—	2,334
TOTALS	2,608	1,117	20	3,745

Jehan, lord of Croy.[1] A force of 389 men-at-arms from Savoy led by Amé de Viry, and Philip of Nevers with some 400 men, arrived too late to take part in the battle. It seems possible that only a few contingents have altogether escaped mention in the sources. If this surmise is correct, then John the Fearless's own army may have amounted to some 5,000 fighting men, of whom about 1,500 were probably archers and crossbow-men and the rest mounted men-at-arms. Monstrelet says that William of Bavaria's army, which included the count of Namur's forces, numbered 1,200 men-at-arms and 2,000 infantry, which would bring the strength of the combined allied army to something over 8,000[2]—a figure which seems more acceptable than the much larger ones suggested by some modern historians.

John the Fearless left Nivelles on 16 September, and it was apparently on the next day, while he was conferring with his allies at Fleurus, in Hainault, that the last and most serious attempt to cut short his campaign was made, this time by the French government on behalf of Charles VI. The chronicler le Fèvre gives the following, perhaps somewhat embroidered, account of this episode:[3]

The king knew of the large-scale mobilization of the two princes, ready for their invasion of the country of Liège. He therefore sent Sir Guichard Dauphin, who later became grand master of the king's house-

[1] For the reviews and payments, see de la Chauvelays, *Armées*, 173–8 and ACO B1554, fos. 226–30; for the other contingents, ibid. f. 230 and ACO B1556, fos. 177–8. For the next sentence, see Monstrelet, *Chronique*, i. 370 and de Stavelot, *Chronique*, 142–3. Not mentioned in the accounts are the earl of Mar and his 80 men (Monstrelet, *Chronique*, i. 351), and the Tournai crossbow-men.

[2] Cf. Relig. de St. Denys, iv. 150, and see Monstrelet, *Chronique*, i. 353–4. For the rest of the sentence, see Kurth, *Cité de Liège*, 58, n. 4 and Schneider, *Johann von Baiern*, 49.

[3] Le Fèvre, *Chronique*, i. 10–11. Cf. *Chron. de J. de Bavière*, 195–6 and Monstrelet, *Chronique*, i. 351–3.

hold, with others in his company, to the duke of Burgundy, to prohibit him in the name of the king and on pain of severe punishment, from attacking the Liègeois or entering their country.

Now it is true that, when Sir Guichard Dauphin and his companions reached the duke of Burgundy and Duke William, they had already entered the territories of Liège, but, notwithstanding this, Sir Guichard accomplished what the king had charged him with, and made the above-mentioned prohibition. To which the duke of Burgundy replied that he had been and was still ready to obey the king, but he had gone so far, and was so near his enemies, that he could not withdraw without great shame. He knew well that the king would not wish him to dishonour himself and, after addressing several remarks to Sir Guichard Dauphin, he asked him, as his friend and relative, if he would help him, adding: 'You have fulfilled your obligations and are no longer an ambassador. As Sir Guichard Dauphin, will you help me to defend my honour?'

Sir Guichard replied that it seemed he could not return honourably without a nearer view of the enemy, and stated that he was ready to live and die with [Duke John] in combat with the rebel Liègeois. He had secretly brought his armour with him [packed] in baskets and, when his companions realized his intentions, they too resolved to arm themselves. And, because they had no armour, the duke provided them from his armoury. Thus they decided to fight with the duke of Burgundy.

John the Fearless crossed the frontiers of Liège with his army on 20 September and, two days later, he joined forces with his allies between Montenaken and Tongres. His own account of what followed may perhaps be preferred to others, particularly as its broad accuracy is confirmed by them. But his figure of 32,000 for the size of the opposing army at Othée must be reduced by at least a factor of two, and the same may be said for his estimate of the number of Liègeois killed in the battle. The chroniclers' conjectures or guesses about the number of Liègeois dead vary from 8,000 to 40,000. Some of them even have the audacity or impudence to give an exact figure. The local Maastricht chronicle, for instance, claims that the Liègeois left 23,917 dead on the field of battle; at Cologne the figure was put at 36,605; and, at Strasbourg, at 34,705! Jehan de Stavelot's figure of 8,368, which is the lowest of all, must be much nearer the mark.[1] Here is John the Fearless's letter to his brother Anthony describing the campaign and the battle.

[1] *Chronijk van Maastricht*, 71–2; *Chron. deutschen Städte. Cöln*, ii. 50; Slecht, *Forsetzung*, 121; and de Stavelot, *Chronique*, 119. The letter which follows is printed in Plancher, iii. no. 260; *Analectes belgiques*, i. 2–6; and *Régestes de Liège*, iii. no. 657. Where these texts differ, I have followed that in *Régestes*.

To my dear and well-beloved brother, the duke of Brabant and Limbourg.

My dear and well-beloved brother, I have received your letters,
which you sent me by the bearer of these, mentioning that you had
heard that, by the grace of God, I had fought the Liègeois, and that, if I
had let you know the day of the battle, you would very willingly have
been present. Be pleased to know, dearest and well-beloved brother,
that in what follows you shall learn how and in what manner things
happened, and then you will realize that I was unable, at the appropriate
moment, to let you know the day.

It is true, dearest and well-beloved brother, that [William of Bavaria],
my brother-in-law of Hainault, and I entered the country of Liège
last Thursday [20 September] with a numerous and excellent company
of knights and squires, and we advanced by different routes across
country to within a league of a town called Tongres in Hesbaye, where
we arrived last Saturday evening; and there we received information
from certain persons that on that very day the lord of Perwez and all the
Liègeois in his company, had raised the siege which they had laid to
Maastricht, in order to come and confront us. Because of this, my
brother-in-law and I sent out some of our scouts on the Sunday morning
[23 September 1408] to ascertain the truth, and these reported to us that
they had definitely seen the Liègeois coming towards us in battle order
and in vast numbers. So my brother-in-law and I arranged our forces
in good order, joining them together in order to meet and oppose the
aforesaid Liègeois.

When we had ridden forward about half a league, we saw them plainly,
above and quite near the town of Tongres, and they saw us. At this
point my brother-in-law and I, together with our people, dismounted in
a fairly advantageous position, thinking that they would come and attack
us there. We placed all our troops in a single mass in order to resist more
effectively the shock and charge which the Liègeois were likely to give us;
and we formed two wings of bowmen and men-at-arms. Soon, they
approached us to within about three bowshots, concentrating somewhat
towards the right, in the direction of the aforesaid town of Tongres,
so that the men of that town, numbering some 10,000, could join them.
There they stopped, drawn up in excellent order, and immediately
opened fire on us with their cannon.

After we had waited a little and seen that they were not going to
move, my brother-in-law and I, with the advice of the good captains and
knights in our company, decided to advance in good order and attack
the enemy where they were. [We also decided] that, to break up their
array and throw them into confusion, we should need 400 mounted men-
at-arms and 1,000 stalwart infantrymen to strike at their rear, while
we engaged them [in frontal assault]; and we appointed the lords of

Croy, of Heilly and of Rasse, your chamberlains and mine, to lead [this force], together with Enguerrand de Bournonville and Robin le Roux, my *écuyers d'écurie*.[1] . . . One hour after midday we marched to attack [the enemy] in the name of God and of Our Lady, in handsome and excellent order, joining battle with them and attacking them in such a way that, with the grace and help of Our Lord, the day was ours. In truth, dearest and well-beloved brother, experienced people say that they have never seen men fight so well as they did; for the battle lasted nearly one and a half hours and, for at least half an hour, no one knew which way it would go. As far as can be ascertained from those who inspected the dead, the lord of Perwez, his son the rebel anti-bishop, another son of his, and a good 24,000 to 26,000 Liègeois, were killed. They were all, or nearly all, armed, and they had in their army 500 mounted men, and 100 archers from England.

It happened that, when the battle was almost over, the men of Tongres sallied forth in arms to come to the Liègeois's aid. They advanced to within three bow shots, but turned in flight when they saw how matters were going, and were forthwith closely pursued by the mounted men on our side, and many of them killed.

However, in this battle, we have lost at least 60 to 80 knights and squires, which saddens me a great deal; for these were not among the worst. God forgive them. And as to the number of Liègeois who may have been in the battle . . . I have discovered for certain from some of their prisoners, taken in the battle, that they left the siege [of Maastricht] last Saturday morning [22 September] 40,000 strong, and went to Liège. There, some 8,000, whom the lord of Perwez considered to be unfit for battle, were left behind; [so] on the Sunday, the day of the battle, about 32,000 or more left Liège to advance towards us.

Moreover, my dear and well-beloved brother, be pleased to know that yesterday my brother-in-law of Liège [John of Bavaria] came handsomely accompanied to my brother-in-law of Holland and me. And today the towns of Liège, Huy, Dinant, Tongres and the other 'good towns' of the country have come to us to make submission, beseeching the said brother-in-law of Liège to have pity on them and pardon them. This he did, through the intervention of the aforesaid brother-in-law of Hainault and me, provided that they surrendered and handed over to him all the guilty persons—of whom there were still many—to do as he pleased with. Moreover, the said towns have asked pardon for everything they may have done in contempt of the said brother-in-law of Liège. All this has been arranged by my brother-in-law of Hainault and me; and to ensure that our decisions are obeyed, each town will give us whatever security we want.

[1] *Écuyer* = squire. The *écurie* was the department of the ducal household responsible for the horses.

Dear and beloved brother, may the Holy Spirit keep you. . . .
Written in my army, in the fields near Tongres, the 25th day of September [1408]. Your brother, the duke of Burgundy. . . .

Other sources add little to what John the Fearless related to his brother about the battle of Othée. Monstrelet, who seems to have based his account of the battle on John's letter, puts the allied casualties at the more realistic figure of 212 knights and squires. He confirms the impression given by others that the battle was planned and directed by John in person, even though he was in the thick of the fight.[1]

There is no need to expatiate on the bravery and coolness of the duke of Burgundy; nor to explain at length how, at the start of the battle, he moved on a small horse from one part of the army to another, exhorting and encouraging his men; and how he bore himself, until the end of the battle. In truth, his conduct was such that he was praised and honoured by all the knights and others of his company; and although he was frequently hit by arrows and other missiles, he did not, on that day, lose one drop of blood. When he was asked, after the defeat, if they ought to cease from killing the Liègeois, he replied that they should all die together, and that he had no wish for them to be taken and ransomed.

Both the strategy and tactics of the Othée campaign seem to have been skilfully planned, and it is hard to deny an element of military genius to John the Fearless. Two points are particularly striking. First, the use made of Anthony, duke of Brabant, who had been in close consultation with his brother John since the end of May, and who had had at least four conferences with him in August and September, must not pass unnoticed; for Anthony's army, mobilized under his personal command at Tirlemont on the frontiers of Brabant between 20 and 27 September, was evidently positioned there to constitute a strategic reserve. Secondly, the well-conceived and decisive flanking movement, led by the lords of Croy and Heilly and others, by means of which John won the battle, is a noteworthy example of his tactical skill. Each side appears to have made at least one major error of judgement: John does not seem to have foreseen the rapidity with which the Liègeois raised the siege of Maastricht and reorganized their forces to attack him; while the Liègeois, for their part, were apparently under the impression, when they marched out of Liège at eight o'clock that Sunday morning, that they would

[1] Monstrelet, *Chronique*, i. 365. Cf. Relig. de St. Denys, iv. 168, 170 and Le Roux de Lincy, *Chants historiques*, 13.

be able to attack and defeat William of Bavaria and his army before John the Fearless could come to his aid.[1]

The battle of Othée had an immediate and decisive effect in the principality of Liège: the collapse of the revolt against John of Bavaria. The surviving elements of opposition were savagely crushed. The allied dukes did not enter Liège itself. A week after the battle they camped outside the city and there presided over the decapitation of the ringleaders of the revolt while, inside Liège, a detachment of men-at-arms drowned in the Meuse the ecclesiastics who had supported or been instituted by the anti-bishop—for their blood could not be judicially shed. This nightmare revenge of John of Bavaria earned him the sobriquet Pitiless, while his brother-in-law John, equally responsible and probably even more merciless, was given the surname of Fearless because of his part at Othée.[2]

The victors made sure of the complete subjection of Liège by demanding 500 hostages from the city. These were shared out between the allies, and it was several years before all of them regained their liberty. Nearly eighteen months later we hear of some of them imprisoned in Artois, apparently at Aire, in the hôtel of a ducal official, Robert de Baincthun, who wrote to the *gens des comptes* at Lille on 21 February 1410 excusing himself from bringing his accounts for audit because of 'the business of the hostages from Liège, who are in my hôtel and who have no desire to please me. So they have pillaged my place and thrown out all my things, so much so that I have no hope, within ten years, of making good all the damage they have done and are still doing.'[3]

The final decision and judgement on the principality of Liège was pronounced at an assembly in Lille towards the end of October 1408. This was a veritable congress, for here was gathered the entire Burgundian clan, which of course included the principal rulers of the Low Countries: John the Fearless, Anthony of Brabant, William of Bavaria, John of Bavaria, Philip of Nevers and William of Namur. The sentence on Liège, pronounced jointly by the victors, John and William, and dated 24 October 1408, was harsh in the extreme. Some of its provisions may be roughly summarized.

  1. Liège and the other towns of the principality to surrender all their charters of privileges to the two dukes at Mons in Hainault on 12 November 1408.

---

[1] For this paragraph, see de Lichtervelde, *Grand commis*, 154–7, and *Chron. de J. de Bavière*, 196–7.
[2] Monstrelet, *Chronique*, i. 371 and 389.   [3] ADN B17612.

2. No new privilege to be granted to the inhabitants of the principality by the bishop or his chapter without the consent of the two dukes.

3. All gilds and confraternities in the city of Liège to be abolished.

4. No assemblies to be held in any of the towns without the bishop's permission.

5. The rulers, John and William, and their successors, to have free right of passage across the Meuse and through the territories of Liège, with or without troops.

6. The money of the two rulers to be legal currency throughout the lands of the bishop and chapter of Liège.

7. A chapel, with six priests, erected on the battlefield of Othée for the welfare of the souls of the slain, to be maintained at the expense of the bishop of Liège.

8. Annual masses on 23 September to be solemnly celebrated in every church in the principality of Liège.

9. Various fortifications to be destroyed, including the walls and towers of Dinant. The gate of Tongres which leads to Maastricht, together with forty feet of wall on either side of it, to be razed for ever.

10. A fine or *aide* of 220,000 gold crowns of France to be imposed on the inhabitants of the principality and paid to the two dukes.[1]

No time was lost in carrying out the terms of this judgement. On the very same day both dukes appointed their commissioners to supervise the demolition of fortifications and the confiscation of the charters, and by the end of the year the work of inventorying the charters and of levying the *aide* had begun. Much opposition was met by the commissioners appointed to collect the *aide*. In December, one of them, Gilbert de Leeuwerghem, wrote to a colleague describing the difficulties he was in and the delays caused by the resistance of the inhabitants. He added a jocular remark which is also a grim comment on the effect of the battle of Othée: 'And if you, who have always been a great lecher, have need of a widow or two besides mademoiselle your wife, you will be able to find plenty here.'[2] In spite, however, of delay and opposition, the whole of the *aide* was eventually levied, John's share of 110,000 crowns being accounted for and paid

---

[1] For this and other printed documents mentioned in what follows, see *Cartulaire de Hainaut*, iii, *Catalogue des actes de J. de Bavière*, and *Régestes de Liège*, iii. For those present at Lille, see O. van Dixmude, *Merkwaerdige geb.*, 47 and Quicke, *Mélanges . . . Pirenne*, 397.

[2] *Régestes de Liège*, iii. no. 672. For what follows, see *IAGRCC* iv. 127–8 and *Régestes*, iii. no. 705.

into his receipt-general of all finances by a special commissioner, Jehan du Buisson. Eventually, in March 1412, John and William gave the bishop and inhabitants of Liège their formal and joint receipt for 220,000 gold crowns of France. Although ostensibly John and William had gone to the aid of John of Bavaria against the Liègeois, it was the bishop-elect, just as much as his people, who was affronted and offended by, and who suffered from, the savage sentence of 24 October 1408. It is true that the revolt against him had been crushed, but the principality which he rightly regarded as his own was now virtually ruled by his brother and brother-in-law. It is hardly surprising then, that during the early months of 1409 a new alignment of persons and interests involved at Liège took place. John of Bavaria now emerges, in support of his subjects, in the rôle of critic and opponent of the sentence of 24 October. His aim, from now on, is its modification in favour of himself and the Liègeois. The victors of Othée were eventually persuaded to publish at Lille, on 12 August 1409, a supplement to, or modification of, the original sentence, in which important concessions were made; but they still insisted on their pound of flesh, that is to say, full payment of the 220,000 crowns, though they now postponed the dates for the remittance of the outstanding instalments. At the same time, some of the confiscated charters were returned. In the succeeding years, John of Bavaria continued to preside over the gradual restoration of the independent political life of his principality. John the Fearless had more pressing and practical matters to attend to than the maintenance of his influence at Liège, and he raised no protest when, on 26 March 1417, King Sigismund, who, as Emperor-elect, was theoretical suzerain of Liège, revoked the sentence John and his brother had promulgated in October 1408, and restored the privileges of the Liègeois. By this time, in any case, the whole situation was changing: William of Bavaria died a few days later, on 31 March, and by September 1417 John of Bavaria had abdicated his bishopric and principality.

In what way was the Othée campaign advantageous to John the Fearless? It was not a conquest, and no territorial gains were made as a result of it. But it was a decisive military and political event in the history of the Netherlands, and even of western Europe as a whole. It considerably enhanced John's prestige in general and his influence in the Netherlands in particular. It demonstrated the solidarity and the practical value of the network of relationships or alliances which had been constructed by Philip the Bold and carefully maintained by his son. More important, it was a crushing and tragic setback to the political aspirations of the urban populations of the Low Countries. Without damaging his own territories, and without alienating the sympathies of his own towns, John the Fearless had struck a blow for the prince's authority against urban privilege and civic liberty which could serve as a severe warning to the turbulent elements in the cities of Flanders. Another benefit was repeated by John from his victory over the Liègeois, for his position in France, uncertain or even insecure ever since the murder of Louis of Orleans in November 1407, was thereby strengthened and consolidated. But John the Fearless's activities in France will concern us in the next chapter. It must suffice to say here that the combination of military skill and ruthless suppression exhibited by him on the expedition to Liège in 1408 contributed everywhere to his growing power and influence.

CHAPTER FOUR

The Mastery of France:
1408-13

Although it was as a self-confessed criminal and a fugitive that John
the Fearless galloped out of Paris on Saturday, 26 November 1407,
his escape to Flanders did not entail an outright breach with France.[1]
The only attempt to pursue and capture him was made by a group of
Louis of Orleans's knights and supporters led by Clignet de Brebant,
and this was apparently called off by the French princes. These last,
who formed the French government and represented the French
king, proved utterly incapable of dealing with the crisis. The assassination of the brother of the king by the duke of Burgundy shattered
and demoralized them; instead of uniting, it divided them. While the
shock paralysed them, the knowledge that there was considerable
public support for John's deed prolonged and deepened their inaction.
Some sought revenge; some wished to pardon John; but the criminal
himself now embarked on a novel and audacious course of action: the
justification of his crime.

Throughout December contacts were maintained between John the
Fearless and Paris. Certain trusted ducal officials, either left behind in
Paris or sent there soon after the crime, worked for the rehabilitation
of their master: the chancellor, Jehan de Saulx; the chamberlain and
councillor Pierre, lord of la Viefville; the ducal secretary, Jehan de
la Keythulle.[2] Envoys from the dukes of Anjou and Berry came to

[1] The following have been used throughout this chapter: d'Avout, *Armagnacs
et Bourguignons*, Coville, *Jean Petit* and *Les Cabochiens*, de Lichtervelde,
Grand commis, Plancher, *Histoire de Bourgogne*, iii (modern authorities); de
Baye, *Journal*, van Dixmude, *Merkwaerdige gebeurtenissen*, *Geste des ducs*,
Journal d'un bourgeois de Paris, Juv. des Ursins, *Histoire de Charles VI*,
Monstrelet, *Chronique*, and the Religieux de St. Denys (chroniclers).
[2] For this and what follows, see Mirot, *AB* iii (1931), 305-42 and Collas,
Valentine de Milan.

67

see John the Fearless at Lille, to propose a meeting, and, by the end of December, this had been fixed for the third week of January 1408, at Amiens. Meanwhile, in Paris, the widow of the murdered duke made two formal public appearances at court, on 10 and 21 December, demanding justice on the murderer. The princes could not easily have agreed to bring John to trial when they were already committed to negotiation with him, but one important concession was made to Valentina Visconti and her sons. By royal *ordonnances* of 26 and 27 December 1407 and 18 January 1408, John the Fearless was implicitly but totally excluded from the government of France. The dauphin, Louis duke of Guienne, was placed under the control and protection of the queen; the coronation of Charles VI's successor was empowered, however young he might be on his father's death; and the government of the kingdom, in the event of both king and queen being incapacitated, was made over to the dauphin.[1]

Directly after his escape from Paris, John the Fearless assembled a conference at Lille. Between 3 and 12 December his brothers Philip of Nevers and Anthony of Brabant were summoned and consulted there and on 9 and 10 December the deputies of the Four Members of Flanders were given a detailed account of the assassination in both French and Flemish. Later in the month, at Ghent, another assembly was held, attended by the three Estates of Flanders, by John of Bavaria the bishop-elect of Liège and his brother William of Bavaria, count of Hainault-Holland, and by many of John's leading councillors and knights, at which a formal justification of his crime was read out by Master Simon de Saulx, ducal councillor and abbot of Moutiers St. Jean. Evidently it was John the Fearless's aim, before he re-entered French territory to confer with the French princes at Amiens, to obtain the support of his Flemish subjects and the rulers of the neighbouring states; or, at any rate, their acquiescence in his crime.

Some historians have supposed that John the Fearless went to Amiens in January 1408 with an army. In fact, he had with him only a medium-sized escort, of 261 knights and squires.[2] Better than an army, though, he enjoyed the support of his brothers; for Anthony and Philip took part personally on John's behalf in the conversations which followed, between 22 and 31 January, and which were conducted, on the French side, by the dukes of Berry and Anjou, and the grand master of the king's household, Jehan de Montagu.

---

[1] *Recueil de diverses pièces*, 32–50; cf. Juv. des Ursins, *Hist. de Charles VI*, 438.
[2] De la Chauvelays, *Armées*, 167–9.

Lawyers too, at this juncture, were more important to John than soldiers, and the legal experts who acted as his paid agents in the Paris *Parlement* were brought to Amiens for the occasion: Pierre de Marigny, Andrieu Cotin, Nicolas de Savigny and the famous Jehan Petit, master of theology and ducal councillor.

The winter of 1407-8 was one of the worst in living memory. The royal dukes, with their cavalcade of attendants, only reached Amiens by employing large numbers of peasants with shovels to clear the snow off the road in front of them. Wine froze on the table; ink froze on the desk or even in the pen of the clerk of the court of the Paris *Parlement*. It became possible to walk over sea from Flanders to Zeeland, and all the rivers of north-west Europe froze over, so that, when the thaw came on 28-30 January, many of the bridges were wrecked.

At Amiens the princes took up separate lodgings. John's love of symbolism was evinced by the painting over the entrance to his hôtel of his coat of arms with, on one side, a sharp combat lance and a plane and, on the other, a blunt jousting-lance. This was taken to signify his readiness to accept peace or war, according to how the talks went. He apparently remained obdurate in his refusal to ask the king's pardon for his deed, insisting on being permitted to present a formal defence and justification of the assassination. The dukes of Berry and Anjou seem in the end to have accepted this, and no opposition was made to John's triumphant return to Paris at the end of February 1408, escorted by some 400 armed men[1] and accompanied by his brother Philip, count of Nevers, his son-in-law Adolf, count of Cleves, and the duke of Lorraine.

At the time of his return to Paris, John the Fearless already enjoyed considerable popularity, above all among the citizenry, who welcomed him back with demonstrations of joy and enthusiasm. But popularity was not enough. He fully intended to clear himself of all reproach by publicly justifying his crime. On 17 February 1408 a Latin manifesto glorifying the assassination as an altruistic act of statesmanship of the very highest quality, and addressed 'To all kings, dukes, counts, and other princes, prelates, barons and others whomsoever, whether ecclesiastical or secular', was submitted to the ducal chancery, but not actually published.[2] However, on 8 March 1408

---

[1] Bazin, *MSHA Beaune* (1897), 67-8 and Plancher, iii. 254-5.
[2] Cartellieri, *Court of Burgundy*, 38-9 and Coville, *Petit*, 103-4. The illuminated frontispiece of the Vienna MS. of the *Justification* is reproduced by Coville, *BEC* lxxii (1911), opp. p. 72.

a solemn justification of the crime, cast in the form of an elaborate syllogism, was verbally presented by Master Jehan Petit to the French royal court in the presence of John the Fearless, and afterwards circulated round European courts in copies both illuminated and plain. This extraordinary document stands out as one of the most insolent pieces of political chicanery and theological casuistry in all history. How much of it was in any sense authentic or sincere is an unanswerable question: we cannot now determine how villainous Louis of Orleans really was. The chronicler Monstrelet copied the *Justification du duc de Bourgogne* out in full, though it took Jehan Petit four hours to read it. I only summarize here what Monstrelet wrote, quoting in part, and omitting the numerous citations from the Canon and Civil law, the Bible, the Fathers and other authorities.[1]

The Justification of the duke of Burgundy

My lord the duke of Burgundy, count of Flanders, of Artois, and of Burgundy, doubly peer of France and doyen of the French peerage, has come here in all humility into the presence of the most noble and most high royal majesty. . . . He felt himself obliged to come to his sovereign as a neighbour, a relative, a vassal, a subject, a knight, baron, count and duke, peer, doyen of the peerage and as father-in-law of the dauphin and Princess Michelle of France. These twelve obligations bind him to love, serve and obey the king, and not only to defend him against his enemies, but to take revenge against them. In addition, that prince of noble memory my late lord duke of Burgundy his father, when on his death-bed, commanded him, above all things, to behave most loyally, honourably, justly and courageously towards the person of the king of France. . . . The deed that has been done was perpetrated, as I shall now proceed to explain, for the safety of the king's person and that of his children, and for the general good of the realm.

My text is from 1 Timothy vi: 'Covetousness is the root of all evil.' My thesis is the following syllogism:

The major: It is permissible and meritorious to kill a tyrant.

The minor: The duke of Orleans was a tyrant:

The conclusion: Therefore the duke of Burgundy did well to kill him.

The major is divided into three articles in which covetousness, the various manners and degrees of high treason and the connection between the two are examined respectively in detail and three examples given of each of the last two, and a fourth article in which eight truths are presented. To prove the third of these truths—that it is permissible to

---

[1] Monstrelet, *Chronique*, i. 177–242. Cf. the account sent to the duchess of Burgundy, printed by Douët d'Arcq, *ABSHF* (1864) (2), 6–26. For what follows, see especially Coville, *Petit*.

kill an infamous tyrant or traitor—twelve reasons are invoked (in honour
of the twelve Apostles), three furnished by the moral philosophers,
three by the Fathers of the church, three by Civil law and three by the
Bible. The other five truths are expounded more briefly, and the major
ends with nine corollaries.

I come now to declare and prove my minor, in which I shall show that
the late duke of Orleans was devoured with covetousness of vain honours
and worldy riches and that, to obtain for himself and his family the
most high and noble kingdom and crown of France by depriving our
king of them, he studied all sorts of sorcery and witchcraft, and practised
various means of destroying the person of the king. . . . So greatly had
ambition and greed and the temptation of the hellish adversary possessed themselves of him that, as a tyrant and as disloyal to his king and
liege lord, he committed the crime of divine and human high treason, in
every manner and degree noticed in my major—that is to say, in the
first, second, third and fourth degrees. In detail, his crimes and misdeeds
were as follows:

1. He resorted to black magic in an effort to kill the king by some slow
   disorder which would not rouse suspicion of murder. To effect this,
   with the help of an apostate monk and three other persons, who
   worked secretly to this end for some days in the tower of Montjay
   near Lagny-sur-Marne, he had his sword, dagger and a ring consecrated by two devils, and suitably treated by contact with the
   cadavers of criminals smuggled from the Montfaucon gallows.

2. He acquired from the same apostate monk a cherry branch which
   had been dipped in the blood of a red cockerel and a white chicken,
   and which possessed such magic powers that no woman could
   resist the advances of its owner. He used this weapon to induce fits
   of sickness or insanity in King Charles VI.

3. He had been encouraged and actively helped in several attempts to
   eliminate Charles VI by his father-in-law, Giangaleazzo, duke of
   Milan, who hoped to see his daughter Valentina, Louis's wife,
   queen of France.

4. He made several attempts to poison the king, and one, with a
   poisoned apple, to murder the late dauphin, Charles.

5. At a fancy-dress ball in Paris [in January 1393], when the king and
   others entered the room disguised as wild animals, he wilfully set
   fire to the king's clothes with his torch.

6. He made a pact with Henry of Lancaster, whereby each promised to
   help the other to usurp their respective thrones. Henry succeeded
   in usurping the throne of England from Richard II in 1399, but
   Louis of Orleans failed to seize that of France. Since Henry IV's

accession, the duke of Orleans had acted as a traitor to France by consistently favouring England.

7. In order to get Queen Isabel and her children into his power, he tried to persuade her to leave France and take up residence in his duchy of Luxembourg.

8. He plotted with Pope Benedict XIII the substitution of himself for his brother King Charles VI on the throne of France. To this end he won Benedict over by supporting him, and attributed all sorts of crimes to the king in the hope of persuading the pope to pronounce him and his children unfit to hold or succeed to the throne of France.

9. To further his aim of taking over the government of France, he posted troops and garrisoned castles in different parts of the kingdom.

10. He imposed heavy taxes on the country, claiming that they were necessary for the war against England, but in fact he used the revenues thus realized to finance his attempts on the throne of France.

Now, if my hearers will unite my minor with my major, it follows clearly that my lord of Burgundy is not deserving of any blame whatever for what has happened to the criminal duke of Orleans. Nor ought the king our lord to be dissatisfied with him but, on the contrary, he should be pleased with what he has done, and requite him for it in three ways, namely, in love, honour and riches. . . . According to my simple comprehension, I conclude that our lord the king ought to declare and publish in his letters patent my lord the duke of Burgundy's loyalty and good fame both within and without the kingdom . . . and God grant that it may be so done.

This final hope expressed by Jehan Petit was indeed fulfilled, for on the very next day John the Fearless, now all-powerful in Paris, received a formal royal pardon, in which the king, recognizing that it was John's duty to protect his royal person, and accepting his word that the duke of Orleans had plotted to usurp his throne, explicitly withdrew any royal disapproval he might have incurred, forgave him for the assassination of his brother, and forbade any moves against him on this account.[1] But the widow and children of the murdered duke, not to mention his numerous sympathizers and supporters, were by no means willing to accept this as the end of the affair. Lawyers were appointed to draw up a refutation of Petit's *Justification* and, as soon as John the Fearless was safely out of Paris and on the

---

[1] Plancher, iii. no. 256. The summary that follows this paragraph is from Monstrelet, *Chronique*, i. 341–8.

way to campaign against the Liègeois, the Orleanists delivered their counter-blast to it. On 11 September 1408, at a special assembly of the royal court in Paris, an abbot presented a detailed defence of Louis of Orleans as well as a list of charges against John, while a lawyer outlined the punishments demanded. The marathon expiation required was vindictive and humiliating in the extreme, though characteristic of the mental or moral savagery of the age.

1. The duke of Burgundy to humbly confess his guilt and ask pardon from the duchess of Orleans and her children, in public, at the Louvre, the Palais, the royal hôtel de St. Pol and, finally, on the spot where the murder was committed. He shall remain on his knees at the last place until priests nominated for the purpose shall have recited the seven penitential psalms and the litany for the soul of the deceased. After this he shall kiss the earth and ask pardon of God, of my lady of Orleans, and of her children, for the offences he has committed against them. Copies of the duke of Burgundy's statement to be circulated to all the French towns and proclaimed there by sound of trumpet.

2. All the buildings in Paris owned by the duke of Burgundy to be destroyed, and the ruins left for all time. On the site of each building a stone cross to be set up with an inscription recording the cause of the demolitions.

3. A similar cross shall be erected on the spot where the murder took place, and the house in which the assassins hid shall be pulled down.

4. The duke of Burgundy shall, at his own expense, found, build, furnish and maintain, at the place where the murder was committed, a collegiate church for six canons, six vicars and six chaplains, appointed by the duchess of Orleans and her successors, to say six masses every day in perpetuity for the soul of Louis of Orleans. An inscription in large letters over the entrance of the church to record the reasons for its foundation.

5. A similar church, but twice the size, to be established by the duke of Burgundy in the town of Orleans.

6. The duke of Burgundy to found two chapels, one in Rome, the other in Jerusalem, where a daily mass for the soul of Louis of Orleans shall be said; each chapel to have a suitable inscription over the door.

7. The duke of Burgundy shall pay the sum of one million francs to found and endow hospitals and chapels, and for other works of piety, for the salvation of the soul of the murdered duke of Orleans.

8. All the duke of Burgundy's lands to be confiscated by the crown and sold.

9. The duke of Burgundy himself to be imprisoned until the whole of the above sentence has been carried out. After this, he shall be banished for ever overseas, or at least for twenty years. After his return, he shall not be allowed within one hundred leagues of the queen or the sons of the late duke of Orleans.

During the spring and summer of 1408 John the Fearless's position in Paris and in the government of France had been insecure and uncertain. He had been faced with the anger and suspicion of John duke of Berry, and the open hostility and hatred of Louis duke of Bourbon; while the duchess of Orleans was planning or dreaming of revenge. As early as 5 July he had had to leave Paris for Flanders to prepare for the campaign against Liège. At first it seemed that the French princes and government might seize this opportunity to act against him, to exclude him altogether from Paris, or even to invade and confiscate his French possessions. No such course of action was even contemplated. There was no one in Paris strong enough to master events in this way. The government of France, divided between the royal dukes, a vacillating and pleasure-loving queen, an insane king, the youthful dauphin and various councillors, was irresolute, decrepit, half-hearted. Apart from drafting royal letters on 2 July 1408 revoking the letters of pardon issued for John on the previous 9 March, the assembly of some troops, and the above-mentioned formal denunciation of John on 11 September, nothing was done. No difficulties were placed in the way of the victor of Othée. Indeed, before he returned to Paris in triumph, as a conquering hero, on 28 November, the entire court, terrified as much by the horrors of a possible popular revolt in Paris, as by the approach of John the Fearless, had fled ignominiously and secretly to Tours during the night of 2–3 November.

John the Fearless did not take his army to Paris in autumn 1408, though he provided for his personal security there by engaging some 700 men-at-arms for service of varying periods at different times between November 1408 and January 1409.[1] His policy in France was based on the possession, or at least the control, of the court and government and, since these had now eluded him, a settlement was essential. Only in this way could the king, queen and dauphin be brought back to Paris under his aegis and into his power. Hence the prolonged negotiations at Tours in the winter of 1408–9 which, considerably facilitated by the death of Valentina Visconti on

[1] De la Chauvelays, *Armées*, 180–4 and ACO B1556, fos. 179a–185b.

4 December 1408, led eventually, in March 1409, to the so-called peace or reconciliation of Chartres. John's chosen instrument in achieving this settlement was his brother-in-law and recent ally of Othée, William of Bavaria, a relative of Queen Isabel whose daughter Jacqueline was married to her younger son John, duke of Touraine. Not only did William labour diplomatically on John the Fearless's behalf through the winter of 1408-9; he also acted in a quasi-military capacity, for in January 1409 he was appointed by the king to command a peace-keeping force of 400 men-at-arms and one hundred archers, which was specially commissioned to keep order during the ceremony of reconciliation.[1]

The critical state of affairs in the month of January 1409 is described in a letter sent to the king of Aragon from Paris by the Aragonese knight whose daughter's adventures with Louis de Chalon have already been described, Pons de Perellos, councillor and chamberlain of the duke of Burgundy.

Most high, most noble and most powerful prince, my redoubted and sovereign lord, I received a letter from your majesty by the bearer of these presents on 22 December last, in which your royal majesty commanded me to certify you of the good estate of my lord the duke of Burgundy, and of all news from here. . . .

Today the queen, the dauphin, [the duke of Anjou] King Louis [of Sicily], the king of Navarre, my lords the dukes of Berry, of Bourbon, of Brittany, and many other lords and all the grand council, are in the city of Tours with the king. My lord of Hainault [William of Bavaria] arrived here in company with my lord the duke of Burgundy, and went at once to the king at Tours, together with a large part of my lord [the duke of Burgundy]'s council, to entreat the king to return to this city [of Paris]. . . . They received a reply to the effect that, for the present, the king would not return here, nor would he listen to anything my lord of Burgundy said or caused to be said to him until he came and submitted to him, and made peace with Monsieur [Charles] of Orleans and his brothers in a certain form and manner. My lord of Hainault has brought back a draft protocol describing this [ceremony] and several other things at length, and this draft [shows that] the honour of my lord of Burgundy would be brought into question and much damaged if he were to carry out [the ceremony] as laid down in it. The queen's brother,

---

[1] *Cartulaire de Hainaut*, iii. no. 966. The letter which follows is from Calmette, *RB* xviii (3-4) (1908), 163-6. For the peace of Chartres and the events leading up to it, see Cartellieri, *SHAWP* iii (1912), no. 11 (2), 10-20; and, more important, Mirot, *AB* iii (1931), 305-42 (the excerpt translated below is from pp. 339-41).

the grand master of the king's household and several others of the council came here as ambassadors from the king, to whom my lord [the duke of Burgundy] replied that the aforesaid draft and its contents was in no way acceptable, and he gave them another, drawn up with great deliberation and counsel, which, if it pleased the king, he agreed to carry out, [adding that] he would always and in all things render the honour and obeisance he owed to the king.

This draft is to be submitted by these councillors to the king at Tours. It is not known if the king and his council will accept it, though the king does nothing except what the queen and the councillors advise, and it is said that they will not refuse it, since it is reasonable and honourable for the king. It is not yet possible to obtain a copy of this draft, until it is accepted and agreed to by the king's party.

If this agreement is confirmed, the affairs of this kingdom will be in a much better state. If it is broken, there will be a great deal of trouble; indeed, more than before. The queen is much afraid of the duke of Burgundy, for various reasons.

Most excellent prince, my most redoubted sovereign lord, there are many troubles and affairs today in this kingdom . . . about which I dare not write to you at all, because if by chance the letter was taken or seen here I should lose my honour and my life. But, as soon as the draft protocol and the other matters under negotiation at the moment are settled . . . I will write again at once to your royal majesty. . . . Most excellent prince . . . [I hope] it will not displease you that the present letter is written in French, for in truth I have no one here who knows how to write any other language, and I write so badly that hardly anyone can . . . read [my writing]. . . .

Written at Paris, the twelfth day of January, 1409.

Pons de Perellos

In the event, after interminable haggling over the exact words to be pronounced by the dukes of Burgundy and Orleans, and after several delays, a ceremony of reconciliation acceptable to both parties was enacted in the cathedral at Chartres on 9 March 1409. A day or two later, a detailed report of this tortuous piece of diplomatic play-acting was sent by John the Fearless to his *gens des comptes* at Lille:

From the duke of Burgundy, count of Flanders, of Artois, and of Burgundy.

Dear and well-beloved, since we only have certain knowledge about earthly things and you want now to hear and receive good news of our estate and our appointment at Chartres, we can certify that, at the time of writing, we are in very good health, thanks to Our Lord. Further, we inform you that, in order to keep our above-mentioned appointment according to the good pleasure and wishes of our lord the king, as we and the duke of Orleans and his brothers have been commanded by him, we arrived at Galardon eight days ago yesterday, which was the third day of this present month of March, thinking that the aforesaid meeting would be held at Chartres on the next day. But because it became necessary to reword the safe-conducts which the duke of Orleans and his brothers and we have to issue to each other, and also because the robes and other things necessary for the meeting were not ready, it was deferred until last Saturday, 9 March; on which day, about eight o'clock, we left Galardon well attended, and arrived at Chartres between ten and eleven.

Because we knew that my lord [the king] and madame the queen were already in the church of Notre-Dame, where the said meeting was to be held, we went directly to dismount there. My lord and lady [the king and queen] were royally enthroned in the church, attended by my lord of Guienne [the dauphin], [Louis duke of Anjou] the king of Sicily, the king of Navarre, our uncle my lord of Berry, Louis of Bavaria the brother of my lady [the queen], the duke of Bourbon, the counts of Alençon, la Marche, Eu and Vendôme, the constable, the count of Tancarville, and several others of the royal blood, all of whom together in noble and fine array awaited the duke of Orleans and his brothers and us. There too were the presidents and lords of the *Parlement*, the *gens des comptes*, the royal *avocats* and *procureurs*, and several others of the grand council. . . . Also in the said church was [William of Bavaria my] brother-in-law of Hainault and most of his troops, fully-armed, to keep the peace . . . as he had been instructed.

We entered the church by one door, and the duke of Orleans and his brothers by another on the other side, and we withdrew to a small chapel completely hung with tapestry, while the duke of Orleans and his brothers did likewise on the other side, opposite us. Soon after, by command of my lord [the king], we went towards him and my lady [the queen] into the place where they were [seated] . . . in the nave of the church, enclosed with a palisade, accompanied by twenty knights only. And, when we had made our due obeisance, we caused our loyal councillor and chamberlain Sir Jehan de Nieles to propose and pronounce the words which had been approved by our lord [the king] and incorporated by his command in a protocol made beforehand, so that no additions or omissions could be made by one party or the other.

After this the duke of Orleans and his brothers entered the enclosure, and the aforesaid protocol was completely accomplished, both as regards the treaty and agreement made between us by means of my lord [the king], and the marriage of one of our daughters to the count of Vertus, brother of the duke of Orleans, without any contradiction whatsoever, or fault. Thanks be to God, the thing was done with all solemnity and much to our honour, and in such a way that everybody on one side and the other was very well content with it. Indeed my lord [the king], my lady [the queen], and the other lords mentioned above made us very welcome, and especially my lord of Guienne our son [-in-law] who, of his own goodwill and without admonition from anyone, came joyfully to greet and embrace us in front of everyone. When all was over and accomplished we left my lord [the king], and the duke of Orleans and his brothers likewise, and returned between twelve and one o'clock to Galardon for dinner, while the duke of Orleans and his brothers returned similarly to dinner in their lodgings outside Chartres —as had been fixed in the above-mentioned protocol. . . .

Dear and well-beloved, may Our Lord keep you in his holy guard. Written at Paris, this Monday evening, 11 March.   Vignier

The reconciliation of Chartres, which was brought about almost exactly a year after Jehan Petit's public justification of John the Fearless, was a victory for John. He had virtually dictated its terms; he now reaped the benefit, and achieved his aim of restoring the king and court to Paris under his supervision and control. An anonymous burgess of Paris recorded this event in his journal in terms which seem to show that, in the popular mind, the return of the king, the restoration of peace, and the triumph of John the Fearless, were inextricably linked together.[1]

On 9 March following, the duke of Burgundy returned with a noble company and, on Sunday 17 March they brought the king to Paris. He was received more honourably than at any time in the last two hundred years, for all the sergeants, as well as the watch, the market people on horseback . . . and all the burgesses, went out to meet him. Before him he had twelve trumpets and a large number of minstrels and, everywhere as he passed by, the people cried Noel! and threw violets and [other] flowers at him. And, in the evening, they supped in joyful mood in the streets, and lit bonfires all over Paris. . . . On the next day, the queen and the dauphin arrived, and the festivity was as great or greater than on the day before, for the queen came more ceremoniously than ever before since her first entry.

After the peace of Chartres, John the Fearless's position in France was completely assured, yet he still did not enjoy unrestrained power. True, the duke of Orleans and his brothers had retired from the seat of government in Paris, but the dukes of Berry and of Bourbon, prompted and encouraged by a powerful and veteran civil servant, Jehan de Montagu, still represented and supported opposition to him.

----

[1] *Journal d'un bourgeois de Paris*, 4–5.

Nor were the royal council and the administrative personnel in any sense creatures of John's—they were French, not Burgundian. During 1409, however, John the Fearless employed his political skill and audacity in a series of moves which, by the end of the year, had resulted in a further strengthening of his position in Paris.

Early in July, he succeeded in winning over one of the leading French princes, Charles III, king of Navarre and duke of Nemours, and on 7 July he signed a treaty with him which went further than the usual princely alliances of those days, for the king of Navarre promised to help John in the event of his involvement in a war with Charles of Orleans and his brothers, in return for John's promise to help him against the king of Castile or the count of Armagnac. But the true character of this 'fraternal confederation' comes out much more clearly in its formal renewal on 8 September 1409, in which, after stating that they had resolved, for the good of the king and the kingdom, to arrest certain 'malefactors and false traitors', John and Charles agree on oath that neither of them will permit anything to be done in the government of France without the consent of the other.[1] But this was in no sense an alliance between equals. True, one partner was a king, the other a duke: but it was the king who now became the instrument of the duke in helping him to rid the French government of his principal rivals and enemies. The mainstay of the opposition to John in France was, and had been for years, the Jehan de Montagu mentioned above, grand master of the king's household, one of whose brothers had just become bishop of Paris, while the other was archbishop of Sens. These were the 'malefactors and false traitors' of the 8 September treaty of alliance. Our most reliable contemporary chronicler, Nicolas de Baye, who was at Troyes at the time, has this to say about the events which followed.

Saturday, 19 October.

Today, at vespers, news has come to Troyes that Sir J. de Montagu, knight and grand master of the king's household, formerly notary and secretary of the king, a man of short stature, thin, with not much beard, gifted and alert, hasty in conversation, quick-witted, subtle and diligent, aged fifty years or more . . . was arrested, Monday eight days ago, between [the church of] St. Victor and Paris, and with him the bishop of Chartres, a general [councillor] on the finances. They were held in the

---

[1] Originals of these two treaties are in ACO B11935. The first is analysed by Plancher, iii. 290; the second is copied into BN Coll. de Bourg. 54, fos. 251 and 260. The extract in the next paragraph is from de Baye, *Journal*, i. 290–2.

Petit Châtelet, by the Petit Pont, and last Thursday the said Montagu was taken thence at about ten o'clock in a cart to the Halles, and there beheaded before a huge crowd. . . .

He had been permitted, through the affection or passivity and simplicity of the king and the princes of the blood-royal, to wield such authority and power that he had, in his time, governed the households of the king, the queen and my lord the dauphin. . . . He had enjoyed considerable power not only in the household of the king and queen, but with the uncles and cousins of the king and, especially, in the household of the duke of Berry. And, while he was the first and principal royal councillor, he had made his two brothers, the one, archbishop of Sens and president of the *chambre des comptes* (and there was hope that he might become chancellor of France), the other bishop of Paris and chancellor of the duke of Berry. . . . He was so haughty that he hardly ever took off his hat when entering the court of *Parlement*, nor even in the presence of the king. . . .

The execution of Jehan de Montagu on 17 October 1409 was undertaken with the theatrical extravagance common to public spectacles of all kinds.[1] He was taken to the block dressed in his livery of white and red, a golden spur on the right foot, and a silver one on the left, sitting high up on the tumbril, with his hands, holding a wooden cross, tied in front of him. Two trumpets preceded him. Further gruesome details are furnished by the Flemish chronicler, Oliver van Dixmude, who describes how his headless body was taken to the gallows at Montfaucon and hung up there by the shoulders with an iron chain firmly secured with a padlock, so that it could not be removed secretly for decent burial. His head remained at the Halles, impaled on a lance.

This macabre event was followed by a purge of royal officials, many of whom were thrown into prison and deprived of their offices. The victim's brother, the archbishop of Sens, managed to escape arrest by flight, and lived to die a soldier's death at Agincourt. Then, on 11 November, John's alliance with the king of Navarre was extended in such a way that his control of the French government was immeasurably strengthened. A new treaty was drawn up at Melun between the king of Navarre; the queen of France Isabel and her brother Duke Louis of Bavaria; William of Bavaria count of Hainault-Holland and his brother John of Bavaria the bishop-elect of Liège; and John the Fearless and his brother Anthony duke of Brabant. It

---

[1] See especially, O. van Dixmude, *Merkwaerdige geb.*, 51 and *Journal d'un bourgeois de Paris*, 6. On J. de Montagu in general, see Merlet, *BEC* xiii (1852), 248–84.

was not that John was now sharing his power with others—far from it. He had in fact won control and personal ascendancy over the queen, titular ruler of France; she, too, now became an instrument of Burgundian power, as a result, if we are to believe Monstrelet, of the mediation or persuasion of William of Bavaria.[1] Next, it was the turn of the dauphin. On 28 December 1409, Master Jehan de le Vigne, a clerk of the duke of Burgundy's councillor Jehan de Nieles, wrote from Paris to the *gens des compte* at Lille with important tidings.

> My very dear and honourable lords, I recommend myself to you as humbly as I can. And may it please you to know that yesterday before dinner, in the castle of Vincennes, the king, in the presence of the queen, my lord of Guienne [the dauphin], the king of Navarre, my lords the dukes of Berry, Brabant, Hainault, Bavaria and Lorraine, and the counts of Alençon and Clermont, the marquis du Pont and other princes of the blood-royal, granted to my lord [the duke] of Burgundy the guardianship and government of my lord of Guienne, under the supervision of the king and queen. Tomorrow, as is said definitely, the queen and my lord of Guienne will come here [to Paris]. Other news I know not at present. . . .
>
> Written at Paris, Saturday, 28 December, very late.

John the Fearless at once converted this titular control over the twelve-year-old dauphin into reality: he surrounded him with trusted and loyal servants of his own. Jehan de Nieles, former second president of the council of Flanders and governor of Arras, was appointed his chancellor; Renier Pot, knight, ambassador, councillor and chamberlain of the duke, was made governor of Dauphiné; and Guillaume de Vienne, another ducal knight and councillor, was made the first chamberlain of the dauphin. These appointments were made in December 1409 or January 1410. At the same time, on 31 December, a royal *ordonnance* formally empowered the dauphin to rule during the king's 'absences'. Now, at last, France was in the hands of John the Fearless. As Monstrelet puts it:[2] 'At that time the duke of Burgundy, being in Paris, had more power than all the other princes,

---

[1] Monstrelet, *Chronique*, ii. 50. The text of the treaty of Melun is in Plancher, iii. no. 263. No less than four originals, all signed (Loys, Ysabel, Charles, Jehan), are in ACO B11892. The letter which follows is in ADN B17612. The text of the royal *ordonnance* of 27 December 1409 granting the government of the dauphin to John is in Plancher, iii. no. 261.

[2] *Chronique*, ii. 66. For the *ordonnance* of 31 December 1409, see *Ords. des rois*, xii. 229-31.

and affairs were carried on by him and his partisans. There is no doubt that this made several people envious of him.'

In fact, a powerful group of princes of the blood were not only jealous of John the Fearless, they were determined to exclude him altogether from the government of France. Some maintained that their ambitions went further than this; that they intended to make the duke of Berry regent of France during his lifetime, and Charles, duke of Orleans, his heir; and that they planned to confiscate all John's territories and divide them up between themselves.[1] During the first nine months of 1410, while John the Fearless held the reins of power, and controlled the royal family in Paris, these princes allied together and prepared if necessary to make war against him. Their vitality and their cohesion came, not from the veterans Bourbon and Berry, neither of whom seems to have had his heart in the project, but from Duke Charles of Orleans and his brothers and, above all, from an ambitious and powerful recruit to their cause, Bernard VII, count of Armagnac. Rightly, if confusingly, this last gave his name to the alliance or party which came into existence at Gien, on the Loire, on 15 April 1410, for he was its driving force.[2]

The league of Gien, as originally formed in April 1410, provided for an army of 5,000 men-at-arms and 4,000 bowmen, to be raised by the dukes of Berry, Brittany and Orleans, and the counts of Alençon, Clermont and Armagnac, and to be used 'for the good of the kingdom'. No mention was made of John the Fearless but, when the league was confirmed in the autumn of 1410, the contracting parties candidly admitted that it was their purpose to attack the duke of Burgundy and, in a manifesto of 2 September circulated throughout France, they announced their intention of 'rescuing' the king and dauphin and restoring them to power. From April on, John can have been under no illusions. In May–June he was trying hard to detach John of Berry from the league;[3] in July and August he issued royal *ordonnances* condemning the league and prohibiting all assemblies of troops; and, from July onwards, he was busy making his own military preparations.

In spite of the crisis of autumn 1410, when both sides mustered

---

[1] *Livre des trahisons*, 63 and *Geste des ducs*, 372.
[2] For the league of Gien, see Durrieu, *MSAF* liv (1895), 167–204. For the recruitment of Bernard, count of Armagnac, see Tardif, *Inventaires et documents*, nos. 1850 and 1851.
[3] ACO B1560, fos. 210, 212, 219; and, for what follows, *Ords. des rois*, ix. 515–17 and 531–4.

troops in and around Paris, there were no serious hostilities between
Burgundians and Armagnacs. Damage, however, was done in plenty.
On 16 September the clerk of the court at the Paris *Parlement*,
Nicolas de Baye, walled up the entrance to the turret of his house to
keep the troops out.[1] On 20 September, according to the monk of
St. Denis, who was infuriated by this intrusion on monastic tranquillity, Duke Anthony of Brabant billeted 6,000 men in the town of
St. Denis, which meant that, for the next six weeks, his abbey had to
be guarded as if it were being besieged by the English! This mobilization and military alert was brought to an end on 2 November by a
peace negotiated at the duke of Berry's castle of Bicêtre, outside
Paris. But the terms of the peace of Bicêtre could not possibly have
constituted a permanent settlement. They signified a slight set-back
for John the Fearless and a mere deferment of further disputes. This
peace was, in fact, a futile rigmarole of unrealistic absurdities, produced by determined men who, if not intent on war, were convinced
of its inevitability. The terms may be summarized thus:

1. The princes of the blood-royal to retire with their troops to their
   own lands, starting on the same day and continuing by equal stages
   each day.

2. In doing so, neither they nor their troops must trespass on each
   other's territories.

3. All garrisons to be reduced to the normal size required for routine
   defensive purposes.

4. The king is empowered to appoint knights to supervise the withdrawal of the princes' forces.

5. None of the princes to return to the king unless specially summoned
   by royal letters-patent. And if the king summons the duke of Berry,
   he will also summon the duke of Burgundy; and vice-versa.

6. The princes to swear not to commit aggression one against the other
   in word or deed, between now and Easter 1412.

7. The king to appoint as councillors certain notable people who are
   not partisans or pensionaries of any of the princes.

8. The dukes of Berry and Burgundy to share the guardianship of the
   dauphin.

9. The provost of Paris to be dismissed and another appointed.

---

[1] De Baye, *Journal*, i. 335 and Relig. de St. Denys, iv. 366. The peace-terms
which follow this paragraph are from Plancher, iii. no. 268.

10. No one to be molested in any way for having obeyed or not obeyed the summonses of the princes.

The supposedly non-party and non-princely government now set up in Paris was a failure from the start.[1] Article nine was carried out by the dismissal of Pierre des Essarts, a councillor-chamberlain of John the Fearless, but John took him with him to Flanders and demonstrated his insincerity by continuing to address him as provost. Later, he managed to have him re-instated. In spite of article seven, the royal council remained dominated by John's supporters, for Guichard Dauphin, Jehan de Nieles, Charles de Savoisy, Jehan de Thoisy bishop of Tournai, Antoine de Craon, Jaques de Heilly, Jehan de Courcelles and Renier Pot were all staunch Burgundians. Article six of the treaty was broken by Charles of Orleans in January 1411, when he arrested three Burgundian ambassadors on their way to see the duke of Berry at Bourges, and held one of them, Jehan, lord of Croy and Renty, ducal chamberlain and councillor, in prison at Blois; and again in March, when he issued a denunciation of Jehan Petit's *Justification du duc de Bourgogne*. Tension grew in the months that followed, but before we describe the first campaigns of the civil war between Burgundians and Armagnacs, in 1411 and 1412, a glance at some aspects of John's situation in France in the preceding years 1408–11 may be instructive.

The basis of John the Fearless's position in France was popular support in Paris. Here the artisans had already, on at least two occasions in the fourteenth century, made a bid to seize power. Their political consciousness and ambitions were carefully nurtured by John the Fearless. Taking the cue from his father, he had begun as an anti-taxer and reformer; he now continued as a champion of the removal of corruption and abuses from the government. The people of Paris seem to have gratefully accepted the elimination of Louis of Orleans and Jehan de Montagu as part of this 'purification' of the government, and their unofficial spokesman to posterity, the anonymous burgess whose journal has already been quoted, is full of admiration for John the Fearless. This popular support in Paris was extended and strengthened by him in 1411, shortly before the outbreak of war, when he made use of the ample supplies of excellent wine available from his southern territories, to marshal the friendship and support, in particular, of the Paris butchers. Nor was the University neglected: in June 1411 eight masters benefited from the

[1] For what follows, see ACO B1558, f. 94 and Monstrelet, *Chronique*, ii. 100–1 and 143; and Valois, *Conseil*, 121–3.

ducal generosity. This urban support, enjoyed and exploited so skilfully by John, was not limited to Paris: in the period May to August 1411 secret embassies were in contact with Rouen, Rheims, Soissons, Laon, Compiègne and Montdidier. But the Burgundian party which emerged in these years by no means lacked a noble and even princely element, for John could always rely on his own family, most of the princes of the Low Countries, and pensionaries or relatives of his like the duke of Lorraine and the count of Savoy.

During the years 1408-11 John the Fearless resided in Paris in the spring and early summer of 1408; intermittently in the winter of 1408-9; and continuously from September 1409 to November 1410, when, according to article one of the treaty of Bicêtre, he withdrew to his own territories. In spite of his popularity, he took care to provide for his personal security there. He maintained a bodyguard, both in his hôtel and when he moved about the streets. Above all, he constructed the famous tower in the hôtel d'Artois which still survives in the rue Étienne Marcel, and goes by the name of the 'tour de Jean sans Peur'. The tower is in fact the only surviving part of that once magnificent range of buildings, the headquarters of the Valois dukes of Burgundy in Paris, which was demolished in 1543 by command of King Francis I. The chronicler Monstrelet briefly mentions this tower—'a strong tower built of masonry, in which he slept at night'—and Perrault-Dabot published a detailed study of it early this century, in which he described and illustrated its inevitable adornment of planes. A great deal more information is to be found in the pages of the accounts of John the Fearless's receiver-general of all finances. From them, and from a separate financial document also preserved at Dijon, it emerges that the tower was built between 9 February 1408 and 15 May 1411; that it cost over 14,000 francs; that it was built under the supervision of the royal *maître des œuvres* Robert de Hellebuterne; and that, below the principal room, which was indeed designed for John's personal safety at night, was his private bathroom.[1]

In an earlier chapter the trickle of money flowing from the royal treasury into the duke of Burgundy's coffers was cited to illustrate the weakness of his position in France. That was in 1405-7; the position now, in 1408-11, was very different. Let us take the years

[1] Monstrelet, *Chronique*, i. 177; Perrault-Dabot, *L'hôtel de Bourgogne et la tour de J. sans Peur*; ACO B486/2 (*Avis* of J. Chousat and L. des Bordes on the works, etc.) and B1560, f. 265a-b. See too, Le Roux de Lincy and Tisserand, *Paris et ses historiens*, 195, n. 2.

1409 and 1410. The facts and figures (in *livres* of Tours) here are all
from Pocquet du Haut-Jussé's admirable study of the gifts of the
king to the dukes of Burgundy.[1]

*Moneys paid or promised to John the Fearless by King Charles VI in 1409
and 1410*

Date	Pretext	Amount promised	Amount recorded as paid into receipt-general
9.10.09	Military expenses	9,000	?
25.10.09	For troops defending Paris	9,000	9,000
7.12.09	Gift of arrears of *aides*	11,250	?
1.10.09	Michelle of France's dowry	120,000	52,907
TOTALS FOR 1409		149,250	61,907
25.3.10	Military expenses on king's behalf	15,000	12,000
15.4.10	Garrison in Picardy, etc.	6,000	5,000
15.5.10	War material in Picardy, etc.	20,000	15,000
7.10	Gift	1,000	1,000
19.8.10	Troops, etc.	10,000	8,900
19.8.10	Troops, etc.	120,000	120,000
9.10.10	Various expenses on king's behalf	6,000	3,000
TOTALS FOR 1410		178,000	164,900

In interpreting these figures, it should be borne in mind that they
do not reveal what was paid to John in cash and what was paid in
assignments. Moreover, although the total of over 150,000 f. paid for
the year 1410 approaches the degree of exploitation or embezzlement
achieved by Philip the Bold, it must be emphasized that this was
John's 'best' year: in 1411 he obtained only 68,000 f. from the king.
Again, while royal funds were diverted to Philip the Bold as un-
explained gifts or in the form of an allowance or pension, John's
payments are all for some specified purpose, suggesting that he could
only obtain money from the king if he had some plausible pretext.
Actually, he was hardly making a profit out of his transactions in
France in these years: he was simply getting the king to pay his

[1] *MSHDB* vii (1940–1), 95–129.

expenses in maintaining his personal power in France. Nevertheless, the change in his position in France is clear. In 1406 he had the shadow of power only; in 1409 he enjoyed its substance and, if this was an expensive game, the king was paying for it, not he.

It was in the summer of 1411 that the opposition to John the Fearless in France was at last translated into military action.[1] But even then, Orleanist military aggression was blurred and blunted with bombast. In April their troops established themselves between Coucy and Soissons; in May, Charles of Orleans wrote to the king denouncing certain Burgundian councillors in the royal service and demanding their dismissal. Meanwhile John the Fearless began the difficult task of negotiating military aid with his Flemish subjects. He also summoned help from the dukes of Lorraine and Brabant, from Savoy, Namur and elsewhere, and sent to Scotland for mercenaries. Nor did he omit to reply to the Orleanist denunciation of his councillors at Paris, by publishing a similar list on 6 June of Orleanists in the French government, whose removal he demanded. John of Berry, alarmed and hesitant, tried to make peace, but, while John the Fearless assured him of his pacific intentions, Charles of Orleans replied to his offers of mediation with a demand for revenge. In July the Orleanist forces advanced to Ham, while John concentrated at St. Quentin. But again, verbiage intervened, and an exchange of challenges and manifestos now took place.

The declaration of Jargeau, which was issued on 14 July and addressed to the king, council and 'good towns' of France, was circulated much further afield, to Namur, Liège and Guelders, for instance. It is a lengthy manifesto in which the three brothers, Charles, duke of Orleans, Philippe, count of Vertus, and Jehan, count of Angoulême, expatiate at length on John the Fearless's crimes, and demand justice. They emphasize the extreme wickedness of the murder of their father, especially in view, first, of John's close relationship to him; secondly, of his friendship with him immediately before the assassination—they maintain that, on the day before, John had asked Louis to dine with him on the following Sunday; and, thirdly, in view of his hypocritical mourning afterwards. They then proceed to denounce the peace of Chartres, as imposed on the king by John, and maintain that, in any case, John has infringed its terms by the arrest, torture and murder of Jehan de Montagu. They go on

[1] For this and what follows, besides the authorities mentioned already, I have used Mirot, *Mélanges . . . Bémont*, 373–95.

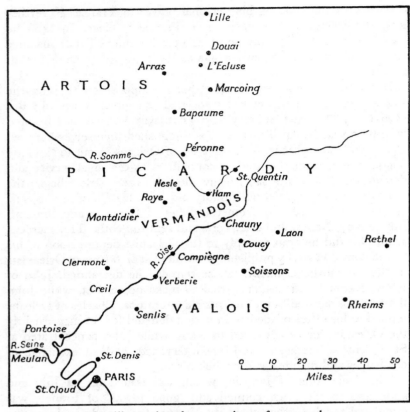

3. Map illustrating the campaigns of 1411 and 1414

to accuse him of usurping the government of the kingdom by detaining the king and dauphin in subjection, and of breaking the peace of Bicêtre by keeping his own men in power in France. Finally, this searching and substantially accurate assessment of John's part in French affairs over the previous four years, ends with a plea for justice against this liar and 'false disloyal traitor'.[1]

The wordy and elaborate declaration of Jargeau was accompanied or followed up by a terse challenge:

> Charles, duke of Orleans and of Valois, count of Blois and of Beaumont and lord of Coucy; Philippe, count of Vertus; and Jehan, count of

---

[1] Text and references in Champion, *Charles d'Orléans*, 84–7. The challenges which follow are in Plancher, iii. nos. 271 and 273.

Angoulême: to you John, who call yourself duke of Burgundy. Because of the hideous murder treasonably committed by you . . . on the person of our most redoubted lord and father Louis, duke of Orleans, only brother of my lord the king, our lord and yours, notwithstanding the oaths, alliances and companionship in arms which you had with him . . ., we cause you to know that from this time on we shall harm you with all our power and in all the ways we can, and we appeal to God and all the prudhommes in the world, to come to our aid against you and your disloyal treason.

Given at Jargeau.   18 July 1411

John the Fearless's characteristically violent reply was not long in coming:

John, duke of Burgundy, etc., to you Charles, who call yourself duke of Orleans; Philippe, who call yourself count of Vertus; and to you Jehan, who call yourself count of Angoulême; who have recently sent me your letters of defiance. We make known to you and wish everyone to know that, to put an end to the abominable treasons conspired, engineered and insanely carried out against my lord the king our most redoubted sovereign lord and yours, and against all his most noble family, by the late Louis your father with the most vilely evil intent, in various and diverse manners, and to stop your aforesaid father, false and disloyal traitor, from achieving the final detestable execution of his plans against our aforesaid sovereign lord and his, and also against his family . . . we, to acquit ourselves loyally and do our duty towards our aforesaid most redoubted and sovereign lord and his family, caused the aforesaid false and disloyal traitor to die and, in this, we have done pleasure to God, loyal service to our aforesaid most redoubted and sovereign lord, and carried out [the demands of] reason. [For Louis of Orleans's plans were] so falsely and notoriously [conceived] that no prudhomme could permit him to live any longer; still less could we ourselves, cousin-germain of our aforesaid lord [the king], doyen of the peerage, and doubly a peer, and more obliged to him and his family than any other of their relatives and subjects, leave so false and cruel a traitor and such a man any longer in this world, except to our own disgrace.

Because you and your brothers are following in the false track and disloyal felony of your father, hoping to achieve the damnable and disloyal aims towards which he aspired, we have [received] your letters of defiance with great gladness of heart. Concerning their contents, you and your brothers have lied, and do lie falsely, evilly and disloyally, like the false and disloyal traitors that you are. For this reason, with the help of Our Lord, who causes and knows the completely impeccable feelings which we have always had and shall have as long as we live, towards our lord the king and his family, and as regards the good of his people and of all his kingdom, we shall loyally ensure that you come to such end and punishment as false and disloyal traitors, malicious, rebel and disobedient felons like you and your brothers deserve in reason to come to. . . .

Given in our town of Douai.   13 August 1411

By the time John the Fearless issued this vitriolic counterchallenge to the Armagnacs, the war had already begun, and Douai, where his brother and military ally Anthony, duke of Brabant, joined him on 16 August, had become his headquarters. But the civil war, which now broke out in France and lasted for almost exactly a year, was fought on at least three fronts: the main forces of either side were assembled first in Picardy, but no pitched battle ensued; at the same time, in August–September 1411, Paris was held for John by Waléran de Luxembourg, count of St. Pol, with the help of the butchers and other craft gilds; while to the south, in Burgundy, the duchess and the local nobility had to face an Armagnac attack on the duchy.

The strategy of the duke of Orleans and his followers, now invariably called the Armagnacs, in the late summer of 1411, seems to have been vitiated by their failure to marshal all their forces towards one objective. Instead, they faltered between the two; between launching an all-out attack on Burgundian Paris, and striking offensively at Artois and Flanders. By mid-August the duke of Bourbon, the count of Alençon, and other Armagnac captains had occupied Vermandois in force, garrisoning the principal towns of Roye, Nesle, Ham and Chauny. Thence they raided Rethel, Bapaume and other places within or near the frontiers of John the Fearless's or his brother's territories. But these preliminary attacks were not developed. John was given time to assemble his men at Douai; to link his army with the troops brought from Brabant by his brother Anthony; and to await the arrival of a contingent of Flemish militia. When all was ready, he moved to the attack through l'Écluse and Marcoing, received the keys of Athies from the terrified inhabitants, and laid siege to Ham on the Somme. Here he was at first held by the Armagnac garrison but, abandoning attempts to take the place by assault from the north, he cleverly caused the garrison to withdraw and the town to surrender by making preparations instead to cross the river to the east and west of it, so that he could invest it all round. Ham capitulated on or about 14 September, and John the Fearless adorned its walls and towers with 3,000 banners which had been specially painted in Cambrai.[1]

[1] *IADNB* iv. 63.

The other Vermandois towns followed suit without further resistance: Péronne and Nesle on 15 and 16 September and, after John had crossed the Somme at Ham, Roye. Finally, five burgesses dressed in black brought him the keys of Chauny. On 22 September he drew up his army at Montdidier.

While the Armagnacs thus evacuated the Vermandois towns they had but recently occupied, Charles of Orleans, who had mustered an army in his county of Valois, rather aimlessly marched to his own town of Beaumont-sur-Oise, suffering losses en route at the hands of the Burgundian garrison of Senlis, captained by one of John's most able and successful military leaders, Enguerrand de Bournonville. In the second half of September, together with the counts of Armagnac and Alençon and the main Armagnac army, Charles of Orleans advanced from Beaumont-sur-Oise to within a few miles of Montdidier. There, at the end of the month, the Burgundian and Armagnac forces were for some days almost face to face; but nothing happened. Each was in fact very badly placed for a pitched battle. John, though he had had the help of a small English contingent throughout the campaign, was still awaiting a much more substantial English force, as well as reinforcements from his other brother, Philip of Nevers; while his Flemish militia, which had been loth to come out on campaign at all, deserted him en masse on 26 September as soon as its leaders had contrived the pretext that there was no enemy to attack. Deprived of his infantry and much of his artillery, and with none of the expected reinforcements, John was forced to withdraw from Montdidier via Péronne to Arras. On the Armagnac side, the failure to act decisively against John at Montdidier is said to have been due to the failure of the allies to agree. More important, perhaps, was the utter insecurity of their strategic position, for behind them not only Paris, but Senlis and Creil and temporarily even Clermont, were held by the Burgundians.

Soon after the campaign in Picardy had been brought to an end by the withdrawal of both sides, the Armagnacs concentrated their forces for the conquest of the most significant military objective in France— the capital. In early October, having retreated across the Oise over a makeshift bridge at Verberie, they laid siege to St. Denis, whose Burgundian captain, Jehan de Chalon, prince of Orange, surrendered on 11 October. Three days later, they took the town and fortress of St. Cloud, on the other side of Paris.

In June 1411, John the Fearless's negotiators had secured a prolongation of the commercial truce between England and Flanders.

Anglo-Flemish contacts were maintained after this and, on 1 September 1411, Henry IV empowered his ambassadors to begin negotiating a marriage treaty between the prince of Wales, his eldest son, and one of John's daughters.[1] Before these negotiations had got under way a substantial English force under the earl of Arundel was despatched, apparently through the intervention on John's behalf of Queen Joan of Navarre or the prince of Wales, or perhaps both of them, to help John against the Armagnacs. This was the contingent which he welcomed in Arras on Saturday, 3 October, and which his enemies made out to have been bought at the cost of the cession or promise to the English of the four principal Flemish ports of Sluis, Dixmude, Dunkirk and Gravelines. But this was mere Armagnac propaganda, which did not make much headway with contemporaries, though some modern historians seem to have fallen for it.[2] Actually, John made no such offer, nor was any formal Anglo-Burgundian treaty made at this time, though negotiations for a marriage treaty continued during the winter of 1411–12.

John the Fearless now demonstrated once more his military skill. Instead of attacking the troops with which the Armagnacs were trying to encircle Paris, he made straight for the city itself, taking the earl of Arundel and his contingent with him. The decision was evidently made at Pontoise, where he was from 16 to 22 October, for he left there after the m:dday meal on 22 October and 'rode all night in arms to go to Paris by Meulan'.[3]

In October, the pamphlet warfare between Burgundians and Armagnacs flared up with renewed vigour. Even before he himself reached Paris John, because he enjoyed control of the city and, with it, the king and court, was able to cause a spate of royal *ordonnances* to be issued in his own favour. On 3 October, the insane and virtually imprisoned king outlawed the dukes of Orleans and Bourbon, the count of Alençon, and the other Armagnac princes, and anyone who pleased was encouraged to attack them. Two days later Charles VI

[1] *Docs. pour servir à l'histoire des relations entre l'Angleterre et la Flandre*, no. 137 = *Procs. and Ords. of the P.C.*, ii. 19–24 = *Foedera*, iv (1), 196. For the relations of the French parties with England in 1411–12 see Boitel, *PTSEC* (1942), 15–20 and, especially, Pocquet, *RH* cciv (1960), 329–38.

[2] E.g. Calmette and Déprez, *France et Angleterre en conflit*, 286; cf. Jacob, *Fifteenth century*, 111 and idem, *Henry V*, 20–1. See Coville, *Premiers Valois*, 337 and d'Avout, *Armagnacs et Bourguignons*, 145–6.

[3] *Itinéraires*, 384. For the next paragraph, see *Ords. des rois*, ix. 635–7 and 640–2. The extract is from royal letters of 6 October 1411 in ACO B11879.

ordered all the royal officers and French towns to give free passage to John and his troops, and on 6 October he ordered the nobles of Artois and Picardy to take up arms for John, claiming that the Armagnac princes Charles, duke of Orleans, Philippe, count of Vertus, his brother, John, duke of Bourbon, the counts of Alençon and Armagnac and the lord of Albret had disobeyed the king, raised troops which were living off the people and, worse still, '. . . had taken several of our towns, killed and ransomed the people and set fire to them; raped married women, violated young girls and taken several of them away by force from their fathers and husbands looking on; robbed churches and abbeys . . .' and so on. On 14 October all royal vassals were summoned to fight against the rebel princes, whose aim was said to be the usurpation of the crown of France.

John the Fearless's propaganda was certainly more effective than that of his enemies. Contemporary chroniclers, almost to a man, supported and admired him. In the autumn of 1411 the Armagnac princes were actually banished the realm by sound of trumpet in all the public squares of Paris. They were solemnly excommunicated and anathematized in the cathedral of Notre-Dame and in all the churches of Paris, by bell, book and candle; and this excommunication was repeated every week until peace was made in August 1412. But military, rather than ecclesiastical, measures were needed to free Paris from the Armagnac blockade, and these were skilfully carried out by John the Fearless. During the night of 9 November he led his army out of Paris and delivered such a well-organized and damaging attack on St. Cloud the next day that the Armagnacs were forced to evacuate both it and St. Denis, and to withdraw from Paris. The mopping-up operations that followed ended with the reduction of almost all the Armagnac strongholds in Picardy and around Paris, including the towns of Dourdan and Étampes. The latter, which belonged to the duke of Berry, was taken early in December by John the Fearless and the dauphin together.

The year 1412 saw John the Fearless at the height of his power in France. The dauphin, now fifteen and married to his eldest daughter, Margaret of Burgundy, was rapidly becoming a useful ally, while the king, the queen and her brother Louis, duke of Bavaria, and the king of Navarre, all accepted John as effective regent and resided with him in Paris. By the end of 1411 the government of Languedoc, which had formerly been entrusted to the duke of Berry, was firmly in the hands of John the Fearless, for it had been transferred to three royal nominees, all of whom were his devoted men: Renier Pot (who was already governor of Dauphiné), Guillaume de Vienne, lord of St. Georges, and Pierre de Marigny.[1] In the early months of 1412 sporadic fighting occurred while both sides were now simultaneously negotiating military help from King Henry IV of England. There was nothing very unusual about this; after all, throughout the previous autumn, both Burgundians and Armagnacs had made use of English mercenaries, but King Sigismund of Germany, who aspired to the title and status of Emperor, disapproved. In the spring of 1412 he wrote reprimanding Henry for permitting this to happen. He claimed that it would only exacerbate the quarrel to have Englishmen fighting on both sides, and he suggested that he and Henry ought to try to make peace in France or, failing this, at least they could agree to support the same side. As a matter of fact, soon after this, in May 1412, Henry IV signed a firm treaty with the Armagnac princes, the text of which became known to John the Fearless and the Paris government, before it was signed, through the arrest of one of the Armagnac ambassadors and the seizure of his baggage. The terms of this treaty, regarded by many as shameful and odious, were disclosed to the court and government in Paris by John the Fearless's councillor, now the dauphin's chancellor, Jehan de Nieles. Indeed they were successfully used to induce the king and dauphin and the other princes in Paris to take up arms, and the *oriflamme* or sacred banner of France and St. Denis, against the rebel Armagnac princes. The actual terms of the treaty of Bourges, ratified in London on 18 May 1412, were in part as follows:[2]

1. The dukes of Berry, of Orleans, and of Bourbon, and the count of Alençon, promise to help the king of England in his just quarrels with their lives and all their power.

2. Among the king of England's just quarrels they agree to include his claim to the duchy of Guienne, which they regard as rightfully his.

3. They offer their sons, daughters, relatives and subjects to make marriages approved by the king of England, and they offer their towns, castles, treasures and other belongings for the assistance of the king of England in his just and lawful quarrels.

4. They also offer their friends and allies to support the said king in the recovery of his duchy of Guienne, and they promise to cede to the king of England twenty stated towns and castles.

---

[1] Devic and Vaissette, *Languedoc*, ix. 1011–14 and Pot, *R. Pot*, 150–8. King Sigismund's letter, mentioned below, is printed in *Acta concilii Constanciensis*, i. 88–92.

[2] Text in *Foedera*, iv (2), 12–14.

5. They also agree to hold certain lands as fiefs of the king of England
John of Berry, for instance, to do homage to the king of England for
the county of Poitou, etc.

6. In return, the king of England promises not to enter into any treaties
with the duke of Burgundy; to help the Armagnac princes to defeat
him and bring him to justice; and to send them at once 1,000 men-at-
arms and 3,000 bowmen, whose wages are to be paid by the princes.

Jehan de Nieles did not content himself with expounding to the
royal council the authentic terms of the treaty of Bourges just summarized. According to Monstrelet, he also produced what purported
to be a programme of reforms to be introduced by the Armagnacs
when they obtained power in France. These obviously bogus measures
were made suitably unpopular, if not horrific:[1]

1. A land-tax was to be imposed on every acre of ground.

2. Every commoner was to be forced to work or leave the country.

3. There was to be one weight and one measure throughout the country.

4. The duchies of Lorraine and Luxembourg and the counties of
Provence and Savoy, were to be conquered by France.

5. The University was to be removed from Paris and set up elsewhere.

If the treaty of Bourges shows to what lengths the Armagnac
princes were prepared to go in their hatred of John the Fearless, the
action now taken by John shows that he was equally extreme in his determination to destroy the enemy regardless of cost and consequences.
The octogenarian duke of Berry, who was far more interested in
art and good living than in politics or warfare, was selected as the
victim of the campaign now launched against the Armagnacs by John
the Fearless and accompanied by John of Berry's nephew, the king
of France, and the dauphin. On 11 June 1412 the royal and Burgundian army laid siege to Bourges, capital city of the duchy of Berry.

The war was now prosecuted on both sides in earnest. An outlying
town, Dun-sur-Auron, south-west of Bourges, offered fierce resistance and had to be battered into submission before Bourges itself
could be invested. The monk of St. Denis was apparently an eye-
witness of this artillery bombardment.[2]

[The besiegers] . . . caused a cannon called Griette, which was bigger
than the others, to be mounted opposite the main gate. It shot stones of
enormous weight at the cost of quantities of gunpowder and much hard

---

[1] Monstrelet, *Chronique*, ii. 241–2. [2] Relig. de St. Denys, iv. 652.

and dangerous work on the part of its expert crew. Nearly twenty men were required to handle it. When it was fired, the thunderous noise could be heard four miles away, and terrorized the local inhabitants as if it were some reverberation from hell. On the first day, the foundations of one of the towers were partly demolished by a direct hit. On the next day, this cannon fired twelve boulders, two of which penetrated the tower, thus exposing many of the buildings and their inhabitants. . . .

It is perhaps of sufficient interest to mention here that Griette had actually been cast at St. Omer by a certain Jaquemart le Mahieu, a *maître charpentier des engins* of the duke of Burgundy, and had been tested there outside the gate near the castle, in the presence of Duke John himself, in May or June 1411. This precise information comes from the meticulously kept accounts of the receiver-general of all finances.[1]

One minor incident in the campaign of Bourges has been described by a participant in his autobiographical writings. This was Guillebert de Lannoy who, with Jaques de Heilly, a noted Burgundian captain, was on his way to join the royal army at the siege of Bourges.

> The lord of Heilly . . . arrived in Berry with six hundred men-at-arms and five hundred bowmen. We billeted [ourselves] and foraged in such a way that, on leaving Déols, the first stop we made was in the town and castle of Limeux. [Here] some thousand men-at-arms arrived one morning, coming from the city of Bourges, together with a number of stalwart bowmen. They attacked us in our lodgings, overcame our barricades and drove us back, grimly and cruelly. Then these forces took all our horses, fifteen hundred in number, and more of our people were killed there than taken prisoner. [As to] the aforesaid lord of Heilly and most of the knights, we retreated into the castle, which they made as if to assault, but in fact they only set fire to the town and went off with their booty. And there, I was wounded in the thigh by a vireton [which penetrated] between my armour, and I carried its point in my thigh for more than nine months. And after we had recovered two or three hundred of our horses by an escapade which our people made at Issoudun, where their booty was, my lord of Heilly and his men came to the king at the siege of Bourges.

Meanwhile, back in Paris, the deity was being constantly implored to bring about a favourable peace settlement, and the people's enthusiasm for one was repeatedly stimulated by a series of solemn processions which continued throughout June. In these the monks of

---

[1] De Laborde, *Ducs de Bourgogne*, i. 24–5. The extract which follows is from de Lannoy, *Oeuvres*, 19.

St. Denis seem to have excelled. On 5 June they arrived in Paris, barefooted, in solemn procession, carrying with them the bodies of no less than seven saints, the *oriflamme* which had been used at the battle of Roosebeke in Flanders in 1382, one of the nails used for the crucifixion, the Crown of Thorns . . . and thirteen banners. But the peace which was sworn in the presence of a grand assembly of princes and representatives of the realm, at Auxerre on 22 August 1412, was due, not to the hand of God, nor even, as one chronicler suggested, to the exhaustion of the available funds on either side,[1] but to the mediation of three princes whose loyalties and sympathies were divided by the war: the dauphin, Louis of Guienne; the count of Savoy, Amadeus VIII; and the king of Sicily, Louis, duke of Anjou.

The terms of the settlement of Auxerre consisted in a ratification of the peace of Chartres, including the promised marriage alliance between the houses of Burgundy and Orleans, and mutual pardons for all save the actual murderers of Louis of Orleans. Moreover, the contracting parties agreed to renounce their alliances with England.[2] This was easy for John the Fearless who, as he stated in his letter of renunciation, in fact had no alliances with England to renounce. But the Armagnac princes now had to buy off the English expeditionary force which they themselves had called into existence by the treaty of Bourges. Thomas duke of Clarence, second son of Henry IV, had landed in the Cotentin peninsula on 10 August 1412 with a considerable army, at a time when only the details of the peace settlement were still to be arranged. After some haggling, the treaty of Bourges was reversed, as it were, by the treaty of Buzançais, signed on 14 November 1412: the English agreed to retire to Bordeaux by 1 January 1413 in return for 150,000 crowns. Meanwhile, the peace of Auxerre had been joyously proclaimed all over France and, according to Monstrelet, the dauphin had gone so far as to issue a decree prohibiting the use of the opprobrious terms Burgundian and Armagnac.

We cannot take very seriously the alliances and protestations of friendship which accompanied the peace of Auxerre: marriage alliance of Burgundy and Bourbon; peace-league of Burgundy, Bourbon,

---

[1] Juv. des Ursins, *Hist. de Charles VI*, 473.

[2] Two of these renunciations are in *Lettres de rois*, ii. no. 178 (Berry) and *Docs. pour servir à l'histoire des relations entre l'Angleterre et la Flandre*, no. 139 (Burgundy). For the treaty, see Plancher, iii. no. 287. The subsequent treaties of alliance are in Plancher, iii. nos. 280 and 286 and ACO B11893 (28 November 1412, alliance of Berry and Burgundy). Other documents are *Choix de pièces*, i. nos. 155 and 158 and *Ords. des rois*, x. 18-24.

Orleans and Vertus; alliance of Burgundy and Berry; not to mention
the treaty itself, the mutual banqueting, and the episode of John the
Fearless and Charles of Orleans riding together on the same horse.
After all, on 13 November 1412 Charles of Orleans had signed a
secret treaty of alliance with the duke of Clarence. Like its predecessors of Chartres and Bicêtre, the peace of Auxerre marked only a
temporary lull in the struggle for power in France.

John the Fearless remained, throughout the rest of 1412 and the
first few months of 1413, in control of the court, the capital, and the
government, of France. Intermittent gifts of Beaune wine helped to
maintain his prestige and his popularity. In December 1412, for
instance, fifty *queues* of wine were distributed to leading members of
the French government—the chancellor, the provost of Paris, the
president and some of the *maîtres* of the *chambre des comptes*, the
governors of the royal expenses, the general councillors on the *aides*,
the *maître* of the *chambre aux deniers*, the *trésorier des guerres*, and
others, including the rector of Paris University.[1] But John had now
to reckon with the growing power of the dauphin, Louis duke of
Guienne, whose sixteenth birthday fell on 22 January 1413. At
Bourges, the dauphin had pleaded with John the Fearless for modera-
tion; and he had been the foremost mediator of the settlement of
Auxerre. When the court returned to Paris after the peace congress,
the dauphin was responsible for the rehabilitation of Jehan de
Montagu—an event almost as macabre as his execution. One evening,
says Monstrelet, the provost of Paris and the executioner, with a
dozen guards, holding lighted torches and carrying a ladder, followed
by a priest in his vestments, went to the Halles and removed the
desiccated head of the former grand master of the king's household
from the lance on which it had been transfixed three years before.
This grisly object was wrapped by the priest in a handsome napkin
and carried on his shoulder to the hôtel de Montagu, where it was
joined to the body, now brought down from the gibbet at Montfaucon.
Both were later given decent burial in the church which Jehan de
Montagu had founded at Marcoussis. Another incident, in March
1413, demonstrated the increasing stature of the dauphin: in a fit of
anger, he dismissed his chancellor, the Burgundian councillor Jehan
de Nieles, from his office.

Until the spring of 1413, John the Fearless had enjoyed mounting
success in France. Every obstacle that the Orleanists or Armagnacs

[1] Plancher, iii. 366. For what follows, see de Pisan, *Livre de la paix*, 29 and
59–61 and Monstrelet, *Chronique*, ii. 300–1.

had raised in his path had been triumphantly surmounted. Slowly but surely he seemed to be establishing his position as regent. But now, in the summer of 1413, events and circumstances conspired against him, and he found himself deprived in a few months of everything he had gained in the preceding few years.

The Cabochien revolt broke out in Paris on 28 April 1413. So called from one of the popular leaders, Simon Caboche, it began with the first (and not the last) mass demonstration before the Bastille in the history of France, and with the arrest and imprisonment by the Paris mob of certain leading figures of the court and government, including the duke of Bar and the recently appointed chancellor of the dauphin, Jehan de Vailly. This revolt was in part an example of the class warfare which was endemic in the urban populations of the later middle ages. In this respect it was just one among many revolts in which the artisans or workers tried by force to seize power in their city. But in part it represented reform rather than revolution, for it was encouraged, supported and exploited by a group of serious men in government and Burgundian circles, who sincerely wished to re- form the government. John the Fearless, placed in an embarrassing position because the leaders of the revolt were his protégés and followers, and because he, alone among the French princes, was popular with the mob, played an exceedingly equivocal rôle: the best construction one can put on it is that he tried to calm and moderate the worst excesses of mob enthusiasm.

The first uprising was preceded by a meeting of the Estates of Languedoil and by the presentation of elaborate reforming petitions. The second outburst of mob activity on 22 May, which achieved the arrest and imprisonment of such notables as Duke Louis of Bavaria brother of the queen, several of the queen's household officers, and some fifteen of her ladies-in-waiting, was followed almost immediately by the formal publication at the request of the Cabochiens of the so-called *ordonnance Cabochienne*, on 26 and 27 May.[1] Only the first ninety-six clauses of this remarkable document were read out on the first day—there were 258 altogether, some of them lengthy. This was not a revolutionary manifesto but a detailed programme of ad- ministrative reforms, many of them designed to make the government more efficient and cheaper, and to remove corruption and abuses; but like so many other *ordonnances* of this period, the *ordonnance Cabo- chienne* was never implemented.

[1] Text in *Ordonnance Cabochienne*, ed. Coville.

The effect of the Cabochien uprising in Paris in summer 1413 on John the Fearless's position in France has been much exaggerated. In fact, all the Cabochien affair amounted to, apart from the agitation for reform, was two serious riots on 28 April and 22 May; the murder of four suspected Armagnacs on 28 April; five or six executions in June and July; and less than fifty persons thrown into gaol. What then was the cause of the reaction in favour of the Armagnacs which set in during the summer, and which ended with the flight of John the Fearless from Paris before the end of August?

The attitude of the dauphin was perhaps the most important single cause of the collapse of the Burgundian party in France at this time. He suffered much at the hands of the Cabochiens in April and May. He was forced to re-instate his Burgundian chancellor, Jehan de Nieles, whom he had dismissed in March; and his hôtel was invaded by the mob, and several of his officials seized and imprisoned. During the summer he is said to have made efforts to escape from Paris, and to have written to the Armagnac princes appealing for their help. In the first half of August, when the Cabochien leaders lost the support of the people of Paris and were forced to flee, the dauphin played a major part in the critical and complex events which brought this about. He seems already to have been detaching himself from John the Fearless in the winter of 1412–13; the Cabochien revolt converted him, temporarily at least, into a staunch Armagnac.

Other equally important factors were involved in the Armagnac coup d'état of 1413. The king recovered his sanity in May and, apart from some lapses, maintained it through most of the summer. Naturally, while sane, he worked for reconciliation and peace; and he tended to support his son the dauphin and the Armagnacs, rather than John the Fearless. Militarily, too, John's situation was weak, and worsening, for when the Armagnac princes mobilized their forces round Paris in the summer of 1413, he became in danger of being cut off and surrounded. These princes, totally dissatisfied with the peace of Auxerre, now consolidated their alliances and resolved at all costs to dislodge John from Paris, where they enjoyed the support, in the summer of 1413, of a growing party of moderates, represented and perhaps led by Juvenel des Ursins, father of the chronicler. The moderates were reinforced in July by sections of the Paris mob itself, as well as by public opinion at large, such as it was, for, once negotiations had started, as they did in July, the desire for peace overrode all other considerations, particularly in view of the ever-present threat from England. By the end of July, John the Fearless, yielding to this pressure, had negotiated and signed the peace of Pontoise, according to the terms of which all the princes promised to disarm, and to confer shortly outside Paris with the king and dauphin.[1]

Early in August, both John the Fearless and the Cabochien leaders were outmanœuvred in Paris by the manipulations of the dauphin, Juvenel des Ursins and other moderate or Armagnac elements. The successful conclusion of peace removed all excuse or pretext for further agitation or reform. The forces of popular enthusiasm were soothed and diverted, as so often in history, by thoughts of peace and prosperity. The dauphin began arresting some of the Cabochien leaders, and even one or two Burgundian partisans. Rumour had it that John was to be secretly assassinated or publicly tried and executed for the murder of Louis of Orleans. Perhaps what he feared more was the prospect of a formal sharing of his power in France, or even renunciation of it. In any case, he fled precipitately from Paris on 23 August 1413 to the safety of Flanders. Earlier in the month his duchess, in Burgundy, had feared he was a prisoner of the Armagnacs in Paris, and had even appealed to Anthony of Brabant and others to rescue him. Now she was assured of her husband's safety, but also of his failure to maintain himself in Paris, by the following letter:[2]

To my most redoubted lady, madame the duchess of Burgundy, countess of Flanders, of Artois, and of Burgundy.

My most redoubted lady, I recommend myself to you as humbly as I can and, because I know that you will want to have news of my lord [the duke of Burgundy], may it please you to know that he left here today, giving out to me and some of his other officials that he was going to see the king, who went to stay yesterday evening at the Bois [de Vincennes]. But in fact he set out for his county of Flanders without having spoken to or taken leave of the king, the queen or my lord the dauphin; and without telling me or his other officials, whom he has left in this town you can imagine in what peril. May God grant that the result will be good and honourable for the duke. My most redoubted lady, it is evident that, to obviate all the fears and panic which may arise because of this affair, you will have to maintain an excellent and secure defence of the duke's possessions down there, for their protection against all eventualities, as I know you have already been doing with all possible care and diligence.

---

[1] On the events of summer 1413 in Paris see, besides the works mentioned on p. 67 above, Champion, *BSHP* xxxvii (1910), 36–9.
[2] Plancher, iii. no. 290.

My most redoubted lady, I pray the Holy Spirit to have you in its holy care, and to give you a good life and a long one.

Written at Paris, 23 August 1413.

Your most humble and obedient servant, Jehan de Saulx, chancellor of my lord [the duke of Burgundy].

On the day this letter was written, at the very moment when John was galloping out of Paris towards Flanders, his troops seized and guarded the vital bridge over the Oise at Pont Ste. Maxence, where he arrived that very evening. An entry in the accounts tells its own tale:[1]

To Guy de Beaufort, squire, the sum of 300 francs, paid to him in cash by ducal command . . . for the wages of himself, 29 other squires, and 44 bowmen who came under him and in his company to serve my lord [the duke] wherever he pleased, and who were reviewed on 23 August 1413 at the bridge of Ste. Maxence by Sir David de Brimeu, knight, deputed to do this by my lord [the duke] in the absence of his marshal, in order that they might wait there or advance to meet my lord [the duke], who was then in danger at Paris.

---

[1] ACO B1576, f. 268.

CHAPTER FIVE

The Means to Power

Finance

Some would have us believe that Philip the Bold left the Burgundian finances in ruin when he died in April 1404. The records show that a quantity of ducal plate had to be pawned to pay for his funeral, and that his debts were still being discharged five years later.[1] The chroniclers support the impression of insolvency: Monstrelet describes how Duchess Margaret of Male, following the custom, renounced all claim to her late husband's belongings and debts by placing her girdle, complete with purse and keys, on his coffin at Arras. The original formal written instrument of her renunciation still exists at Dijon, and along with it another document, recording the sale by John the Fearless to his mother, for 40,000 francs, of part of her husband's belongings which he had inherited. The fact is, of course, that Philip the Bold's effects were worth a large sum of money, and his succession was by no means so encumbered with debts as to be valueless. There were debts, naturally, but there were credits too: the king, for instance, owed him some 75,000 francs, and the normal revenues of the Burgundian state continued to flow in. No valid conclusions about financial exhaustion can be deduced from the picturesque though banal action of the widowed duchess. She renounced her dead husband's succession not because his finances were in ruin, but to elude his creditors, who would otherwise have had a claim on her as well as on her son John. The historian of Burgundy, Ernest Petit, in a much-repeated passage, gives a very misleading impression when he says: 'The situation, on Philip's death, was so

---

[1] Plancher, iii. 200–1 and ACO B1560, f. 190b. For what follows, see Monstrelet, *Chronique*, i. 89 and ACO B307 = Plancher, iii. no. 218, dated 9 May 1404, and Plancher, iii. no. 220. For the rest of the paragraph, see Plancher, iii. 213–14 and Pocquet, *MSHDB* vi (1939), 123. The quotation is from Petit, *Philippe le Hardi*, 11.

burdened with debt, that Margaret of Flanders renounced the succession by depositing her purse and girdle; and the bailiff of the *Parlement* took possession of the furniture of the hôtel d'Artois under the very eyes of John the Fearless.' The second part of this statement is in any case probably quite irrelevant in this connection, for it seems to refer to an incident in 1414.[1]

Philip the Bold was not an egocentric spendthrift who had dissipated the revenues of Burgundy and left his lands and family in poverty and debt. The creator of the Burgundian state had in fact maintained and augmented its financial resources. Because of this wealth, he enjoyed extensive credit. No wonder that he died in debt: every successful ruler did, just as every modern state and business lives on borrowed money.

We must be equally chary of drawing too hasty conclusions about the ruinous state of Burgundian finances under John the Fearless. Coville, for instance, thought that, after the expensive campaigns of 1411, John was impoverished in 1412.[2] He talks of drastic economies in court expenses and of the suppression or diminution of pensions and wages. But there is no sign in the accounts, of household economies at this time, and restrictions on the payment of pensions and wages were in force intermittently throughout John's reign. We may be equally suspicious of the contemporary records themselves. What debtor has not solemnly informed his creditor that he is absolutely broke? Do we have to believe the literal words of John the Fearless when he writes to his sister, Catherine, duchess of Austria, to say that he *cannot afford* to pay her the rest of her dowry, still owing to her? Of course not. It was simply a matter of deciding on priorities; a sister must learn to wait. When she threatened to come and live in the duchy or county of Burgundy at John's expense, until he paid up, he wrote off to the *gens des comptes* at Dijon on 27 February 1412 telling them that he could not afford to pay his sister and that, at all costs, she must be dissuaded from descending on his territories in this way. The man to pacify her was the abbot of Lure. He must be sent on embassy to her, and all moneys owing to *him* must be promptly paid.

It would be churlish for the historian to complain of the gaps in the original financial records for the reign of John the Fearless. After all, the material that survives is probably more abundant than that

[1] See below, p. 196.
[2] *Les Cabochiens*, 158. For what follows, see below, pp. 115–16 and 118 and ACO B307, original letters close of 27 February 1412.

Surviving accounts, for John the Fearless's reign, of the receipt-general of all finances and the two regional receipts-general

Year (approx.)	Rec.-gen. of all finances Ref. no.	Period covered	Rec.-gen. of two Burgundies Ref. no.	Period covered	Rec.-gen. of Flanders Ref. no.	Period covered
1404	ACO B1538	1.10.03–16.6.04				
1405						
1406	ACO B1543	5.11.05–19.11.06				
1407	ACO B1547	22.11.06–22.11.07				
1408	ACO B1554	22.11.07–22.11.08				
1409	ACO B1556	23.11.08–31.1.09				
	ACO B1558	1.2.09–1.2.10				
1410	ACO B1560	1.2.10–1.2.11	ACO B1559	12.4.09–31.12.10		
1411	ACO B1562	1.2.11–17.4.11	ACO B1563	31.3.11–3.11.11		
	ACO B1570	17.4.11–30.4,12				
1412	ACO B1571	1.5.12–16.10.12	ACO B1569	1.1.11–31.3.11 4.11.11–31.12.12	ADN B4086	24.6.11–24.6.12
1413	ACO B1576	21.2.13–31.12.14				
1414	ADN B1903	19.3.14–18.4.15			AGR CC2704	1.6.13–24.6.14
1415						
1416			⎱ ACO B1588	27.11.15–31.12.17	ADN B4088	24.6.15–24.6.16
					ADN B4089	24.6.16–26.11.16
					ADN B4090	26.11.16–24.6.18
1417						
1418			ACO B1594	1.1.18–31.12.18		
1419	ACO B1601	1.1.19–30.6.19	ACO B1598	1.1.19–31.12.19		
	ACO B1603	1.7.19–10.9.19				

for any other early fifteenth-century ruler. Yet the incompleteness of the existing series of accounts does make it very difficult to calculate or even estimate John the Fearless's annual revenue. The state of completeness of the three series of accounts important in this connection is shown in the table on page 105.

Unfortunately there is insufficient overlap between these series for a direct calculation of John's revenues. The best we can do is to estimate them from certain annual averages for the years 1407–14. Thus, by adding together the average annual extra-ordinary receipts of the receiver-general of all finances and the average annual receipts of the two regional receivers, a rough figure of 416,000 l.t. is arrived at. Another method of assessing the annual revenues, by adding the expenses recorded in the account of the receipt-general of all finances to the *local* expenses of the regional receivers, gives an approximate total of 436,000 l.t. per annum. It may thus be surmised that, in the years 1407–14, the annual income of John the Fearless was between 400,000 and 450,000 *livres* of Tours.

What changes took place in John the Fearless's revenue during his reign? The years we have perforce used for the foregoing estimates were years of stability and prosperity for the Burgundian finances.

Estimate, from receipts, of John the Fearless's annual revenue in the period 1407–14
l.t. = *livres* of Tours; l.p. = *livres* of Paris

Receipt-general of all finances	The total extra-ordinary receipts—mainly royal gifts—of the receipt-general of all finances for most of 1408, 1409 and 1410–11 (ACO B1554, 1558 and 1560) = 368,117 l.t. These accounts cover exactly three years, therefore the annual average = 122,705 l.t.	122,700 l.t.
Receipt-general of Burgundy	The total receipts of the receipt-general of the two Burgundies for 1411 and 1412 (ACO B1569 and 1563) = 125,079 l.t., giving an annual average of 62,539 l.t.	62,500 l.t.
Receipt-general of Flanders and Artois	The total receipts of the receipt-general of Flanders and Artois for 1411–12 and 1413–14 (ADN B4086 and AGR CC2704) = 369,336 l.p., giving an annual average of 184,668 l.p. Multiply by $\frac{5}{4}$ to convert to l.t. = 230,835 l.t.	230,800 l.t.

ESTIMATED TOTAL AVERAGE ANNUAL REVENUE   416,000 l.t.

Estimate, from expenses, of John the Fearless's annual revenue in the period 1407–14
l.t. = *livres* of Tours; l.p. = *livres* of Paris

Receipt-general of all finances	The total expenses of the receipt-general of all finances for most of 1408, 1409 and 1410–11 (ACO B1554, 1558 and 1560) = 1,079,329 l.t., giving an annual average of 359,776 l.t.	360,000 l.t.
Receipt-general of Burgundy	The total expenses of the receipt-general of the two Burgundies in 1411 and 1412 (ACO B1569 and 1563) = 149,510 l.t. The total paid to central accounting officers = *c*. 93,400 l.t. Therefore, the total expended locally = 56,110 l.t. This gives an annual average local expenditure of 28,255 l.t.	28,000 l.t.
Receipt-general of Flanders and Artois	The total expenses of the receipt-general of Flanders/Artois in 1411–12 and 1413–14 (ADN B4086 and AGR CC2704) = 346,762 l.p. The total paid to central accounting officers in this period = 269,587 l.p. Therefore, the total expended locally = 77,175 l.p. This gives an annual average local expenditure of 38,587 l.p. Multiply by $\frac{5}{4}$ to convert to l.t. = 48,234 l.t.	48,000 l.t.

ESTIMATED TOTAL AVERAGE ANNUAL REVENUE   436,000 l.t.

Military expenses may have been heavy at times, but the success of the ducal army at Othée in 1408 brought John a windfall of 123,750 l.t. A major change occurred in August 1413, when John the Fearless was forced to leave Paris. Up to then, over the whole period 1406–12 inclusive, he had been receiving on average about 70,000 l.t. per annum from the king of France.[1] After then, this source of revenue dried up completely, apart from a mere trickle of funds from royal *aides* in Artois, traditionally shared between crown and count. Unfortunately the disappearance of the accounts of the receipt-general of all finances for the years 1415–18 makes it impossible to examine in detail the effect of this on John the Fearless's finances. We can be sure, however, that it was not catastrophic. Moreover, late in 1417,

[1] Averaged from Pocquet's figures, *MSHDB* vi (1939), 115. For John the Fearless's receipts from mints in Burgundy see Dumas-Dubourg, *AB* xxxiv (1962), 5–45.

Improvements in John the Fearless's financial situation in 1417–19

Figures are for one calendar year and in *livres* of Tours unless otherwise stated

Year	Royal gifts to John and Charolais (from Pocquet)	Receipt-gen. of all finances	Total receipts of rec.-gen. of Burgundy	Profits from royal mints in the two Burgundies	Total receipts of rec.-gen. of Flanders (in livres of Paris)
1411	68,500	Annual av. receipt in 1408, 1410 and 1411 c. 360,000	Period of 2 years, 125,079 Halved, to represent one year's revenues	Period of 2 years 6,364 Halved, to represent one year's revenues	156,771
1412	38,000		62,539	3,182	
1413	14,266				212,565
1414	—				
1415	—				151,172
1416	—		Period of 2 years and 35 days 312,058 Halved, to represent one year's revenues	Period of 2 years and 35 days 184,403 Halved, to represent one year's revenues	Period of 2 years 288,919
1417	200,000		156,029	92,201	
1418	17,000		302,171	264,783	
1419	18,596	Receipts for first 6 months only, 237,101 Doubled to represent one year's revenues 474,202	272,423	211,203	Halved, to represent one year's revenues 144,459

French finances once again became available and, in 1418–19, John the Fearless actually enjoyed outright control of the entire financial administration of France. Furthermore, in the same period, from 1417 on, he was able to exploit certain valuable coinage concessions in the two Burgundies, which he had extracted from the French crown. Thus, after 1417, while the income from Flanders and Artois remained static, the profits of the royal mints at Dijon, Troyes and elsewhere more than quadrupled that from the two Burgundies.

The accompanying table is designed to show these improvements in John the Fearless's finances at the end of his reign. It does not take account of his direct control of the finances of France in 1418–19, simply because this did not much affect the Burgundian finances. What happened was this. The French financial personnel was re-placed in 1418 by a predominantly Burgundian one, and John ap-pointed his own receiver-general of the French finances, Pierre Gorremont, whose accounts have been admirably studied and pub-lished by Pocquet du Haut-Jussé.[1] But these accounts show clearly that John the Fearless, instead of transferring funds on a large scale from one treasury under his control to another, kept the two separate. He made use of French finances for his own purposes in France, and retained Burgundian finances for his own purposes in Burgundy. Thus Pierre Gorremont compensated or rewarded the duke's followers and supporters of 1413 with French money; Burgundian garrisons on French soil were paid for by him in 1418–19; and John the Fearless's diplomatic expenses were partly met by Gorremont from French funds. In fact, the Burgundian finances continued much as before, while John's new and considerable commitments in France were financed by these newly available French funds.

The three major elements in the revenues of the Burgundian state under John the Fearless were (1) the ordinary domanial income which contributed largely to the regional receipts-general; (2) the extra-ordinary *aides* or taxes which the duke could raise from time to time with the consent of his subjects; and (3) the income from the French crown. Enough has already been said about this last,[2] and we may turn to look at the *aides* which John the Fearless succeeded, though often with difficulty, in imposing from time to time on the subjects of his different territories. The figures here are sums voted, not sums paid, though there is no reason to believe that these taxes, even if

[1] *BEC* xcviii (1937), 66–98 and 234–82 and *La France gouv. par J. sans Peur.* See, too, Mollat, *RH* ccxix (1958), 299–304.
[2] Besides the foregoing pages, see above, pp. 41–3 and 85–7.

sometimes delayed for a time, were ever evaded altogether. This table, though perhaps virtually complete for Flanders and the duchy of Burgundy, is by no means so for the smaller territories, and Malines is altogether omitted.

Aides *granted to John the Fearless, 1404–19*
Figures in *livres* of Tours

Year	Flanders	Artois	Lille-Douai-Orchies	Duchy of Burgundy	County of Burgundy
1404					
1405		?		36,000	20,000
1406					
1407					
1408	324,000	? 14,000			
1409					
1410	180,000	? 14,000		20,000	8,000
1411					
1412			? 4,500		
1413		? 14,000	2,756	15,000	6,000
1414					
1415	15,000		4,500		
1416	180,000				
1417	300,000	?		7,000	5,500
1418		? 10,000			
1419	c. 30,000			12,000	
Totals	1,029,000	? 52,000	? 11,756	90,000	39,500
Average p.a.	68,600	3,467		6,000	2,633
Combined totals		1,092,756		129,500	
Combined av. p.a.		72,850		8,622	

While the *aides* from the Burgundies, declining in amount during the reign, brought a mere irregular trickle of funds into the ducal treasury, those from Flanders were clearly of considerable importance, representing perhaps one-sixth or one-seventh of John's total revenues. It is particularly interesting to compare the revenue from Flemish *aides* under John the Fearless with that obtained by Philip the Bold. The figures, juxtaposed, speak for themselves: John was far more successful than his father at extracting money from the tight-fisted but wealthy Flemings.

Flemish aides voted to Philip the Bold and John the Fearless
Figures in *livres* of Tours

Philip the Bold		John the Fearless	
1384	c. 30,000	1405	
1385		1406	
1386	c. 10,500	1407	
1387		1408	324,000
1388	100,000	1409	
1389		1410	180,000
1390		1411	
1391	98,182	1412	
1392		1413	
1393		1414	
1394	141,818	1415	15,000
1395		1416	180,000
1396		1417	300,000
1397	218,182	1418	
1398		1419	c. 30,000
1399			
1400			
1401			
1402			
1403			
1404			
TOTAL	598,682	TOTAL	1,029,000
Av. p.a.	29,934	Av. p.a.	68,600

If, on a long view, John the Fearless's financial situation was basic-ally sound, in the short term he was faced with one perpetual prob-lem: the urgent need to raise funds for immediate use. In particular, he needed supplies of specie, of hard cash, to pay household, military and diplomatic expenses. Whenever they were gullible or weak enough, his creditors were fobbed off with assignments, or promis-sory notes. But troops in the field, like the numerous personnel of the ducal hôtel, had to have food. Every time an army was mobilized, barrels of coin were collected and despatched from all parts of the ducal territories. In the autumn of 1405, for instance, three ducal officers had to borrow 6,000 francs in the county of Burgundy, and pack the coin in barrels to be sent to Dole and thence on to Paris, to pay the troops assembled there.[1] A month later a group of officials with an escort of twenty-two men-at-arms took 20,000 francs in coin to Montbéliard, to hand over to Catherine, duchess of Austria, as part

[1] For this and the next sentence, see Blondeau, *MSED* (10) viii (1938), 69–70 and, for what follows, *IADNB* iv. 71.

of her dowry. In 1412 Pierre Gorremont, who was then the clerk of John the Fearless's *maître de la chambre aux deniers* Jehan de Velery, was sent on several missions to fetch coin to pay the troops on the Bourges campaign. On one occasion, while passing the castle of Mont-faucon on his way back from Nevers with saddle-bags loaded with specie, he was attacked by the enemy, and his horse died under him as it reached safety in the royal camp after galloping two leagues weighted down in this way.

The people who suffered most from the urgent ducal need for cash were the local receivers. They were the unwilling recipients of count-less letters from the duke or the duchess, asking often for the most paltry sums. For instance, on 31 August 1410, the treasurer of Vesoul, Perrenot le Moniat, was sent the following letter from the duchess:[1]

From the duchess of Burgundy, countess of Flanders, of Artois and of Burgundy.

Dear and well-beloved, from letters which we have recently received from the captains of the troops which monsieur [the duke] has sent from Burgundy into the county of Charolais in order to defend it and to resist the evil designs of his enemies, who have been reported in number on the frontiers near the said county of Charolais . . . [it appears that] there is an urgent need to furnish as quickly as possible provisions, artillery, gunpowder and suitable men. . . . The necessary money to do this cannot be found in time except by enlisting the aid of you and the other ducal officers. . . . We do not believe that my lord [the duke] has ever had such difficulties in the defence and security of his aforesaid land [of Charolais] as he has at the moment. . . . So we earnestly beg you and indeed order and command you as firmly as we possibly can on behalf of my lord [the duke] and ourselves, that at once without any delay, on receipt of these letters, you hand over and pay to the bearer—whom we are sending to you for this reason—the sum of twenty-five francs, to be used for the above-mentioned purposes. And we shall send you your receipt for this sum by the same messenger. Do not default in any way in this matter, whatever moneys you may have to owe as a result, if you desire and love the well-being and honour of my lord [the duke] and the safety of the county of Charolais and the whole of his land of Burgundy. . . .

May Our Lord keep you. Written at Rouvres, on the last day of August, 1410.

J. de Maroilles

In this case, as in nearly all the others, the receiver was authorized

[1] Bazin, *MSHA Beaune* (1897), 81–2, from BN Coll. de Bourg. 57, f. 139.

or instructed to recoup himself out of his receipt for the following year. He was, in fact, being made the victim of a forced loan. Here is another example: a letter written in March 1413, and evidently sent to all the ducal receivers and other local accounting officers in the southern territories:[1]

From the duke of Burgundy, count of Flanders, of Artois and of Burgundy.

Dear and well-beloved . . ., because of the latest plans that have been laid against us by certain lords, both English and otherwise, who are intending to do all in their power to damage monsieur the king and us, and his lands and subjects and ours . . . and indeed because without considerable and prompt finance we shall neither be able to continue the war nor raise armed men to resist the enemy . . . and to defend our lands and you and our other subjects against them, we earnestly pray and require you to aid and succour us according to your power and ability by lending us at once the sum of fifty francs, to recover it later from the revenues of your receipt. Bring this sum to our town of Dijon, to our dearly beloved companion the duchess, before the thirtieth day of this present month, notwithstanding any delays, and deliver it to our receiver-general of Burgundy, Regnaut de Thoisy, or to Jehan Moisson, our receiver of Dijon, who will give you a sufficient receipt. And take care, in so far as you love and fear us and desire our honour and well-being, that you do not default in any way, however you may become indebted as a result, because we assure you that, if there is any fault, we shall not be obliged to make it good. Also, make sure you are at the appointed place on time and in person, to hear certain things which the duchess has to say to you from us about the defence and security of our country of Burgundy and Charolais. And do not fail us in this, on pain of incurring our perpetual indignation and of dismissal for ever from your office for disobedience.

Dear and well-loved, may the Holy Spirit keep you. Written at Paris, on the eleventh day of March.

Saulx

These forced loans, usually of small sums, may have been fairly easy to raise. Doubtless the receiver could extract or borrow moneys locally by intimidating his underlings and those who paid him rents and the like. But heavier demands were made on these local accounting officers, especially on those who were wealthy nobles with a

---

[1] ACO B11942, no. 21, addressed to the castellan of Montréal. Similar letters to the treasurer of Dole, asking for 150 francs, are in BN Coll. de Bourg. 57, f. 211, and to the castellan of Verdun, asking for 100 f. in ACO B11841, 11 March 1413.

recognized place at the ducal court, for they were frequently asked or compelled to stand surety for the duke's debts in their own persons and goods. In June 1406, for instance, a group of receivers were sent copies of the following letter, in which each was required to stand surety for part of a loan which John the Fearless had raised in Paris.[1]

To our dear and well-beloved Jehan de Chanceaux, castellan of Aignay [-le-Duc], from the duke of Burgundy, count of Flanders, of Artois and of Burgundy.

Dear and well-loved, with the good wishes of monsieur the king and madame the queen, and with the aid of God, we propose, before next 12 July, to celebrate the marriage of monsieur [Charles, count] of Ponthieu, the son of monsieur the king, to our daughter Agnes; also, the marriage of our daughter Mary to the count of Cleves; and [that] of our daughter Joan to the count of Penthièvre.

For these festivities and weddings, which very much concern the well-being and honour of us and our subjects, considerable expenditure both in provisions and household expenses and in purchase of jewellery, as well as otherwise in various ways, will be necessary. We cannot accomplish these things without a large sum of money which, at the moment, we cannot obtain from our revenues for this present year. Yet nevertheless, whatever happens, we must have it.

For this reason we have arranged to receive and borrow about 10,000 francs from Michaut de Laillier, merchant of Paris, but he will not give this, or any part of it, to us, without first having in his hands before everything else good surety in the form of guarantees and obligations to repay this sum to him, at two terms, one at the end of next February and the other at the end of April following. This we cannot do, except through you and the other receivers of our country of Burgundy. Therefore we pray you as earnestly as we can, and indeed we order you, as soon as you have received these letters, to obligate yourself and agree on our behalf to the said Michaut in your own and private name to pay and render to him, as your portion of the said sum of 10,000 francs, the sum of forty gold francs, and send this obligation by our messenger, the bearer of these, without any dissent. . . .

For the sake of all the pleasure you would like to afford us, and as you love our well-being and honour, you had better not fail us in this matter, on pain of dismissal from your office, because otherwise our affairs will suffer a great deal and we should be unable to celebrate the said weddings and festivity, which would be most displeasing to us, and damaging, both now and in the future. . . .

---

[1] Printed by Petit, *Itinéraires*, 583–4, and here corrected from his source, BN Coll. de Bourg. 54, f. 148 (Petit addresses it to the castellan of Arnay-le-Duc, and dates the letter 12 June).

May Our Lord be your guard. Written at Paris, on the twenty-second day of June, in the year 1406. Bordes

The loyalty of John the Fearless's officials and partisans was perhaps more severely tested by the repeated use of another financial stratagem designed to make funds available at short notice. This was the simple but crude device of temporarily withholding payments of salaries and pensions.[1] Sometimes, it was explicitly stated that the money thus raised was to be collected then and there and paid over at once to the duke. These forced loans were in operation intermittently throughout John the Fearless's reign as duke, but the ducal orders for the limitation or cessation of payments of wages and pensions, the surviving examples of which are listed here, were invariably followed

List of ducal letters restricting payments of pensions and wages, 1404–19

Date	Reference	Period of restriction	Nature of restriction
26.7.07	ADN B1600, f. 53b	17.11.06 until further notice	All pensions granted since 1405 stopped
24.5.08	ADN B1600, f. 69	1.1.08–31.12.08	All pensions and wages in northern territories halved
3.4.09	BN Coll. de Bourg. 54, f. 204	Until further notice	All pensions stopped
16.8.10	BN Coll. de Bourg. 54, f. 302	For one year	All pensions, wages and other payments halved
20.4.12	ADN B1600, f. 144b ADN B17614 BN Coll. de Bourg. 55, f. 35	1.1.12–31.12.12	All pensions stopped; all wages halved
10.8.13	BN Coll. de Bourg. 55, fos. 92–3	1.1.13–31.12.13	All pensions and wages in southern territories halved
19.10.13	ADN B1601, f. 26	1.10.13–31.12.13	All pensions and wages stopped
7.4.15	BN Coll. de Bourg. 55, f. 160	1.1.15–31.12.15	All pensions and wages in southern territories halved
13.2.16	ADN B1601, f. 115b	Until further notice	All pensions in northern territories stopped

[1] See, besides what follows, Pocquet, *MSHDB* viii (1942), 149 and Lameere, *Grand conseil*, 22 n. 1.

by partial exemptions and relaxations. The actual effect on the remuneration of civil servants was to make payments irregular and uncertain, rather than to stop them altogether. There seems, incidentally, to be no clear distinction, in contemporary accounting usage, between pensions and wages (*gaiges*), though a pension was usually an annual grant made to a ducal knight or supporter, while wages were annual or daily payments made by way of salary to ducal officials.

The different devices used by John the Fearless to raise funds included the pawning of jewellery and plate; the sale of offices, of privileges, and even of the ducal domain lands; as well as the forced loans from civil servants already described. The loan was almost certainly the most important of these devices.[1] The sums involved, borrowed from individual persons or institutions, varied from three or five francs to the 32,300 francs which John the Fearless owed to the Parisian merchant Guillaume Sanguin when he fled from Paris in August 1413. In the receipt of the two Burgundies only three loans of importance appear in the accounts which survive, one of rather under 10,000 francs, and the other two of between 15,000 and 20,000 francs. They were raised from the towns, clergy and people of the two Burgundies in September 1411, October–December 1415 and in winter 1417–18.[2] In the receipt-general of all finances, and in the accounts of the ducal household, loans are of even less significance, but they do occur occasionally: for example, 12,000 francs lent by the duke of Bar in November 1409, and 2,500 crowns lent by the dean and chapter of Notre-Dame of Paris in December 1410 to pay for troops. It is only in the receipt-general of Flanders and Artois that loans form a significant element among the sums recorded as receipts. Their regularity and importance there is illustrated in the accompanying table. All these loans were raised from the officials, towns, and populace of the northern territories; the bulk of them were borrowed by ducal accounting officers from the revenues of their receipts. Some represent advance payments of *aides* already granted.

So far, in this section, discussion has been confined to John the

---

[1] See Bigwood, *Régime juridique et economique du commerce de l'argent*, 17, 28, 37, 40, 84–5, 88 and 93; Lobry, *Relations entre la cour de Bourgogne et les milieux d'affaires parisiens sous Jean sans Peur*, 57–82; and Humbert, *Finances de Dijon*, 166. For what follows, see, for example, ACO B1563 fos. 31 ff. For the moneys owing to Sanguin, see ACO B486/2, paper cahier.

[2] See the relevant sections of ACO B1563, 1588 and 1598. For what follows, see ACO B1558, f. 41b and 1562, f. 14b.

Loans recorded among the receipts of the accounts of the receipt-general of Flanders in John the Fearless's reign
Figures in *livres* of Paris

Reference	Approx. period	Total receipts	Total loans recorded
ADN B4086	1411–12 one year	156,771	13,803
AGR CC2704	1413–14 one year	212,565	145,780
ADN B4088	1415–16 one year	151,172	18,347
ADN B4089	1416 five months	193,250	69,135
ADN B4090	1417–18 nineteen months	95,669	34,528

Fearless's receipts and his methods of raising funds, and virtually nothing has been said about his expenses. Here there is a major point of difference between Philip the Bold and John the Fearless: on the whole, Philip did not fight wars, but John did. Unfortunately we cannot hope to ascertain exactly what proportion of John's revenues was dedicated to warfare, for the entries in the accounts, recording payments to troops, are certainly incomplete, and those recording payments for war materials and other military purposes are not classified or grouped separately. Moreover the accounts of the receipt-general of all finances for the years after 1414 have not survived. The table which follows shows all the important payments for troops in the three main series of accounts. No large payments occur in the accounts of the receipt-general of Burgundy until 1415, and almost no military expenses are entered in the accounts of the receipt-general of Flanders. A very rough estimate, based on a careful scrutiny of the entries in the accounts recording these payments, puts John the Fearless's total expenditure on troops and other military purposes in a year of warfare, or of general mobilization, such as 1408, 1410, 1411, 1412, 1414 and 1417, at something approaching 100,000 *livres* of Tours. But this is only guesswork. Incidentally, the Othée campaign of 1408 against Liège must have paid for itself, for John's share of the indemnity exacted by the victors was 123,750 l.t.

The household expenses of John the Fearless remained very similar to those of Philip the Bold. About 100,000 l.t. continued to be spent each year on the duke's own household, while in the south, Duchess Margaret of Bavaria had to be content with a mere 16,000 l.t. per annum. In Flanders, Philip, count of Charolais, was instructed

Principal payments for troops entered in the accounts of the receipts-general of all finances and of the two Burgundies under John the Fearless
Figures, approximate only, in *livres* of Tours

Approx. year	Reference number	Total
Receipt-general of all finances		
1407	ACO B1547	8,000
1408	ACO B1554	40,000
1409	ACO B1556 and 1558	22,000
1410	ACO B1560	93,000
1411	ACO B1570	15,000
1412		
1413	ACO B1576	40,000
1414	ADN B1903	35,000
Receipt-general of Burgundy		
1415		
1416	ACO B1588	74,000
1417		
1418		
1419	ACO B1598	34,000

by his father to find his own expenses out of the revenues of the northern territories.[1] The figures for the ducal household, which are to be found in the surviving hôtel accounts, are set out here.

Receipts and expenses of John the Fearless's household
Figures in *livres* of Tours

Reference no.	Period	Total receipts	Total expenses
ACO B1568	1411–12: 1 year	117,160	98,174
ACO B1578	1412–14: 2 years	154,160	198,794
ACO B1581	1414–15: 1 year	66,512	63,505
ACO B1589	1415–18: 3 years	313,418	291,630
	TOTAL	651,250	652,103
	AVERAGE PER ANN.	93,035	93,157

The earlier accounts are missing, but it is reasonable to assume, if this very high level of expenditure could be maintained in these critical years after 1411, that in the years 1405–11 the household expenses may have somewhat exceeded 100,000 l.t., giving an overall

[1] Plancher, iii. 352–3 and ADN B1601, f. 84.

average for the reign of about that amount. This does not by any means represent the *total* annual expenditure on the ducal court, but only what was paid out for everyday use by the *maître* of the *chambre aux deniers*, Jehan de Velery. Other payments, for jewellery and the ducal wardrobe, for instance, were made by the receiver-general of all finances, or some other receiver, and entered on their accounts. As with military, so with household expenses, it is not possible to give a complete answer without analysing every single entry in every single one of the many hundreds of accounts surviving for John the Fearless's reign. Only with the aid of a computer and a team of dedicated research students will the historian be able to provide a comprehensive analysis of ducal expenditure, to show what proportion of the revenues was devoted to administration, to buildings, to warfare and to the court. Meanwhile, these few rough guesses and tentative suggestions must suffice.

The duke himself made repeated attempts to ascertain his financial situation, though nothing approaching a budget has survived in the Burgundian archives for John the Fearless's reign. It would be interesting to have the detailed reply to the following letter which perhaps initiated an attempt, on the part of the duke or his central government, to achieve a more satisfactory distribution of expenses among the different receipts.[1]

To our loyal friends the *gens des comptes* at Dijon, from the duke of Burgundy, count of Flanders, of Artois and of Burgundy.

Dear and well-beloved, because we want to know accurately the value of the receipts and revenues of our country of Burgundy and other lands belonging to us which are accounted for to you, including our land of Jaucourt and our rents and revenues which are enclaves in the county of Tonnerre, and also the usual expenses [of these territories], we command and expressly enjoin you, as soon as you receive these letters, to cause to be carefully written down in a clear and accurate statement the value of each of our receipts, castellanies, granaries and the like, which are accounted for to you. [Do this] in such a way that, in this statement, one can see exactly, or as clearly as possible, what surplus there is available in our southern territories to spend during the coming year. You should value and convert corn and other products into money, according to their worth in normal years, and make sure that, after the statement [of revenues] of each receipt, castellany or granary, the usual expenses are declared. And because there are profits of justice and other extra-ordinary revenues in these receipts, which you cannot know about

---

[1] BN Coll. de Bourg. 57, f. 72.

until our officers have accounted for them, you are to include in your statement whatever sum these officers usually enter in normal years. The same goes for fines, eighths, and other extra-ordinary receipts—you should put down for each receipt whatever they are worth in a normal year. When you have done this, we wish you to send it to our well-loved receiver-general of [all] our finances, Jehan de Pressy. Take care, if you fear our anger, not to fail us in this, and notify us of your receipt of these presents by the next messenger. May Our Lord keep you. Written at Paris, on 25 June [1407]. Vignier

The general state of the Burgundian finances under John the Fearless was much the same as under his father Philip the Bold, the revenues being maintained at something over 400,000 l.t. France, apart from the years 1413–17, was exploited in a similar way, though to a lesser extent. Expenditure by both dukes was on the grandest possible scale. Both maintained an elaborate court, which must have cost them at least 150,000 l.t. per annum, or more than one quarter of their annual revenues. But Philip the Bold undertook a number of extravagant projects which together probably cost more than John the Fearless's armed struggle for power in France. The Charterhouse of Champmol and the tour de Bourgogne at Sluis cost Philip over 300,000 l.t., and the crusade of Nicopolis and the ransom of John of Nevers, as he then was, cost half a million. John the Fearless did not try to emulate, still less surpass, these lavish and grandiose disbursements of his open-handed father: he needed every penny for more urgent and immediate purposes. Like his father, he drove the Burgundian financial machine as hard as he could, but it did not break down. In spite of the debts, the dubious devices, the temporary difficulties, the constant trading on the loyalty and devotion of the ducal officials; in spite of all this, money was invariably forthcoming to nourish and support the vital purposes, the projects, and the campaigns, of John the Fearless.

The Civil Service

When John the Fearless succeeded his father Philip the Bold in 1404–5 as ruler of the Burgundian state, he inherited with it a numerous, experienced, salaried administrative staff or secretariat, a civil service, in fact, which continued to function smoothly, and so far as we can tell, efficiently, throughout his reign. Without the industry and support of these men who, because they were mostly recruited locally, formed a vital link between the ruler and his subjects,

Burgundy would have been inconceivable. Behind John the Fearless, through all the vicissitudes of his reign, stood this devoted and loyal personnel, ready to lend him money, to move their homes at his command, even to suffer imprisonment by his enemies. Whatever the dukes achieved was done with their help, and many of them devoted the greater part of their lives to their service. Who were these men?

Towards the end of John the Fearless's reign there were seven principal financial officers in the ducal service: three of whom were central officials, and four regional. Three receivers-general, (1) of all finances, (2) of the two Burgundies, and (3) of Flanders and Artois; and three household accounting officers, the *maîtres* of the *chambres aux deniers* (1) of Duke John, (2) of Duchess Margaret, and (3) of Philip, count of Charolais, all acted under the supervision and control of the chief of the Burgundian financial administration, the treasurer and governor-general of finances. The succession to these offices is set out on the following page, along with information, where this is available, about the domicile of their holders.[1]

This list shows how the central financial officials might be recruited from almost anywhere, though there is a curious bias in favour of Artois, while the regional receivers-general were invariably local men. It also shows that a high proportion of these men were already in the ducal service before John the Fearless's accession. Dreue Suquet, for instance, had begun his career on 8 December 1395 as a clerk in Philip the Bold's *chambre des comptes* in his home town of Lille and, two years later, had been promoted *maître des comptes*.[2] He had in fact served the duke as *maître des comptes* at Lille for sixteen years before his promotion to head of the financial administration in 1413. Joceran Frepier and Pierre de Montbertaut had both served previously as treasurers and in other important financial offices under Philip the Bold, and Jehan Chousat had been receiver-general of all finances in 1401-4. On the other hand, the few newcomers in this list seem, as it were, to have appeared out of the blue. Jehan Fraignot, who first emerges in 1410 in charge of the Chalon fairs, was suddenly promoted in 1415 to be receiver of the bailiwick of Chalon and, in the same year, appointed receiver-general of the two Burgundies. Three

---

[1] Data from Pocquet, *MSHDB* iv (1937), 5-77; Bartier, *Légistes et gens de finances*; Vaughan, *P. the Bold*; Proost, *Financiele hoofdambtenaren*. These and Pocquet, *France gouv. par J. dans Peur* and *Mémoires*, ii. have been used throughout this chapter.

[2] ADN B1598, fos. 28 and 75.

Holders of the principal offices in John the Fearless's financial administration
Names occurring more than once are italicized; * indicates service in some
office under Philip the Bold

Name	Period of service	Region and place of domicile
Treasurers and governors-general of finances		
*Jehan Chousat	5.11.05–19.5.07	County of Burgundy, Poligny
*Pierre de Montbertaut	19.5.07–31.1.09	Artois, Arras
Jehan Saquespee	31.1.09–9.5.10	Artois, Arras
		ACO B1554, f. 67
*Jehan de Pressy	9.5.10–15.8.10	Artois
*Joceran Frepier	14.5.10–12.4.11	Duchy of Burgundy, Chalon
*Jehan Despoullettes	12.4.11–16.10.12	Artois, Arras
Joceran Frepier	16.10.12–28.10.13	
*Dreue Suquet	31.10.13–16.10.14	Flanders, Lille
		ACO B1570, f. 81b
Jehan de Pressy	16.10.14–10.9.19	
Receivers-general of all finances		
Jehan Chousat	5.11.05–19.11.06	
Jehan de Pressy	19.11.06–31.1.09	
*Jehan de Noident	1.2.09–17.4.11	Duchy of Burgundy
*Robert de Bailleux	17.4.11–16.10.12	Picardy, Amiens
		ACO B1603, f. 38b
Joceran Frepier	16.10.12–21.2.13	
Jehan de Noident	21.2.13–10.9.19	
Receivers-general of Flanders and Artois		
*André de Douay	1.8.04–January 09	Flanders
*Godefroy le Sauvage	January 09–May 13	Flanders, Sluis
		ADN B4090, f. 106
Jehan Utenhove	1.6.13–26.11.16	Flanders, Ghent
		AGR CC21787, f. 7b
Barthelemi le Voogt	26.11.16–10.9.19	Flanders. Sluis
		ADN B4090, f. 109
Receivers-general of the two Burgundies		
*Guillaume Chenilly	6.8.1400–12.4.09	Duchy of Burg., Dijon
		AD B147, f. 1
*Regnaut de Thoisy	12.4.09–26.11.15	Duchy of Burg., Autun
		IACOB ii. 177
Jehan Fraignot	26.11.15–10.9.19	Duchy of Burg., Dijon, Chalon ACO B457 and 3627
Maîtres of the chambres aux deniers		
(1) *Jehan de Velery	1404–1419	With Duke John
(2) Guiot le Jay	11.4.05–1419	Duchy of Burg., Flavigny, Rouvres ACO B1598, f. 69
(3) Jehan Sarrote	1.5.08–1419	Flanders, with Philip, count of Charolais

years later, he was enobled by John the Fearless.[1] Likewise Jehan Saquespee, receiver-general of the royal *aides* in Artois, was drawn into the ducal financial administration late in 1408 in the very minor post of receiver of the Liège indemnity, then suddenly promoted.

These top-ranking officers were kept busy in all kinds of ways not directly connected with their offices. Joceran Frepier was employed on a special mission to Flanders at the end of 1414, after he had 'retired'; and in 1410 and 1418 he was sent on embassies to Savoy.[2] Jehan Sarrote had to be specially recompensed by the duke in April 1411 after his embassy to Venice had been prolonged by sickness and interrupted by his imprisonment at the hands of Christoph von Liechtenstein in the castle of Pergine, whence he had to struggle back on foot over the Brenner pass to the help and hospitality of Catherine of Burgundy, duchess of Austria, then at Vienna. He was not the only local ducal financial officer to suffer in this way, for a similar accident befell the receiver-general of all finances Jehan de Noident. On 1 February 1414, while travelling towards Burgundy from St. Denis, he was arrested near Meaux by Clignet de Brebant and other Armagnacs, and imprisoned until his ransom money was paid. During his chief's enforced absence his clerk, Pierre Macé, found himself suddenly promoted by John the Fearless, on 19 March 1414, to be acting receiver-general of all finances.

Perhaps the most notable of all John the Fearless's *gens de finances* was Jehan Chousat of Poligny. Under Philip the Bold he had added to his local financial office in his native county of Burgundy the post of receiver-general of all finances. At the beginning of the new reign he was seconded for a time to John the Fearless's brother Anthony, being appointed on 9 April 1405 'financial councillor, treasurer and receiver-general of Brabant'. Then, late in 1405, still a pluralist, he was recalled to Burgundy to combine for a time the office of receiver-general of all finances, which he had held before under Philip the Bold, with that of treasurer and governor-general. But this was too much for him. In November 1406 he confided to the *gens des comptes* at Dijon that he hoped and wished to resign his offices,[3] and he was

[1] ACO B15, fos. 100 and 119a–b; *IACOB* i. 430–2; and ACO B457. For the next sentence, see AD A12/1; ACO B1554, f. 35b, 1556, f. 17b, 1558, f. 30b, etc.; *Cartulaire de Hainaut*, iii. 362–3.

[2] ADN B1601, fos. 89a–b, ACO B1562, f. 77 and 1598, fos. 113a–b. For the next sentence, see *IAC* i. no. 96 = ADN B1600, f. 124b.

[3] BN Coll. de Bourg. 57, f. 26b. For what follows, see Plancher, iii. 244; *Ords. des rois*, ix. 137; and above, p. 42.

in fact relieved of one of them, but it was May 1407 before he persuaded the duke to allow him to resign the other. Although he does not, after this, appear again among the holders of high financial office, he did not cease to devote his time and energies to the ducal service. Moreover, on 15 September 1406, Charles VI had appointed him a *général conseiller sur le fait de la finance des aides*: that is to say, he had entered the French financial administration, a fact which probably explains why, on 25 May 1407, the duke charged him with the difficult or even impossible task of recovering the sum of 347,591 francs which, John the Fearless claimed, the king of France owed him.

Thus was Jehan Chousat kept busy. On his own assertion, he devoted 511 days to the duke's service between 14 April 1409 and 30 November 1410—511, that is, out of a possible 596.[1] At this time he was *premier maître des comptes* both at Dijon and Lille, and in the next year he excelled himself by being away from home on the duke's business for exactly 396 days between 1 December 1410 and 31 December 1411! He was the most highly paid ducal official after the chancellor. For the period 12 April 1409–31 December 1412, he was paid instalments totalling 1,200 f. of his annual pension of 400 francs, and 2,267½ f. in wages at the rate of 2½ f. per day: a total of 3,467½ f., or nearly 1,000 francs per annum. This at a time when ducal orders were in force abolishing all pensions and halving wages! Besides his work in the ducal civil service, Jehan Chousat found time to establish a collegiate church at Poligny, and to entertain the duke to supper in his Paris hôtel.

Among the duke's financial officers we have not included the resident *maîtres des comptes* at Dijon and Lille, for they formed a group of officials which was somewhat distinct from the other senior financial officers so far considered. In spite of important connections between the two *chambres*, such as the appointment of Jehan Chousat and Jehan Bonost to both of them,[2] they remained quite separate, and each was separately staffed by men of its own locality, who normally worked their way up to the rank of *maître* through that of clerk and *auditeur* in their own *chambre*. In the list which follows, only active, full-time *maîtres des comptes*, are included. Those, like Amiot Arnaut

---

[1] ACO B1559, f. 57b. For the rest of this paragraph, see Andt, *Chambre des comptes*, 96 and n. 185; ACO B15, f. 125; ACO B1569, fos. 81a–b; above, p. 115; and ACO B1547, fos. 67b and 97b. For the chancellor's remuneration, see below, pp. 134 and 136.

[2] Andt, *Chambre des comptes*, 96 and ADN B1601, f. 31b.

and Jehan Chousat at Dijon, who were only honorary or part-time, and were not paid as *maîtres des comptes* nor given their traditional annual grant of 50 f. for robes, are therefore omitted. Dates are approximate only.

Active maîtres des comptes *at Lille and Dijon during John the Fearless's reign*
† indicates date of death

Name	Period of service	Previous posts	Notes and references
Chambre des comptes at Lille			
Jehan de Pacy	1386–1413†	Notary in Paris	For him and the
Dreue Suquet	1397–1413	Clerk in Lille	others listed here,
	1414–19	*chambre des c.*	see de Seur, *Flandre illustrée*, 66–7
David Bousse	1397–1419	Clerk in Lille *chambre des c.*	
Barthelemi a la Truye	1413–19	*Auditeur* in Lille *chambre*, 1411–12	ADN B4086, fos. 54b–5
Jehan de Lanstais	c. 1416–19	Receiver of castellany of Lille, 1404–5	*IADNB Rép. Num.*, i. 137
Guerin Suquet	c. 1416–19	Clerk in Lille *chambre des c.* 1406–15	ADN B1600, f. 36b; ADN B4086, f. 55 and 4089, fos. 80b–1
Chambre des comptes at Dijon			
André Pasté	1373–1412†	Clerk in Dijon *c. des comptes*	*Inventaires mobiliers*, i. 583 n. 4
Regnaut Gombaut	1384–1415†	Clerk assigned to keep hôtel accounts	
Nicolas le Vaillant	1386–1416†	Clerk in Dijon *c. des comptes*	
Guillaume Courtot	1407–19	Clerk (1390) and *auditeur* (1406) in Dijon *comptes*	Andt, *Ch. des c.*, 85 n. 157
Jehan Bonost	1408–19	Clerk (1400) and *auditeur* (1407) in Dijon *comptes*	Andt, *Ch. des c.*, 85 no. 157
Dreue Mareschal	1409–19	Clerk (1400) and *auditeur* (1407) in Dijon *comptes*	Andt, *Ch. des c.*, 85 n. 157
Estienne de Sens	1411–19	?	
Odot de Varranges	1416–19	Ducal councillor in Dijon bailiwick, 1386	D'Arbaumont, *Armorial*, 122. He succeeded le Vaillant as *maître*

Virtually all the Dijon *maîtres* listed here lived at Dijon, and we may assume that many of them were natives. Certainly these men formed an important link between the ducal administration and the capital of the duchy: Odot de Varranges's father had served as mayor of Dijon; Jehan Bonost was a public notary there; Estienne de Sens a merchant draper of the town.[1] By John the Fearless's reign too, in both *chambres*, family traditions of service were being established. At Lille, the two Suquets may have been father and son, and Barthelemi a la Truye was Jehan de Pacy's son-in-law. At Dijon, Jehan Bonost and Odot de Varranges were cousins, and Jehan Bonost's son of the same name became a clerk in the *chambre des comptes* in 1412. Three generations of Pastés worked there: André, who appears in the foregoing list; his son Estienne, who died in 1416 having been clerk since 1405 and *auditeur* since 1410; and Pierre, who became a clerk there in 1416.

On the whole, the *maîtres des comptes* were sedentary, or resident, officials, only occasionally, like Estienne de Sens, who was ducal *maître-général des monnaies* and who only kept his post in the *comptes* because of his special knowledge in this field,[2] holding other offices, and seldom travelling on special missions. Some of the *maîtres*, at any rate at Lille, evidently disliked leaving their place of work. Thus Dreue Suquet, in Dijon on the duke's affairs in 1412, ended a letter to his colleagues at Lille with the words: '. . . I was in some fear of the Armagnacs in coming here but, thank God, I have managed to escape them up to now, though I was in danger. God grant that I may return safely. . . .' David Bousse, whose commitments in Lille included a hôtel, landed property, and an illegitimate daughter, apparently found the occasional help, which John the Fearless had ordered him to give to his brother Anthony in the *chambre des comptes* of Brabant at Brussels, extremely irksome. In May 1411 Duke Anthony wrote complaining that Bousse had come to Brussels, but had left after only a week with the excuse that he must return to Lille for the audit of the Flemish accounts. Earlier, in May 1406, the senior *maître des*

---

[1] ACO B15, f. 68b and d'Arbaumont, *Armorial*, 121 and 122. For what follows, see Fremaux, *BCHDN* xxviii (1911), 136; d'Arbaumont, *Armorial*, 122; ACO B15, f. 101b; quittance of Jehanne de Vitel of 14 December 1408 in ACO B3; ACO B15, fos. 70b and 87; and *Mémoires* ii. 157 and 158.

[2] D'Arbaumont, *Armorial*, 121. For what follows, see ADN B17614, original letter of 14 January 1412, and *Cartulaire de St. Pierre*, ii. nos. 1308 and 1336, and ADN B1602, f. 31b.

comptes at Lille, Jehan de Pacy, had received an urgent letter from Anthony, worded in part as follows:[1]

My dear and good friend, a short time ago we wrote to Master David Bousse asking him to return at once to us in order to apply himself to the affairs of the accounts here, where, as he well knows, nothing can be done in his absence. But he has done nothing about this, excusing himself on the grounds that one of your and his colleagues is away in Paris at the moment and that a great deal of business is accumulating day by day in the *chambre* at Lille. These excuses seem to us to be of very little moment, considering that work on the accounts [in the *chambre*] at Lille, which has for a long time been in excellent order, can very well continue in his absence. But this cannot be done in this [*chambre*], which concerns our very dear lord and brother the duke of Burgundy as much as it concerns us, or more. Also, as you know, our lord and brother has ordered him to work here.

The so-called *conseil de Flandre*, at Ghent from 1407 onwards, was similar in general character to the *chambre des comptes* at Lille. It comprised a group of experienced, responsible, officials, recruited locally, but specializing in legal and administrative work. Their names and some facts about them are listed on p. 128. Here, far more than with the *maîtres des comptes*, we have to deal with a rather ill-defined group of men, and this list includes only full-time permanent councillors who were paid at the full rate. For instance Eulart des Aubeaux, canon of Tournai, is excluded because, though he was supposed to be a resident councillor at Ghent, he absented himself: in 1411–12 his name appears in the accounts as due for his councillor's salary of 300 f. per annum, but he was not paid because of absence. Thereafter his name disappears.[2] The same goes for Guillaume de Halewin, paid nothing in 1415–16 because of his absence, and thereafter not even mentioned, and others. As a matter of fact, Halewin had only been appointed a resident councillor in 1411; while des Aubeaux's appointment dated from 1398.

In Flanders we can only with difficulty distinguish the hard core of veteran regular councillors from the shifting irregular and more numerous fringe; at Dijon, this is impossible. There, the council was by no means fully differentiated from the *comptes*, for the two were

---

[1] ADN B17613, letter of 26 May 1411, and ADN B17609, letter of 30 May 1406.
[2] Hautcœur, *Église de St. Pierre de Lille*, ii. 461 and ADN B4086, 51b. For what follows, see ADN B4088, f. 87; de Lichtervelde, *Grand commis*, 190; and ADN B1598, f. 88b.

128 JOHN THE FEARLESS

Permanent full-time resident councillors at Oudenaarde and, from 1407 on, Ghent. 1405–19

Name	Period of service	Notes and references
Daniel Alarts	1402–19	Native of Flanders; became ducal secretary in 1385 and later served as *m. des comptes* at Lille. Vaughan, *P. the Bold*, 212 and 216
Henri Goedhals	1405–19	Native of Ghent and dean of Liège. Huguet, *Aspects de la guerre de cent ans*, i. 54 and see AGR CC21787, f. 8b
Simon de Fourmelles	?–1418	Native of Ghent; appointed *chef du conseil* in 1411; resigned to go on pilgrimage to Jerusalem, 1418. ADN B4086, f. 52 and AGR Acquits de Lille 432, payments for July 1418
Jaques de la Tanerie	? 1405–19	Had served Philip the Bold as *procureur général* of Flanders and *maître* of the *chambre aux deniers*. Vaughan, *P. the Bold*, 219
Danckaert d'Ogierlande	? 1411–16	Bailiff of Ghent, 1389–1411. *IAGRCC* ii. 383

not physically separated, as they were in Flanders between Ghent and Lille. As a result, at Dijon the hard core of veterans in the council was supplied by the resident *maîtres des comptes*, who were also councillors. Apart from them we find a substantial number of part-time councillors attending irregularly, and including after 1411 a *chef du conseil*, Richard de Chancey, who was also bailiff of Dijon, *maître des requêtes*, and quite often absent on missions for the duke. Like himself, his colleagues were local men who held other posts.[1] Jehan Couillier (†1408) was dean of the ducal chapel and *garde des chartes*; Hugues le Vertueux (†1412) was lieutenant of the ducal chancery at Dijon and received only 50 f. p.a. as councillor, as opposed to the 300 francs per annum of the councillors at Ghent; and the councillor's salary of Jehan de Vandenesse, dean of Beaune, was only 40 f. p.a. These three had all been councillors of Philip the Bold, but the same is true of the new arrivals recruited by John the Fearless: Regnaut Gastellier, appointed councillor in 1413, combined this office with the governorship of the castellany of Beaune and was, too, a titular *maître des comptes*; Jehan Juliot became lieutenant of the chancery at Dijon soon after his appointment as councillor in 1410; and Hugues

[1] For this and what follows, see ACO B15 and 94; *IACOB* i–v; Billioud, *États de Bourgogne*; *Mémoires*, ii; and Plancher, iii. On Chancey, see, too, below 191 and Bossuat, *CHCLG* vii (1962), 301–17.

Morel of Auxonne, a Dijon councillor from 1406 with a salary of only 40 f. p.a., became dean of the ducal chapel and *garde des chartes* in succession to Couillier. The connection between these men and the town of Dijon was close: Chancey and Juliot both held civic office there at one time or another.

The ducal secretaries did not, perhaps, form a particularly homogeneous group: after all, they were distributed throughout the ducal territories. Yet everywhere their duties were similar in character. They were responsible for the issue and signing of ducal letters; they were key men personally known to their ruler, who were constantly employed for confidential missions. They were few in number, but of vital importance in John the Fearless's administration. Sometimes, too, they were used as diplomats: George d'Ostende crossed to

The more active secretaries of John the Fearless

Name	Where 'attached'	Period of service	Notes and references
George de la Boede	Chancellor	?1411–14	ADN B1601, f. 50
Jehan de la Keythulle	? Flanders	1405–17	Native of Bruges or neighbourhood; councillor at Ghent, 1417–19. Schoorman, *ASHAG* xii (1913), 109–74
Quentin Menart	Philip, count of Charolais	1412 on	From Flavigny, duchy of Burgundy, Simonnet, *Docs.*, 80 n. 1
Jehan de Maroilles	Duchess Margaret of Bavaria	1401–19	Lived at Dijon, AD L350, f. 87; had been attached to Duchess Margaret of Male, 1393–1404
Jehan Seguinat	Duke John	1412–19	*Clerc des offices* of Duke John's hôtel in 1411, ACO B1569, f. 97b. See Bartier, *Légistes*, 410–11. By letter of 17.12.16 Duke John ordered that only these four secretaries be permitted to sign letters concerning gifts and finance. Plancher, iii. 458 = ADN B1601, f.135b
George d'Ostende	Duke John	1408–18	
Baude Des Bordes	Duke John	1405–19	
Guillaume Vignier	Duke John	1403–19	
Jehan Fortier	Duke John	1402–?16	
Jehan de Saulx	Duke John	1405–19	Bastard son of Duke John's chancellor, Pocquet, *France gouv. par J. sans Peur*, 99 no. 157

England at least twice on ducal service.[1] The list on page 129 includes only those signing most frequently.

The only one of these secretaries to have had the advantage of a biographer is Jehan de la Keythulle. The career of another, Guillaume Vignier, would be worthy of attention.[2] He was apparently a Frenchman from Paris or the area of the Loire, propertied, and therefore probably of bourgeois extraction. He became secretary of Philip the Bold in or before 1403, and his Burgundian loyalties never wavered thereafter. Like the other ducal secretaries, he received, apart from his daily wage of one franc when on special missions, an occasional gift of 200 francs which, averaged out over the years, might possibly have amounted to 100 francs p.a., and a minor office in Flanders worth 130 crowns p.a. = 146 *livres* of Tours. With this annual revenue from ducal sources he and the other ducal secretaries were paid as much as anyone in the ducal service, apart from a very few high-ranking councillors and financial officers. The *maîtres des comptes* at Lille, for instance, received no more (200 *livres* of Paris p.a. = 250 l.t.).

Vignier was a keen soldier. Whenever the duke mustered an army, he was there, serving along with two companions and seven or eight horses, at his own expense. Well-armed too, though the duke did buy him a basinet at St. Omer in November 1406. He was entrusted with secret diplomatic missions: in 1410, to the duke of Berry in Poitou; in April 1411 to Paris, to rescue some fine jewels which the duke had left there in November 1410. Then, disaster came. Already, in summer or autumn 1410, a hôtel of his near Paris had suffered from being commandeered for seven weeks by the Armagnac troops of the count of Richemont. In August 1413 Paris was seized by the Armagnacs, and everything Vignier possessed, save his wife and children, was destroyed or taken from him. He and his family fled to Flanders but, early in 1416, while on his way through Brie on the duke's business, he was attacked by the Armagnacs, robbed of his personal effects and the official documents he was carrying, and imprisoned until his ransom-money was collected and in part subscribed by the duke. It was only after John the Fearless's triumphant

---

[1] *Foedera*, iv (2), 162 and iv (3), 4.
[2] This account of Vignier is put together from Pocquet, *France gouv. par J. sans Peur*, 72 no. 63 and 114; *Mémoires*, ii. 115 n. *l*; ADN B1600, fos. 119a-b and 139b and 1601, f. 41; ADN B17616, memo. of 15 May 1414; ACO B1538, f. 118, 1543, f. 108b, 1547, f. 100, 1558, f. 71b. 1560, fos. 98b and 212, 1570, f. 88b, and 1588, f. 150.

return to Paris in 1418 that Guillaume Vignier was indemnified, by his appointment as *trésorier des guerres* of the king of France and a royal notary. Years before, in 1409, Duke John had stood godfather for Vignier's son; now, in 1418, the king did him that honour for another son.

Another group of ducal civil servants which was distributed, like the secretaries, throughout John the Fearless's lands, and included, like them, some of the duke's most trusted officials, were the *conseillers et maistres des requestes le lostel de monsieur le duc de Bourgogne* —to give them their full and rather grand title in contemporary French. Their names and activities are much easier to determine than their titular functions. Many, perhaps most, of the *maîtres des requêtes* were clerics, and they seem to have been as often used for diplomatic missions abroad as for judicial functions at court. Here are some facts about the most notable of these men.[1]

Some of John the Fearless's maîtres des requêtes
† indicates date of death

Name	Period of service	Ecclesiastical office	Missions
Jehan Mercier of Mâcon	1407–19		Savoy, Venice and Foix
Philibert de Montjeu	1406–18	1412: archdeacon of Beaune 1418: bishop of Amiens	
Raoul le Maire	1406–14	1411: provost of St. Donatian, Bruges 1414: canon of Tournai (*IAB* iv. 77 and ADN B1601, f. 66)	England (at least twice)
Jehan Langret	1405–19	1404: archdeacon of Grand Caux 1412: bishop of Bayeux	Spain, Italy, Savoy, Brittany, etc.
Jehan Rolin, brother of Nicolas	1409–15†		Italy and Savoy (Valat, *MSE* (n.s.) xli (1913), 26–8)
Jehan de Thoisy	1404–19	archdeacon of Ostrevant 1409: bishop of Auxerre 1410: bishop of Tournai	Anglo-Flemish negotiations, 1406–9 (Champion and de Thoisy, *Bourgogne-France-Angleterre*)

[1] This list is based on scattered references in Pocquet, *France gouv. par J. sans Peur*; *Mémoires*, ii; Plancher, iii, and the three main series of Burgundian accounts.

Leaving aside the various lesser categories like clerks, sergeants, minor household officials and the hordes of lawyers employed locally by the duke as *avocats* and *procureurs*, there remains, for discussion here, the knightly, or noble, element in the ducal civil service. By far the most important and numerous group of officials supplied by the nobility were the bailiffs, who, because they formed the backbone of the Burgundian administration, deserve to be briefly listed here. Let us start with some of the more important Flemish bailiwicks.[1]

Some Flemish bailiffs under John the Fearless

Names occurring more than once are italicized; asterisks denote those who had already served Philip the Bold as bailiffs.

AALST

*Jehan d'Ogierlande[2]	Dec. 1403–Oct. 1405
Robert de Leeuwerghem	Oct. 1405–May 1407
*Jehan de Latre	May 1407–Nov. 1411
*Pierre Boudins	Nov. 1411–Aug. 1414
*Francois de Haveskerke	Aug. 1414–Mar. 1417
Louis de le Hole	Mar. 1417–Jan. 1421

BIERVLIET

Baudouin Janssone	Feb. 1406–Apr. 1409
Francois de Haveskerke	Apr. 1409–June 1411
*Nicolas Utenhove	Nov. 1411–Jan. 1418
Pierre Alarts and Jehan Ratgeer	July 1418–Nov. 1419

BRUGES

Henri Reynghervliete	Sept. 1404–May 1407
*Robert de Capples	May 1407–Nov. 1411
Francois de Haveskerke	Jan. 1412–Aug. 1414
Pierre Boudins	Aug. 1414–Dec. 1417
Girart de Maldeghem	Dec. 1417–Nov. 1419

COURTRAI

Jehan de le Berghe	Jan. 1405–May 1407
Robert de Leeuwerghem	Aug. 1407–Apr. 1412
Louis de Moerkerke	Apr. 1412–Dec. 1413
Robert Boudins	Dec. 1413–Sept. 1414
Jehan de Stavele	Sept. 1414–Mar. 1416
Wautier de Calonne	Mar. 1416–Jan. 1417
Louis de Haveskerke	Jan. 1417–Nov. 1419

[1] Information from *IAGRCC* ii. The bailiffs of Artois and of Bergues, Bourbourg and Cassel are here omitted, together with all the minor Flemish bailiffs.
[2] Brother of Danckaert, ADN B17608, ducal letter of 9 May 1405.

FURNES

Jehan de Latre	Sept. 1404–May 1407
Jehan de le Berghe	May 1407–Nov. 1411
*Girart de la Tanerie	Nov. 1411–July 1414
Mathieu le Teldre	July 1414–Sept. 1417
Nicolas le Teldre	Dec. 1417–May 1419
Pierre Boudins	May 1419–Jan. 1421

GHENT

*Danckaert d'Ogierlande	Dec. 1389–Nov. 1411
Jehan de Latre	Jan. 1412–Mar. 1417
Francois de Haveskerke	Mar. 1417–Nov. 1419

OUDENAARDE

Jehan du Molin	July 1404–May 1407
Girart de la Tanerie	May 1407–July 1409
Robert le Brune	Aug. 1409–Aug. 1414
Daniel le Huusman	Aug. 1414–Nov. 1419

TERMONDE

*Simon Rym	Jan. 1400–May 1407
Louis Salart	May 1407–Aug. 1414
Girart de Maldeghem	Aug. 1414–Nov. 1417
Guy de Ghistelles	Nov. 1417–Nov. 1419

YPRES

*Pierre Gherbode	Sept. 1404–May 1407
Louis de Moerkerke	May 1407–Apr. 1412
Jehan Belle	Apr. 1412–Jan. 1416
Girart de la Tanerie	Feb.–March 1416
Roger de Lichtervelde	Mar. 1416–Aug. 1419

The frequency of changes is a striking feature of this list, many of the bailiffs serving in two or three different bailiwicks during the course of John the Fearless's reign. These men were certainly devoted and loyal, though some at least were by no means unconcerned with their own advancement. One of them, Louis de Moerkerke, bailiff of Ypres and also, like many of his colleagues, a knight and titular ducal councillor, wrote to the *gens des comptes* at Lille on 1 September 1409:[1]

And besides, may it please you to know that I have heard from some of my friends that my honoured lord monsieur the chancellor has been pleased to write to you asking you to let him know which of the [duke's] Flemish officers have comported themselves, in exercising their office, well and diligently to the profit of my redoubted lord [the duke]. I suspect that he has not done this without cause, and I believe that it is in order to make some changes among those who are not efficient. I have

---

[1] ADN B17611, letter of 1 September 1409.

considerable talent and good will to serve my very redoubted lord well and loyally, therefore I pray you earnestly and in all friendship that you may be pleased to recommend my humble self in the reply which you send to my very honoured lord monsieur the chancellor. . . .

The bailiffs of the two Burgundies, like those of Flanders, were recruited from the local nobility, but in Burgundy, in contrast to Flanders, there was practically no movement from one bailiwick to another. The list opposite is based on Bouault's paper,[1] with some modifications and the addition of the two county bailiwicks of Amont and Aval and that of Charolais, which was combined with Autun until May 1408.

Another group of ducal officials who were recruited from the nobility were the *maîtres d'hôtel*. It was they who supervised the day-to-day administration of the ducal household, a job of no mean complexity, when we remember that this institution, constantly on the move, comprised several hundred men and horses. Normally, four of these highly-paid (usual salary, 240 l.t. p.a.) officers were on duty at court at any one time. Among those who served in Duke John's reign, Louis de Poissy, who was *maître d'hôtel* for Duchess Margaret of Bavaria, Philibert de St. Ligier, Jehan Pioche, Jaques de Busseul, a *maître d'hôtel* of Philip count of Charolais, and Pierre de Fontenay, were perhaps the most notable.[2]

Philip the Bold's civil service had been directed by a bishop, Jehan Canard; the head of John the Fearless's administration was a nobleman, Jehan de Saulx, lord of Courtivron in the duchy of Burgundy, who was appointed *chancelier de monsieur le duc* on 9 April 1405, and remained in office until his death in October 1420, having resided, at different times, in all parts of the Burgundian territories.[3] For instance, throughout the critical year 1411 he remained at Ghent, helping the youthful and newly-installed count of Charolais, Philip, to administer the northern territories. Perhaps the most notable thing about the chancellor was his remuneration. Besides his annual pension or salary of 2,000 f., he was paid *gaiges* or wages at the rate of eight francs per day when away from his hôtels at Courtivron, Beaune or Couchey, on ducal business. The accounts show that he was away a great deal, almost continuously in fact. During the four years between 26 November 1415 and Duke John's death on 10 September 1419,

[1] Bouault, *AB* ii (1930), 7–22.
[2] Plancher, iii. 286 and *Mémoires*, ii. 134–5.
[3] D'Arbaumont, *Armorial*, 6 and *Mémoires*, ii. 94 and n. *a*. For the next sentence, see, e.g., *IAB* iv. 61, 67, 69, 79 and 118.

The bailiffs of Burgundy under John the Fearless

Asterisks denote those who had already served Philip the Bold as bailiffs;
† indicates date of death

AMONT
Evrart du Four   1404–18   *IADB* i. 31; ACO
                                                 B287; *IACOB* ii. 157

AUTUN
*Guy Moreau   Jan. 1398–1404
Nicolas Chrestien   Jan. 1405–Dec. 1407
Guillaume Saichet   Dec. 1407–1408
Josseran du Sercey   Sept. 1408–Mar. 1412
Hugues de Montjeu   Mar. 1412–1418   *IACOB* i. 248

AUXOIS
*Jehan de Rochefort   Dec. 1391–1411
Guy de Bar   Apr. 1411–Dec. 1422

AVAL
Bon Guichart   ?–1405   ⎫ ACO B15, f. 71 and
Jehan de Champdivers Jan. 1406–1409   ⎬ *IADB* i. 29
Guy Armenier   1409–Mar. 1414   ⎱ Blondeau, *MSED*
Guillaume de   Mar. 1414–?   ⎰ (10) x (1940–2), 44
Champdivers

CHALON
*Guichart de St. Seine Dec. 1403–Sept. 1409†
Jehan de St. Hilaire   Sept. 1409–1417

CHAROLAIS
[Nicolas Chrestien   1405–07   *IACOB* ii. 36]
Guillaume Saichet   May 1408–1409   ACO B348, letters of
                                                 17.5.08, and *IACOB*
                                                 ii. 36
Girart de la Guiche   1413–14   ⎫ Bazin, *MSHA Beaune*
                                              ⎬ (1897), 92–3, 97–8 and
Jehan de Veyre   July 1418–?   ⎭ 120 n. 5

DIJON
*Antoine Chuffaing   Sept. 1400–Aug. 1406†
Pierre Bourgeois   Aug. 1406–Aug. 1412†
Richard de Chancey   Aug. 1412–Sept. 1423

LA MONTAGNE
Jehan de la Rochelle Jan. 1405–Aug. 1412†
Jehan de Chappes   1412–15†   ACO B348, letters of
                                                 1.6.15 and 14.11.15
Jehan de Neuville   Aug. 1415–July 1418
Guillaume de la
Tournelle   July 1418–1436

he enjoyed only two periods off duty, one of twenty days, and the other of ten.[1] There is no point in setting out in detail the recorded payments to him, because the loss of certain accounts would make the picture incomplete. In any case, the facts about his remuneration are abundantly clear from those which survive: he received few gifts; his annual pension was regularly, fully and punctually paid, normally by the receiver-general of the two Burgundies, but in 1411–15 by the receiver-general of all finances; and his daily wage of eight francs was invariably fully paid up, until 1415 by the receiver-general of all finances and after then by the Burgundian receiver-general. Since, on average, he took something like ten days' holiday each year, when his wages were not paid, his total annual income from the duke was $2,000 + (355 \times 8) = 4,840$ livres of Tours. This is comparable to, or perhaps slightly larger than, the salary of his predecessor Jehan Canard under Philip the Bold.[2] Evidently the repeated ducal restrictions of payments of salaries and wages were aimed at lesser fry than the chancellor; certainly they had no effect whatever on his princely remuneration.

In the fifteenth century it was scarcely courteous to send an embassy to another country without at least a knight or two at its head, even if a lawyer or a cleric accompanied it to do the talking. John the Fearless made much use of his nobles as diplomats, and some of them acquired considerable experience in this field. Renier Pot went four times to Bohemia and Hungary in 1408–9, thrice to Paris in 1415, and in 1416 he was sent to Brabant and to King Sigismund of Germany at Lyons.[3] Guillaume de Champdivers had been to England, Cambrai and King Sigismund on John the Fearless's behalf. Diplomatic embassies like these were everyday affairs, and almost any and every knight was employed on them. Yet there are some signs of specialization. John the Fearless's embassies to the Iberian peninsular were often entrusted to natives in the ducal service: the Portuguese squire, Diego d'Oliviere, was sent on two embassies to Spain, and the Catalan knight, Pons de Perellos, went to Aragon.[4] Being nearest to Constance, the nobles of the county of

[1] See ACO B1588, f. 150b, 1594, f. 107b, and 1598, fos. 104b–5.
[2] Vaughan, *P. the Bold*, 222.
[3] Pot, *R. Pot*, 115–17, 122, 129, 175, 177, 178, 178–9 and 181–3. For G. de Champdivers, see *Mémoires*, ii. 125 n. *c*; ADN B18842/29386; Valois, *Schisme*, iv. 242 n. 2.
[4] Pocquet, *France gouv. par J. sans Peur*, 106; ACO B1560, f. 75; ADN B6762, f. 30; Calmette, *RB* xviii (3–4) (1908), 139–96.

Burgundy found themselves given the task of representing their count at the Council. The leading lay members of the important embassy sent there in early 1415 were Gautier de Bauffremont, lord of Ruppes, Guillaume de Vienne, lord of Ste. Croix and St. Georges, and Jehan de Neufchastel, lord of Montagu, all of them from the county of Burgundy.[1] Not unnaturally, nobles from the northern territories were normally chosen to cross the Channel on the duke's service: in 1411 it was Pierre, lord of la Viefville, and Roland d'Uutkerke, along with a bishop, a councillor and a secretary; and both these knights went to England on other occasions for Duke John.

A few of John the Fearless's most prominent civil servants have been purposely omitted or only briefly mentioned here, because they have been the subject of scholarly studies by historians or descendants. These are the Italian financier Dino Rapondi, studied by Mirot; the *garde des chartes* of Flanders, Thierry Gherbode, whose life under John the Fearless was almost wholly devoted to negotiating with the English; Jaques de Lichtervelde, lord of Koolskamp in Flanders, whose descendant Count Pierre de Lichtervelde published his admirable biography in 1943; Renier Pot, described by an admiring but not quite so scholarly descendant in 1929; Guy Armenier of Besançon; Jehan de Thoisy, bishop of Tournai, who enjoyed the benefit of collaboration, for his biography, between a historian

Annual pension or salary and daily wage of certain officials of John the Fearless

Figures in *livres* of Tours

Officer	Pension	Wage
chancellor	2,000	8
treasurer and governor of finances	500	3
senior Flemish councillors	500	3
receiver-general of all finances	400	2 or 3
ordinary Flemish councillors	300	2
Dijon *maîtres des comptes*	300	2
Lille *maîtres des comptes*	250	
maîtres d'hôtel	240	
marshal of Burgundy	200	5
procureur général of Flanders	200	2
maître de la chambre aux deniers	200	
maîtres des requêtes	200	2 or 4
bailiffs of Burgundy	120–200	1
part-time Dijon councillors	40–50	

[1] Coville, *Petit*, 512. For the next sentence, see ACO B1570, fos. 108 and 117a–b.

and a descendant; and, finally, the ducal secretary, Jehan de la Keythulle.[1] On the whole, it is clear from the accounts that the ducal orders restricting payments of pensions and wages had little effect on the remuneration of his officials. His most prominent officers enjoyed exemption from them; some lesser ones had to wait; few or none actually suffered permanent reductions in salaries. There is more evidence of reductions and delays in the payments of pensions to the duke's noble or princely clientele of allies and partisans, but this does not concern us here. Broadly speaking, the duke's civil servants were paid a daily wage when away from their homes on ducal business and an annual retaining fee or pension. The secretaries were a special case, for they relied in the main on gifts of one kind or another to supplement their daily wages. The list above, on p. 137, sets out some typical examples of the pensions and wages of John the Fearless's higher-ranking officials.

The Army

In December 1407, before John the Fearless's military skill, or his army, had been put to the test of active warfare, a merchant wrote as follows to the *podestà* of Lucca:[2] 'You may be quite sure that the duke of Burgundy will remain the most influential and powerful prince of this kingdom. His power is based on the troops which he can raise in his lands. He can muster so many that he fears no one.'

The distinction between peace-time and war-time armies held good in the middle ages as it does in modern times. In those days, however, the peace-time army was an even more truncated relic than it often is nowadays; while the war-time army, instead of being a quasi-permanent institution, called into being for the duration of the war, was normally something mobilized and created for one expedition or campaign. When the above-quoted prediction was made, John the Fearless had only assembled one such army, in August 1405, and that had not been engaged in battle. Others, however, followed, and abundantly justified the Italian merchant's claim. The most

[1] Mirot, *BEC* lxxxix (1928), 299–389; de Coussemaker, *ACFF* xxvi (1901–2), 175–385; de Lichtervelde, *Grand commis*; Pot, *R. Pot*; Blondeau, *MSED* (10) viii (1938), 57–76 and (10) x (1940–2), 38–66; Champion and de Thoisy, *Bourgogne-France-Angleterre*; and Schoorman, *ASHAG* xii (1913), 109–74.
[2] Calmette, *Grand ducs*, 132. Throughout this section I have leaned heavily upon de la Chauvelays, *Armées des ducs de Bourgogne*.

important armies mustered by John the Fearless may be listed as follows:

John the Fearless's principal armies, 1405–17

Figures from de la Chauvelays represent approximate number of men reviewed

Date	Purpose	Approx. size	Notes and references
Aug.–Sept. 1405	Defence of Paris against Duke Louis of Orleans	3,500	Plancher, iii. 224 (3,527); de la Chauvelays, *Armées*, 160 (3,339)
Sept. 1408	Campaign of Liège	5,000	above, p. 58
Aug.–Oct. 1410	Defence of Paris against league of princes	8,700	de la Chauvelays, *Armées*, 201–16 and ACO B1560, fos. 283–325
Aug.–Sept. 1411	Campaign against Armagnacs in Vermandois	10,000	de Lichtervelde, *Grand commis*, 173, n. 48 10,000 Flemish were promised; presumably many did not arrive, but the duke had a sizeable body of men-at-arms with him
Nov. 1411	Defence of Paris against Armagnacs	2,600	Relig. de St. Denys, iv. 476 and 526
May 1412	Royal campaign of Bourges	3,000	This was the number promised by Duke John, BN Coll. de Bourg. 55, f. 33
Jan. 1414	Attack on Armagnac-held Paris	3,500	de la Chauvelays, *Armées*, 223–7
Summer 1414	Defence of Artois against royal/ Armagnac attack	2,250	de la Chauvelays, *Armées*, 227–33
Aug.–Sept. 1417	Attack on Armagnac-held Paris	10,500	de la Chauvelays, *Armées*, 244–9

Most of the figures given here are based on the detailed reviews of troops printed by de la Chauvelays. Unfortunately it is impossible to distinguish clearly between the Burgundian army proper and the allied contingents, which are for the most part excluded from this list. In 1405, for instance, we know that forces from Brabant, Liège, Austria and Württemberg joined the Burgundian army in Paris, but these were not then reviewed by Burgundian officers, though on other occasions they were. Nevertheless, even allowing for the omission of some allied contingents from these figures, particularly those for 1405 and 1410, when, for instance, Duke Anthony of Brabant's forces are omitted, it is clear that the estimates or guesses of most contemporaries and some modern historians, concerning the size of John the Fearless's armies, are much exaggerated. How can we suppose, in view of the scale of these figures, that in September 1411, as one modern historian has it, John marched at the head of 50,000 men? If he did, the great majority must have been non-combatants. Juvenel des Ursins enumerates the 1411 army in detail, but still on an exaggerated scale: 3,000 knights and squires; 4,000 crossbow-men, each with two assistants; 4,000 pioneers; 4,000 archers; 600 men-at-arms and 1,000 archers from Artois; 1,200 men-at-arms from Flanders, etc. One chronicler says that John the Fearless had 16,000 men on this campaign, another says 66,000![1]

In fact, we may be fairly sure that the number of combatants put in the field by John the Fearless, even including allies, seldom exceeded ten or fifteen thousand. Medieval armies, however, probably had an even longer 'tail' than modern ones, though this is nowhere enumerated in the surviving documents. On this subject, writing of John the Fearless's army of 1417, one contemporary chronicler is interesting, though probably inaccurate:

This army numbered 3,600 men-at-arms and more than 2,000 bowmen. And one would have found in it, on any one day, 200,000 persons, and at least 150,000 horses, including the transport, which was very considerable and took up more than two great leagues when on the move. This transport was loaded with every sort of war equipment, so that never was so fine an army seen by the subjects of a single prince.

More interesting perhaps than the absolute size of John the Fearless's armies, is their composition or make-up. Where did his troops come from? We can answer this question, at least in part, by further analysis of the records of reviews of the various captains and their companies or *chambres*, to use the contemporary term for these groups, which have been printed by de la Chauvelays in his invaluable *Armées des trois premiers ducs de Bourgogne*. The figures in the accompanying table represent the number of persons, including sometimes an occasional trumpet or minstrel. The place of origin is that of the captains.

It seems reasonable to conclude, from these figures, that the real basis of John the Fearless's military power lay in the nobility of

[1] D'Avout, *Armagnacs et Bourguignons*, 146; Juv. des Ursins, *Hist. de Charles VI*, 462–3; le Bouvier, *Chron. de Charles VI*, 422; and *Chronique des Cordeliers*, 210. The extract which follows is from *Chron. des Cordeliers*, 237.

The composition of some of John the Fearless's armies

All figures, except those italicized, represent numbers of men reviewed, and are taken from data in de la Chauvelays

	Army of 1405	Army of 1408	Army of 1410	Army of 1417	TOTAL	%
Artois	1,274	1,859	957	3,723	7,813	29
Two Burgundies	854	1,411	1,800	3,536	7,601	29
Flanders	111	475	1,307	572	2,465	9
TOTAL OWN LANDS	2,139	3,745	4,064	7,831	17,879	67
Bar and Lorraine			1,177			
Brittany	109		337			
France	383	*130*	1,598	1,307	3,418	13
Fribourg, count of	333					
Hainault			411			
Nevers, count of		*400*	492			
Rethel	79					
Savoy	?	389	348	780	1,517	
Scotland		*80*				
Spain	38					
Unidentified				286		
TOTAL 'FOREIGN'	940	999	4,363	2,373	8,675	33

Artois and the two Burgundies, which together provided over half his troops. It is evident too, that the duke's northern territories made a rather larger contribution to his armies than the southern—a disproportion which is increased if one includes the French contingents, for most of these came from Picardy.

Those parts of France, like Picardy, which were or became Burgundian in sympathy, formed useful recruiting grounds for John the Fearless, but many others were available. Some, like England or Scotland, were used only occasionally, though sometimes to good effect. The intervention of a force of English mercenaries under the earl of Arundel, on John's behalf, late in 1411, tipped the balance decisively in his favour. Other recruiting grounds, like Savoy, which was conveniently near, were regularly used to raise a force of mercenaries, in the case of Savoy with the permission and co-operation of Amadeus VIII, John's brother-in-law.[1] Sometimes John the Fearless persuaded his relatives to reinforce the Burgundian army by appearing

[1] See Cognasso, *Amedeo VIII*, ii.

in person on his behalf with their own troops, though on these occasions payment was made, or at least consideration of some kind passed. In 1405, for example, John of Bavaria, bishop-elect of Liège, and Anthony, duke of Brabant, both brought troops to Paris to reinforce John's army there, and in 1411 Philip, count of Nevers, invaded Tonnerre on John's behalf at a time when the main Burgundian forces were fully engaged in Picardy and elsewhere. Other methods employed by John the Fearless to supplement the forces provided by his own territories were the granting of pensions, the imposition of homage, and the formation of alliances. Thus Count Eberhard IV of Württemberg, who provided a contingent for John's Paris army in 1405, had done homage to him;[1] the duke of Lorraine, who helped Philip of Nevers to invade Tonnerre in 1411, was an ally and 'pensioner' of John the Fearless; and the count of Fribourg, Maxim de Ribeaupierre, and others, provided military assistance on occasion as allies or vassals.

So far not a word has been said, in discussing the composition of John the Fearless's armies, about the citizen militia of Flanders. The fact is that the men whose fathers stood and died on the field of Roosebeke in armed opposition to their count, Philip the Bold, and whose ancestors had won the battle of Courtrai against the chivalry of France, were loth to turn out and fight for John the Fearless—unless, of course, their country was threatened by the English, as it was in 1405. Understandably, they much preferred to discharge their obligations to him by voting taxes, instead of trusting their lives to the dubious issue of the battlefield. Nevertheless in 1411, after some tricky negotiations at Ghent in the third week of July conducted by John in person,[2] the Flemish towns agreed to provide 9,000 infantrymen and 1,000 crossbow-men for his campaign against the Armagnacs in Vermandois.

How many men the Flemish actually provided in August–September 1411 it is impossible to say. Their presence in the ducal army caused endless trouble, and their defection at a critical moment of the operation caused John the Fearless to end it abruptly. They had hardly started out on campaign when a dispute arose which had

[1] Juv. des Ursins, *Hist. de Charles VI*, 424; Stouff, *Catherine de Bourgogne*, 16 and n. 2; and *DRA* vi. 257–8. For the duke of Lorraine, see *Mémoires*, ii. 99 and n. *h*. For Fribourg and Ribeaupierre, see Stouff, *Catherine de Bourgogne*, 16–21; Bazin, *MSHA Beaune* (1897), 98–9; and ACO B1570, f. 287b. See, too, below, p. 258.
[2] Described in detail by O. van Dixmude, *Merkwaerdige geb.*, 59–60.

to be settled hurriedly and in a manner scarcely calculated to further military efficiency. The official instrument of arbitration has survived to tell its own tale:[1]

John, duke of Burgundy, count of Flanders, of Artois and of Burgundy, palatine, lord of Salins and Malines, to all those who see these presents, greetings.

A dispute has arisen, on this present expedition, between our well-loved subjects of the Franc of Bruges with its dependencies and the inhabitants of the towns and castellanies of Furnes, Bergues, Bourbourg, Nieuport, Poperinge, Dunkirk and those who follow them, on the one hand, and our well-loved subjects the inhabitants of the town of Ypres and their followers on the other hand. The men of the Franc and the rest of their party say and maintain that, when on the move in arms, they ought to march directly behind the men of our town of Bruges, thus preceding the men of Ypres; while the men of Ypres say and maintain, on the contrary, that they ought to march ahead of the men of the Franc and their followers.

For the benefit of peace and so that no inconvenience or delay may arise from this, and having discussed it with those of our council and the other Members of our country of Flanders who are with us, we cause it to be known that we have ordained and we do now ordain by these presents that, on this occasion in this present army, the men of the Franc and the above-mentioned towns and castellanies and their followers shall march in front of the men of Ypres on the first day after leaving here, and the men of Ypres shall march ahead of them on the second day, and so on, each party leading on alternate days. This decision shall not in the future prejudice either of the parties concerned, and, after our return from this present expedition, we shall do right and reason to the aforesaid parties as we ought to do, within a month after their return to Flanders and their appeal to us.

Given in our army, in the fields near Marcoing, 6 September 1411, by my lord the duke, my lord the duke of Brabant, Sir Jehan de Ghistelles, Sir Lourdin de Saligny, the lord of Roubaix, Sir Jehan de Bailleul, the lord of Steenhuize, and others present.   Bordes

Whether or not this cumbersome compromise obviated disputes among themselves, it evidently did not check the Flemings' proclivity to quarrelling with others. The chronicler Monstrelet is hyperbolic, as always, yet, as he wrote for our benefit, it seems unfair to disregard him altogether.

[1] Text in *Analectes historiques* (15), BCRH (3) xi (1870), 358–9 and in *IAEB* i. no. 284. The extract following this one is from Monstrelet, *Chronique*, ii. 173.

With regard to the Flemings, they thought that no towns or fortresses could withstand them. . . . When they marched on foot from one night's quarter to another they were usually fully-armed and in companies according to the different towns and the customs of Flanders. And even though they marched on foot, as mentioned above, most of them wore leg armour. As to their discipline in marching through the country, whatever they could lay hands on was seized and stolen by them and, if portable, loaded onto their carts. They were so proud, on account of their vast numbers, that they paid no attention to noblemen, whatever their rank. When the army was to be quartered, they brusquely drove away other soldiers, especially if they were not their countrymen, and took from them whatever provisions they might have collected. . . .

In spite of the abuse which the French and French-speaking chroniclers showered on the Flemish, none denied that they played a decisive part in the conquest of Ham. Not unnaturally, the Flemish went further than this. The chronicle of Ghent, refreshingly brief after Monstrelet, but equally hyperbolic, has this entry under the year 1411.[1] 'In this year Ham in Vermandois was conquered by the citizens of Ghent on 12 September.'

Soon after they had burnt and looted the town of Ham, the Flemish resolved to return home. According to them, because no battle was offered, or because, in spite of assurances to the contrary from John the Fearless himself, their scouts could find no sign of the enemy. According to others, because their scouts, contrary to ducal assurances that the enemy van was small, found it numerous and powerful. Be this as it may, the Flemish refused to advance further towards Paris, though, according to van Dixmude, they offered to stay where they were while the duke and his nobles rode on to Paris, and to return to Flanders only when he had arrived safely there. But John could not risk this, and all accounts agree that he made every effort to induce the Flemish to stay with him. Letters were produced, dated at Paris on 21 and 23 September, from the king of France, the dauphin, duke of Guienne, the dauphiness Margaret of Burgundy and from the municipality of Paris, congratulating the Flemish on their admirable efforts so far, and exhorting them to continue the good work. Although, at the time, 'the men of Ghent believed that these letters had been written in Duke John's tent', Léon Mirot has upheld

---

[1] *Memorieboek der stad Ghent*, i. 154. For what follows, see de Budt, *Chron. Flandriae*, 359–60; O. van Dixmude, *Merkwaerdige geb.*, 63–5; and Relig. de St. Denys, iv. 486.

their authenticity.[1] The originals have actually been preserved among the muniments of the city of Ghent, where they still are. For my part, I believe that the men of Ghent were right—the letters were forged by John the Fearless. But, be this as it may, in spite of them, and in spite of Duke John's urgent entreaties, and very possibly against the advice or orders of some of their leaders, the Flemish packed their bags precipitately during the night and dispersed homewards at dawn on 27 September in considerable confusion, causing further trouble on their way. Not until July 1414, when the county of Artois was invaded by the Armagnacs, did John the Fearless apply to them again, and this time, though they professed themselves willing to defend Flanders, they refused outright either to fight in the same army as their duke, or to leave Flemish territory.[2]

In every period of prolonged or repeated warfare captains emerge on either side, but John the Fearless was perhaps especially fortunate in the number and skill of the military leaders who brought contingents to his army or campaigned more or less independently on his behalf. His own territories certainly provided their share of these. His marshal, who had already served as marshal under Philip the Bold, was Jehan III de Vergy, lord of Fouvent in the county of Burgundy. As supreme commander of the ducal armies, the marshal of Burgundy's duties were by no means limited to the southern territories, and Jehan de Vergy was employed in the north intermittently from the first days of John's reign as duke.[3] He left his castle at Fouvent on 7 May 1404 in answer to the duke's urgent summons to him to help arrange the funeral of Philip the Bold and, from then on until his death on 25 May 1418, he played an active part in all the military events of the reign. He left Fouvent again on 15 August 1405 to take command of the ducal army in Paris, and only returned at the end of November. In 1408 he left home in mid-August for the

[1] See *Mélanges . . . Bémont*, 373–95, where he also prints the text of four of them. Three of these letters had been published long before Mirot printed them: royal letters of 21 September 1411 in *Petit cartulaire de Gand*, no. 30; royal letters of 23 September 1411 in *Analectes historiques* (4), *BCRH* (2) viii (1856), 69–71; letters from Paris of 23 September 1411 in Kervyn, *Flandre*, iv. 170 n. 1. My quotation is from O. van Dixmude (*Merkwaerdige geb.*, 64), apparently not used by Mirot.
[2] AGR Acquits de Lille 430, certificate of payment of 24 July 1414 and O. van Dixmude, *Merkwaerdige. geb.*, 85–6.
[3] For what follows, see *Itinéraires*, 574; ACO B1547, fos. 161b–162; ACO B1556, f. 177a–b; Plancher, iii. 291 and Duchesne, *Hist. de la Maison de Vergy*.

campaign against Liège, but did not return till January, when he was awarded a special gift of 800 crowns for his important services in the battle of Othée, and in taking possession of the city of Liège afterwards. In autumn 1409 we find him directing the siege of Vellexon, only ten miles from Fouvent; but in 1411 he was in Paris again, and in 1412 on the campaign to Bourges.

The marshal was a ducal officer with important military responsibilities, in particular, the assembly and review of troops and the command of the van of the ducal army, but there were other Burgundian officials, whose posts were not specifically military in character, who were or became notable captains. Guy de Bar, the bailiff of Auxois, was one of those responsible for the brilliant recapture of Paris from the Armagnacs at the end of May 1418. Others of John the Fearless's captains, some of the most famous among them, were not his subjects at all: the Savoyard knight, Amé de Viry, for example, and the French knight Elyon de Jacqueville, not to mention the Picards, Enguerrand de Bournonville and Jaques, lord of Heilly.

Of all John the Fearless's captains, Enguerrand de Bournonville was the most successful and famous. No wonder that Monstrelet, himself a squire and enthusiastic admirer of all deeds of chivalry, describes Enguerrand as 'renowned as the flower of all the captains of France'. A more significant testimonial to his fame is to be found in the chronicle of Oliver van Dixmude, a magistrate of Ypres, and the very opposite of Monstrelet in almost everything except the amount of first-hand information at his disposal, for this Flemish burgher says that Enguerrand was 'an outstandingly good man-at-arms, and a great captain' who had carried out many 'fine deeds of arms against the enemies of my lord of Burgundy'.[1]

Enguerrand de Bournonville first appears in the surviving records in 1405 when, as John the Fearless's *écuyer d'écurie*,[2] his ransom was paid, or at least contributed to, by the duke, after he had been captured by the English during a skirmish at the castle of Marck outside Calais. He cannot have remained a prisoner long, for he was sent to Pisa by the duke in 1406. In 1408 he was at Othée. In 1411 he was one of the most active of the Burgundian captains, holding Senlis for John in August, and commanding a division of the ducal army

---

[1] Monstrelet, *Chronique*, iii. 10 and O. van Dixmude, *Merkwaerdige geb.*, 77 and 82. For what follows, see ACO B11886, quittance of 30 June 1405; *IACOB* i. 144; Relig. de St. Denys, iv. 152, 480, 558 and 646–8; *Geste des ducs*, 520–2; and Plancher, iii. 402.

[2] See above, p. 61 n. 1.

at the battle of St. Cloud in November. In October, while helping to defend Paris against the Armagnacs, he undertook numerous sallies against them, one of which is described in full and picturesque detail by the author of the *Geste des ducs de Bourgogne*. In 1412 he was responsible for bringing a large body of reinforcements to the royal and ducal army outside Bourges. Then, early in 1414, he was appointed captain of Soissons by John the Fearless. It was here that his brief career was brought to its close. Summoned to surrender by the advancing royal forces, he refused and, on 11 May 1414, the royal army encamped outside Soissons and laid siege to the town. Inside, the citizens, or a large part of them, were loyal to the Armagnacs and the king, and fighting soon broke out between them and Enguerrand's garrison, which consisted of a small group of Burgundian knights from Artois and Picardy, and a detachment of English mercenaries. His position rapidly became impossible, and on the afternoon of 21 May the besiegers took the town by assault with the connivance and collaboration of many of its inhabitants.[1]

A few days later, on 25 May, Enguerrand de Bournonville was publicly executed in Soissons, an unchivalrous deed which was said to have aroused universal criticism. It was explained, though not justified, on the ground that the duke of Bourbon had ordered it as an act of private vengeance: his bastard brother, Hector de Bourbon, having been shot in the throat and killed during the siege by one of Enguerrand's crossbow-men, while he was reconnoitring the defences virtually unarmed. Enguerrand's execution was described to Oliver van Dixmude by an eyewitness. Arrived on the scaffold, he asked for a drink, and coolly toasted the health of the duke of Burgundy with the words: 'Lord God, I ask your forgiveness for all my sins, and I thank you with all my heart that I die here for my true Lord. I ask you, gentlemen, to punish the traitors who have basely betrayed me, and I drink to my lord of Burgundy and to all his well-wishers, to the spite of all his enemies.'

John the Fearless's captains would have availed him little without some military skill on the part of the duke himself. This he undoubtedly possessed, and demonstrated at Othée in 1408 and during the fighting in 1411, as well as on other occasions. Yet his military

---

[1] On the fall of Soissons, I follow O. van Dixmude, *Merkwaerdige geb.*, 83; *Journal d'un bourgeois de Paris*, 51–3; and *Chronique des Cordeliers*, 222, rather than Monstrelet, *Chronique*, iii. 6–11 and Juv. des Ursins, *Hist. de Charles VI*, 495–6. For the next paragraph, see Juv. des Ursins, *Hist. de Charles VI*, 495 and O. van Dixmude, *Merkwaerdige geb.*, 83.

reputation could equally well be based on a remarkable and, for the middle ages, perhaps unique document: a detailed plan of battle, issued by him and his military advisers on 17 September 1417, at Versailles, when he was moving in a cautious semicircle towards Armagnac-held Paris with one of the largest armies ever assembled by him. Before he drew up this document, which displays abundant evidence of prudent and experienced generalship, he had conducted a careful review of the whole of his army on 12 September 1417.[1]

> When the whole army had crossed the bridge [at Meulan] and the duke found himself in the open fields of a fine plain, which lay at the foot of a hill, and before he had passed it, he halted the army and ordered all his men into battle order, to ascertain how well-equipped they were. There he found a very fine company of gentlemen and of bowmen, well-armed and mounted, each to the best of his ability. His van was in front, with 400 men-at-arms and the standard of his *fourrierie*[2] supported by 60 men-at-arms; while Castelain Vast, with his troop of about 100 men-at-arms, remained in the rearguard. The duke of Burgundy was well content with all his men, and very happy to see them in such fine order.

The exceptional interest of the plan of battle drawn up a few days after this review has led me to translate it in full, apart from its solitary disciplinary clause and the marginal additions ordering the implementation of the various articles.[3]

> On the 17th of September, in the army of my lord before Versailles, and with the approval of my lord [the duke] and his council, it was decided as follows, on the question of a battle.
>
> 1. My lord the marshal and the other lords of the van must be ordered and enjoined to send out reliable mounted scouts diligently and continually and in sufficient number to ascertain the state of the enemy; and [they must] see that what [these scouts] discover is at once made known to my lord [the duke], so that he is always well informed about what needs to be done.

---

[1] *Chronique des Cordeliers*, 239–40. The person I have identified here as Castelain Vast, who had 285 men under him at the start of the 1417 campaign (de la Chauvelays, *Armées*, 245) and was perhaps from Savoy (Bossuat, *Gressart et Surienne*, 6 n. 3), appears in the *Chron. des Cordeliers* as 'Castelinba'.

[2] The department of the ducal household responsible for finding and preparing lodgings for the night.

[3] Text in Chastelain, *Oeuvres*, i. 324 n. 2 (pp. 324–7), with corrections in de Lannoy, *Oeuvres*, 478–9. See, too, Verbruggen, *RIHM* xx (1959), 443–51.

2. If the enemy arrives and takes up position, my lord [the duke] ought on no account to give them battle if they are near Paris, whence they can easily and plentifully supply themselves with cannon, caltrops,[1] ribaudekins and other similar armaments, but should withdraw wherever seems best to him, if necessary providing a powerful rearguard to oppose the enemy.

3. My lord of Salenove, Hector de Saveuse, Jaques de la Baulme, the lord of Gaspaines, Jehan de Gingin, Charles Labbé, Clavin and Jehan du Clos and Sir Castelain Vast, commanding in all about 1,000 men-at-arms, together with all their available varlets who possess arms, are to exclude from their ranks those either poorly mounted or inexpert on horseback, and send them, under any captains they like, to reinforce the van. And if, after this, they have fewer than 1,000 men-at-arms, they may make up their numbers from any detachment they choose.

4. As soon as news comes of the enemy's approach, these 1,000 men-at-arms, who shall be mounted, are to withdraw from the main division of the army and the van to one side and, if they see any disorder in the approaching enemy's ranks, or any mix-up between their cavalry and infantry, they are to attack them vigorously.

5. If the enemy approaches in good order, the said force of 1,000 men-at-arms shall withdraw far enough to one side of the van to permit them afterwards to do whatever they see to be expedient, whether this be to charge the enemy's cavalry, if he has any, or his bowmen, or to make their way round him to attack his rear, a manœuvre which might prove of great value.

6. If the enemy attacks us, the whole van is to draw itself up on foot in the most advantageous position possible, and my lord [the duke] will reinforce it with as many men as he withdraws from it to use as cavalry, or more.

7. All the archers and crossbow-men in this present army, except for 300, are to place themselves in front of the van in two wings under two small standards, and these men shall be led by two notable and valiant gentlemen who shall command the said standards and bowmen.

8. Officers shall be appointed, in the van by monsieur the marshal, and in the main division of the army by the duke.

9. If there is sufficient space, the main division of the army, under the duke, shall station itself on foot on one side of the van, near it or about 40 paces behind it, so that if the enemy forms one division only, our van and main division can join together under a single command.

---

[1] See above, p. 39 n. 1. A ribaudekin was a kind of cannon.

10. If there is not enough room, the van with the bowmen shall place itself as explained above, and the main division shall be drawn up about 50 or 60 paces behind it.

11. After this main division, and about a bowshot behind it, shall be placed 400 mounted men-at-arms with their varlets, together with the 100 bowmen mentioned above. This, as a rearguard, to provide a remedy, both with men-at-arms and bowmen, in case any of the enemy cavalry is ordered to attack our army in the rear.

12. On the advice of my lord [the duke], it seems desirable that my lord the marshal and others whom he thinks suitable, to the number of 16 or 20 notable, wise and valiant men from the van, should be posted behind the van, mounted on horseback so that they can rally any who fall back and encourage them to do their duty, and so that there are some gentlemen to fill any breaches which may be made in the line formed by the van.

13. In the same way, if necessary, certain people are to be placed by my lord the duke behind his own division of the army.

14. The captains of the companies of bowmen shall inform the two commanders of the bowmen of the numbers of reviewed men under them, so that they know how many bowmen there are in all.

15. If possible, and as quickly as possible, all the transport waggons shall be placed, battened down, behind the rearguard to fortify it. The transport commanders to be charged with this task.

It is difficult to assess the military importance of artillery in the Hundred Years War. Certainly John the Fearless made frequent use of it. All accounts agree, for instance, that the conquest of Ham in 1411 was achieved so rapidly partly because of the Flemish artillery, and it was also used to good effect at the siege of Bourges in the summer of 1412: the duke of Berry, defending the city, was said to have been forced to change his place of residence seven times because of the accuracy and persistence of the royal and Burgundian artillery fire.[1] In Burgundy itself, artillery was used at the sieges of Vellexon, Rougemont and Château-Chinon, probably with decisive effect, and by 1419, twenty-three ducal castles in the duchy were equipped with cannon. Nor was the use of artillery confined to siege warfare: the men of Liège used cannon at Othée and, among the transport of John the Fearless's 1417 army, was a small artillery train.

John the Fearless himself evinced a personal interest in artillery, and his reforming energies were usefully applied to this part of his

[1] Relig. de St. Denys. iv. 686–8. What follows is based on Garnier, *Artillerie des ducs de Bourgogne.*

military forces during his visit to Burgundy in 1414–15. It was then that the Dijon *gens des comptes* were obliged by him to open an artillery book, a register in which documents concerning the artillery, and inventories of it, were regularly copied. At the same time, the duke reorganized the administration of his artillery by appointing a new central officer, a single *maître d'artillerie*, Germain de Givry, to look after cannon and siege-engines of all kinds in all the ducal territories. Finally, on 13 May 1415, John the Fearless ordered all the artillery in the two Burgundies which was not actually in use in his castles, to be brought together in a special arsenal in Dijon.[1]

Thus far John the Fearless's war-time army. But something must be said of the permanent peace-time army of the duke, even though this was limited to the ducal escort or bodyguard, the garrisons of ducal castles, and the appointment of captains-general in parts of his territories. The personal ducal guard seems to have been a permanent institution. We hear of it in November 1408, in 1410 and in 1412–13; and it was captained successively by Jehan de la Viefville, David de Brimeu and Enguerrand de Bournonville. Its size increased from fifteen squires in 1408 to fifty men-at-arms and twenty bowmen in 1413.[2]

Unfortunately, it is not possible to estimate the strength of John the Fearless's peace-time garrisons, but they must have comprised several hundred men in all, scattered throughout the ducal territories under castellans or captains. For the most part, these garrisons were small. Girart de Bourbon, captain of Semur castle, disposed of only six squires and six crossbow-men; and when John the Fearless garrisoned his sister's castle of Belfort, in the county of Ferrette, he sent only a castellan, nine squires and one cannoneer, with varlets and horses. The largest peace-time garrison was that of the castle of Sluis, which in 1415 comprised twenty-five men-at-arms, thirty crossbow-men, twenty-five pikemen, two cannoneers and six porters. In emergency or time of war, the garrisons were quickly reinforced: in the face of possible English landings in 1405, 770 men were sent to occupy Gravelines.

Although the governors who were appointed in some of John the Fearless's territories were not primarily military officers, mention of them is not wholly irrelevant here, since they were often war-time ducal captains, and they frequently combined their post with the more

---

[1] BN Coll. de Bourg. 55, f. 178 and ACO B15, fo. 115b.
[2] *IADNB* iv. 57; ACO B1560, f. 105b; ACO B1572, f. 58 and 1576, fos. 262a-b.

military one of captain-general. The distribution and the status of these governorships followed closely on the lines laid down by Philip the Bold. In the southern territories[1] there was no permanent governor of the duchy, but the marshal, Jehan de Vergy, held the office of governor of the county for some years after 1404, as he had done before. Other appointments seem to have been of a temporary or *ad hoc* nature. In April 1411 John appointed four captains-general in the two Burgundies, ordering them to collaborate in the defence of his southern territories, but a different arrangement was made when John the Fearless left Burgundy at the end of 1415, for on 14 November Jehan de Neufchastel, lord of Montagu, one of the four, became solitary captain-general and governor of both the duchy and county of Burgundy. He seems to have remained in office until the end of John the Fearless's reign.

In the northern territories, there seem to have been two permanent governorships, those of Arras and Lille; the former new to John the Fearless's reign, the latter old-established.[2] Guillaume, lord of Bonnières, became governor of Arras about 1410 in succession to Jehan de Nieles; the governorship of Lille was held from August 1414 by Hugues de Lannoy. The other governorships in the north, like those in the duchy of Burgundy, seem to have been on a purely temporary basis. For instance, on 17 March 1416 Jehan, lord of Fosseux, was made governor and guardian of the county of Artois and, though he was still holding this post in 1417, there is no trace of a successor to him after his death in 1418. In Flanders where, as in the duchy, the posts of governor and captain-general seem to have been either combined or synonymous, William, count of Namur, and Jehan, lord of Ghistelles, both appear in this office briefly, and at intervals, just as they had done under Philip the Bold. Thus Jehan de Ghistelles was captain-general in 1406, and the count of Namur held office in 1410.

[1] Vaughan, *P. the Bold*, 114–15; Plancher, iii. no. 270 and p. 440; Richard, *MSHDB* xix (1957), 103.

[2] Vaughan, *P. the Bold*, 126–7; *IADNB* i (2), 4 and iv. 70, 76 and 84, ACO B1558, fos. 171b–2 and Fremaux, *BCHDN* xxviii (1911), 137–8; Potvin, *BCRH* (4) vi (1879), 117–38 and Lannoy, *H. de Lannoy*; Mirot, *BEC* lxxv (1914), 313–14 and 321–4; ADN B1601, fos. 117a–b, *IADNB* iv. 81 and Monstrelet, *Chronique*, iii. 288; ADN B17609, letters of 16 February 1402 and 20 March 1406, AGR CC14109, account of 10 May–20 September 1406, f. 17, ACO B1560, f. 102 and ADN B1903, f. 62. The full titles of the two permanent governorships were (*a*) governor of the bailiwicks of Arras, Lens, Avesnes, Bapaume and Aubigny and (*b*) governor of the sovereign bailiwick of Lille, Douai and Orchies.

CHAPTER SIX

Flanders under Philip, Count of Charolais

The peculiar position of Flanders in the Burgundian state was really twofold: both her wealth and her concentrations of urban population marked her out from the other ducal territories. Moreover, these peculiarities were coherently expressed in a political form, for the wealth and population of the Flemish towns had led to the emergence of a representative institution, the Four Members of Flanders. For this reason, the relationship of subjects and ruler was more important in Flanders than elsewhere in the Burgundian territories, where representative institutions were less powerful. This relationship underwent marked, indeed almost revolutionary, changes, during John the Fearless's reign and as a result of his policies. Already, in the years immediately after 1405, John or his wife Margaret had visited Flanders and resided there for extended periods—a thing which Philip the Bold and Margaret of Male had never done; indeed in their time, there had been little or no personal contact between the ruler and his Flemish subjects.[1] Although in 1409 and 1410 the Flemish were again for a time ignored, John the Fearless soon reverted to his earlier policy. In 1411, acceding to the requests of the Flemish themselves, which had been reiterated at the end of 1410, he installed his only legitimate son, the fifteen-year-old Philip, count of Charolais, later Philip the Good, at Ghent as his resident personal representative in Flanders.

Although Philip of Charolais seems to have had no official title in 1411, he certainly acted as ruler on John's behalf, with the help of the ducal chancellor Jehan de Saulx. It was Philip, for example, who

---

[1] Above, p. 15 and Vaughan, *P. the Bold*, 172–3. For this chapter in general, see Kervyn, *Flandre*, iv; *Geschiedenis van Vlaanderen*, iii; and de Lichtervelde, *Grand commis*.

handled the crisis in October of that year, 'having, in the absence of his father, the government of the land and county of Flanders'; and letters from him first appear, among the correspondence received by the *chambre des comptes* at Lille, in September 1411.[1] It seems likely that he took up his governmental duties, and his residence at Ghent, in September 1411, when John the Fearless left Flanders after a stay there of nearly a year. Certainly he governed and resided in the autumn and winter of 1411 and throughout 1412; and, though he left

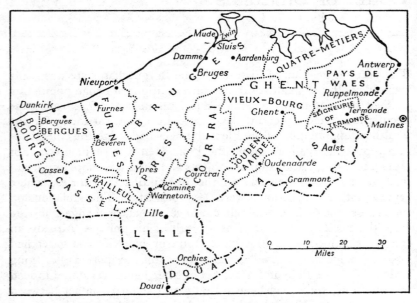

4. Flanders, showing places mentioned in the text.

Flanders in December 1412 to join his father in Paris, he was back again, as a result of renewed Flemish requests to John the Fearless, by June or July 1413. Thereafter he seems scarcely ever to have left Flanders again during his father's lifetime. When John himself visited Flanders, as he did from September 1413 to October 1414 and from February 1416 to July 1417, he automatically took over the government from his son when he arrived there and, after the first visit,

[1] The earliest is dated 15 September 1411, ADN B17613. For the rest of this paragraph, see *Itinéraires*; *IAB* iv; *IADNB* viii. 3–4; Stasino, *Standenvertegenwoordiging*, and letters of 6 October 1414 appointing Philip of Charolais, in ADN B1601, f. 85, mentioned in de Barante, *Histoire des ducs*, i. 335, n. 4.

and doubtless after the second as well, Philip's commission as 'lieutenant and governor-general in our absence of our lands and counties of Flanders and Artois', was formally renewed again when he left the country. Never, since Philip the Bold became count in 1384, had the Flemish received so much personal attention from their rulers. Once again, as before the accession of the Burgundian dynasty, they possessed a ruler of their own, resident among them.

The documents leave no doubt whatsoever that, from September 1411 onwards, with the exception of the first half of 1413, Philip, count of Charolais, was effective and active head of the government of Flanders, though he ruled in close collaboration, at times, with the chancellor, and, always, with the council at Ghent. How fitted he was to rule the Flemish at this time, we do not know. Though we might consider him a trifle youthful, according to contemporary standards he was old enough; his twenty-first birthday fell on 30 July 1417.[1] From the age of three onwards he had had a tutor charged with instructing him 'to read, write and speak Flemish', but he does not seem to have progressed very much further in this language under his *maîtres en école* Pierre Taquelin and Jehan de Rasseghem, than his father had under his tutor Baudouin de la Nieppe, for we learn of a document returned by Philip to the Ghent council in April 1418 *because it was written in Flemish.* Actually he had no need of a knowledge of the language, for among his own councillors, attached to his hôtel, were two Flemish nobles, Guillaume de Halewyn and Jaques de Lichtervelde, both of whom were also members of the *chambre du conseil* at Ghent, whose permanent Flemish personnel, Daniel Alarts, Henri Goedhals, Simon de Fourmelles and the rest, were frequently called in to afforce Philip's personal council. The position of Henri Goedhals is interesting in this connection, though a little obscure. He was certainly a regular member of the *chambre du conseil* and was paid as such. Yet in 1415 he was attached to the hôtel of the count of Charolais as a councillor and, in a document of 1418, he is referred to as 'chief of the council of my lord of Charolais'. It seems almost certain, in fact, that by this is meant the *chambre du conseil*, Goedhals having probably succeeded de Fourmelles as chief or president in 1418.[2] The *chambre du conseil* at Ghent was a permanent institution,

---

[1] *Itinéraires*, 591. For what follows, see Pocquet, *MSHDB* viii (1942), 148; Doutrepont, *Littérature*, xxii–xxiii; and AGR Acquits de Lille 432, roll of payments for April 1418.
[2] ADN B4086, fos. 51b–2; AGR Papiers d'État et de l'Audience, 22, f. 3b (with Goedhals spelt Gonstal); ADN B6762, f. 27b. See, too, above, p. 128.

equipped with its own messengers and clerk, and staffed with skilled, salaried, resident councillors, and it is only natural that Philip of Charolais, acting with the advice and help of the councillors attached to his hôtel, among whom were several members of the *chambre du conseil*, should rule through it and with its close co-operation.

If John the Fearless's relations with the Flemish were better than those of any other Valois duke of Burgundy, the installation of his son at Ghent as his lieutenant, to rule with a council predominantly Flemish, was certainly one of the reasons. In this, John had appreciated the sentiments and satisfied the demands of his Flemish subjects; but there were other causes of his relative popularity and success with them. In the first place, John, or his son acting for him, took care to uphold the interests of the Flemish in their relations with their neighbours and partners in commerce. He issued or confirmed the usual trading privileges to the merchants of Portugal, of Aragon, of Genoa, and elsewhere; he took part in commercial negotiations with the Hanse; he intervened in a dispute between some Scottish merchants and Malines, which the former had taken to the *Parlement* of Paris; and on 4 September 1414 he signed a commercial treaty with William of Bavaria which settled a number of disputes between Flanders and Holland-Zeeland.[1]

Because of the age-old rivalry between the Flemish town of Malines, and Antwerp in Brabant, Flemish commercial relations with Brabant were much more involved and difficult than those between Flanders and Holland; but, here again, John the Fearless and Philip of Charolais did their best to promote the interests of the Flemish. The historian of Antwerp devotes pages to the quarrels of Antwerp and Malines at this time, but pages more could be written.[2] It was probably in January 1411 that John the Fearless and his brother Anthony, duke of Brabant, in conference at Malines, had the angry exchange on this subject which is recorded, partly *ad verbum*, by the assiduous chronicler and secretary of four dukes of Brabant in succession, Edmond de Dynter.

The duke of Burgundy told his brother the duke of Brabant that he had little love for those who had persuaded and advised him in this

---

[1] *Cartulaire de l'Estaple de Bruges*, i. nos. 589, 606, 608, 610 and 622; *Hanserecesse* v, vi and viii; and *Hansisches Urkundenbuch*, v.

[2] Prims, *Geschiedenis van Antwerpen*, vi (1), 24–58. The extract which follows is from *Chron. des ducs de Brabant*, iii. 188–9; cf. *Brabantsche Yeesten*, iii. 102–4 and see *Itinéraires*, 18 January 1411 and Quicke, *Mélanges . . . Pirenne*, 401. For the conference of chancellors, see ADN B288/15,179.

affair, and that he would benefit more from his affection than from that of others. To which Duke Anthony, without taking advice, replied:

My lord and brother, I recognize that you are my elder brother, and, so long as you do not interfere with me in my own jurisdiction, I shall take care to fulfil promptly whatever service and friendship I owe you because of your primogeniture. However, as duke of Brabant . . . I am not prepared to allow you, as count of Flanders, to encroach on my frontiers, in the conservation of which you, more than anyone else, are bound to assist me with aid, counsel and goodwill.

Others became involved in this quarrel between Antwerp and Malines, or were interested parties: Louvain and Brussels in Brabant, for instance, not to mention the Four Members of Flanders. In March 1411 the chancellors of Burgundy and Brabant opened a conference at Antwerp which was later adjourned to Malines. A lengthy paper roll, preserved in the archives at Lille, describes twenty-seven points disputed between the two countries at this conference, many of them concerning Malines and Antwerp. Protracted negotiations took place throughout 1412 and 1413, and it is not clear whether they were prolonged or expedited by the economic blockade of Antwerp proclaimed by John the Fearless. The agreement drawn up between John and Anthony in December 1413 seems to have had little effect, and in 1414 both Malines and Antwerp appealed to King Sigismund, the uncrowned Holy Roman Emperor; but he only made matters worse, by granting the two contestants identical, though in fact meaningless, commercial privileges! The following summary of the 1413 agreement well illustrates the trivial but complex nature of this interminable quarrel.[1]

Tuesday, 12 December 1413. Settlement and agreement made by the duke of Burgundy and Anthony of Burgundy, duke of Brabant, with the mediation of the count of St. Pol, between the towns of Louvain, Brussels and Antwerp, on the one hand, and the town of Malines on the other. This agreement contains the following stipulations:

1. As to the misdeed committed by the people of Malines, who carried away and buried the body of a man killed on the territory of Duffel, the agreement lately made at Lille will take effect, and if they carry it out before the twentieth day of January next, the authors of the misdeed or those accused of it will be completely exonerated.

---

[1] I have followed the version in *IAM* ii. no. 960, where 1412 is an error for 1413. Prims has a different version, *Geschiedenis van Antwerpen*, vi (1), 44–5.

2. As regards the Louvain boat, laden with salt, which was seized by the people of Malines, it is to be released without indemnity. In transporting salt on the Senne and Dyle, the inhabitants of Louvain and Brussels must observe the usages which existed in the year before and the year after the death of the [late] duke of Burgundy.

3. The duke of Burgundy shall send commissioners to the towns of Louvain, Brussels and Antwerp, and the duke of Brabant to the town of Malines, to examine there the charters and privileges invoked by these four towns in their disputes, and to take copies of them.

4. As regards damages done and prisoners made on one side and the other, the princes' commissioners, who have been furnished with the [necessary] information, shall assemble on 20 January at Termonde, to come to a reasonable decision.

5. The duke of Burgundy and the duke of Brabant, accepted as arbitrators in the dispute between the towns of Antwerp and Malines, shall be empowered to judge not only on the main point at issue, but also on the complaints of those of Antwerp about the staples of Malines.

6. The duke of Brabant, on the request of his brother the duke of Burgundy, will pardon Jaques Dordebout and Jehan Stamelaert for the misdeeds perpetrated by them.

More important to Flanders, as a trading-partner and neighbour, than either Holland or Brabant, was England; and John the Fearless was involved throughout his reign in endless negotiation with the English which succeeded, in a turbulent age and in difficult circumstances, in maintaining more or less good relations between the two countries, and thus protecting the commercial interests of the Flemish. In this respect, at any rate, John the Fearless earned their goodwill.[1]

The course of these negotiations, in the early part of John's reign, has been outlined in Chapter One. They achieved, in June and

---

[1] For what follows, see especially, *Actes concernant les rapports entre les Pays-Bas et la Grande-Bretagne*, no. 7; *Calendar of letter-books of London*, I, 83, 104 and 162–3; de Coussemaker, *ACFF* xxvi (1901–2), 333–63; *Docs. pour servir à l'histoire des relations entre l'Angleterre et la Flandre*, nos. 124–63; *Foedera*, iv (1–3); Huguet, *Aspects de la Guerre de Cent Ans en Picardie Maritime*, i. 119–25 and ii. nos. 16–20; *IAB* iv. 37–42, 60–75, 137, 255; de Lichtervelde, *Grand commis*, 237–43; Owen, *EHR* xxviii (1913), 27–8; *Précis analytique*, (1) iii. 198–208; *Procs. and Ords. of the P.C.*, ii. 232–3 (other docs. here are printed in *Docs. pour servir . . .*); Stasino, *Standenvertegenwoordiging*; Varenbergh, *Relations diplomatiques*, 500–8 and 572–8; and Wylie and Waugh, *Henry V*, ii. 297–305.

August 1408 respectively, a three-year commercial treaty, and a treaty for general security at sea north-east of a line between St. Valéry and Winchelsea. These were to remain in force for three years, and they did so, in spite of repeated violations, which caused continual negotiations at Calais and elsewhere, and led to an exchange of letters and embassies between the Four Members of Flanders and the king of England. One of these letters, although a little partisan, shows well how the complex question of infringements of the truce dragged on from year to year. This particular letter, written on 5 May 1411, is notable for the number of well-known people, on both sides of the Channel, mentioned in it: Simon de Fourmelles, whose trip to England on this occasion was paid for by John the Fearless, was a leading member of his council at Ghent; Godefroy le Sauvage became receiver-general of Flanders in 1409; William Longe had been mayor of Rye in 1407 and 1409–10; and John Prendergast achieved immortality because of Monstrelet's inclusion, at the beginning of his chronicle, of his lengthy correspondence with the Aragonese squire Michel d'Oris, who had sent an open challenge to any English knight.[1]

Most high and excellent prince, the king of England, lord of Ireland. Most high and puissant prince, your majesty knows how, in the year 1407, certain truces for merchandise were drawn up, agreed and published by some English ambassadors in your name on the one hand, and by the commissioners of our most redoubted lord and prince, our lord of Burgundy, for his land of Flanders, on the other, to remain in force for a period of one year, beginning on 15 June 1407.

On the Flemish side, these truces were so well and firmly adhered to that there is nothing to say. Yet, notwithstanding, considerable damage was done during these truces by the English, notably by a certain Stoutbury of Rye and his accomplices, who seized a quantity of madder and other lawful goods which Godefroy le Sauvage and other merchants of Bruges and Sluis had hoped, relying on these truces, to send to the river Seine. Because of this seizure, proceedings were duly instituted with you, your chancellor, and your council, and sentence on it, and on the legal costs, was given by your commissioners; but, nevertheless, has not been executed.

Your majesty also knows that, before they had expired, these one-year truces were continued and extended by the common accord of you and of our very redoubted lord, for a period of three years, which will expire

<hr>

[1] ACO B1562, f. 74b; Vidler, *New Hist. of Rye*, 158; Monstrelet, *Chronique*, i. 11–31. The text is from *Docs. pour servir à l'histoire des relations entre l'Angleterre et la Flandre*, no. 131.

on 15 June next. These truces have been observed in such a way by the
Flemish that, up to now, to the best of our knowledge, no Englishmen
have been damaged or molested by way of pillage or robbery by anyone
from Flanders. But, on the part of the English, various misdeeds,
injuries and damages have been perpetrated against the Flemish, in
violation of the truces, as has been lately explained to you in detail by
Master Simon de Fourmelles, councillor of our most redoubted lord,
who also asked for restitution.

By way of reply, you were pleased to inform Master Simon, according
to what he has related over here, that it was your intention to maintain
the said truces made and published between your kingdom of England
and the country of Flanders, and that you had appointed a knight, a
clerk and a merchant, to be in Calais on St. George's Day last, empowered
to prolong the existing truces or make new ones, and also to deal with
infringements on one side and the other. Yet, notwithstanding this reply,
on or about the said St. George's Day, William Longe of Rye, accompanied by Sir John Prendergast, knight, and several other Englishmen,
with men-at-arms and bowmen, came aggressively and seized by force
eleven Flemish ships sailing towards Flanders from La Rochelle and
laden with wine from Poitou, together with the people in them. . . . This
action, carried out by your people and subjects at this particular moment,
amazes us, since it was done expressly against the terms of the truces
and of your majesty's reply to the above-mentioned Master Simon de
Fourmelles, and because the conferences fixed for discussing the treaty
of Calais had been agreed to by our most redoubted lord [the duke of
Burgundy]'s people. . . .

Therefore, most high and puissant prince, we entreat you earnestly
and warmly to take notice of these matters and to be pleased, in maintaining the said truces, which our very redoubted lord wished and still
wishes to keep and observe on his side . . ., to cause the above-mentioned eleven Flemish ships, together with the wines and other goods
and merchandise and the Flemish people thus arrested by your subjects,
to be entirely released, and to ensure that a similar thing does not
happen again. If you please, send us your favourable reply on this.

Most high and puissant prince, may Our Lord keep you. Written on
5 May, under the judicial seal of the town of Bruges, on behalf of us all,
burgomasters, *avocats*, *échevins* and councils of the towns of Ghent,
Bruges and Ypres, and of the Franc of Bruges.

Another conference at Calais, on 27 May, was crowned with
success, and in June all parties concerned, Henry IV, John the Fearless and King Charles VI of France, proclaimed the extension both
of the truces and of the treaty of general security at sea for a further
five years from 15 June. The main interest of this treaty lies in the

institution which it created, for it declared that 'conservators of the truces' were to be appointed on both sides of the Channel. John the Fearless's version of it runs in part as follows:[1]

John, duke of Burgundy, count of Flanders, of Artois and of Burgundy, palatine, lord of Salins, greetings to all those who see or hear these presents.

With the licence, power and authority given to us by my lord the king, as well as by our own volition and in our own name, certain points and articles were agreed by our deputies with the English ambassadors, originally for one year and then extended for three years. [These points and articles], which are due to expire on 15 June next, provided for the safe exchange of merchandise between the kingdom of England and our country of Flanders, and the passage of pilgrims from one to the other; for English clerks travelling to the papal court; and for fishermen generally fishing at sea. [They applied] even in the event of a war between my lord the king [of France] and his kingdom and England. Moreover, to increase the safety of commerce, a general security at sea between the harbours of St. Valéry and Winchelsea and everywhere north and east of that line, was granted and agreed, besides the points and articles above-mentioned, to run for the same three-year term.

Because the various provisions made in the above-mentioned points and articles, and in the [treaty for] general security at sea, both of which are now prolonged and continued for five years from 15 June . . ., have been badly observed up to now by land and sea because of seizures, arrests and damages done on one side and the other, to the prejudice and harm of the subjects of both parties and their merchandise . . ., and in order that from now on during the coming period of five years the above-mentioned agreements may be properly observed . . . certain additional points have been agreed to, as follows:

1. Conservators, living on the frontiers and empowered to see that the truces and security are not infringed, and to punish offenders, shall be appointed by both sides. They shall swear to act diligently and impartially.

2. When any prize is brought into an English or Flemish port, the conservators of the truces or the port authorities are to take it into safe custody; make an inventory of its contents; and arrest those responsible for the outrage.

3. As soon as the owners of the prize, being merchants of England or Flanders, establish their identity, the goods, ships and persons in them are to be returned to them.

---

[1] Varenbergh, *Relations diplomatiques*, 572–8 = *IAB* iv. 70–4. The additional clauses are here summarized.

4. If the goods and ships have been sold, lost or ransacked, then those who seized or profited from them must offer security for adequate restitution, or else remain in gaol until they do so.

5. The high contracting parties agree not to use letters of marque or reprisals against each other's subjects, and to execute judgements and make legally established reparations, within three months.

Although a conference sat in Calais throughout August 1411 fixing reciprocal reparations and restitution, and although conservators on both sides were duly appointed, mutual damages and disputes, with their concomitant negotiations, continued. In 1412, 1413 and again in 1414, the Four Members had to send deputies to Calais to confer with the English about infringements of the truce. Sometimes, in these years, the commercial truce was strengthened by a closer political relationship between John the Fearless and England: this happened in 1411, and again in 1414. Sometimes, as in May 1412, when the Armagnac princes signed the treaty of Bourges with Henry IV, it was severely strained. On this occasion, however, when Henry wrote to the Four Members on the eve of John the Fearless's campaign against the duke of Berry and the other Armagnacs, asking them if they intended to remain neutral and maintain the truces in spite of their duke's involvement in a war with England's allies, they replied in the affirmative, if slightly equivocally.[1] In the summer of 1415, while Henry V was preparing the invasion of France which led to Agincourt in October, a bout of seizures and reprisals caused the intervention of Philip, count of Charolais, who wrote a series of letters to Henry V on the Flemish behalf. After Agincourt, in December 1415, the Four Members sent a deputation to John the Fearless in France, asking him to take the necessary steps to prolong the truces, due to expire in June 1416, and in February he appointed twelve ambassadors from among Philip of Charolais's entourage and his leading Flemish officials, who succeeded in extending both the truces and the general security for a further year from 15 June 1416. Even after this, in spite of growing difficulties, John the Fearless managed to maintain the truces: they were continued from 15 June 1417 to Easter 1418; from Easter 1418 to Easter 1419; and from then

---

[1] Henry IV's letter of 16 May is printed in *Foedera*, iv (2), 12 and, wrongly dated 1407, in *Docs. pour servir à l'histoire des relations entre l'Angleterre et la Flandre*, no. 119. Monstrelet, *Chronique*, ii. 260-1, copied it out, and it and the Flemish reply are described by O. van Dixmude, *Merkwaerdige geb.*, 74-5. See, too, Kervyn, *Flandre*, iv. 184-5 and *IAB* iv. 138.

until 1 November 1419.[1] In these years too, special commissions were set up, one by John the Fearless in August 1417 and another by Philip of Charolais in March 1418, to enquire into damages done to Flemish merchants by the English. Thus, by his vigorous, repeated and successful efforts, John the Fearless protected and nourished the commercial interests of his Flemish subjects by maintaining the Anglo-Flemish truce and the machinery for more or less permanent negotiation which was its necessary concomitant.

There were other reasons, besides his installation of Philip of Charolais at Ghent and his careful protection of Flemish commercial interests, for John the Fearless's more or less pacific reign in Flanders. Although the opposition to him was enshrined in the politically powerful Four Members of Flanders, these did not form a truly representative institution. They did not speak for all the Flemish towns, but only for the three largest and the Franc or castellany of Bruges; still less did they represent Flanders as a whole.[2] On the other hand, the theoretically more representative body, the three Estates of Flanders, which was convened from time to time by the Four Members or, more often, by John or Philip of Charolais to handle political questions like the peace of Arras (nine meetings in 1414–15 on this) or to receive requests for military or financial aid, met only twenty-six times between 1412 and John's death, as against about 260 meetings or *Parlementen* of the Four Members. Although the three Estates were sometimes so poorly attended that the meeting had to be deferred, on some occasions at any rate they were dominated and exploited by their ruler or his nominees. For instance, in November 1414 they consisted of the deputies of the Four Members for the commons; the abbot of St. Peter's, Ghent, and the ducal councillor Henri Goedhals, dean of Liège, for the clergy; while the nobles were represented by another ducal councillor, Jaques de Lichtervelde, the castellan of Furnes, and one other.

While the harsh or extremist politics of the Four Members were thus tempered by their unrepresentative character or softened by the duke's manipulation of the Estates, opposition to him was far more seriously hampered by commercial or class rivalries between and within the Four Members, or between them and other Flemish towns. Such disputes gave the duke an opportunity to intervene in

---

[1] For this and the next sentence, see ADN B6762, fos. 35, 37, 38a–b and *Foedera*, iv (3), 127–8.
[2] For what follows, see Stasino, *Standenvertegenwoordiging* and de Lichtervelde, *Grand commis*, 226.

Flemish affairs, to extend his authority in Flanders, and to add to the number of his partisans among the Flemish generally and within the Four Members in particular.

In the last year of John the Fearless's reign, when Bruges and the Franc were at loggerheads over their commercial rights and privileges, the Franc opened separate negotiations with the duke, thus to some extent undermining the common negotiating machinery which was part of the strength of the Four Members.[1] Already in 1416 a dispute between these two Members had led to the appointment of a ducal commission of mediation; and a similar outcome attended the disputes between Ypres and Warneton in 1413 and Bruges and Furnes in 1412. Within each Member, too, disputes tended to play it into the hands of the duke. The struggle for power in Bruges, which led to a pro-ducal government there between 1407 and 1411, continued throughout the rest of John's reign. At Ypres, a similar situation came to a head in 1414, when a deputation of citizens invited the duke to reform the constitution of their town so that power was no longer monopolized by a single group of magistrates. The existence of a pro-ducal element in Ypres is further revealed in a document of April 1417, which records the disclosure to the ducal council at Ghent, by certain magistrates of Ypres, of a plot against the bailiff and magistrates. Thus divisions, disputes and diverging interests among the Flemish themselves helped to undermine their opposition to John the Fearless, and enabled him to maintain or even extend his authority over them.

Another way in which John the Fearless was able to gain the support of at least some of the Flemish, and at the same time to undermine their solidarity, was by the grant of special privileges to individual towns or Members. Sometimes this device was used as a political bribe: in September 1411 both Ghent and Bruges were granted important new privileges, in an unsuccessful effort to persuade their militias to remain on campaign with their ruler. More often it took the form of an outright sale. In 1410 John the Fearless sold to the Franc of Bruges for 10,000 crowns, the privilege of

---

[1] Stasino, *Standenvertegenwoordiging*, 90, n. 10. For what follows, see Schoorman, *ASHAG* xii (1913), 142; *IAB* iv. 257-8, *IAY* iii. nos. 767, 768, and O. van Dixmude, *Merkwaerdige geb.*, 87-90 (Ypres v. Warneton); *IAB* iv. 219-20 (Bruges v. Furnes); Zuylen van Nyevelt, *Épisodes*, 222-4, *IAB* iv. 135-6 and 252, ADN B4086, f. 80a-b (Bruges); O. van Dixmude, *Merkwaerdige geb.*, 90-1, *IAY* iii. nos. 772, 773, AGR Acquits de Lille, 432, roll of payments for April 1417 (Ypres).

exemption from the punishment of confiscation of goods. In 1411 a similar privilege, along with two others, was sold to Ypres, which paid 15,000 crowns for the three; in April of the same year Bergues and Furnes each bought identical privileges, one of which was the right for their citizens to go about Flanders armed, for 7,000 crowns; and in 1412 Termonde bought the right to levy assizes, or local taxes, without its ruler's permission. Many other examples could be cited, to show that John the Fearless was always prepared to cede rights and privileges in individual cases—for a consideration.[1]

Because of the care he evidently took to ingratiate himself with the Flemish, and because of the skilful political manœuvring of himself and his son Philip, John the Fearless, unlike the other three Valois counts of Flanders, never found himself in serious difficulties with the Four Members, still less with the Flemish as a whole. There were, however, three occasions in the later part of his reign when relations between the ducal government and the Flemish became important. The events of autumn 1411, when only Bruges was involved, and of 1414, when the Flemish failed to obtain the concessions they demanded, may be described as crises. The third occasion, in July 1417, was simply a bargain struck between ruler and subjects.

The crisis of 1411 began at the end of September, when the Flemish militia, refusing to campaign beyond Montdidier or for longer than a month, returned home in disorder.[2] The men of Ghent set fire to the duke's camp as a parting gesture, and attacked and pillaged at least one place on their way home; the men of Ypres were only narrowly dissuaded from attacking Lille as they passed it, and refused to return home until they had extracted certain concessions, including two months' pay, from the magistrates of Ypres. But it was the Bruges contingent which caused the real trouble. Its behaviour is described in the official report sent, at his request, to Philip, count of Charolais, by the magistrates of Bruges.

[1] For this paragraph, see *Coutumes . . . Gand*, i. no. 59, and *IAB* iv. 87–8; *Coutumes . . . Franc de Bruges*, ii. no. 32; *IAY* iii. nos. 753–5, 758–62 and O. van Dixmude, *Merkwaerdige geb.*, 59; *Ords. des rois*, ix. 582–90 and ADN B4086, f. 38a–b; ADN B1601, fos. 149b–150b; and, in general, de Budt, *Chron. Flandriae*, 358–9.

[2] For what follows, see O. van Dixmude, *Merkwaerdige geb.*, 65–9; Kervyn, *Flandre*, iv. 175–8 and 499–506; *IAB* iv. 113–36; *IAEG*, no. 676; Fris, *BAAB* (1911), 253–67; Zuylen van Nyevelt, *Épisodes*, 213–19; de Lichtervelde, *Grand commis*, 177–86. In the extract which follows, from Kervyn, *Flandre*, iv. 499–503, Bruges magistrates' letters of 11 October 1411, I have summarized the seven points.

On Thursday 6 October last the army was quartered three leagues from Bruges, at a place called Ter Belle, and when the magistrates knew that it was going to halt there, they sent Monsieur Baudouin le Vos the burgomaster, with Jehan Oste, Jaques Breydel and George de le Stichele, *échevins*, together with a pensionary of the town, to find out at what time the men wished to enter the town on the next day. But they replied, that this expedition had cost them a good deal; that they had spent considerably more than the wages of eight groats per day which had been fixed for them; and that they wanted, besides these eight groats per day, a further two groats, to be paid for two whole months. On this, after some discussion, the burgomaster and *échevins* agreed that they would be paid these wages, which they had asked for, as soon as they returned home. This satisfied them, and the deans and other officers [of the craft gilds] promised that they would enter the town [next day] between nine and ten o'clock before dinner. During the night, however, certain people caused a general agitation, and Lievin le Scuetelaar, the burgomaster who was with the army, sent a message to the above-mentioned Baudouin, his colleague, asking him to come, together with Jehan Oste, Jaques Breydel and some other magistrates who were in favour with the commons, to St. Michel at eight or nine o'clock next morning, in order to calm down the common people, who were extremely agitated, and persuade them to enter the town peacefully. This Messire Baudouin did, taking with him Jehan Oste, Jaques Breydel, George de le Stichele, Jehan le Hond and Clais Willemzone. But when the deputies from the army arrived at St. Michel, where these magistrates were, it became clear to the magistrates and captains that the common people would not on any account enter the town until they had been satisfied on seven points, as follows:

1. Abolition of the procedure of summoning burgesses of the town by the sound of a bell and, when they failed to appear, sentencing them for default.

2. Abolition of the tax, levied by the municipality on corn sold in the town, called *cueillote*.

3. Restoration of the payment to the burgesses and gilds of certain emoluments called *maandgeld*.

4. Payment of the extra wages of two groats per day already demanded by the militia.

5. Surrender by the duke of the one-seventh part of all the town's revenues, or seventh penny, which had been ceded to him in May 1407, and restoration of the earlier annual payment to him in lieu of this.

6. Cancellation of the so-called *calfvel*, the document of 24 May 1407, in which the craft gilds had bound themselves not to unfurl their

banners in the market-place before those of the duke and the town of Bruges (see above, p. 27).

7. Restoration of the privilege of exemption from the punishment of confiscation of goods.

On this, the magistrates and the captains replied that the people of Bruges had been away in the service of my lord [the duke], and that they were much more in his good graces than any of the other Flemish contingents who had been with him; therefore they implored them for God's sake not to lose the favour of my lord [the duke], but to enter peaceably and if, after resting and settling down, they still wanted to make certain requests to the duke, the captains, and the magistrates, they would gladly be heard and answered reasonably and satisfactorily for them.

Thereupon they shouted at the tops of their voices: 'No! No! We won't be deceived as we have been in the past. We demand attention to our requests before we return to the town.'

'All right my good sirs,' replied the magistrates and captains, 'but if you must make these requests, for God's sake make them in a reasonable manner, and don't put forward matters which have never been within the competence of the captains and magistrates, for it is not within their power to answer three of your requests. The seventh penny, which you want abolished, is the duke's; and the document concerning the banners, which you want cancelled, is in his possession, and the captains and municipality cannot provide you with it.'

They were told that the other four requests would be dealt with in such a way as to make them, in reason, satisfied, provided that they entered the town peacefully and quietly. Some of them seemed to be quite content with this answer, provided they had it in writing, but others shouted, 'No! No! We want to have everything. . . .'

Things having turned out thus, the captains and magistrates returned to the town much perplexed and, hastily assembling the municipality, they invited Sir Jehan de Ghistelles, Sir Louis his brother, the lords of Uutkerke and la Chapelle, Sir Roland d'Uutkerke and the bailiff of Bruges [Robert de Capples], ducal councillors, to join them in the council chamber. When they were all assembled, the captain, Felix de Steenhuize, and the magistrates concerned, related everything that has been said above, and asked the above-mentioned lords for their advice; but they excused themselves from giving counsel. It seemed, however, to a number of those present that the magistrates could well issue letters granting the four requests which concerned the town, in order to content the people and avoid greater inconvenience, and that these letters might be taken to them. If they again introduced the three requests which concerned only my lord [the duke], they could well be told that if, in due time and place, they wished to pursue these with the duke, and if they would appoint three or four deans [of the gilds] or others of their people to speak for them, the magistrates would gladly send their deputies with them to expedite their business to the best of their ability.

This decision thus made was put into execution on the next day, which was last Thursday morning. But the common people did not wish on any account to accept the above-mentioned letter, though it was taken to them duly sealed with the great seal of the town. Instead, they yelled at the tops of their voices, 'We want to have everything together and not in bits and pieces.' Nevertheless, the captains and magistrates spoke so sweetly to them that, in the end, they agreed that they did not wish to take or have anything from my lord [the duke] without [addressing themselves to] him and, because of this, they no longer wished to press for the abolition of the seventh penny, but would be content to be free [from the punishment of confiscation] as they had formerly been. Finally, they insisted that the letters concerning their banners should be brought to them and cancelled and torn up in their presence before they left their camp. . . .

The upshot of all this was a deputation from Bruges to Philip, count of Charolais, then at Ghent, and his eventual surrender to the 'common people' of Bruges as represented by her citizen militia. On 18 October the decision was taken to hand over the *calfvel* and related documents and, at the same time, Philip drew up a solemn notarial act of protest, declaring that the transference of these documents was carried out under pressure of force, and adding, quite untruthfully, that this was done without the consent of his father John the Fearless. The *calfvel* itself, when it was surrendered on 20 October, was cut into pieces after the dean of each of the fifty-five craft gilds which had originally assented to it, had removed his seal from it. Then, and only then, did the triumphant militia of Bruges, the crossbow-men and archers in their red hats embroidered with the letter B; the artillery-men wearing blue hats; and the mounted men-at-arms carrying the standards and banners of the town, file peacefully into Bruges and, after a brief word of thanks in the market-place from their captain, disperse quietly to their homes.

But this was by no means the end of the affair, for a further surrender was forced on the ducal government by the magistrates of Bruges, acting under popular pressure. In November 1411 John the Fearless had to remove both the principal ducal officers in Bruges, the bailiff Robert de Capples and the *écoutète* Pierre Boudins, causing a major reshuffle among the Flemish bailiffs which is reflected by the number of changes in November 1411 recorded in the list of bailiffs on pages 132–3 above. Unrest at Bruges, too, continued well into 1412 and, in spite of John the Fearless's efforts, nothing occurred there during the rest of his reign to swing the rather delicate internal political balance back again in his favour. The events of autumn 1411 had in fact reversed the ducal victory in Bruges in the spring of 1407, and restored a more or less anti-ducal government there. Not until twenty-five years later, when he was ruling as Philip the Good, was Philip of Charolais able to exact his revenge by bringing the town more or less completely under his control. John the Fearless had to rest content, in the autumn of 1411, with the implausible but useful fiction that the concessions had been wrung from his son, and not from him. 'What is done by you', he had written to Philip on 15 October, 'will be less damaging to my honour and government.'[1]

The crisis of 1414 was very different from that of 1411, for in 1414 all Four Members attempted to exploit John the Fearless's political and military difficulties, but they were unsuccessful. These difficulties, which will be described in a later chapter, may be briefly summarized here. In February 1414 John the Fearless failed to recapture Paris and the person of the king from the Armagnacs who had seized both in August 1413. Their counter-attack, led by the king in person, with the apparent aim of seizing and confiscating all John's territories, was at first extremely successful. Artois was invaded, and Flanders itself threatened; but Arras, besieged from about 25 July 1414, held firm and, early in September, military operations were halted by a negotiated peace.

The part played in all this by the Flemish was equivocal and at times obscure, but certain facts are clear.[2] From December 1413 onwards John had been trying to persuade them to vote him an *aide* of 100,000 crowns. They temporized; they had granted him substantial subsidies in 1408 and 1410. In May 1414 John's military situation had grown so desperate that, forgetting or disregarding the bitter lesson of 1411, he applied to the Flemish for troops. They refused. In June they were in contact with the Armagnacs, on whose behalf the king opened negotiations with them, in the hopes of detaching them from their count. But the Flemish were apparently unwilling to contemplate the alternatives to John the Fearless which would result in his defeat by the Armagnacs: direct rule by France or the

---

[1] De Lichtervelde, *Grand commis*, 180.
[2] What follows is based on O. van Dixmude, *Merkwaerdige geb.*, 79–87; de Lichtervelde, *Grand commis*, 215–25; and Stasino, *Standenvertegenwoordiging*. See, too, Fris, *BSHAG* xix (1911), 295–321.

installation of a new dynasty in Flanders. By July they actually agreed to mobilize for John the Fearless, though on terms quite unacceptable to him, and in September and thereafter they were involved, on John's behalf, in making peace with the Armagnacs.

But the Flemish had not rested content, through the critical year 1414, with neutralism. Apart from doing little or nothing to help their count in his hour of need, they attempted to exploit his difficulties by offering him troops in July, and an *aide* in August 1414 and after, when it was once more cash rather than troops that he needed, in return for his acceptance of twelve requests. These twelve points are partly summarized by the chronicler Oliver van Dixmude. They included demands for Flemish-born councillors at Ghent and Flemish-born ducal officials in general; for Flemish captains of Sluis and Lille; for a coinage, agreed by all, to last for John's lifetime; and for the abolition or removal of various novelties and exactions imposed by himself and his father. According to van Dixmude, John was prepared to grant eight or nine of these requests, not more; while the Flemish held out for them all. What is certain is that both sides remained firm. The attempted purchase by the Flemish, in exchange for a subsidy of 100,000 crowns, of the privileges and concessions enshrined in their coveted twelve points, never came off. The duke refused to sell; but the haggling only ceased in August 1415, and, as late as February 1417, when Ghent refused an advance on the *aide* granted by her and the other three Members in 1416, the municipality wistfully remarked to the ducal council that ' . . . if it had pleased my lord [the duke] to grant the twelve points formerly requested from him, his land would have been rich and powerful to aid him; and, if he now agreed to those points, they would acquit themselves towards him like good and loyal subjects.'[1]

Soon after the 1416 *aide* had been paid a bargain was struck between ruler and subjects which at first sight looks like a ducal surrender, though in fact it was the Flemish who on this occasion virtually gave way to John the Fearless by reducing their twelve points to an anaemic five. In July 1417, on the eve of his ultimately victorious campaign in France, they voted him another *aide*, of 300,000 *livres* of Tours, in return for a document in which John the Fearless made only one or two small concessions; otherwise it merely confirmed his earlier practice or repeated promises already made. It took the form of a statement of five requests made by the Flemish, with the duke's replies, and may be compared with the similar

[1] AGR Acquits de Lille, 432, roll of payments for February, 1417.

document drawn up at the instigation of the Four Members in 1405.[1]

1. *Request:* That we appoint our son the count of Charolais to rule Flanders on our behalf during our absence, with the help of councillors familiar with the country.
   Reply: Agreed.

2. *Request:* That the Anglo-Flemish truces and general security at sea should be prolonged for ten or twelve years, or for as long a period as possible; and that the enquiries into damages done by the Flemish be expedited, so as to give the English no cause for breaking off negotiations.
   Reply: Agreed.

3. *Request:* That a new gold and silver coinage be minted, of weights and values laid down by the Four Members.
   Reply: Agreed to strike these coins next Michaelmas unless an assembly of ducal councillors and experts, to be held in August, can devise a more profitable coinage.

4. *Request:* That we abolish the general commissioners set up to enquire into alienations, gifts and payments made to the prejudice of the count, etc., and that the inhabitants of Flanders be subject only to the rights, laws and customs of their own country.
   Reply: Agreed that the general commissioners shall no longer exercise their power, which we revoke, along with all proceedings initiated by them touching Flanders.

5. *Request:* That the frontiers of Flanders with France be kept open and all hindrances to commerce there be removed.
   Reply: Agreed.

As in 1405, when he first came to Flanders as count, so in 1417, on his last visit, John the Fearless made an effort to carry out his promises to the Flemish. Philip continued, as before, to rule Flanders as his lieutenant; efforts continued, as before, to maintain or prolong the Anglo-Flemish truces. A new coinage, after much discussion with the Four Members, was eventually minted in summer 1418; and the powers of the general commissioners, whose activities had apparently been confined at first to Artois, and Lille, Douai and Orchies, were revoked.[2] These minor concessions, however, by no means

[1] See above, pp. 14–15, and Stasino, *Standenvertegenwoordiging*, 67. The document summarized here as printed in *Verzamelingen van XXIV origineele charters,* no. 8: *Analectes historiques,* (15), no. 393 = *BCRH* (3) xi (1870), 359–64; and *IAEB* i. no. 316.
[2] On this 'reformation', see ADN B1281/15,335 and 15,335 bis and B1282; Marc, *MSBGH* xxi (1905), 328–30 and 330, n. 2. On the coinage,

halted the friction between rulers and ruled; and Philip, count of Charolais, had to face further difficulties with the Flemish in the last two years of his lieutenancy at Ghent. In March or April 1418, for instance, they presented four complaints to him, three of which concerned minor disputes; but the fourth was a request for the removal of the *procureur général* of Flanders, the count's principal legal officer there. The Four Members, too, delayed payment of the *aide* they had voted in July 1417, taking two years over it, instead of the one they had agreed to. Nevertheless, it is clear that relations between John the Fearless and the Flemish had improved during his reign, especially after Philip of Charolais's installation at Ghent in 1411, and that they continued to improve right to the end.

When the history of Valois Burgundy is surveyed as a whole, the reign of John the Fearless stands out, in Flanders, as a relatively pacific period of acceptance by the Flemish of their Burgundian dynasty and of concessions on the part of the dynasty to its Flemish subjects. It may be argued that John the Fearless was too weak, politically, to do otherwise, or that he was not interested in maintaining his authority in Flanders, but only in France. These are falsifications of the truth. The facts are that John the Fearless devoted considerable care to his position in Flanders; that he extracted more money from the Flemish than his father had done; and that he avoided the rebellions, bloodshed, pitched battles and other horrific events which the Flemish initiated or suffered under his predecessor and successors; avoided them, not only through chance or because of external events, but also by the arts of statesmanship, that is, the subtle manipulation of circumstances in his favour.

see Deschamps de Pas, *Revue numismatique* (n.s.) vi (1861), 228–32 and van Gelder, *RBN* cvii (1961), 147–8.

CHAPTER 7

Burgundy under Margaret of Bavaria

It must have been John the Fearless's intention, from the early years of his reign, to make use of his wife Margaret of Bavaria and his only legitimate son Philip, count of Charolais, in the government of his territories. At first, as we have seen, Philip was installed at Dijon while Margaret took up residence at Ghent; but this arrangement was reversed in 1409–11. Unlike her son in Flanders, the duchess was never formally appointed John's lieutenant or governor in Burgundy, and she invariably styled herself, in all her letters, grandly but vaguely: 'Margaret, duchess of Burgundy, countess of Flanders, of Artois and of Burgundy, palatine, lady of Salins and of Malines, having the government of the above-mentioned countries and places in the absence of my lord [the duke].' She lived in Burgundy from May 1409 onwards, dividing her time between Dijon and neighbouring Rouvres, and visiting other places in the duchy and county from time to time. The earliest evidence I find of her governmental activity there is a letter of the Dijon *gens des comptes* of 12 October 1409, in which they excuse themselves to her for their failure to obey the marshal's request for the immediate despatch to him, for the siege of Vellexon, of supplies of powder, and of the ducal cannoneer, Jehan Manus. They inform her that gunpowder is not to be had and, in any case, there is no money to buy it, and that Manus is away in France.[1]

We know a great deal about the duchess's movements in 1410 and 1411 because of the fortunate survival of the daily accounts or *contrerolle* of her household for these years. In 1410 she was at Rouvres till September, then moved to Dijon for the rest of the year. In 1411 she forsook Rouvres for Dijon in April, June, and the last four months of the year. Her periodic consultations with the councillors and

---

[1] BN Coll. de Bourg. 54, f. 252. For the next paragraph, see BD MS. 1107, fos. 65 and 99b and MS. 1108, f. 31b. There are extracts from the duchess's *contrerolle* of 1414 in BN Coll. de Bourg. 55, fos. 107–8b.

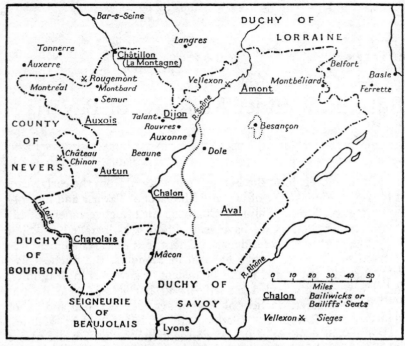

DUCHY OF LORRAINE

Bar-s-Seine

Tonnerre
• Auxerre
Langres
Châtillon
(La Montagne)
Belfort
Basle •
Ferrette

× Rougemont
Montréal
• Montbard
• Semur
Vellexon ×
Montbéliard
Amont

Talant • Dijon
COUNTY
OF
Auxois
Rouvres •
Auxonne
Besançon

NEVERS
Château
Chinon
• Autun
Beaune
•
• Dole

Chalon
Aval

R. Loire
DUCHY
OF
BOURBON
Charolais
• Mâcon

SEIGNEURIE
OF
BEAUJOLAIS
DUCHY OF
SAVOY
R. Rhône
Lyons

0 10 20 30 40 50
Miles
Chalon Bailiwicks or Bailiffs' Seats
Vellexon × Sieges

5. The two Burgundies and neighbouring territories

officials of the duchy are noted in these accounts, at any rate when
they took place at Rouvres:

Wednesday, 14 May 1410. At Rouvres, where Sir Jaques de Courtiambles, the bailiff of Dijon, and other ducal councillors came to dinner.

Tuesday, 22 July 1410. At Rouvres, where Sir Jehan de Champdivers
and several other ducal councillors spent the day.

Thursday, 26 February 1411. At Rouvres, and Sir Jehan de Chalon, the
lord of St. Georges, the marshal of Burgundy, the lord of Pagny, and the
ducal council at Dijon were there.

On 24 April 1410 the duchess summoned an assembly of nobles and
ducal officials to Rouvres, and in June she presided in person over
meetings of the Estates of the county of Burgundy at Dole, and of the
duchy at Dijon, to obtain financial assistance for her husband, who
was at this time faced with the formation of the league of Gien by the

French princes hostile to him.[1] By ducal letters-patent of 27 January 1411 she was empowered to strengthen and repair the ducal castles and to take all measures necessary for the defence and security of the duchy; but this investment with specifically military responsibilities added little or nothing to the implicit authority she already enjoyed and wielded as duchess, and the same is probably true of her power to appoint ducal officials, which was explicitly granted to her by the duke on 11 December 1411. Although she invariably ruled in the closest co-operation with the ducal council at Dijon and with the Burgundian nobles mentioned in the extracts above and others who were likewise ducal councillors and chamberlains, there is ample evidence to demonstrate that she was in sole and effective command of affairs. Moreover, it seems that she was by no means lacking in administrative skill, though much of the efficiency and mastery of detail in her government may probably be attributed to her veteran secretary, Jehan de Maroilles.

Although the duchess was very much left on her own in Burgundy after 1409, she remained in close and constant touch with her husband in Paris or elsewhere. Nor did John the Fearless entirely ignore his southern territories, for he was there from October 1414 to November 1415, and again, for three months, in the early summer of 1418.

It is scarcely surprising that military affairs dominate the history of the two Burgundies in John the Fearless's reign. The civil war in France, between Burgundians and Armagnacs, which broke out in 1411 and continued intermittently during the rest of the reign, was bound to have repercussions there. From 1411 on, in fact, Margaret of Bavaria and her government were preoccupied with defence, and their success in confining actual warfare to the frontiers of the duchy, or to neighbouring territories, was as much the result of the effective and expeditious precautions which they constantly took by way of mobilization, garrisoning and reconnaissance, as of John the Fearless's prudent strategy.

As a matter of fact, the military organization of the two Burgundies was put to the test in 1409, some time before the outbreak of civil war in France. The count of Blamont in Lorraine had defied a sentence of the *Parlement* of Dole by retaining possession of the powerful fortress of Vellexon in the county of Burgundy, which John the Fearless thereupon ordered the marshal of Burgundy, together with the

---

[1] Plancher, iii. 310–11. The ducal letters of 27 January 1411 are in ACO B11844, copied thence into BN Coll. de Bourg. 54, f. 318. The letters of 11 December 1411 are in ibid., f. 350.

bailiffs of Amont and Aval, to seize. But this was not so easy, for reconnaissance showed that it was too powerful to be taken by assault. In September 1409 preparations for a formal siege were got under way, while the defenders showed their determination by burning down the village of Vellexon. In October over a hundred pioneers and workmen were employed building palisades round the castle, assembling artillery from Chalon, Dijon and elsewhere, and fashioning stone cannon-balls from the neighbouring quarries, though shortage of cash delayed operations. By December a small army, about 500 strong, consisting of many of the Burgundian nobles, supported by communal contingents from Dijon, Auxonne, Besançon and other towns, was encamped at Vellexon, while the artillery was now directed by the ducal cannoneer, Jehan Manus, who had arrived from Paris. Even then, it was not until 22 January 1410 that the castle finally fell to the besiegers as a result of a combination of mining and bombardment. Of the thirty or so defenders, nearly all were released after a spell in prison, though some were first branded on the forehead with the ducal arms. Finally, in February, the towers of Vellexon were mined and the castle demolished.[1]

In the summer of 1412 a military operation of a similar kind took place just outside the western borders of the duchy. The garrison of the fortified town of Château-Chinon, which belonged to one of the Armagnac princes, John I, duke of Bourbon, had apparently been raiding the duchy. At any rate, John the Fearless resolved to reduce this place—a decision which seems to have been inspired, strategically, by the desire to keep his enemies at arm's length, so to speak, and avoid warfare on his own territories. In mid-June 1412, while forced loans were raised in the neighbouring parts of the duchy to help pay for the siege, casks of gunpowder were scrounged from the towns of the county. Between 10 and 17 July over 800 men were reviewed by the ducal commissioner at the siege, but it was only towards the end of the month that the captain of Château-Chinon surrendered, in return for a payment of 500 *livres* of Tours, and the fortifications were demolished.[2]

---

[1] For this paragraph see Bertin, *BSASH* (3) xxxi (1900), 1–190. See, too, Plancher, iii. 291–7; Clerc, *Franche-Comté*, ii. 310–11; Garnier, *Artillerie des ducs de Bourgogne*, 17–30; de la Chauvelays, *Armées*, 191–9; Bazin, *MSHA Beaune* (1897), 72–6; Camp, *Auxonne*, 57–8 and ACO B11877.

[2] For this paragraph, see *Mémoires*, ii. 94 n; Plancher, iii. 348–50; Garnier, *Artillerie des ducs de Bourgogne*, 42–3; de la Chauvelays, *Armées*, 219–20; and Bazin, *MSHA Beaune* (1897), 89–91. For the following paragraphs, see Plancher, iii. 339 and no. 269, 340–1, 363–3, etc.; Bazin, *MSHA Beaune*

The sieges of Vellexon and Château-Chinon were isolated and successful military enterprises, but the hostile activities of Louis de Chalon, count of Tonnerre, forced a protracted and costly war on the duchess of Burgundy and her government, and constituted a standing military threat to the duchy from 1411 onwards. Since his indiscretion in 1406–7, in abducting one of the duchess of Burgundy's ladies-in-waiting from court, and the subsequent seizure of his lands in the duchy and county by John the Fearless, Louis de Chalon had come to an understanding with the duke, in May 1410, whereby most of his lands were to be restored to him. Before this had been done, however, he was suspected of being in treasonable contact with the Armagnacs, and John the Fearless at once took action against him. In January 1411 he contrived the issue of royal letters confiscating the county of Tonnerre to the French crown and appointing himself its governor. Soon afterwards, his troops occupied Louis's lands and castles in the county of Burgundy; his officials were installed in the county of Tonnerre; and proceedings were once more initiated against Louis in the high court of the county of Burgundy, or *Parlement* of Dole.[1]

In these circumstances, it can hardly have surprised John the Fearless when, at the very time when the duke of Orleans sent him his formal challenge or declaration of war, and the Armagnac princes embarked on a campaign against him in the north, Louis de Chalon did the same in the south. Louis's letter, sent to John's captain-general in Burgundy, who happened to be Louis's cousin, runs in part as follows:

> Dear cousin Sir Jehan de Neufchastel, lord of Montagu and of Fontenay in Vosges, captain-general of the duchy and county of Burgundy and of Charolais for the high and puissant prince the duke of Burgundy your master and lord. . . . A letter you have written and sent to me Louis de Chalon, count of Tonnerre, by [the hand of] the herald Rethel, dated Châtillon-sur-Seine, Saturday, 8 August 1411, states in effect that if by dinner-time the following Monday I have not made good the various and considerable damages which you claim I and my people have done in your master's territory . . ., you will provide a remedy by all the means at your disposal. . . .

To reply to your letter: even if it were true, as you claim, that injuries have been done by me or the people from my garrisons on the territory of your master, in view of the shortness of the time you allow—not even one whole day from my receipt of your letter—it would be quite impossible for me to do anything about it. . . . I have been requesting and entreating the said duke [of Burgundy] for the last four or five years to give back and restore to me my lands in the county of Burgundy, which he has held and holds improperly and unreasonably, and for which I was his loyal vassal and subject. But he has done nothing about this in the past, nor is he doing anything now, and I wish to declare to him and to all others, that I, deprived and foreclosed of my aforesaid lands wrongly, without cause and without reason, am no longer his man, nor his subject, nor well-disposed towards him: but his enemy, and [enemy also] to all those who choose to help him in this matter. Nor [shall I be] against my very redoubted lord monsieur the duke of Orleans, whose loyal vassal and subject I now am, just as formerly I was the duke of Burgundy's. To him and to all his allies, I certify that I shall serve my very redoubted lord monsieur the duke of Orleans against all his enemies. . . . Please declare and make known all this to the high and puissant prince the duke of Burgundy. . . .

Dear cousin, I commend myself to you. Please recommend me to all my other relatives in Burgundy, and tell them that, apart from the quarrels of our masters, I am ready at all times to do for you and for them whatever one relative ought to do for another. Dear cousin, may God by his grace give you success in arms in some other war than against me. . . .

Written at Tonnerre, Monday, 10 August 1411.

This formal defiance was sent some weeks after Louis de Chalon had opened hostilities by seizing and garrisoning his town of Tonnerre and the other places in the county of Tonnerre which had been taken over by John the Fearless at the beginning of the year. In July or August 1411, too, he had placed a strong garrison in the strategically valuable castle of Rougemont, the ruins of which now overlook the main railway line into Burgundy from Paris, and which lay right on the borders of the duchy. He had even organized sorties thence into ducal territory. But the duchess of Burgundy acted with expedition. Garrisons were strengthened, munitions gathered, the nobility of duchy and county mobilized, and the marshal sent for to advise on a plan of campaign. At Semur, by mid-August, John the Fearless's brother, Philip, had arrived with a contingent of his own from his neighbouring, and likewise threatened, county of Nevers; and the growing army was soon swollen by the troops of a military ally of

John the Fearless, Charles, duke of Lorraine, whose help had been sought. Between them, the duke of Lorraine and the count of Nevers successfully undertook the siege of Rougemont in the last week of August, helped by the ducal cannoneer Jehan Manus, who arrived in person to direct the use of a rather motley collection of artillery, which included the 'great bombard of Burgundy' as well as privately owned pieces lent by the lord of Villars, the lord of Arlay, and other nobles. After initial supply difficulties, the *gens des comptes* at Dijon managed to send 400 lb. of bread each day to Montbard, escorted by the pennons of Lorraine and Nevers. The fall of Rougemont caused Louis de Chalon to evacuate most of his castles in the county of Tonnerre, though he held onto the castle of Tonnerre itself until November. By the end of 1411 the whole of the county was again in the hands of John the Fearless, administered by a bailiff appointed by him, and garrisoned by his own forces.

In 1412 and the first half of 1413, when John was at the height of his power in France, Louis de Chalon was scarcely in a position to re-open hostilities; nor could he do anything to defend himself against the legal warfare which, now military operations were over, John waged against him. In January 1412 he made over most of Louis's lands to his son Philip, count of Charolais, and in July 1413 Louis was again banished for ever from the county of Burgundy by decree of the Dole *Parlement*, and all his lands there confiscated. But John the Fearless's expulsion from France by the Armagnacs in August 1413 might well have been a signal for renewed activity by Louis de Chalon, determined as ever to reconquer his county of Tonnerre.

The duchess and her advisers were fully aware of the strategic importance of Tonnerre. Provided they could hold it and the neighbouring castles, the duchy was secure from actual invasion by the Armagnacs. Witness this letter, sent by her to the ducal *maîtres des comptes* at Dijon on 22 September 1413:[1] 'Dear and well-beloved, be pleased to know that our cousin of Arlay will be with us on Monday . . . to advise about the defence and security of this land, because, if we surrender Tonnerre, we shall have a war on our hands . . . . So we command you to be with us without fail next Monday evening or the following Tuesday morning. . . .' In the following month, the duchess was still preoccupied by the hostile threat of Louis de Chalon,

---

[1] BN Coll. de Bourg. 56, f. 66. The letter which follows is from *Itinéraires*, 602.

as another letter to the *gens des comptes*, written on 26 October, shows:

> Dear and well-beloved, according to the letters of our cousins of Arlay and St. Georges, enclosed within, we ought to send to Troyes, Bar-sur-Seine and Tonnerre to ascertain the attitude and intentions of the count of Tonnerre and his brothers, who are said to be masters of Bar-sur-Seine and Montagu-sur-Troyes, so that if they place garrisons there to damage my lord [the duke] and his lands, similarly, my lord [the duke] can place garrisons of men-at-arms at Châtillon-sur-Seine, Montbard, Montréal and elsewhere as necessary for the security of the land. And for this reason we are sending Guillaume de Mandres there, with two companions, so that he and his friends can discover the situation and plans of the said count of Tonnerre and his brothers and report what they discover to us. So we command you to see that Regnaut de Thoisy pays the aforesaid Guillaume. . . .

As a matter of fact, Louis de Chalon was biding his time, His opportune moment came in the spring and early summer of 1414, and he opened his offensive at the end of April with an attempted seizure of Châtillon-sur-Seine, at the very moment when the Armagnac campaign against John the Fearless in the north began with the capture of Burgundian-held Compiègne. Once again, as in 1411, John had to fight a war on two fronts. In June and July 1414, while the victorious Armagnac forces were moving in on Arras, capital of the county of Artois, and soon after over 2,000 men had hurried northwards from the two Burgundies to help defend it, Louis de Chalon invaded and reconquered the county of Tonnerre. He was also credited with deploying 80–100 well-disguised mounted spies in the duchy of Burgundy. Once again, as in 1411, the duchess and her military advisers reacted vigorously. In June she reinforced the garrison of Châtillon-sur-Seine, and made provision for her own safety by forming a personal bodyguard for herself 'during this time of uncertainty and danger', and by building a special tower at Rouvres, on the lines of that added by John to the hotel d'Artois in Paris, in which she and her children could take refuge in case of need.[1] While Louis de Chalon raided the duchy, she mustered an army to meet him and eventually, in late October or early November, the castle of Tonnerre was once more captured, this time by the Burgundian forces returning from Artois, after the armistice had been signed at Arras in early September and after the town and the castle bailey had been taken by the duchess's forces. No heed was taken of the royal letters of 11 November 1414,

---

[1] BN Coll. de Bourg. 55, fos. 123 and 124, and 56, f. 208.

if indeed they arrived in time, ordering John to desist from his attacks on the castle of Tonnerre which, the king claimed, were in direct breach of the armistice.

Thus ended the war of Tonnerre, for, in spite of numerous, indeed almost constant, scares, threats and raids in the two Burgundies during the rest of John's reign, it seems that most of these were not the work of Louis de Chalon. His county of Tonnerre was henceforth administered by John, to whom it was formally transferred by royal grant on 25 July 1419. The whole affair was a nice combination of private revenge, strategic advantage and aggression by the duke.

By the seizure of Château-Chinon, Rougemont, and Tonnerre, outside the western borders of the duchy, John the Fearless was keeping his potential enemies there on the defensive. This judicious strategy was at first pursued to the south of the duchy, where Beaujolais, belonging to the duke of Bourbon, was unsuccessfully invaded in 1412 by the Savoyard captain Amé de Viry at John's instigation. But the threat from the duke of Bourbon was thereafter parried by diplomatic means: by a projected marriage alliance in 1412 and 1418; and, in June 1414, by a treaty of 'abstinence from war' which effectively neutralized both Beaujolais and Château-Chinon. By the terms of this treaty the dukes of Burgundy and Bourbon agreed not to make war in each other's territories, Beaujolais and Château-Chinon being both expressly mentioned, and each bound himself to give the other at least three weeks' notice in the event of a declaration of war. Later, in February 1418, this treaty was confirmed, strengthened and extended by the inclusion in the areas it neutralized of the town and bailiwick of Mâcon, between the duchy of Burgundy and Beaujolais.[1]

The seizure and occupation of the royal bailiwick of Mâcon by John the Fearless in September 1417 was not a strategic move; indeed it had little or nothing to do with the defence of the duchy. It was an act of pure aggression, by means of which John secured an important addition of territory to the Burgundian state. It happened in September 1417, and was carried out under cover of John's plan to persuade the principal towns of France to swear loyalty to him, or else to conquer them. Nogent-sur-Seine and Troyes surrendered to John's forces in July; Rheims and Rouen submitted at about the same time to persuasion; Senlis and other places swore loyalty to John in September; and Tours became Burgundian in November. But the case of Mâcon was different, for, though it was persuaded to declare

---

[1] Leguai, *Ducs de Bourbon*, 63 and 73; BN Coll. de Bourg. 55, fos. 121–2b = 309b–10b, and ib., 267–8b.

its allegiance and support for the government of John the Fearless in France on exactly the same terms and in the same manner as the other French towns, its fortified places were thereupon seized by Burgundian troops and its administration was taken over by Burgundian officials; not to mention the revenues of its tolls and its mint, its courts of law, and the jurisdiction of its royal legal officers. In short Mâcon, city and bailiwick, was virtually annexed by John the Fearless and incorporated into the Burgundian state. Dreue Mareschal, one of the *maîtres des comptes* at Dijon, who was sent to Mâcon to collect whatever cash he could lay hands on, wrote to his colleagues in Dijon on 25 September 1417, not without humour, giving some account of the situation there.[1]

> Dearest sirs and brothers, I commend myself to you, and may it please you to know that last Monday [20 September], after the end of the Chalon fair, which was a good one, and the closing of the merchants' accounts, I left Chalon and came to this town, as I had been expressly commanded by my lord the chancellor, my lord of St. Georges, and Sir Jehan Chousat, though I would have much preferred to return to you, rather than come here. I found the chancellor here, together with the lord of la Marche-sur-Saône his son-in-law who has now left to look for 25 or 30 men-at-arms, the lord of Laubespin, Sir Philibert de St. Ligier, the bailiff of Chalon and other notable knights and squires, armed and mounted like St. George, to the number of about 100 or 120 well-equipped men-at-arms; and they are needed too, because, although the inhabitants of this town have permitted us entry and done us obeisance, and though we are masters of the castle and the whole town and have their letters produced today in the form of those of Langres, all the same, some of them pull faces and smack of the Armagnac. But most are openly Frenchmen and Burgundians.
>
> Monsieur the *pardessus*[2] and I began yesterday to examine the accounts of the masters of the mints, the receivers of the domain and of the *aides*, and the master of the ports of this town, but we've found very little to savour there. . . . Whatever anyone tells me, I cannot help thinking that my lord the chancellor, monsieur the *pardessus* and I would be more securely lodged over there with you, than here.
>
> We have no benefits whatsoever in this town. You, my comrade Master Guillaume [Courtot], know the people of Mâcon well, and what sort of wine we use here. The inhabitants of Lyons still haven't replied to us, but the bailiff of Mâcon [Philippe de Bonnay] is there, doing his

---

[1] Richard, *AB* xxxiii (1961), 88–98, prints this and other letters concerning the occupation of Mâcon.

[2] The *pardessus* was the ducal officer in charge of the salt-works at Salins; in this case Jehan Chousat, Mareschal's colleague on his mission to Mâcon.

best to oppose us. If you, Master Estienne de Sens,[1] were at Cuisery, we would get you over to see the state of the mint here, which is hard at work. . . . I certainly shan't remain behind when our troops set out for home; indeed if monsieur the *pardessus*, Joceran Frepier and I hadn't promised my lord the chancellor to remain with him all the time, we should already be at Chalon, or with you. Some of the people here are extremely hostile, and we shall have to deal with them as at Troyes and Langres. We are sending to Lyons yet again.

I pray you, dearest sirs and brothers, send me news of my lord [the duke]; God grant him grace to bring his affairs and good intentions to a satisfactory conclusion. May Our Lord have you in his holy guard, and give you a good life and a long one. Written at Mâcon, 25 September.

Monsieur the *pardessus* recommends himself to you a hundred thousand times—he has permission to go to Dole on St. Rémy's Day for the farms of the treasury of Dole,[2] but he has promised faithfully on oath to return soon. Master Jehan Mercier commends himself to you and lets you know that he has today entertained my lord the chancellor and 54 knights and squires and other people of substance, not counting servants, to dinner on a grand scale. Please give my regards to the bailiff of Dijon [Richard de Chancey].

Your brother and servant, Dreue Mareschal.

At Lyons, in spite of the chancellor's attempts to cajole or compel its citizens to join the Burgundian party, John the Fearless was unlucky. The nearest he got to success was at the end of 1417. In November Hugues, lord of Laubespin, found a squire who offered to capture the bailiff of Mâcon, Philip de Bonnay, who, having fled Mâcon, had installed himself at Lyons and rallied the Armagnacs there, provided he was given a suitable boat, 25–30 men-at-arms, 12 crossbow-men and 100 crowns. The boat was built, at a cost of over 200 francs; the troops were provided; and, on 21 December 1417, the project was launched with the enthusiastic support of the chancellor. But, alas! The water in the Rhone was so low that the boat ran aground several times when they were still two or three leagues from Lyons, and the expedition had to be abandoned.[3]

[1] Estienne de Sens was a *maître des comptes* and master-general of the mints of Burgundy.

[2] The annual award of farms or contracts for certain of the provostships in the bailiwick of Aval, the revenues of which were paid to the treasurer of Dole, took place on 1 October. Jehan Chousat was also treasurer of Dole.

[3] Letters of Jehan de Saulx, 11 January 1418, in ACO B11879. See, too, Déniau, *Commune de Lyon*, 286–7, 290, 323–6, 336–7, etc. For what follows, see above, pp. 13–14; Clerc, *Franche-Comté*, ii. 322–7; Piquard, *MSED* (10) i (1931), 96–7; and Blondeau, *MSED* (10) viii (1938), 75–6.

Another city in the area of the two Burgundies, over which John the Fearless attempted to extend his control, was Besançon, an imperial enclave in the heart of the county of Burgundy. The citizens, at loggerheads with their archbishop, had tried to tempt John the Fearless into helping them undermine his authority by offering him the lordship of the city. In 1408 he had all but accepted this offer, and was preparing for the installation at Besançon of administrative and judicial institutions for the county of Burgundy; but the project was dropped in 1409.

Disputes and negotiations continued at Besançon during the following years, but in 1412 peace was at last made between the archbishop Thibaud de Rougemont and the city, and his six-year interdict over it was raised. At the same time, in May 1412, the citizens once again took up with John the Fearless the question of the lordship of the city. Again, they offered it to him in exchange for the establishment of Besançon as the administrative capital of the county of Burgundy, and again, in May 1412, he signed a treaty with the city, which was very similar to that of 1408: he bound himself to transfer the high court of the county, the *Parlement* of Dole, to Besançon; and to set up there a *chambre des comptes*, a council, and a chancery court, on the lines of those at Dijon. He agreed also to defend the inhabitants of Besançon and maintain their privileges. In return they transferred to him the lordship of their city.

The interest of the Besançon affair does not lie in its intrinsic importance, for the events of 1408–9 and 1412–13 scarcely altered the status quo, but in the detailed advice John the Fearless received on it from more than sixty councillors, officials, bailiffs, nobles and deputies from the towns, of his southern territories, which was submitted at a special series of assemblies held in Dijon by the duchess in February 1413, on the command of the duke. The individual written recommendations of these persons have survived in the archives at Dijon.[1] The question at issue, on which the duke may have sought advice because he was genuinely perplexed, was whether he should honour the treaty already made with the city of Besançon in the previous year, or whether he should strike a bargain instead with the archbishop, by the terms of which archbishop and duke would share the lordship between them, as they had agreed to do in the recent past, on the basis of the duke enjoying the judicial rights involved, while the archbishop kept the rents and lands.

There was little disagreement, among those consulted, about the

[1] ACO B1055/2 = BN Coll. de Bourg. 55, fos. 4–11 and 16–23.

value of the lordship of Besançon, if it really could be acquired by the duke; but no one seriously suggested that outright possession, or indeed any kind of rule over the city, was a possibility at this stage. They recognized that King Wenzel's grant of the regalian rights to the duke was invalid for various reasons, and the feeling was that the citizens' offer of the lordship of Besançon was fraudulent and invalid: it simply was not theirs to give. Jaques de Courtiambles thought that the city of Besançon was 'extremely haughty, quarrelsome and arrogant'; that it had no respect for lordship in any case; and that the limited lordship it offered to the duke was not worth having. Rather, he urged, and here most of the others supported him, the duke should accept the judicial rights which the archbishop was prepared to give or sell him, that is, a share in the administration of justice, care of the keys of the city gates, the inheritances of intestate bastards, and the like. While many argued, on various grounds, that John the Fearless's 1412 treaty with the city was in any case invalid, and that he was by no means bound to keep the promises he made in it, the ecclesiastics, playing safe, recommended him to obtain a dispensation. Jehan Langret's advice was the most detailed and expert of all. He had been personally involved in the negotiations at Besançon and he fully agreed that the treaty with the city should be disregarded, though he insisted that care be taken to preserve the goodwill of the authorities and inhabitants. Others thought that the whole scheme was against the 'public interest'. Naturally, the deputies of Dole opposed the transfer of their *Parlement* to Besançon, and many opposed its establishment there on the more altruistic grounds that appeals from it would then lie to the Emperor, whereas at Dole it was a sovereign court of justice.

John the Fearless readily accepted this impressive consensus of opinion; his treaty with the civic authorities of Besançon was disregarded and dishonoured in favour of an arrangement with the archbishop, and he made no further attempts to extend Burgundian influence or control over the city. Perhaps the chancellor was disappointed. His advice on the Besançon affair is interesting enough to permit him to have the last word on it here: [1]

1. On the question put to the full council by madame the duchess at the duke's command on 16 February 1413, that is, whether or not he should hold his *Parlement* in the city of Besançon. Considering the

---

[1] Translated and partly abridged from the summary in BN Coll. de Bourg. 55, f. 23.

appeals which will probably be taken thence before the Emperor, it seems inadvisable to hold the *Parlement* there until the duke has obtained imperial letters removing this possibility; in which case Besançon seems more suitable for the said *Parlement* than any other place—provided, that is, that the duke has the lordship of the city. However, in present circumstances, it seems best to defer this move.

2. On the second question, that is whether or not the lordship of Besançon would be advantageous for the duke. It would be most unwise for him to abandon it, especially in view of the popular saying, 'He who is not lord of Besançon, is not lord of the county'. For this reason an immediate agreement should be reached with the archbishop.

3. The duke has accepted too many obligations towards the inhabitants of Besançon in his treaty with them, which should therefore be disregarded.

4. As to installing a *chambre du conseil* and a chancery court at Besançon, they would be very advantageous to the duke and his subjects, provided always that he has the lordship of the city as well.

5. In this affair there is one thing that ought especially to be borne in mind, and that is the conduct of the late duke [Philip the Bold] in similar circumstances. In order to achieve better justice in his land of Flanders, he set up a *chambre du conseil* there, which still exists. He took infinite trouble over this, and it cost him more than 20,000 *livres* before he got a penny from it. But today we see that it enjoys the most extensive jurisdiction of any court in Flanders. Presumably, when Duke Philip accepted the *garde* of Besançon for 500 francs,[1] he only did so because he envisaged a greater advantage from it later. Without doubt he would much rather have had the lordship than the *garde*. It is very true that, in all things, when one starts them, one ought not to consider only the immediate advantage. 'He who takes things step by step goes far.' It is in this way that large lordships have been built up, and those who have tried to acquire them in some other way have found them of short duration and little profit.

John the Fearless's attempt to extend his rule over Besançon was linked to a project of administrative reform, which probably appealed to him almost as much as the possible acquisition of Besançon. He was, in fact, both a reformer and an administrator; perhaps too much of a reformer to be a really successful administrator. The *ordonnance Cabochienne*, partly inspired by him, is in some ways typical of the man: a comprehensive and detailed scheme of reform which was far

[1] Vaughan, *P. the Bold*, 105.

too radical to be actually implemented; and the Besançon plan was rather similar: it was bold and imaginative, but did not take account of practical possibilities and actual circumstances. An even better example, from the southern territories, is the *ordonnance* of 7 April 1415. This was an elaborate and indeed revolutionary scheme to reorganize the whole administration of all the southern territories at one and the same time. The idea was to save money by drastically reducing the number of ducal officials; restricting their wages; and, wherever possible, by farming out their duties. As a matter of fact, a total saving, in cash and kind, of 11,133 *livres* of Tours per annum was calculated by the duke's advisers if this *ordonnance* were implemented. It would have reduced the money-wage bill for the entire administrative personnel of the southern territories from 15,560 l.t. p.a. to 8,429. But, even though the ducal administration was undeniably clumsy, over-staffed and unreasonably extravagant, there never was any hope that the *maîtres des comptes* and the councillors at Dijon would accept this scheme which, incidentally, entailed a reduction in their own numbers. Like the *ordonnance Cabochienne*, it was shelved. Its radical character, its total failure to appreciate the facts, or weaknesses, of human nature, may be judged from a few of its 197 clauses, chosen more or less at random.[1]

22. The forester at Talant, who looks after the woods there, to be paid 60 *l.* per annum instead of 100 *l.* p.a.

25. At Saulx, where there have been three watchmen, each paid 16 francs and three measures of corn, there are to be only two in future, paid 10 francs and two measures of corn.

62. The number of councillor-advocates in the bailiwick of Chalon is to be reduced from two to one, and he is to be paid 25 *l.* per annum, instead of the 50 *l.* p.a. which he and his colleague each used to receive.

157. The wages of the bailiff of Amont are to be reduced from 222 francs per annum to 150 f. p.a.

John the Fearless's reforming zeal sometimes went so far in the southern territories as to cause confusion and muddle on a large scale. The fact is that he quite often acted so precipitately or inadvisedly that he afterwards had to reverse what he had done. We have seen what happened, twice, at Besançon. In Burgundy under John the

---

[1] BN Coll. de Bourg. 55, fos. 153–9b. See Lameere, *Grand conseil*, xiv–xv and Plancher, iii. 432–4, 454 and 456.

Fearless the recipients of ducal gifts of land or of judicial revenues
might find this generosity annulled by a subsequent general revocation of all such donations.[1] The *gens des comptes* at Dijon often had to
have dispensations from oaths they had sworn at the ducal behest.
For instance, on 27 February 1415 John the Fearless had to send
urgently from Rouen to the bishop of Langres, Charles de Poitiers.

> Because our *gens des comptes* at Dijon have sworn to obey and carry
> out certain instructions and *ordonnances* of ours, according to which,
> among other things, they cannot and ought not to execute letters of ours
> touching certain stated matters unless they are sealed with the seal held
> by our chancellor, they have delayed and still delay executing several of
> our letters which have been presented to them, but which were only
> sealed with our privy seal in the absence of the great seal which our
> chancellor, at present in Flanders or Artois, has with him. [It would be
> a considerable inconvenience to have to send these letters to the chan-
> cellor for sealing,] therefore, reverend father in God, our dearest and
> well-beloved cousin, we pray you to dispense our said *gens des comptes*
> from their aforesaid oaths in so far as this particular matter only is
> concerned. . . .

The inadvertent appointment of two persons to the same office at
the same time must have been a commonplace of every late medieval
state, but it happened in John the Fearless's Burgundy on a grand
scale. In May 1417 the duke abolished all the *greniers à sel*, or ducal
salt warehouses. A year later, when he found it necessary to re-
establish them, the officials who had formerly administered them were
re-instated, while at the same time their posts were filled by a series
of new appointments![2]

The periodic special commissions which were appointed by John
the Fearless in his southern, as well as northern, territories, may be
taken as evidence of a certain misplaced reforming zeal, though they
were at least partly inspired by the duke's financial needs. The
special judicial commission of 1405, mentioned in Chapter One, was
replaced on 27 June 1415 by a similar one, with similar far-reaching
powers. The chancellor Jehan de Saulx; the veteran financial officer
Jehan Chousat; the *maître des comptes* Guillaume Courtot; and two
others, were appointed 'judges and general reformers in all the bailiwicks and provostships of our duchy and county of Burgundy and of

---

[1] E.g., see BN Coll. de Bourg. 55, fos. 178 and 200. The extract which follows
is from ibid., 56, f. 193.
[2] See Plancher, iii. 463–4 (texts in BN Coll. de Bourg. 55, fos. 224 and 226)
and 495–6 (texts in ibid., fos. 286–7 and 288); and ACO B15, fos. 125b–129.

Charolais', and empowered to call before them any judicial proceedings in any court whatsoever in this area, and to prosecute and punish anyone who had committed any crimes, or acted in any way prejudicial to the ducal government.

Finance, as well as justice, continued to receive special attention of this kind, and the clean sweep which in March 1409 temporarily deprived nearly all the ducal financial officers in the south of their posts, was repeated two years later, when Richard de Chancey, who was appointed president of the ducal council at Dijon later in the year, and Jehan Moreau, at that time serving temporarily as receiver-general of the two Burgundies, were ordered to dismiss all the accounting officers in the two Burgundies who had failed to submit their accounts for audit at the right time. In September 1415 another special financial commission was appointed, this time to raise loans in the southern territories.[1]

It would be unfair to pass judgement on John the Fearless's administrative skill on the basis of the radical schemes and special commissions just mentioned. In fact, many of his administrative reforms were timely, effective and well conceived. In the southern territories, mention has already been made in Chapter One of his defence *ordonnance* of 1408 and his reform of the *chambre des comptes*; and in Chapter Five of his admirable reforms of the artillery there. In an attempt to establish a rational and uniform financial year he ordered, on 2 January 1411, all the Burgundian financial officers to make out their accounts in future from 1 January to 31 December, and copies of this order were circulated to all the officers concerned. On 9 March 1412 he ordered the *gens des comptes* at Dijon to see to the calendaring and rearrangement of those of his muniments there which had not yet been inventoried; and on 21 March they were instructed to submit a detailed report on the state of the *gruerie* or forestry service, to the duke or his chancellor. Another valuable reform was the establishment in 1413 of a permanent *élu*, or official to supervise the levying of *aides* in the duchy. Thus, in spite of his sometimes misplaced enthusiasm and failure to appreciate the detailed circumstances, John the Fearless did do something to improve the administration of his southern territories.

---

[1] For this paragraph, see above, p. 12; BN Coll. de Bourg. 55, f. 170a–b and 54, f. 323; Lameere, *Grand conseil*, xv; *IACOB* ii. 325 and 340; Plancher, iii. 320–2 and 436. For the next paragraph, see above, pp. 10–12 and 150–1; BN Coll. de Bourg. 54, f. 315 and ACO B15, f. 93; BN Coll. de Bourg. 54, f. 353a–b and 55, f. 29; and Plancher, iii. no. 282.

This chapter cannot be closed without some reference to the capital and largest town of the duchy of Burgundy, Dijon, and to its relations with John the Fearless and Margaret of Bavaria.[1] On the whole these were excellent, and the duke found Dijon reasonably co-operative both in defence and in financial matters, though the town shared the dislike of military service that was so noticeable in Flanders. Indeed, if the citizen-militia of Dijon had been as numerous and powerful as those of Bruges in 1411, they would probably have behaved in exactly the same way. At the siege of Vellexon in 1409 the troops from Dijon proudly displayed a new banner with the arms of their town; but it was only with difficulty that they were persuaded to stay there for more than a month—a month which they claimed began on the date of their departure from Dijon rather than on their arrival at the siege, and which they maintained fulfilled all their military obligations to the duke. Two years later Dijon sent a contingent to the siege of Château-Chinon. This time its behaviour was even more reminiscent of the Flemish: mutiny, or even rebellion, seems not have been far from the thoughts of these stalwarts, whose letter to the magistrates of Dijon of 20 June 1412 is still preserved among the civic muniments:

> Dearest sirs, we recommend ourselves to you, and may it please you to know that although you, monsieur the mayor, promised that we would receive our pay at Lucenay-l'Évêque, nevertheless we haven't had a penny so far.
>
> As to news from here, the evening we arrived we pitched camp before the castle and had wind and rain to keep watch in as an inaugural ceremony. We should have spent our money to good purpose if we'd had any. The bearer of these, Demoingeot Colinet, will tell you more about the state of the siege than we can write.
>
> We cannot be back by the Nativity of St. John [24 June] for the mayoral election as we had hoped, but if you don't act to our liking, we shall elect another mayor when we return.

Besides military assistance, the inhabitants of Dijon afforded financial help to their duke. They contributed to the *aides* voted to him from time to time by the duchy as a whole, and they advanced him loans and made him gifts, though with some reluctance, as this

---

[1] For what follows, I have used Bertucat, *RB* xxi (2) (1911), 150; Humbert, *Finances municipales; Chartes de communes*, i. no. 72; *Correspondance de la mairie de Dijon*, i. nos. 2–19; and AD B146–50 and L 350–5.

characteristic entry in the minute-book of the council-meetings shows:

28 May 1415. To help pay for affairs he has on hand at the moment, my lord the duke asked the magistrates for a gift of 3,000 francs. However, he was told that we can only give him 800 francs, because of the poverty of the town. But, according to today's report, his people are not content with this. Resolved to give my lord [the duke] 1,000 francs, to please him.

Actually the town of Dijon lent or gave John the Fearless a total of 5,900 frances between 1405 and 1417. What did the duke or duchess do for the town in return for these military and financial favours? They helped to force the clergy to pay their share of the cost of the municipal fortifications; they intervened in disputed mayoral elections; and they saw to it that Dijon was efficiently administered. In 1414 the duchess ordered the mayor to see that the clock of Notre-Dame, now called the Jacquemart, was repaired. More important, in July 1416 the duke temporarily made over all criminal first instance jurisdiction to the mayor and aldermen. But the real reason for the good relations between the ducal government and the town of Dijon lay in the identity of the personnel concerned in them, for the wealthy bourgeois families of Dijon, who provided her mayors and aldermen, also provided the duke with many of his councillors and administrators.

Several natives of Dijon were prominent at this time in the service of both duke and municipality. Richard de Chancey, who lived in the rue des Forges, was one of the four senior aldermen of Dijon in 1407-8. He became president of the *chambre du conseil* at Dijon in 1411, and ducal bailiff there in 1412. Jehan Gueniot graduated from being *procureur* of the municipality in 1405-8 to clerk of the *chambre des comptes* in 1409; and Guillaume Chenilly, who served both Philip the Bold and John the Fearless as receiver-general of the two Burgundies, was an alderman in 1407-10. Perhaps more important than any of these, in the years 1409-19, when the effective ruler of Burgundy was Duchess Margaret of Bavaria, was her secretary Jehan de Maroilles. He was almost certainly a native of Dijon; he had a house there, and also a room in the duchess's château at Rouvres.[1] He was her confidant. He seems to have signed every single letter she ever issued or wrote, except a handful signed by herself, perhaps in his absence. Yet he was in close touch with the civic authorites of Dijon,

[1] *IACOB* ii. 312. The letter which follows is AD B450/3.

whose interests he seems to have consistently represented, and furthered, with the duchess. An undated letter has survived to illustrate this:

Your clerk, Jehan de Maroilles, to the mayor of Dijon, Guy Poissonier, Rouvres, Tuesday . . . at 10.0 p.m.

Sir Jehan de Maigney came to see madame [the duchess] between seven and eight o'clock, just as she was going out into the garden, and complained a great deal, alleging that he had been arrested without cause and taken to the prison where burglars are held, and that he'd never said anything against you or the town of Dijon. . . . Madame has given him an appointment for Thursday. . . . Please let me know if you think it would be expedient for some people from the town, or at least the *procureur*, to be here to refute him . . . though I shall sufficiently advise madame and the council of what needs to be done. . . .

CHAPTER EIGHT

Exiled from Paris: 1413–18

After the collapse of John the Fearless's commanding position in France and his precipitate flight to Flanders on 23 August 1413, his enemies gathered in Paris and tried to consolidate their new-found supremacy by means of a veritable barrage of edicts and proclamations in the name of King Charles VI. On 29 August all those involved in the recent troubles in Paris, except for a list of named Cabochien leaders, were officially pardoned; early in September, all the edicts which the king had formerly passed against the Armagnac princes, including their banishment on 3 October 1411, were revoked; the famous *ordonnance Cabochienne*, with all its 258 articles, was solemnly torn up by the clerk of the court at the Paris *Parlement*; an official version of the events of May 1413 and of the subsequent actions of the princes was drawn up and circulated as widely as possible; and requests were sent to Bruges and Ypres, abroad to England and probably elsewhere, and even to John the Fearless himself, for the extradition and return to Paris under armed guard of over sixty named fugitive Cabochiens. Further salvoes of this verbal or legal offensive were recorded in October and November by the chronicler Monstrelet, who took the trouble to transcribe nearly all the texts from the versions received by his local bailiff of Amiens, including proclamations against taking arms and assemblies of men-at-arms, and against disturbers of the peace and the use of factious epithets. To complete the series, the chronicler Juvenel des Ursins gives the text of a royal decree of 14 November which explicitly accuses the duke of Burgundy of assembling troops in breach of the royal proclamations, and orders the captains and inhabitants of various towns to deny access and transit both to the duke and his men.[1]

[1] For this paragraph, see *Ords. des rois*, x. 163–5 and 167–70; *Quelques textes*, 158–67; Boutaric, *AMSL* (2) ii (1865), 291–2 = AGR Trésor de Flandre,

This mass of verbiage hurled at John the Fearless was accompanied by the systematic replacement of his sympathizers in the French government by Armagnac partisans; by the persecution of Burgundians among the burgesses and population of Paris; and by an attempt by the leaders of the new government, Bernard, count of Armagnac and the dukes of Berry, Anjou and Orleans, to enlist the support of the University and the *Parlement*.[1] John the Fearless, who had sent a solemn embassy to Paris in September to try to justify his flight, wrote in November to the king and others at length in the same vein. But events were moving towards war, not peace. In November came the insulting affront to John of the repudiation and return of his daughter Catherine to him by the duke of Anjou, to whose eldest son Louis she had been married since 1410; and in November, too, the whole question of the murder of Louis of Orleans was reopened in Paris by the meeting of a Council of the Faith, convened to examine and, if possible condemn, not only the doctrines of Jehan Petit, but also various other assertions attributed either to Burgundians or Cabochiens.

By the end of 1413, though Burgundian garrisons held out defiantly in Caen and some other towns of Normandy and Picardy, John the Fearless had been successfully and completely excluded from the government of France. Moreover, the Burgundian party in Paris had been virtually suppressed. But, though his situation seemed weak and his future position in France uncertain, John the Fearless now acted with characteristic decision, or impetuosity. In January he seized the initiative in the paper warfare that had been almost continual since early September, by publishing and circulating everywhere numerous copies of no less than three letters purporting to have been sent to him from Paris by the dauphin in December 1413, asking for his assistance. John claimed that the dauphin, who was his son-in-law, had been held a virtual prisoner by the Armagnacs in the Louvre, where he had had almost nothing to do to while away the time except play the organ. Although the dauphin's letters have been

---

(i) 2524; Gachard, *Notices et extraits*, i. 334–5 and *Foedera*, iv (2), 46–8. In this chapter I have relied particularly on the following: de Baye, *Journal*; *Chronique des Cordeliers*; de Fauquembergue, *Journal*; de Fenin, *Mémoires*; *Journal d'un bourgeois de Paris*; Juvenel des Ursins, *Histoire de Charles VI*; Monstrelet, *Chronique*; Religieux de St. Denys, *Chronique*; d'Avout, *Armagnacs et Bourguignons*; Coville, *Les Cabochiens*, *Jean Petit* and *Premiers Valois*; David, *Du nouveau sur Jean sans Peur*; and Mirot, *Les d'Orgemont*.
[1] De Baye, *Journal*, ii. 151–4 and Relig. de St. Denys, v. 196–202.

accepted as authentic by contemporary chroniclers and by modern historians, there is no evidence at all to support this belief, and nobody has ever seen an original. They are perhaps more likely to have been forged by John in an effort to manipulate events in his favour. The text of the first of these letters runs as follows:[1]

> To our dearest and well-loved father, the duke of Burgundy.
>
> Dearest and well-loved father, we command you, as soon as you have seen these letters and without any excuses, to come to us well accompanied, for the security of our person: and do not fail us in this if you fear our anger. May our Lord be your guard. Written by our own hand, at Paris.
> 4 December 1413.   Loys

Judging from the efforts made by the Armagnac government in Paris to deny and disprove the authenticity of these letters, their publication by John the Fearless in January 1414 must have had some effect. A further manifesto of his, distributed on 23 January to the towns of Picardy, was accompanied by action, for on that very day he left Lille for Paris, collecting en route a two-thousand-strong army mustered in his northern territories.[2] On Friday, 2 February, after an early dinner, he reached Compiègne and joined forces with his brother, Philip of Nevers. On 7 February he was at St. Denis, outside Paris, having been reinforced by a Burgundian contingent of over a thousand mounted men, and by Jehan de Luxembourg with the vassals of his uncle the count of St. Pol. Militarily and strategically the Armagnac government in Paris, meeting in clumsy grand councils attended by both queen and dauphin, had been completely outmanœuvred by John the Fearless's speed and organization. On 26 January, when John was at Bapaume, they had summoned the loyal vassals and subjects of the king to assemble in arms at Montdidier on 5 February following. But John had already by-passed Montdidier on 1 February. Although Péronne and Senlis, appealing to the royal command, refused him entry, John the Fearless had little difficulty in entering Roye, Compiègne and St. Denis. At Compiègne he gained entry by showing the dauphin's letters asking him to come to Paris to rescue him. At St. Denis, where he set up his headquarters at the Sword Hotel, his own partisans let him in.

For a tense week in Febuary 1414 John the Fearless waited, poised

---

[1] Coville, *Les Cabochiens*, 389.
[2] De la Chauvelays, *Armées*, 223-7 and *Itinéraires*. For this campaign, see map 3, above, p. 88.

outside the walled-up gates of Paris, hoping to effect an entry. The government, fearful of a revolt in his favour, arranged demonstrations of armed men and public processions to overawe or distract the populace, while those manning the walls and gates were ordered to make no hostile move. The clerk of the court at the Paris *Parlement* has this, among other entries describing these events, in his journal.[1]

Saturday, 10 February. Today, about nine o'clock, before dinner, the lords of the court of *Parlement* rose and left the Chamber because of a report that the duke of Burgundy, with a large force, was drawn up in order of battle between the Porte St. Honoré and the Porte St. Denis in the fields outside Paris. To discover something of this, I went up to the top of the Tour Criminelle here and saw these troops in the fields between Le Roule and Montmartre.

The government's policy of sitting tight in Paris and refusing either to do battle or negotiate was soon crowned with success, and John the Fearless was compelled to withdraw. The only military advantage he had gained by this brief and bloodless campaign was the installation of Burgundian garrisons in the French towns of Soissons and Compiègne. The absence of fighting, however, was made up for on either side by a great deal of hot air and propaganda. While he was at St. Denis, letters justifying John's actions were smuggled into Paris by a messenger disguised as a Franciscan, and posted up on the doors of Notre-Dame, the Palais Royal and other public buildings. Other letters or pamphlets were left by the Artois herald on a cleft stick outside the Porte St. Antoine, and still others were shot into the city with arrows.[2] But the Armagnacs now recovered the initiative in the field of propaganda which they had lost over the dauphin's letters to John. Not content with the publication of letters and proclamations against John condemning all his actions in detail since the murder of Louis of Orleans and exposing his traitorous designs on Paris and the person of the king, they had him publicly banished in the streets of Paris, as a traitor and murderer; on the pretext of a case brought against John by one of his creditors, they ordered the sequestration of his furniture and belongings in the hôtel d'Artois;[3] and finally, on 25 February, Jehan Petit's *Justification du duc de Bourgogne* was solemnly burnt in front of Notre-Dame cathedral, and it was even suggested that his bones should be fetched from Hesdin to be burnt in the same place as his arguments.

[1] De Baye, *Journal*, ii. 167–8.
[2] Van Dixmude, *Merkwaerdige geb.*, 78 and Champion, *Charles d'Orléans*, 121.
[3] *IADNB* i (2), 4. See above, p. 104.

It was not until April that the all but fatal irresolution of the Armagnac government in Paris gave place to decisive military action. A vigorous counter-attack, with the aim of crushing John and conquering or confiscating his territories, was resolved on and executed. The insane king set out on the road to Arras with the white bend of the Armagnacs over his arms, just as happily as he had left for Bourges two years before, decked out with the Burgundian cross of St. Andrew. There is little evidence of widespread enthusiasm for this campaign: the constable of France contrived a broken leg, while the admiral fell victim to a timely attack of gout. But, while these military leaders excused themselves, the dauphin, now seventeen and almost as unstable as his father, demonstrated more than mere military fervour on this occasion, and in a manner insulting in the extreme to his father-in-law John the Fearless.[1]

My lord the dauphin was in a jovial mood. He had a handsome standard covered in beaten gold and adorned with a K, a swan (*cigne*) and an L. The explanation was that there was a very beautiful girl in the queen's household, the daughter of Sir Guillaume Cassinel, who was popularly known as La Cassinelle. She was as good-natured as she was good-looking . . . and, so it was said, the dauphin was passionately in love with her. Hence these symbols. . . .

Throughout the summer of 1414 the Armagnac or royal army held the field against John the Fearless, but its advance into his territories was so uncertain and slow that it was not until mid-July that it reached its first major objective, the capital city of Artois, Arras.[2] In fact, between the surrender of the Burgundian garrisons in the French towns of Compiègne and Soissons in May, and the invasion of Artois, the fall of Bapaume and the beginning of the siege of Arras itself in July, the Armagnacs enjoyed no important military successes, apart from the abject submission early in June of Philip of Nevers, defender of Laon for his brother John, who evidently feared for his neighbouring county of Rethel, or else just lost his nerve. In spite of the aggressive intentions of leaders of the royal army like the count of Armagnac and the duke of Anjou, Bapaume was the only Burgundian town it succeeded in conquering, and the siege of Arras was tamely abandoned early in September in favour of a negotiated peace. Paris, during this protracted campaign, was convulsed with the mass religious frenzy customary on occasions like this. Public processions proliferated in the streets, just as they had done during the

<hr>

[1] Juv. des Ursins, *Hist. de Charles VI*, 494.
[2] For this campaign, see map 3, above, p. 88.

campaign of Bourges in 1412. And now, as then, it was the monks of St. Denis who excelled: after all, they possessed more relics than any-one else—they even had a spare *oriflamme*, as the following extract shows:[1]

Contemporary annals furnish no example of a procession more solemn than that organized by the royal monastery of St. Denis on 25 June [1414]. What induces me to mention it here for the instruction of pos-terity is neither the size of the crowd which watched it, nor the enormous number of processions from other churches which preceded it, but rather the prodigious quantity of relics, which were carried with unusual pomp and respect. The monks, preceded by men dressed in tunics and dalmatics of silk, carrying on their shoulders reliquaries containing the holy bodies of SS. Osman, Hilary, Eugenius, Hippolytus, Eustace and the head of St. Benedict . . ., sang canticles in honour of these and other saints. At their head was the precentor, wearing a most precious cope, and followed by other ecclesiastics, who carried the gold cross, the royal *oriflamme*, the chin of St. Mary Magdalene and the finger of St. Louis . . ., gilt statuettes of St. Mary and St. Nicholas, and the hand of the apostle Thomas. Finally came the reverend abbots of St. Denis and Pontlevoy, with the . . . insignia of the passion of our Lord, that is to say, the Crown of Thorns, the Holy Nail, and [a piece of] the cross of our Lord.

The failure of the Armagnac campaign of 1414 was partly due to the diplomatic skill of John the Fearless, who enlisted his brother Duke Anthony of Brabant, his sister Margaret, wife of William of Bavaria, count of Holland-Hainault, and the representatives of the Four Members of Flanders, to negotiate on his behalf with the king, the dauphin, and those princes or nobles who were not, like the count of Armagnac, intent on his unconditional surrender. But it was also due to his military skill, for the defence of Arras was undertaken in a systematic and masterly manner. The suburbs were mostly destroyed before the siege began; artillery was assembled and put to excellent use; and John took advantage of the slowness of the Armagnac advance to muster a garrison over 1,500 strong. The exact composition of this garrison is not now ascertainable, but there does seem to be some truth in the statement of the Flemish chronicler Oliver van Dixmude, that Arras was defended by men from the county of Bur-gundy who, as subjects of the Empire, could not be accused of fight-ing against their suzerain when attacked by the king of France. Cer-tainly a large proportion of the defending troops were from the

---

[1] Relig. de St. Denys, v. 342–4.

county of Burgundy, and another very sizeable contingent consisted of English mercenaries.[1]

While John the Fearless's diplomatic efforts, as well as his military skill in the stubborn defence of his territories, contributed to the failure of the Armagnac attack against him, there were other factors of great importance. One was the pro-Burgundian element in the royal army, which was apparent at all levels, from the dauphin himself, whose love of peace and, perhaps even more, of ease and luxury, led him, after his initial bravado, to repeat his 1412 rôle of peacemaker, to the humble engineer at the siege of Arras mentioned by the monk of St. Denis in the following passage:

> I am not ashamed to admit that the progress of the royal expedition was hampered by a friendly disposition towards the enemy both among the knights and squires and among the artillerymen. The man in charge of the largest piece, called the Bourgeois, frequently directed his shots on purpose into the air or in the wrong direction. When the count of Richemont saw this and threatened him several times with death, he took the first opportunity to escape in secret to the enemy, who discovered from him the number of combatants and the names of the captains directing the siege on the royal side; not to mention the existence of three or four mines which were being constructed underground to bring down the walls. . . .

Of all the reasons for the failure of the attack on John the Fearless, which was marked by the abandonment of the siege of Arras early in September 1414, perhaps the most important was the state of the French army, which had evidently been kept in the field much too long for military efficiency and, above all, for its good health. Monstrelet explicitly attributes the peace to dysentery. The anonymous bourgeois of Paris has this to say in his journal about the appearance of the returning army:

> All, or nearly all, those who had been at the siege of Arras were so emaciated, pale, and ill, when they arrived [back in Paris], that they looked as if they had been in gaol for six or eight months on bread and water. They brought back nothing but sins, and more than 11,000 of them died.

Peace was eventually made at Arras on 4 September, as announced

[1] See Finot, *Paix d'Arras*, 13-14 and O. van Dixmude, *Merkwaerdige geb.*, 85. On the siege of Arras, see d'Héricourt, *Sièges d'Arras*. The extracts which follow are from Relig. de St. Denys, v. 372 and *Journal d'un bourgeois de Paris*, 56.

in a letter written to John the Fearless on the very same day, probably by the ducal councillor Henri Goedhals, dean of Liège.[1]

May it please you to know, most redoubted lord, that today, at about 9.0 p.m., peace was made and publicly proclaimed on the king's behalf by the chancellor of France, in the presence of [the dauphin] my lord of Guienne, in a way very much to your honour, which we shall tell you about on our return to you. My lord of Guienne caused this peace, which was first sworn to by my lord of Brabant and madame of Hainault, your brother and sister, and by us in your name, to be sworn to by my lord the duke of Orleans, my lords the counts of Alençon, Richemont, La Marche, Vendôme, Marle and Roucy, my lords the chancellors of France and Guienne, the archbishop of Sens, the bishop of Laon and several other great lords, barons, knights, squires and others present at this proclamation, amid a large crowd [of people] all shouting Noel! at the tops of their voices and in joyful mood.

My lord of Guienne promised to keep the peace and to cause it to be kept and sworn to, before he left, by all the princes of the blood present there but absent at this proclamation; and, when he arrived in Paris, by all the others. . . . Then my lord of Guienne ordered everyone to remove his bend or saltire,[2] and prohibited, under penalty of the gallows, the use on either side of injurious or slanderous terms such as 'Burgundian' or 'Armagnac', as well as the singing of songs or any other insults of whatever kind, and ordered everyone to cease from all kinds of warlike deed, and to be good friends together. Soon afterwards we took leave of my lord of Guienne, who told us to write to you [asking you] to cease from all deeds of war outside your castles.

Towards midnight we went with my lord and lady your brother and sister to one of the gates of the city of Arras, to inform those within of the peace, in case they unknowingly violated it, and to ask them, as a sign of it, to ring the bells of the city as requested by my lord [the dauphin] and his councillors. Tomorrow, the keys of the city will be taken to the king and the city formally thrown open according to the terms of the peace. As to the rest of this treaty, we shall report it to you as soon as possible. . . .

There is nothing else that we can tell you about at the moment, except that it seems to us desirable and expedient that you should write a gracious letter of thanks to my lord of Guienne in the nicest possible terms because, in everything that has come to our notice, he has shown himself your good and true friend and son.

The peace of Arras was a triumph of John the Fearless's duplicity,

[1] *IADNB* i (2), 523 and Finot, *Paix d'Arras*, no. 2. See Thomas, *RH* cxviii (1915), 308 n. 4 and ADN B4089, f. 123a–b.
[2] Heraldic badges of the Armagnacs and Burgundians respectively.

as well as of his military and diplomatic skill. The main provisions of this masterpiece of ambiguity were as follows:[1]

A. The Public Treaty

1. Duke Anthony of Brabant, Duchess Margaret of Hainault, and the deputies of the Four Members of Flanders, acting as the duke of Burgundy's proctors, are verbally to request the king's and dauphin's pardon for any wrongs the duke may have done them since the peace of Pontoise.

2. They shall surrender the keys of Arras and those of such other places held by the duke of Burgundy as the king and dauphin may require. Royal banners are to be placed over the gates of Arras and royal officers are to be appointed there and elsewhere, if the king so desires.

3. The duke of Burgundy is to hand over the castles of Crotoy and Chinon to the king.

4. The king and dauphin are free to decide whether or not to grant the duke of Burgundy's request for a general pardon for his supporters. Meanwhile, Duke John agrees not to assist those banished by the king.

5. The above-mentioned proctors promise on Duke John's behalf that he will make no treaties with the English against the interests of the king or his kingdom.

6. The duke of Burgundy will promise not to harm anyone who has been in the royal service, and to restore any lands or possessions confiscated by him from those in the royal service.

7. Duke Anthony, Duchess Margaret of Hainault and the deputies of the Four Members will swear, in the name of Duke John, to keep this peace, and they promise to obtain his ratification of it.

B. The Secret Articles

1. As to the surrender of Arras, the dauphin agrees that the royal officers permitted entry will be few in number, will do no damage, will exercise no jurisdiction there, and will depart within four or five days at the most, leaving the city in the possession of the duke of Burgundy.

2. As to Duke John's request for a free and general pardon for all his supporters and subjects, the dauphin agrees to pardon all his nobles, vassals, councillors, officers and servants and, in general, all his subjects.

---

[1] Texts, discussion and references in Thomas, *RN* v (1914–19), 193–215.

This thoroughly equivocal document left all the major points at issue unsettled. Moreover, by his use of proctors, John the Fearless removed himself, as it were, outside the field of dispute and made it possible for him to disown whatever was done on his behalf in the negotiations which were bound to follow. The treaty of Arras was thus a resounding victory for him. A forged version of it, circulated at the time by his enemies, and copied out by an Italian diarist, perhaps represents the kind of terms which the more extreme Armagnacs had hoped for:[1]

1. The duke of Burgundy is to found, build and endow a magnificent monastery in which masses and prayers are to be constantly said for the soul of Louis of Orleans.

2. The duke to pay annually to the French crown the sum of 200,000 francs.

3. The duke to cede seven of his territories to the king of France for seven years.

4. The duke of Burgundy to go on a personal pilgrimage to the Holy Land for the sake of Louis of Orleans's soul.

It would be tedious here to narrate in full the prolonged negotiations over the implementation of the peace of Arras, which continued for nearly a year.[2] They were conducted with the utmost chicanery on either side, and John made full use of the fact that he was acting through proctors. As early as November 1414 he had strengthened his bargaining position by accusing the Armagnacs of infringing the treaty of 4 September and thus appearing as an aggrieved party. But the situation was complicated by differences of opinion and even a dispute for power in Paris, between the pacific dauphin on the one hand, apparently eager to implement the promises he had made to John at Arras; and the Armagnac princes, Berry, Orleans, Bourbon and the rest, on the other, who could not countenance a royal pardon for John the Fearless's Cabochien supporters. The result of this, during the autumn and winter of 1414–15, was a gradual hardening of feeling against John. Slowly but surely the Armagnacs in Paris

---

[1] Morosini, *Chronique*, ii. 10–12.
[2] Documents concerning these negotiations are printed by Finot, *Paix d'Arras*; Caillet, *MAA* (2) xxxix (1908), 220–35; Cartellieri, *SHAWP* iv (1913), no. 2; Mirot, *BEC* lxxv (1914), 253–327; Thomas, *RH* cxviii (1915), 305–14; *Cartulaire de Hainaut*, iv. Still unprinted are ADN B17618, letters of Guillaume de Bonnières, of 17 January 1415 and 13 March 1415. See, too, Champion and de Thoisy, *Bourgogne–France–Angleterre*, 131–4.

increased their influence, and the dauphin was persuaded or compelled to pursue their policies. In October John's proctors were put
off with the excuse that they had insufficient powers. Early in January
1415 a Burgundian conspiracy to raise the common people of Paris by
parading the dauphin round the streets one night, was disclosed to
the duke of Orleans by the bell-ringer of the church of St. Eustace
who was supposed to give the signal for it.[1] This plot coincided, on
5 January, with a series of elaborate memorial services for Louis of
Orleans in the cathedral of Notre-Dame and elsewhere, at which the
preachers demanded humiliation and punishment for John the Fearless. Both events strengthened the hands of his enemies in Paris.

John the Fearless's continued exclusion from French affairs and
the further decline in his influence in Paris became even clearer in
February and March 1415, when his brother Anthony and the deputies of his sister Margaret and the three Estates of Flanders, acting
as his proctors, as well as his own personal ambassadors, found it
necessary to consent and solemnly swear—though not without protest and qualification—to a unilateral royal *ordonnance* of 2 February
which excluded 500 named supporters of John the Fearless from the
promised amnesty. All over France, in March and April, people were
busy swearing to keep the peace of Arras, and notaries were engrossing
declarations that this *ordonnance* had been promulgated. Yet neither
John himself nor the extreme Armagnacs would accept the settlement: the former refused outright to swear; the latter only did so
with reluctance. John's views are well expressed in a letter he sent
to the bishop of Tournai, Jehan de Thoisy, and his other ambassadors
to the dauphin, protesting against their acquiescence in the royal
ordonnance of 2 February 1415.[2]

And so, dearest and well-loved reverend father in God, since you
must know and understand plainly, just as we, who are not of such
great intelligence as you, know for certain, that the proceedings [you
have reported to us] have been and are . . . to the very great damage
and dishonour of us, our line and posterity, as well as all our lands,
subjects, servants, friends, partisans and supporters, and that those in
my lord of Guienne's entourage are only trying by all the means that
they can think of and imagine to bring about the total destruction of us
and of ours without any regard to the maintenance of the peace recently
made before our town of Arras, nor to the oaths that have been made

---

[1] Cousinot, *Geste des nobles*, 153-4 and ACO B11894, royal letters close to
John the Fearless of 12 January 1415.
[2] Finot, *Paix d'Arras*, no. 14.

204 JOHN THE FEARLESS

concerning it . . . we inform you that the things that have been done are and will be displeasing to us . . . and we do not want you to proceed with them in any way whatsoever. And if, which God forbid, my lord of Guienne . . . remains and persists absolutely in this purpose and there is no possibility of another arrangement honourable for us and ours, we would like you to depart and take leave of him. . . .

Thus, in spite of its apparent finality and the universal enthusiasm with which it was welcomed and sworn to by the populace, the settlement of February 1415 neither effectively implemented the peace of Arras nor pleased either party. John the Fearless, whose moral failings did not include disloyalty to friends and supporters, refused to accept the banishment of 500 of them, even though most of these were Parisian mob-orators or Cabochiens. As a result of repeated pressure from John, the dauphin eventually agreed at the end of June 1415 to reduce the number to 200, and assured him that after he had sworn to the peace, the royal amnesty would be extended to all. But John still refused to swear, and only finally did so on 30 July 1415. Even then he had a formal but secret statement made out by apostolic notaries, recording that his oath was conditional on the dauphin keeping his promise to extend the amnesty to all his supporters; and he included a clause, in the letters he sent to the king and dauphin recording his oath, implying that he would only regard it as valid if the Armagnac princes swore similarly and implemented their part of the treaty. Not unnaturally, the dauphin disliked this clause, but John only agreed to remove it, and reissued the letters in September (though still dated 30 July) without it, after he and all but forty-five named Cabochien partisans of his had been formally pardoned by the king on 31 August 1415.[1] But, though he had at last sworn to abide by the terms of the treaty of Arras, John the Fearless, not content with sheltering and maintaining the Cabochien refugees at his court or in his territories, continued through the autumn of 1415 with his attempts to obtain their pardon from the king. His failure was due, not to lack of endeavour on his part, but to the intransigence of a dauphin now firmly under the influence or in the power of the Armagnacs.

It was at this critical point in the internal history of France, when Burgundians and Armagnacs, quibbling over a patched-up peace, were still really in the grips of civil war, that the youthful and

---

[1] Finot, *Paix d'Arras*, no. 18; BN Coll. de Bourg. 55, fos. 173-5 = ACO B11894, letters of 30 July 1415; Plancher, iii. 420-2 and no. 298 etc.; and Juv. des Ursins, *Hist. de Charles VI*, 511-14.

ambitious Henry V of England, one of the most aggressive and shifty products of an age of violence and duplicity, prepared and executed an invasion of France for his own advantage and renown, behind the usual smoke-screen of ambassadors.

John the Fearless's reaction to the English threat was somewhat equivocal: his attitude was conditioned by his previous relationship and negotiations with Henry V. In 1411 and 1412 both parties in France had negotiated one after the other with Henry IV; now, in 1413–14, they were both negotiating with Henry V at the same time, and Catherine of France and Catherine of Burgundy were rivals for his hand. On the whole, Henry IV had been inclined towards the Armagnacs; his son was more of a Burgundian. As the French chronicler, Juvenel des Ursins, observed:[1] 'Even the English princes were divided by the quarrel between Burgundy and Orleans, for the dukes of Clarence and of Gloucester, the king's brothers, and with them the duke of York, favoured the Orleanists; while the king and the duke of Bedford, likewise his brother, were inclined to the Burgundians.'

Throughout the first three years of Henry V's reign, from May 1413 on, Anglo-Burgundian political negotiations were in progress side by side with the commercial negotiations between England and Flanders over the trade truces in the Channel; and side by side, too, with Anglo-French negotiations over Henry V's claims and demands from France. It was in the summer of 1414, when John the Fearless was seriously threatened by the initially successful royal and Armagnac campaign against him which culminated in the siege of Arras, that his negotiations with the king of England became somewhat more earnest. The perfidious Henry V, fully resolved on his French adventure, probably hoped, by negotiating with John in May–September 1414, to convert him into a military ally against France and, by simultaneous negotiation with the dauphin and king, either to trick them into major concessions, or to lull them into a false feeling of security. But John the Fearless, even in May, when he ought to have been willing to make almost any concession in exchange for instant military assistance from England, was aloof and evasive and after September, when he made peace with the Armagnacs at Arras, he withdrew altogether from the negotiations. The points made by the Burgundian and English ambassadors in conference at Leicester in May 1414 were detailed in the so-called treaty of Leicester, which was not a treaty at all. They reveal an atmosphere of intense

[1] *Hist. de Charles VI*, 497.

suspicion, even incredulity, on the English side, and of evident
equivocation on the part of the Burgundians.[1]

Proposals of the Burgundian Ambassadors

1. One of the duke's marriageable daughters, Catherine aged thirteen
   or Anne aged eleven, to marry Henry V.
2. The duke of Burgundy and the king of England to sign a military
   alliance, and each to supply the other, whenever so requested and
   without payment, with 500 men-at-arms or 1,000 bowmen, for
   three months.
3. The duke of Burgundy to help the king of England in the conquest
   of the territories of the count of Armagnac, the lord of Albret and
   the count of Angoulême. Also, the king and duke to conquer jointly
   the lands of the dukes of Orleans, Anjou and Bourbon, and of the
   counts of Alençon, Vertus and Eu.
4. Neither party to make an alliance with any of the above-named
   without the consent of the other.
5. This alliance to be aimed against all, except the king of France, the
   dauphin, and their successors; the dukes of Brabant and Nevers;
   those who are or shall be married to daughters of the duke of Burgundy; the count of Savoy, the count of Hainault, the 'king of
   Spain', and the duke of Brittany.

Questions raised by the English Deputies, with the Burgundian replies

1. Where will the duke of Burgundy's 500 men be recruited from?
   Reply. Burgundy, Picardy and Flanders.
2. If the king of England decides to cross over in person, who will
   command the duke of Burgundy's contingent?
   Reply. The duke of Burgundy himself. The ambassadors were sure
   he would rather lead 1,000 men in person than send 500.
3. If, when King Henry and Duke John were on the battlefield
   together, the king of France ordered the duke to make peace, withdraw, or attack the English, what would his reaction be?
   Reply. In spite of anything his suzerain the king of France might say
   to him, the duke of Burgundy would in no circumstances abandon
   his ally.
4. If the king of France attacked the forces of King Henry and Duke
   John, what would the duke do?

---

[1] Printed, Cartellieri, *SHAWP* iv (1913), no. 9, 12–20, from ACO B296
= PRO E30/1531. Other documents are in *Foedera*, iv (2), 78–80. The most
detailed recent account of the Anglo-Burgundian negotiations of summer
1414 is Calmette and Déprez, *France et Angleterre*, 299–305, which supple-
ments and corrects Wylie and Waugh, *Henry V*, i. 413–16 and others.

Reply. Though they thought they should consult the duke on this point, his ambassadors believed he would try to explain and justify his actions to his suzerain and do all in his power to help his ally.

5. What would the duke do if King Henry did not come in person, but sent one of his brothers, or some other notable captain? *Reply*. He would behave exactly as he would if King Henry was present.

6. Granted that King Henry and Duke John are traversing France victoriously with their armies, how would the duke treat the Armagnac territories they passed through? *Reply*. In an orderly and peaceful way, paying for all victuals.

7. What would the duke's reaction be if, while he was campaigning with King Henry, the king attacked a castle or contingent which belonged to the king of France, rather than his Armagnac enemies? *Reply*. The ambassadors neither dared nor knew how to answer this question without consulting the duke.

8. If, after they have together conquered the Armagnac lands, the king of France attacks them, should King Henry and Duke John assist each other? *Reply*. Yes.

9. If King Henry, after embarking on campaign, found it necessary to return to England, would Duke John still help him? *Reply*. Yes.

10. If this alliance is made, what guarantees will Duke John give for his observance of it? *Reply*. The usual ones—sealed and signed letters, solemn oaths on the Gospels, etc.

When, nearly a year after the failure of these prolonged but fruitless negotiations, King Henry V invaded Normandy, John the Fearless did nothing to help him. He had in fact, in spite of Armagnac claims to the contrary, actually honoured the terms of the treaty of Arras, which he ratified a fortnight before the English landing, by not making an alliance with Henry V. Moreover, in spite of insinuations to the contrary both by contemporary and modern historians, it seems that John the Fearless at first fully intended to join the French army in autumn 1415 in person with all his available troops. This is suggested by the following letter:[1]

Oudenaarde, 10 October 1415. The count of Charolais to the *gens des comptes* at Lille.

---

[1] ADN B17618, letters of 10 October 1415. For what follows this extract, see ADN B17620, letters brought to the *chambre des comptes* on 14 October 1415 from Robert Bourée in Paris; Plancher, iii. 438; and ADN B4090, f. 106b.

Dearest and well-beloved, my father has recently informed me of his
departure with all his power to advance against the English in the service of the king . . . and he wishes to have with him everyone in his
lands who is accustomed to bear arms, including we ourselves in person
and [the knights and squires] of Flanders and Artois. . . .

Moreover an observer in Paris reported on about 11 October 1415
to the *gens des comptes* at Lille that letters from John the Fearless to
the king stating his intention of coming in person at the head of his
troops instead of merely sending a contingent, as the king had asked,
had been read out in the royal council and approved by a majority.
It seems too, that on 12 October John was still preparing to join the
royal army, for he sent an embassy to the king on that day announcing
his mobilization and imminent arrival. Soon after 13 October the
count of Charolais set out from Oudenaarde with the evident intention of joining the royal army assembled at Rouen. But neither father
nor son was present at the battle of Agincourt, fought on 25 October
1415. John himself never set out; Philip of Charolais was restrained
at Aire in Artois, probably on John's orders, from following the
example, and perhaps fate, of his uncle Anthony who, dashing ahead
of his forces in his enthusiasm for battle, arrived virtually alone at
Agincourt and was killed there wearing a chamberlain's armour, a
herald's tabard and no helm.

John the Fearless was by no means the only French prince not
present on the disastrous field of Agincourt. The duke of Brittany
had just the same difficulties in getting there, though he was much
nearer to start with: he somehow found it impossible to advance
beyond Amiens.[1] The battle was regarded with some justification, by
John the Fearless's supporters in Paris, as an Armagnac defeat: after
all, most of the Armagnac leaders were liquidated by it. The duke of
Alençon and the lord of Albret, constable of France, were killed; the
dukes of Orleans and Bourbon were taken prisoner. Yet this shatter-
ing defeat, which so drastically changed the balance of power between England and France, and prepared the way for the conquest
of Normandy by Henry V in 1417-19, had surprisingly little effect
on the internal situation in France. John the Fearless moved slowly
towards Paris in November, hoping for a reaction in his favour, and
in December 1415 he was lodged with a considerable military force
at Lagny-sur-Marne, some twenty miles east of the capital. Yet,
though the atmosphere was tense and more than one Burgundian plot
was unearthed, the government remained firm and the people of

[1] See Knowlson, *Jean V et l'Angleterre*, 95-6.

Paris quiet. The chronicler Juvenel des Ursins gives a lively impression of the situation in Paris in the late autumn of 1415:[1]

> It was rumoured in Paris that those who governed the city at that time—the provost of the merchants and the magistrates—intended, in the event of the duke of Burgundy trying to enter the city, to put to death all those known to sympathize with him. To do this, it was said that they had had 4,000 axes with blades blackened so that they would not be visible by night, and 4,000 black jackets, distributed in various places about the city; and that they had introduced troops into the city to help them carry out this evil intention. . . .
> During several nights in the last week of November the whole city was in fear and on tenterhooks, and not everyone slept all night. The worst [moment] was the Wednesday evening, 4 December, when it was thought that they would execute their plan that night, so much so that the monks of St. Martin-des-Champs and others . . . kept fires burning all night in their houses.

Two weeks later an event occurred which considerably strengthened the Armagnac government in Paris: the dauphin, who, in spite of his youth and debaucheries, had been statesman enough to form a moderate party around himself, and to try to pursue a restrained and pacific policy, fell sick and died on 18 December. The clerk of the court to the Paris *Parlement* provides this pen portrait of him:[2]

> Wednesday, 18 December 1415.
> Today my lord Louis of France, eldest son of our lord the king, dauphin of Vienne and duke of Guienne, died at the age of twenty or thereabouts. Of handsome features, [he was] large and fat of body, heavy and slow, not at all agile, much given to fine clothes and jewels for the adornment of his person. . . . He spent a great deal on ornaments for his private chapel, especially on large and elaborate statuettes of gold and silver. He took very great pleasure in organ music. . . . Recently he had been in the habit of staying up at night, doing very little, and sleeping during the day: he would dine at three or four in the afternoon, sup at midnight, and go to bed at dawn or sunrise. For this reason it did not seem likely that he would live very long.

The death of Louis of Guienne, unlike the battle of Agincourt, had an immediate and decisive effect on John's position and prospects in France. On 27 December Bernard, count of Armagnac, arrived in Paris; on 30 December he became constable of France. All John's hopes of returning to power were dashed to the ground, and the

---

[1] *Hist. de Charles VI*, 524–5.   [2] De Baye, *Journal*, ii. 231–2.

government of France now fell into the hands of his avowed enemies. On 29 January 1416 he decamped from Lagny-sur-Marne and made his way northward to Brabant and Flanders. In spite of a Burgundian plot at Easter 1416; in spite of the oppressive nature of the Armagnac regime in Paris; in spite of all John the Fearless's efforts, he remained totally excluded from power in France throughout the next two years.

During the years 1414–16 the struggle between Armagnacs and Burgundians, between the majority of the French princes of the blood on the one hand, and John the Fearless on the other, was not only fought out on French soil, but was taken to Constance, where prelates from all over Europe had gathered together in October 1414 in an effort to end the schism which had divided the papacy since 1378.[1] The Council of Constance attracted all kinds of disputes besides that between the followers of the rival popes. The French, locked in a deadly military struggle with England, waged ideological warfare at Constance against their secular enemy, and even tried to have the English 'nation' there, as each country's prelates were termed, abolished altogether by merging it with the Germans. Moreover, disputes between the bishop-elect and the civic authorities of Strasbourg, and between the bishop of Trent and Frederick of Habsburg, occupied the attention of the assembled divines when they were not engaged in discussion or controversy over church reform or the extirpation of heresy.

It was due mainly to the aggressive French prelate Jehan Gerson that the case against Jehan Petit and his *Justification du duc de Bourgogne* was taken to Constance in the summer of 1415. A protégé and subject of Philip the Bold, Gerson had shown no overt signs of hostility towards John the Fearless before 1413, when he suffered considerably at the hands of the Cabochiens, who broke into and pillaged his house and forced him to live in hiding for some days in the rafters of Notre-Dame cathedral. It was apparently because of this incident that Gerson, whose belligerent tendencies and inquisitorial energies were also expended on John Hus, the Friars, and others, turned against the Burgundians. From summer 1415 onwards, the work of the Council for church reform, and its efforts to end the papal schism, were constantly interrupted and at times severely hampered by the Burgundian-Armagnac dispute over the

---

[1] For what follows I have used Bess, *Frankreichs Kirchenpolitik* and *ZK* xxxvi (1916), 1–61; Coville, *Petit*; Schoenstedt, *Tyrannenmord im Spätmittelalter*; and Valois, *Schisme*.

doctrines of Jehan Petit, in which of course the honour, the reputation, and the prestige of John the Fearless were closely involved. The results of this struggle at Constance over the condemnation of Jehan Petit were inconclusive, for, though the royal embassy sent there by the Armagnac government in Paris under the leadership of the queen's brother Louis of Bavaria, took up the cause of its most formidable member, Gerson, Jehan Petit was defended with equal tenacity and skill by John the Fearless, who used every conceivable means to protect his interests at the Council. His embassy there consisted of a group of able and respected ecclesiastics and laymen, his councillors, servants or partisans. These men acted under firm instruction from the duke. The bishop of Arras, Martin Porée, was to be president. The members of the embassy were to avoid quarrelling among themselves; they were not allowed to receive gifts of any kind nor to accept invitations to dine or sup outside their lodgings; and they were sworn to secrecy. Their president Martin Porée and another Burgundian ecclesiastic, Pierre Cauchon, who later earned an unenviable place in history as Joan of Arc's judge, resided permanently at Constance. Martin Porée, who left Dijon for Constance on 1 March 1415 and returned to the duke at Troyes on 31 March 1418, was paid during this absence of over three years at the rate of four francs a day, a total for the 1,695 days involved, of 4,500 francs.[1] His colleague Pierre Cauchon was there even longer, for he had set out for Constance on 11 January 1415. Both these men were skilful debaters and ardent supporters of the duke, and the lay members of the embassy seem to have been equally effective. One of them, Gautier de Ruppes, a nobleman from the county of Burgundy, councillor-chamberlain of the duke, in defending John the Fearless against the allegations of Louis of Bavaria, who had accused the duke of Burgundy of a plot against King Sigismund's life, actually achieved the distinction of having his brief but forceful speech in the Council quoted by a chronicler: 'The person who said that, told a lie; the person who says it now, is telling a lie; the person who says it in future, will be lying; and that person is Louis of Bavaria, whom you see here.'

Other methods used by John the Fearless to protect his interests at Constance seem to have included both bribery and force. The bribery is well attested, and this was not only monetary, for plate and jewels, books and quantities of wine were despatched to Constance by him

[1] ACO B1594, fos. 216b–17b. The extract which follows is from de Roye, *Chronique*, 167–8.

and distributed to the prelates assembled there. In one order to pay of 26 July 1415 the purpose of this liberality is clearly stated.[1] 'Eight queues of Burgundy . . . delivered to . . . Pierre Cauchon, vidame of Rheims, who has been and is in embassy for us at Constance, for him to distribute and present this wine on our behalf to several cardinals, archbishops and bishops and other ecclesiastics at the said Council, in order to expedite our affairs there. . . .' As to the use of force, it is hardly surprising that when, in June 1415, some members of the French royal embassy to Constance were arrested and imprisoned at Pagny in Barrois, John the Fearless was accused of complicity in the outrage. Be this as it may, it is clear that the main reason for his success, in avoiding an outright condemnation by the Council of Constance of Jehan Petit and his defence of tyrannicide, was the pertinacity of his ambassadors there. In October 1415 they even managed to pass to the attack, and momentarily turned the tables on Gerson by requesting the detailed examination of twenty-five propositions of a doubtful nature extracted from Gerson's own writings.

Throughout the period when the Armagnac and Burgundian ecclesiastics were locked in battle at Constance, John the Fearless was totally excluded from power in France. But the death of the dauphin Louis of Gienne in December 1416, though it led to the immediate consolidation of the Armagnac government in Paris, provided Duke John with a pretext for intervention in France, since the new dauphin John, duke of Touraine, was married to Jacqueline of Bavaria, the daughter of Duke William of Bavaria, count of Holland and Hainault, and John the Fearless's sister Margaret, at whose court he was residing. John the Fearless's first action after decamping from the neighbourhood of Paris in January 1416 was to confer with Duke William of Bavaria and John of Touraine at Biervliet in Zeeland on 29 February 1416. Apparently John the Fearless favoured a triumphant and armed march on Paris to install the new dauphin there, and of course himself, while William of Bavaria proposed a more pacific approach. At a further conference, at Valenciennes in Hainault in November 1416, John the Fearless, Duke William and the dauphin John entered into a firm alliance, the explicit aim of which was to install the dauphin in Paris with the help of the queen. Implicitly, the restoration of Burgundian rule there was obviously envisaged. But, though William had hoped to take the dauphin to Paris in

---

[1] Coville, *MA* xii (1899), 332. For what follows after this extract, see Jarry, *RHD* vi (1892), 173–93.

person, the plan was delayed by the opposition of the Armagnac government, and then foiled by the dauphin's death on 4 April 1417 and Duke William's on 31 May.[1]

Meanwhile John the Fearless had turned once more to England, though again, as in 1414, no firm treaty was achieved or even probably intended. In July 1416 the existing commercial truce had been reinforced by a treaty of 'abstinence from war' in Picardy and Flanders. This was followed by a meeting at Calais in October between Henry V and John the Fearless. Mutual suspicion and mystery surrounded this conference at the time, and the mystery remains. But it seems that Henry V hoped to achieve what he had attempted in 1414: the conversion of John the Fearless into a useful and active ally in his conquest of France, and even into a vassal of the king of England; while John the Fearless's only firm aim was to avoid any such commitment. He only agreed to go to Calais after suitable measures had been taken to ensure his personal safety.[2]

> The duke of Burgundy went to see the king of England at Calais about certain secret matters which never came to the knowledge of the common people. Arrangements were made for the security of his person during the visit. On leaving the town of St. Omer, he was accompanied by his son the count of Charolais and a large number of knights and squires. They rode in fine array to a stream which flows between St. Omer and Calais, where the king of England's brother, the lord of Gloucester, was waiting well escorted by men-at-arms. The dukes of Burgundy and of Gloucester arrived opposite one another, ready to cross the stream, the duke of Burgundy on the way to Calais, and the duke of Gloucester en route for St. Omer. They did reverence to one another right in the middle of the water, and, after remaining a short while together in the stream, they passed on their respective ways. . . . The duke of Burgundy was escorted to Calais by the English, while the duke of Gloucester was accompanied to St. Omer by the count of Charolais as hostage for the security of the person of the said duke of Burgundy.

It is perhaps hardly surprising that modern scholars have disagreed about what actually happened at the conference of Calais on 7–11 October 1416. After all, the talks were held in the strictest secrecy, and nobody at the time discovered what decisions had been made.

[1] For this paragraph, see especially *Chronique de Tournai*, 358–9, 363 and 365–6; Monstrelet, *Chronique*, iii. 164–8; and Plancher, iii. 452–4. For what follows, see Bonenfant, *Meutre de Montereau*, 11 and notes, and Monstrelet, *Chronique*, iii. 147.
[2] *Chronique des Cordeliers*, 235.

The anonymous English chronicler of Henry V's reign knew no more than his French counterpart quoted above:[1]

> What conclusion was reached by these mysterious discussions and negotiations did not emerge beyond the royal mind or the reticence of the council. I who write this know that the feeling of the people was that the duke had detained our king all this time with evasions and ambiguities and had so left him, and that finally, like all Frenchmen, he would prove to be a double-dealer, one person in public, and another in private.

In fact, the three champion double-crossers of the age were all in Calais together in October 1416, for King Sigismund, the emperor-designate of Germany, was there too. On the diplomatic evidence alone, it is quite clear that no treaty was made, secret or otherwise, between John and Henry V, though some historians have maintained that the document printed by Rymer, which is in fact a draft treaty produced by the English chancery in the hopes that John could be induced to accept it, was a traitorous and 'infernal pact' made by John the Fearless with the English and written in his own hand. It was nothing of the sort. Here is the text:[2]

> John etc. to all those who see or hear these letters, greetings. The most high etc. Henry, by the grace of God king of England, who styles himself king of France, has informed us of his rights and title to the kingdom and crown of France, and how . . . to avoid bloodshed, he asked Charles his adversary of France, to cede the crown and kingdom of France to him . . . to which request his above-mentioned adversary did not wish in any way to assent, nor would he agree to any other peaceful proposal. For this reason the king of England has told us that, with the help of God, Our Lady and Monsieur St. George, he intends to proceed by way of force to the recovery of the kingdom and crown of France. . . .
> We, recognizing the rights of the said king of England etc. and considering the great victories which God of his grace has given . . . to him . . . and to his predecessors . . ., promise by these letters, written

---

[1] *Gesta Henrici quinti*, 103–4.
[2] PRO E30/1609(1), 1609(2), 1068 and 1273 = *Foedera*, iv (2), 177–8. Against Wylie and Waugh, *Henry V*, iii. 28–9, Calmette and Déprez, *France et Angleterre*, 336–7, and even Jacob, *Henry V*, 122 and *BJR* xxvi (1942), 315–16, see for instance Boitel, *PTSEC* (1942), 19 and Bonenfant, *Meutre de Montereau*, 9–10 and especially, 9 n. 5. I have examined the copies of this 'treaty' in the Public Record Office and, needless to say, none of them is sealed or dated, or written in anything remotely resembling the handwriting of John the Fearless. They are drafts only.

with our own hand and sealed with our privy seal . . ., that from now on we desire to support him and we shall support him and his heirs as those who by right are and shall be kings of France. . . .

Although the king of England is refraining from asking us to do homage to him for the time being, though we ought to do it, nevertheless we promise by these presents that, as soon as the king of England, with the help of God, our Lady and Monsieur St. George, has recovered a notable part of the kingdom of France, we shall do him liege homage and [swear an] oath of fealty [to him] just as every subject of the king of France ought to do to his sovereign lord the king of France. . . . And also [we promise] that we shall help him . . . to realize his plan of enjoying actual and peaceable possession of the aforesaid crown and kingdom of France, and that, during the whole time that the king of England is engaged in the reconquest of the said kingdom and crown of France, we shall make war with all our power on our enemies in the kingdom of France, that is, A. A. B. C. D. etc., and on all their people, lands and supporters. . . .

And, so that everyone knows that these our letters proceed from our pure and free will, and that we wish to keep and observe them in each and every point . . . we swear and promise [to do this] by the faith and loyalty of our body and on the word of a prince.

Written and signed with our own hand and sealed with the privy seal . . . at Calais, the   day of October

In spite of this flirtation with the English, and in spite of his plans for making use of the new dauphin, John of Touraine, John the Fearless made little headway during 1416 towards his aim of recovering power in France. The Armagnacs held sway in Paris, subjecting its populace to what hostile chroniclers depicted as a veritable reign of terror, and its burgesses to a series of forced loans.[1] Even in the late summer of 1417, when John the Fearless mounted an all-out military offensive against the capital timed to coincide with the beginning of Henry V's conquest of Normandy, the Armagnacs held firm. Nevertheless, 1417 was a crucial year for John, in the course of which he transformed and immeasurably strengthened his position in France.

Proceedings were opened in characteristic manner: a wordy but forceful manifesto was issued at Hesdin in Artois on 25 April 1417, signed by John the Fearless himself and distributed all round France, but especially to the towns.[2] In this apparently effective and

---

[1] Bossuat, *RHDFE* (4) xxviii (1950), 351–71.
[2] Signed originals are AN J963/7 and in ACO B11895; printed by Plancher, iii, no. 303. This manifesto also found its way into the chronicles of Monstrelet and the Religieux de St. Denys.

certainly vigorous piece of propaganda, John charged the Armagnacs with all sorts of crimes, including the murder of both dauphins and the violation of all the treaties they had ever made. He also accused them of deliberately permitting Henry V to invade France and win the battle of Agincourt! He called on all those loyal to the crown to join him in attacking them, and promised to abolish or reduce taxation. This document, which inaugurated a renewed Burgundian-Armagnac civil war, ended as follows:

We promise you, by the faith and loyalty which we owe to God, to my lord [the king] and to the common good of his kingdom, that our only intention and desire is to do all in our power to ensure that neither the king nor his kingdom are ruined by the above-mentioned [Armagnac] traitors, destroyers, pillagers and poisoners. . . . By these presents we offer peace to all those who want to enjoy it with us . . . in the pursuit of our good intention, which is directed towards the welfare of my lord [the king] and his kingdom. . . . We shall persevere until death in this holy, loyal and necessary task, without any further delay or lenience in dealing with the said traitors, destroyers and poisoners, for this business has already been delayed too long. Everyone must fully appreciate that they are determined to destroy the said noble house of France, the nobility, and, in general, everyone in this kingdom. . . . We shall do everything in our power [to ensure] that in future [the people] pay no taxes, forced loans, subsidies, impositions, salt-duty or any other exactions. . . .
In witness of this, we have signed these presents with our own hand. . . . Given in our castle of Hesdin on 25 April 1417.　　　Jehan

The civil war that followed in the summer and autumn of 1417 consisted, in the main, of a process of piecemeal conquest and persuasion, whereby many of the principal towns of France were won over to John the Fearless. Gradually the Burgundian ring round Paris tightened, but the Armagnac government there held firm, even in September and October, when John the Fearless actually marched his army right round the capital, approaching as near as Versailles, and virtually reducing Paris to a state of siege. The accompanying map illustrates the pattern and chronology of the recruitment of the French towns to the Burgundian interest or their conquest by Burgundian troops. While all this was going on, incidentally, the English were quietly embarking on the conquest of Normandy.

John the Fearless's treatment of the French towns in the summer and autumn of 1417 varied considerably. Some went over to him without a blow, while others, like Lyons, remained firmly Armagnac and obeyed the government's instructions to send his letters to Paris

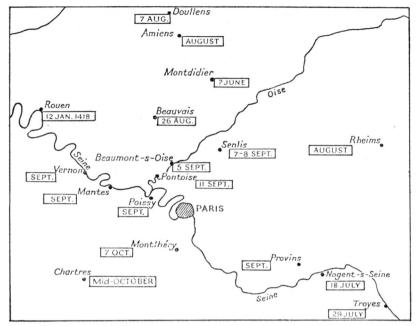

6. The fall of French towns to John the Fearless in 1417

unopened.[1] At Tournai, which was almost an enclave in Burgundian territory, the magistrates found themeslves skating on very thin ice indeed. A resolution they made on 1 July 1417 shows that they recognized the delicacy of their situation: 'Agreed that it was desirable that the town should hold out firmly for the king, provided that it could also remain in the good grace of my lord of Burgundy.' With those towns which were willing to submit to John the Fearless a treaty was often made, like that with Doullens near Amiens, of 7 August 1417, which happens to be preserved in the pages of Monstrelet. Its terms were roughly as follows:

1. The magistrates and burgesses of Doullens will help the duke of Burgundy in his efforts to restore the king to the full enjoyment of his power.

---

[1] Caillet, *AUL* (2) xxi (1909) and Déniau, *Commune de Lyon*. For Tournai, see Houtart, *Les Tournaisiens et le roi de Bourges* and Champion and de Thoisy, *Bourgogne–France–Angleterre*, 156–66. The extract is from *Extraits analytiques*, 134–5, and the Doullens treaty is in Monstrelet, *Chronique*, iii. 184–7.

2. They agree to allow the duke and his troops free access to their town, and to provide them, against payment, with whatever provisions or necessities they may require.

3. The duke promises not to imprison any inhabitant of Doullens without trial.

4. All citizens of Doullens to have free passage through the territories of the duke of Burgundy.

5. The town of Doullens promises not to admit any garrison from the enemies of the duke, and to punish anyone hindering or injuring him.

In almost every French town Burgundians and Armagnacs were both represented, and the question of whether or not a given town would opt for John the Fearless or the Armagnacs, often resolved itself into a struggle between the two parties inside the city walls. A letter sent jointly to the duchess of Burgundy on 1 August 1417 by a knight and a senior civil servant of John the Fearless's, Antoine de Toulongeon and Jehan Fraignot, describing the fall of Troyes to the Burgundians, illustrates this well. Here, the Armagnacs were in a minority.[1]

Most redoubted lady, we recommend ourselves to you as humbly as we can. . . . May it please you to know . . . that last Wednesday my lords of Argueil, of Neufchastel and other knights and captains of our contingent, wrote . . . to the clergy, burgesses and inhabitants of the town of Troyes asking them what they intended to do about our lord [the duke]'s letters patent expounding . . . his solicitude for the welfare of the king, but there was no reply to these letters. For this reason, last Thursday morning [29 July 1417] we went to the gates of Troyes with Sir Gautier de Ruppes and Sir Henri de Champdivers . . . to ask for a reply. We arrived at about the hour of prime and there, that is to say at the gate of the suburb of Croncel, the bailiff came to parley with us. He could not have had more than thirty persons with him, all of them [Armagnacs]. . . . Although we talked with the said bailiff a long time about these [ducal] letters . . . which had earlier been sent to Troyes, and which he had not permitted to be published or read aloud before the people, [and although] we asked him for leave to enter the town in order to read and publish these letters . . . nevertheless the bailiff would not do anything. We were saddened and angered by this but, after his reply and departure, we found means to enter quite easily into the said suburb of Croncel, and we found our way through it with some other knights and squires to the city gate, which the bailiff had closed. . . . Because the crowd of people who had gathered within the city, near this gate, having

---

[1] *Itinéraires*, 610–12.

heard about the ducal letters . . . and wanting to ascertain their contents, became hostile to the bailiff and his partisans, and because of the intervention of certain influential individuals who had the duke's interests at heart, some of the citizens came to parley with us, and to such good effect that within an hour we entered the city of Troyes. Before the people gathered there, who numbered some six or seven thousand persons . . ., the duke's letters were read out aloud by me Fraignot . . . in the principal square of Troyes, called the Cornmarket. . . . After this the crowd, in very happy and joyous mood, cried out 'Noel! Long live the king and the duke of Burgundy!'

[Some time after this], with the agreement of the townspeople I, Toulongeon, was appointed to the guard and government of the said town, which has made a complete submission, and is and will be entirely for our lord [the duke], as has been promised and agreed by the people. . . .

The actual fighting, in the summer of 1417, was confused, sporadic and indecisive. There were no pitched battles, though a number of towns only fell to John the Fearless after a more or less prolonged siege. Chartres, for instance, held out a month. Corbeil resisted stoutly for a fortnight, and then saw the Burgundians decamp at the end of October. An incident described by an anonymous chronicler is probably typical of many:[1]

While the duke of Burgundy was on his way to Tours [at the end of October 1417], and most of his troops remained in their lodgings in the villages around Chartres, the Armagnacs in garrison at Dreux and Dourdan sallied forth one night at dawn and forced their way into a village called Sours about two leagues from Chartres, where the bastard of Thian was lodged, guarding the lord of Inchy's standard. . . . The Armagnacs did a great deal of damage in the village and seized a number of people in their beds. . . . They also took all the horses, equipment and other things . . . and captured the lord of Inchy's standard and took it away with them.

Now it so happened that the lord of Inchy's brother and the said bastard escaped capture and, after the Armagnacs had left, the bastard sounded his trumpet to rally those who had fled from his hôtel. He soon had some twenty horses with him and, swearing that he would never return until he had discovered who it was who had carried off his brother's standard, he set out after them without delay, still sounding his trumpet. At that moment, men-at-arms of other Picard lords, such as those of [Sir Jehan de] Luxembourg and the lord of Antoing and others, lodged in the neighbouring villages, were on their guard,

---

[1] *Chronique des Cordeliers*, 243–4.

having been woken up by the noise which the Armagnacs had made, and when they noticed the said bastard pursuing them, some of them decided to follow. They mounted their horses, calling out to one another, to such good effect that the bastard found himself strong enough to attack the men who had despoiled him. And he rode so hard, he and those who had followed him, that they caught up with their enemies and then assaulted them so vigorously that they defeated them all, captured most of them, and recovered the shaft of their standard. . . . The standard of the bastard of Ste. Terre, who was the captain of these Armagnacs, was taken to Chartres and hung up in the cathedral there, in front of the statue of our Lady.

Although the Armagnac government in Paris was reinforced at this time by the emergence of a youthful leader and figurehead, the new dauphin Charles, appointed royal lieutenant-general on 6 November 1417,[1] nevertheless, John the Fearless's efforts to overthrow the government and seize the capital came within a hair's breadth of success. The nearest he got to it was on 23 November, when a carefully-laid plot was treacherously revealed to the government at the last moment:

The duke of Burgundy and his partisans were always trying to find some way of entering Paris. There was a gang of people consisting of a cleric and some wicked Parisians, who planned to let him in on a certain day through the Porte Bourdelle, and they hatched their plot in a house near this gate. Some said that a locksmith of their company forged some keys, and that they had files, muffled saws . . . and [other] instruments for secretly opening the aforesaid gate. They fixed the day and hour for doing this, and let the duke of Burgundy know . . . and he promised to bring or send troops at the appointed time, and that he himself would approach. . . . And he did indeed send troops and approach himself, at the time agreed and, among other captains of war, he sent the valiant knight Sir Hector de Saveuse there.

Now it is true that there was a furrier in the rue St. Jacques, who was in the conspiracy; but, when he thought about the troubles that might ensue, he went to see Sir Tanguy du Chastel, the provost of Paris, on the very evening that the plot was due to be carried into effect, and offered to disclose a conspiracy against the city to him, provided he would pardon him for what he had done wrong. The provost promised what he asked and also promised to reward him, whereupon he related what has been said above, and told him that he would find the conspirators at

---

[1] *Ords. des rois*, x. 424–6. The extract which follows is from Juv. des Ursins, *Hist. de Charles VI*, 538–9. Cf. Relig. de St. Denys, vi. 158–60.

about 10.0 p.m. in the house of Master Jaques Braulart, who was a councillor of the king in the *Parlement*.

The provost . . . went to this house and found them there. They were all arrested and taken to the Châtelet, and a guard was put over the gate, and reinforced with some Parisian crossbow-men, armed with very powerful crossbows. When the Burgundian troops arrived, Sir Hector de Saveuse and his men were among the first. They were received with a volley of shots, Sir Hector was wounded, and they had to withdraw. Of those taken to the Châtelet, a number were executed.

Even before the failure of this plot, John the Fearless had brought off a coup which immeasurably strengthened his position in France: he had lured or rescued the queen from the hands of her Armagnac custodians. He joined her at Tours on 2 November and, during the winter of 1417–18, first at Chartres and then at Troyes, duke and queen together set up a rival and alternative government of France to that of the dauphin Charles and the Armagnac princes in Paris. A spate of proclamations explained and justified these proceedings to the French people: 11 November 1417, the queen writes to the towns exhorting them to obey her and the duke of Burgundy; 10 January 1418, the queen empowers John, duke of Burgundy, to govern France on the king's behalf with the same powers as she herself enjoys; 16 February 1418, the *Parlement* and *chambre des comptes* at Paris are formally abolished and new ones set up at Troyes.[1]

At the same time, the new administration of France was staffed with Burgundian partisans and servants and councillors of John the Fearless, and the revenues of France were taken over and entrusted to a Burgundian civil servant, Pierre Gorremont. In Languedoc, which John the Fearless had lost in 1413 when, soon after his flight from Paris in August, the duke of Berry had been reappointed governor on 29 October, he now strove to regain his power, and, by the spring of 1418, a large part of the country had recognized the new government of duke and queen at Troyes.

Meanwhile in Paris, still held in the iron grip of Bernard, count of Armagnac and constable of France, and still nominally ruled by the dauphin Charles, the end was not long in coming. During the spring of 1418 the Burgundian net, already cast round it in 1417, was drawn relentlessly tighter. In May, two cardinals arrived on a peace-making

[1] Monstrelet, *Chronique*, iii. 230–4; Plancher, iii. no. 302; *Ords. des rois*, x. 436–43. See, in general, Pocquet, *France gouv. par J. sans Peur*, and, for the next paragraph, *Recueil de diverses pièces*, 79–80, and Dognon, *AM* i (1889), 433–509.

mission from the new pope, Martin V, but, compared with the obvious sincerity of the dauphin's government, the attitude of John and Queen Isabel was evasive to the point of truculence: they were winning and they knew it. At a conference on 23 May the ambassadors of the queen and the duke of Burgundy proposed the following:[1]

1. A general amnesty.
2. Revocation of all confiscations.
3. Return of all goods to rightful owners.
4. Offices in the French government to be disposed of with the advice of the duke of Burgundy and the queen.
5. The queen, the duke of Burgundy, and the other princes to have free access to the king.
6. The queen's acts of the previous six months to remain in force.

The ambassadors of the dauphin and the king agreed to all these points, though they asked for the addition of the phrase 'and of the other princes and the council' to the fourth article. They went on to make some very reasonable proposals of their own, but the Burgundian ambassadors' replies to these proposals show that John the Fearless's intention was far from peaceful.

Proposals of the Dauphin's Ambassadors with the Burgundian replies

1. The duke of Burgundy to return all royal towns and castles occupied by him.
   Reply. In occupying these castles the queen and duke of Burgundy have no intention of depriving the king and dauphin of them. They are held on the king's behalf.
2. All other castles and places, wrongfully seized or held by any of the princes, to be restored to their rightful owners.
   Reply. This is covered by the second of our proposals, revoking all confiscations.
3. The duke of Burgundy to annul all his infringements of royal rights, including his establishment of a court of *Parlement* and *chambre des comptes* at Troyes.
   Reply. This is covered by the sixth of our proposals, leaving the queen's acts in force.
4. The duke of Burgundy to renounce all pacts, truces and conventions

---

[1] Relig. de St. Denys, vi. 208–22 and de Fenin, *Mémoires*, 255–67. My summary follows the text in de Fenin.

he may have made with the king of the Romans, the English, or other enemies of France.

Reply. In this matter, the duke of Burgundy has never done anything disloyal, and he will always remain a loyal vassal and servant of the king of France.

5. The duke of Anjou and the queen of Sicily and all the other royal princes are to be included in the peace.

Reply. Agreed, reserving to the duke of Burgundy the pursuit of his own interests.

The final coup, the seizure of Paris, was being meditated and planned by John under cover of these specious peace negotiations. Indeed the replies of his ambassadors just quoted were probably couched on purpose in terms which the dauphin and constable were bound to reject, thus bringing on themselves, in the eyes of the people, the odium of refusing to make peace. Paris actually fell to the Burgundians during the night of 28-29 May, but the dauphin escaped in his nightshirt to the Bastille, with the help of the provost of Paris. These dramatic events are narrated, rather drily, by the new clerk of the court at the Paris *Parlement*, Clément de Fauquembergue, who had succeeded Nicholas de Baye in 1417.[1]

Sunday, 29 May 1418

My lords Claude de Chastellux, Guy de Bar, Jehan de Villiers the lord of l'Isle-Adam, knights, servants and officers of the duke of Burgundy, accompanied by some 200 men-at-arms, entered the city of Paris through the Porte St. Germain-des-Prés, which had been secretly opened for the lord of l'Isle-Adam by a group of nine or ten common people, between one and two hours after midnight. Some of these people went to the royal hôtel de St. Pol and remained there to guard the king; others went to the rue St. Honoré to arrest and imprison the count of Armagnac; and some went to different parts of the city to seize various officers of the king, the dauphin, the count of Armagnac, and others who had been concerned with the government of this kingdom. Many of these were captured, but some of those who escaped led my lord the dauphin [safely] into the Bastille St. Antoine. Others did not have time to get there. Many were arrested in Paris on this and the succeeding days, including the count of Armagnac, then constable of France, [and several of his captains and officers] . . . also Henri de Marle, chancellor of France . . ., the archbishops of Rheims and Tours, and the bishops of

---

[1] *Journal*, i. 126-7. See too, on this and what follows, besides the chroniclers, de Fenin, *Mémoires*, 268-9; Vielliard, *ABSHF* (1940), 124-53; Garnier, *BSHP* iv (1877), 47-53; and ADN B17624, letter of 31 May 1418.

Laon, Lisieux and Evreux. . . . On this occasion the [Burgundian] troops met with no resistance, and there were only two or three persons killed in the streets of Paris. These, it was said, had tried to rally support for the count of Armagnac by shouting 'Long live Armagnac!' in the presence of the [Burgundian] troops.

Although the dauphin Charles was only fifteen, he seems to have acted in this crisis with some decision and vigour, and within a few days of the Burgundian coup he launched a counter-attack on Paris which came very near to success. An account of this, sent to King Alfonso V of Aragon by an Aragonese knight in King Charles VI's service who took part in the enterprise, has survived. It reads in part as follows:[1]

Then the dauphin sent a messenger to the marshal of France, who was at Meaux in Brie, some ten leagues away . . . with 700 men. As soon as he received the dauphin's message he left, and we took the road for Paris, as the dauphin had ordered us. When we arrived at the bridge of Charenton, two leagues from Paris, we found the dauphin already there. Altogether we were about 1,000 men-at-arms or a little less. Upon my faith, señor, there was nobody in the world who would not have taken pity on the dauphin at that time, seeing him in the state we found him in. He was in the middle of a field with two other people, without any armour or arms . . ., with a wretched coat, and an even more wretched hat on his head, despoiled of all his kingdom by his own vassals. . . . No one would have guessed who he was, seeing him in this state.

He held council . . . and, though the most pressing matter was the personal security of the dauphin himself, it was agreed that since the Bastille St. Antoine was held for him, they would try to regain Paris through it or lose everything rather than live in this way. It was recognized that there were as many people in Paris favourable to the dauphin as there were rebels against him and that, with the men-at-arms already there, numbering 700, and we ourselves, numbering 1,000, we would give them confidence. This was an enterprise of rash young people rather than wise men but, with an enthusiasm born of desperation and in order to rescue the constable, all were prepared for martyrdom.

The thing was resolved on and organized in the following way. That very evening, which was the Tuesday [31 May] after the rebellion of Paris, the marshal of France with 300 men would enter the Bastille on foot, while the dauphin, with the rest of the force, mounted, would proceed to the Porte St. Antoine. The infantry was to leave the Bastille at dawn on Wednesday and enter Paris and, while some held off the enemy, others were to open the Porte St. Antoine. If it could be opened, the

---

[1] Vielliard, *ABSHF* (1940), 137–53.

provost of Paris, who was much feared in the city, was to enter first, with 300 men-at-arms. . . . Then, my lord of Barbazan and Perron de Luppé with 200 men-at-arms would follow after them, and the dauphin would enter with 2,000 more men-at-arms. . . . The thing was well planned, but more was needed than just thinking it out.

Towards midnight, we entered the Bastille with the marshal and 300 men-at-arms and, at dawn, the dauphin arrived before the Porte St. Antoine. Then the marshal, who in truth is a notable and valiant knight, made a sortie from the Bastille, while 100 men were ordered to attack the Porte St. Antoine and open it. They went there and met some fifty Parisians guarding the gate, who did not give way without first making use of their arms. Some of [our men] were killed, but the party got hold of the keys, opened the gate and lowered the drawbridge.

Those of us with the marshal numbered 200 men-at-arms and, while the gate was being opened, we advanced along the rue St. Antoine in the best possible order. The first encounter we had was with the Burgundian watch posted near the bombards which were trained on the Bastille. They numbered about fifteen men-at-arms, but they were asleep when we came across them and we soon got rid of them. Then, continuing our advance, we met with the main watch, perhaps seventy or eighty men-at-arms with a standard. They began to defend themselves behind their barrier, but we captured their standard and, upon my faith, I don't think many of them escaped, for the marshal would not allow us to take prisoners. . . . These men discomfited, we advanced again and at another barrier we met with a few men who looked as if they might be going to defend themselves, but were too polite to wait for us. In truth, señor, it was as if we were entering a deserted city as we rode the whole way down the street to the church of St. Antoine. There we stopped for two reasons: mainly because of fatigue, but also because many of our men, having lost all their belongings in Paris, had entered the houses for purposes of plunder. This was true to such an extent, señor, that upon my faith there were only 100 men-at-arms left around the marshal's standard where we had halted. . . .

At this juncture, the Porte St. Antoine was open and the provost entered . . . and advanced further than us, as far as the Porte Baudet. After him my lord of Barbazan entered and followed the same route. All this señor, was not done without taking up a considerable time, during which the news spread round Paris, and the cry went up that the Armagnacs were entering. What was worse, and proved our undoing, rumour had it that we were massacring the inhabitants just like the Burgundians, and that we were sacking the town.

In fact, the Burgundian troops now assembled and, with those of the city, attacked the provost. . . ., and things came to such a pass that the provost's standard, together with six others (for my lord of Barbazan had already joined forces with him), turned in full flight with all the men-at-arms. As for us, who were on foot, and waiting for the dauphin to enter, your majesty can imagine our joy when we saw our cavalry flee—especially as we were tired and far from safety, with half our contingent dispersed in the houses. What was worse for us was that, while we were withdrawing, our own people came upon us in the middle of the street and, in their haste to pass, showed no more regard for us than for strangers. They rode at full tilt through our midst, knocking people over here and there, so that it was our own people who discomfited us and, upon my faith, I believe that, without them, the Burgundians would not have done us great harm. . . .

With the seizure of Paris at the end of May 1418, John the Fearless also seized control of the government of France. His position was further consolidated by means of a reign of terror in Paris, where the count of Armagnac, the chancellor of France, and nearly all the Armagnacs who could be found were put to death in brutal and revolting circumstances. Not until the turmoil of mob enthusiasm and riot which accompanied this process had begun to subside did John and Queen Isabel enter Paris in triumph on 14 July, with the accompaniment of a suitable demonstration of military force. An anonymous letter-writer describes the event.[1]

May it please you to know that on Thursday, the fourteenth day of this month, at about four o'clock in the afternoon, the queen and my lord of Burgundy, who was always as close as possible to her carriage, entered the city in the following manner.

First, about 1,200 burgesses of Paris, all dressed in blue, were drawn up in fine order nearly half-way to the bridge of Charenton. In front of them passed the advance-guard, in which there were about 1,500 archers, marching together in close array. Next came five standards accompanied by 1,000 men-at-arms from Picardy, led by Sir Jehan de Luxembourg, the lord of Fosseux, the vidame of Amiens, the lord of Aucourt and other nobles from Artois. Afterwards came a column led by my lords of Arlay and St. Georges, in which there was only one standard, that of the duke of Burgundy, comprising at least 1,500 men-at-arms, with their lances adorned with planes. . . .

All these proceeded through the city as far as the Louvre, where the queen and my lord [the duke of Burgundy] . . . knelt before the king, who stepped forward and embraced the queen with the words 'You are most welcome.' Then he said to my lord [the duke], 'Fair cousin, you are very welcome'; and he thanked him for what he had done for the queen. . . . There were many people there who wept for pity. Finally, wine and spices were brought, but neither the queen nor my lord [the

---

[1] Longnon, *BSHP* ii (1875), 104–9.

duke] would eat or drink. . . . Then . . . the duke saw the que͟c
room, and went to stay in his hôtel d'Artois. After this, on the follᵤ
Friday, which was yesterday, a deputation from the University came
excuse themselves for their hostile actions towards my lord [the duke],
claiming that they were the fault of adversity, not the University.

As to the government of Paris, of those who were open Armagnacs,
some have been killed, others imprisoned, and still others have fled and
their houses have been pillaged and robbed. . . . As to offices, there are
six applicants for every post. Everything is in the control of my lord of
Burgundy. May God by his grace give him salvation for his soul and
good government for the well-being and honour of the king and himself,
Amen.

Although the refugee of 1413, attacked in his own territories and
wholly excluded from French affairs, had skilfully repaired his broken
fortunes, and in the summer of 1418 had returned triumphantly to
Paris, yet his power in France was by no means unlimited or un-
questioned. The pre-eminence, and the easy exploitation of French
resources, which John the Fearless had enjoyed in the years before
August 1413, were no longer even possible. Now, the bitter memories
of civil war in the intervening years; the open violence of both sides;
the flagrant duplicity of almost everyone concerned, had brought
about a deeply and bitterly divided France. Above all, the new
dauphin Charles had refused to be submerged in the tide of Burgundian victory. Although a mere boy, he had already behaved like a
hero, and now, defying his parents, the duke of Burgundy, and almost
all his other relatives, he set up a kind of provisional government in
exile at Bourges, supported not only by a band of stalwart knights,
but also by a considerable proportion of the population of France,
covering a wide area south of Paris. In fact, though the capital and
the government were now Burgundian, France as a whole had eluded
John the Fearless—as it turned out, for ever.

CHAPTER NINE

The European Ruler

In everything but the title of king, John the Fearless was a European monarch. That is to say, he acted in Europe in his own interests as an independent ruler. He wielded as much influence, or power, as the other rulers of his time; he took part in their conferences and made alliances and diplomatic contacts as he chose; he sent deputations to church Councils and he maintained the court life typical of a great prince. Burgundy, along with Aragon and Castile, France and England, Venice and Genoa, was one of the major powers of the west European continent. Her ruler, influential in France and master through family connections or direct rule of most of the Netherlands, was one of the dominant figures of the age.

The purpose of this chapter is to examine John the Fearless as a ruler and to analyse his position and power in Europe. It is proposed to review in turn his character as a ruler, his aims and his court; to investigate the additions of territory he made to the Burgundian state; to show how he utilized and promoted family or matrimonial connections; and, finally, to look at some of the diplomatic contacts he made and maintained with the other European powers.

The ruler and his court

John the Fearless's aims as a ruler were similar to those of his contemporaries: he wanted to augment his own power, extend the influence and wealth of his house and consolidate his family's position in Europe. He may not have thought of his lands as forming an independent political entity, but he certainly thought of them as Burgundian, not French, and as his own. His father Philip the Bold had created or presided over the emergence of a new power for himself and his family; John aimed to consolidate it, and he succeeded. If, as some have maintained, John the Fearless was a typical French prince, he was typical only in the sense that he was out for himself for, as the chronicler put it, the French princes at that time 'were only concerned with their own private advantage'.[1] Like most medieval and many more recent rulers, John the Fearless placed first, and above all else, the pursuit of his own interests and those of his house. Some historians have drawn attention to John the Fearless's activities in France and suggested that French affairs occupied his energies to the detriment of his own interests and those of Burgundy but, as a matter of fact, the murder of Louis of Orleans not only permitted John to make freer use of the material resources of France, it also permitted his brother Duke Anthony of Brabant to annex the duchy of Luxembourg. The future of Burgundy in a large measure depended on the exploitation or at least the friendship of France, and the influential position there which had been enjoyed by Philip the Bold was bound to be sought after by his son. Thus the impulse behind the struggle for power in France was neither an attempt on the French throne, nor mere lust for power in France, it was specifically Burgundian. John the Fearless was compelled to intervene in France by the situation he inherited, by circumstances, and by the interests and financial needs of himself and his house. But intervention, as so often happens, led to involvement. He was drawn further and further into the vortex of French events, until at last personal disaster overtook him and he fell victim, on the bridge of Montereau, to the very hatreds and passions which he had initially stirred up to suit his own ends.

What were the personal characteristics of John the Fearless as a man and as a ruler? His more apparent qualities, or weaknesses, have often been described. He was violent and unscrupulous, brutal and cruel, ambitious and hypocritical. In all this, he was no different from the other rulers of those days, though some may feel that his recourse to political assassination, or tyrannicide, as Jehan Petit euphemistically put it, has left a more enduring stain on his character than that suffered, for instance, by King Sigismund, in permitting John Hus to be burnt at Constance while bearing his safe-conduct. One quality which John the Fearless completely lacked was prudence.

[1] Juv. des Ursins, *Hist. de Charles VI*, 430, 'ne pensoient qu'à leurs profits particuliers'; see above, p. 29. On this paragraph, see especially d'Avout, *Armagnacs et Bourguignons*, 105; Bess, *Frankreichs Kirchenpolitik*, 4; Bonenfant, *Meutre de Montereau*, 1–2 and 2, n. 3; Heimpel, *GWU* iv (1953), 258; Mirot, *RQH* xcv (1914), 338; Pirenne, *Hist. de Belgique*, ii. 225–6; Rössler, *OW* v (1958), 127–8; Steinbach, *RV* ix (1939), 62–3; and, above all, Pocquet, *AB* xiv (1942), 181–96 and *RUB* vii (1954–5), 385–404, and David, *Du nouveau sur Jean sans Peur*, 45, 48 and 87.

He was a masterful opportunist who acted impulsively, with speed and decision, on the spur of the moment. As a ruler, one of his principal failings was his inability, or refusal, to weigh the consequences of his actions.

There was something insidious or stealthy about John the Fearless, an element of cunning, which some of the chroniclers noticed, and which was reflected in his use of spies, his passion for secrecy, the various conspiracies he organized, and in his devious diplomacy. More evident, even than this, was John the Fearless's suspicious nature. He lived in fear of his life; he was apprehensive and nervous by temperament; he trusted no one.[1] In Paris he locked himself up in the famous tower of the hôtel d'Artois and employed a bodyguard whenever he went out. The assassin, who died by assassination, lived in fear of it; his surname sans Peur is a mockery of reality.

The dark and sinister element in John the Fearless's reputation as a ruler was exploited to the utmost by his enemies long before the eye of history began to see him as a depraved and execrable tyrant. The following letter, evidently circulated by the Armagnacs, was copied out by a diligent though obscure chronicler, and has even found its way into print:[2]

Lucifer, emperor of the deep Acheron, king of hell, duke of Erebus and Chaos, prince of the Shadows, marquis of Barathrum and of Pluto, count of Gehenna, master, regent, guardian and governor of all the devils in hell and of those mortal men alive in the world who prefer to oppose the will and commandment of our adversary Jesus Christ, to our dearest and well-loved lieutenant and proctor-general in the West, John of Burgundy. . . .

We pray and request, indeed we order and command, you to persevere, as you have begun, in obeying and carrying out the wishes of Satan. Ever since you were old enough to carry arms, we have given you —and we do give you by these presents—full power and irrevocable authority, and we are very well informed of your evil enterprises, which we shall help you to accomplish. Rest assured that we shall keep the promises which we have made to you . . . through the . . . grand proctor of our court, Satan, inviolably and without fault. Furthermore, we wish you to know that our court is completely void of devils in our service,

---

[1] De la Marche (Mémoires, i. 83) says he 'fut homme subtil, doubteux et souppechonneux, et ne se fioit pas en chascun'. For his character and interests, see especially Mirot, ABSHF (1938), 129–245 and JS (1942), 66–81.

[2] Durrieu, ABSHF xxiv (1887), 193–224.

[because] they have all entered the hearts of your trusted people, accomplices and allies. . . .

It is true that the greatest joy and pleasure that we can have is in the destruction . . . of churches, cathedrals . . ., abbeys, monasteries, chapels, oratories and all buildings dedicated to the honour and reverence of our adversary Jesus Christ, and you deserve praise for the good start you have made with this. . . . After you have carried out our orders in the area of your commission . . . we shall help you to cross the sea . . . and then we shall cause you to be crowned king of Turkey, emperor of Constantinople . . ., king of Jerusalem, Babylon and Carthage and of several other kingdoms, both christian and pagan. . . .

In witness of this we have sealed these presents with our very horrible signet, present several troops of devils, in our most dismal consistory . . . in the year of our doleful reign six thousand six hundred and six.

To return to reality: of John the Fearless's more statesmanlike qualities, his approachability, and his interest in and apparent respect for the opinions of his officials, is noteworthy. Far from being arbitrary and despotic, he appears, in his relations with councillors and servants, as cautious and enlightened, and even deferent. How else can one explain the tone of this letter, written to him by his councillor, Thierry Gherbode, in September 1409?[1]

Most redoubted lord, I recommend myself to you as humbly as I can. May it please you to know, my most redoubted lord, that the day before yesterday, when I returned from Bruges . . . I found here [at Lille] in my hôtel a letter-close, delivered in my absence, written by you on the ninth of this month, in which you were pleased to ask me to . . . engross the judgement recently delivered in your town of Lille by you and my lord of Hainault your brother [-in-law], and send it to you without fault or delay.

As to this, may it please you to know, my most redoubted lord, that, although in this and all other matters I am ready to obey your commands . . . nevertheless . . ., to be truthful, I am not aware that this judgement has [yet] been made out in draft, nor have I been in a position to take advice and collate the text in order to publish it in the form of letters [as you require]. Moreover, my most redoubted lord, even if I had made out the draft of this judgement . . . it would still be necessary, in my humble opinion . . . to have it examined and discussed most carefully before it is engrossed in the form of letters. . . .

This letter shows that John the Fearless's officials were by no means afraid on occasion to give him advice, or to protest mildly at

[1] Thomas, *RH* cxviii (1915), 309–11.

some of his more drastic administrative procedures. Once, at least, John organized a large-scale consultation among his civil servants. This was in 1412, when the project of making Besançon the administrative capital of the county of Burgundy was, as it were, put to the vote of the senior civil servants of the two Burgundies. They resolved against the project, and this decision was respected by the duke.[1]

In spite of the dramatic and violent events in which he became involved in France, where he was able, incidentally, to put his skill in military matters to good use, John the Fearless was keenly interested in the administration of his own territories. Even in France he appeared as a reformer as well as a party leader; after all, he was the instigator of the famous *ordonnance Cabochienne*. In Burgundy we have already had occasion to examine his reforms or reforming projects in both the northern and southern territories: he reorganized his artillery; he set up special financial commissions; he reformed the *transport* or taxation of Flanders; he issued detailed instructions regulating the procedure and behaviour of his councillors and officials. True, he often went too far, but all this points clearly to a certain enthusiasm for reform, a definite interest in the administration and good government of his lands. As to their rule in general, he established an arrangement which had been adumbrated by his father Philip the Bold. A kind of federal or family organization was set up, and worked admirably. In the northern territories, John's eldest child and only legitimate son, Philip, count of Charolais, resided and ruled; in the south, his capable wife, Margaret of Bavaria, did so. John the Fearless himself followed his father's example and remained, at least when this was politically possible, in Paris. The hôtel d'Artois there was not just a centre of French intrigue, it was the seat of the government of Burgundy, and there is abundant evidence to show that John, while he was there, kept in constant touch with his wife and son, and that they never acted in important matters without his advice. In fact, John ruled Burgundy from the most convenient place, Paris, where he could be in equally close contact with both groups of territories. At the same time, he obviated many of the disadvantages of the geographical division of his lands by appointing his wife and son as his representatives there.

Although the character and interests of Philip the Bold and John the Fearless certainly differed, historians have over-emphasized the contrast between the chivalrous, generous, statesmanlike patron of

[1] Above, pp. 13–14 and 184–6.

the arts, who founded the Charterhouse of Champmol, and his mean, cunning, unscrupulous and brutal successor. We can hardly expect to find one of them patronizing the artists and musicians of the day, and not the other, for all the princes of those days patronized artists and book-illuminators, just as all of them worshipped elaborately, gave alms generously, and spent large sums of money on New Year's Gifts for each other. The assumption, or assertion, for instance, that under John the Fearless 'musical activities' at the Burgundian court 'were reduced to a minimum', is completely unfounded.[1] A group of secular musicians regularly belonged to John's household, and on Christmas Eve 1412 the duke hired Master Nicolas Grenon as chaplain, and specifically charged him with looking after and teaching music to Cousin Dupuy, Jehan Dupuy, Philibert l'Arbalestrier and Jehan Pousset, former choir-boys of the duke of Berry, now retained as *enfants de chapelle* of the duke of Burgundy. Music in fact, like hunting, jousting and sartorial extravagance, went on as before.

The same is true of sculpture and painting. Nor was the Charterhouse of Champmol neglected by John the Fearless, who visited it whenever he was in Burgundy; went on pilgrimage to his father's tomb there; and saw to the enclosure against the weather of Claus Sluter's *puis de Moïse*.[2] John the Fearless maintained the succession of *maîtres des œuvres*, of court sculptors, and of official ducal painters. Claus Sluter was commissioned to complete Philip the Bold's tomb and, after his death, his nephew Claus de Werve succeeded him as ducal *tailleur d'ymaiges*. Philip the Bold's painter Jehan Malouel was continued in office by John the Fearless and employed in decorating armour, in painting the ducal arms and devices, in colouring the effigies of Philip the Bold and Margaret of Male and, in 1412, he was required to execute a portrait of the duke for despatch to King John I of Portugal. When he died, he was replaced by Henry Bellechose of Brabant, who found time from painting the inevitable banners and pennons to complete some pictures for the Charterhouse of Champmol.

Just as the painting and sculpture of Philip the Bold's reign was continued without serious intermission or diminution under his son, so too the art of book illumination was patronized by John the Fearless in the same way, though perhaps not quite to the same extent, as it

---

[1] Bowles, *GSJ* vi (1953), 45. What follows is from ACO B1572, f. 23.
[2] For this paragraph, see Monget, *Chartreuse de Dijon*, ii. 5–57; Dimier, *GBA* (6) xvi (1936), 208–9; Kleinclausz, *RAAM* xx (1906), 161–76 and 253–268; and Canat de Chizy, *BM* lxiii (1898), 245–72, etc.

had been by Philip the Bold. John the Fearless undertook the completion of illuminated books commissioned by his father; he looked after the library which his father and mother had put together; and he and his wife enriched this library with some forty books, increasing the total number from about 200 to 250 volumes. Among the most notable illuminated manuscripts commissioned or purchased by John, which still survive, are the famous Breviary he had with him when he died, which is now divided between two manuscripts in the British Museum; a Book of Hours almost certainly executed in Ghent some time after 1408; a copy of the history of the discovery of the Canary Isles in 1402–4 by two French adventurers, called *Le Canarien*; and superb manuscripts of Laurence de Premierfait's French translations of Boccaccio's *Decameron* and *De casibus virorum et feminarum illustrium*.[1] In other artistic fields too, John followed in his father's footsteps. Philip, for instance, had commissioned a set of tapestries depicting the battle of Roosebeke, John did the same for his victory over the men of Liège at Othée.

In many of John the Fearless's manuscripts his favourite device or emblem appears. This was a carpenter's plane, which he had chosen to smooth away symbolically the duke of Orleans' club, and he used it in excessive profusion on every possible occasion. All his contemporaries had their chosen emblems, but none broadcast them on the scale on which John the Fearless employed his plane. In 1406 he gave away 315 gold planes, many of them embellished with diamonds and inscribed with the ducal motto, and he appeared at jousts with planes decorating his armour. In 1411 he presented 200 gold planes to the gentlemen of his household and 300 silver ones to the servants. Gold wood-shavings frequently accompanied these planes: on one occasion John ordered 3,000 scarlet pennons for his troops, each of them to be emblazoned with a plane and wood-shavings in gold. At least two manuscripts in the Bibliothèque Nationale, one the *Réponses* of Pierre Salmon, the other a collection of tracts on travel called the

---

[1] These manuscripts are respectively BM Add. MS. 35311 and Harley MS. 2897; BN MS. nouv. acq. 3055; BM Egerton MS. 2709; BV MS. Pal. 1989; and BA MS. 3193. See, on this paragraph, Doutrepont, *Littérature* and *Inventaire de la 'librairie' de P. le Bon*; Durrieu, *Le Manuscrit*, ii (1895), 82–7 and 162–8, etc. and *BEC* lxxi (1910), 58–71; Leroquais, *Livre d'Heures de J. sans Peur*; Mirot, *BEC* ci (1940), 225–9; Panofsky, *Early Netherlandish painting*, i. 118–19; Prost, *AHAL* ii (1890–1), 337–53; and the relevant catalogues of manuscripts. For what follows, see Plancher, iii. 289 and Bauyn, *BSHF* (1847–8), 232 and 242. For the next paragraph, see Plancher, iii. 233–4 and 342–3 and Bazin, *MSHA Beaune* (1897), 60–1.

Livre des merveilles du monde, show the duke, with his customary black hat and characteristic profile, wearing a robe embroidered all over with planes.[1]

The connections of John the Fearless with the literary world of his day were as tenuous as those of his father. Yet he did patronize or inspire a certain amount of literary activity. The indefatigable poetess Christine de Pisan continued to address or offer works to him, just as she did to the other French princes, and to receive suitable financial recompense from time to time, as recorded in the Burgundian accounts:[2]

> To Demoiselle Christine de Pisan, widow of the late Master Estienne du Castel, a gift of 100 crowns, made to her by my lord the duke, for and in acknowledgement of two books which she has presented to my lord the duke, one of which was commissioned from her by the late duke of Burgundy, father of the present duke . . . shortly before he died. Since then she has finished this book and my lord the duke has it instead [of his father]. The other book my lord the duke wanted to have himself, and . . . he takes much pleasure in these two books and in others of her epistles and writings. . . .
> Let these books be entered in the inventory and kept for my lord the duke.

The writings which seem to have been directly inspired by or undertaken for John the Fearless form a rather motley, if not bizarre, collection of literary curiosities.[3] The battle of Othée was the subject of a mediocre 500-line poem, comprising little more than a list of the Burgundian captains who took part. A treatise on the schism was presented to John about 1405, and a tract advising princes not to dabble in fortune-telling was dedicated to him in 1411. To these we may add Petit's *Justification du duc de Bourgogne*; the *Mémoires* of John's secret agent at the French court, Pierre Salmon; and two quasi-historical poetic works which provide a kind of literary apotheosis of John the Fearless, and manifest an extreme Burgundian enthusiasm. These are the *Pastoralet*, which is a sort of epic poem in praise of John the

---

[1] BN. MSS. fr. 23279 and 2810. For the former, see *Demandes faites par le roi Charles VI*.
[2] De Laborde, *Ducs de Bourgogne*, i. 16, no. 63 = ACO B1543, f. 107. On Christine de Pisan, see the references in Vaughan, *P. the Bold*, 198 n. 2. See, too, Prost, *AHAL* ii (1890–1), 346–9. Prost also prints this extract, ibid., 346.
[3] What follows is from Doutrepont, *Littérature*. The poem on Othée is printed in *Mémoires*, i. 373–9. For the tract on the schism, see Bayot, *RHE* ix (1908), 728–35.

Fearless, but disguised as a rustic allegory; and the *Geste des ducs de Bourgogne*, which, though equally propagandist and partisan on John's behalf, conceals behind its doggerel a detailed and valuable history of the events of 1411.

In all this, the differences between Philip the Bold and John the Fearless seem to be differences of degree only, a fact which is true also of the love life of these dukes. Philip the Bold as a young man seems to have indulged in sexual adventures which he afterwards eschewed, for it is said that the proprietor of the Stag Inn at Hal, where he died, was an illegitimate son of his, born about 1360. But John the Fearless was of a more amorous or wanton disposition. *Mulierosior patre multo fuit*, as the sixteenth-century Dutch historian Pontus Heuterus put it.[1] This propensity, or weakness, seems to have been transferred to his children, especially Philip the Good. John, bastard of Burgundy, provost of St. Donatian's at Bruges and of St. Peter's at Lille, bishop of Cambrai and archbishop of Trier, who once celebrated mass at Cambrai attended by thirty-six of his illegitimate sons and grandsons, was the bastard son of John the Fearless and Agnes de Croy, whom he had seduced at a dance. John is credited with other illegitimate children, three of them by Marguerite van Borsselen, and among his mistresses was supposed to have been the lady of Giac, Jehanne du Peschin, who was closely involved in the events which led to his assassination.

Territorial expansion

It is often claimed that John the Fearless was diverted by the affairs of France from paying proper or sufficient attention to the addition of new territories or lordships to the Burgundian state. Actually, he appears to have exploited every conceivable opportunity for territorial expansion, and there is no evidence at all that this activity, which was, after all, pursued as a matter of course by every ruler and landowner in Europe from the emperor to the humblest rustic nobleman, was neglected by him.

We have already had occasion to notice John the Fearless's successful expansion in the area of the two Burgundies. It is true that he failed to extend his rule over the imperial city of Besançon, which might thereby have become the administrative capital of the county of Burgundy, but he did acquire two important groups of lands adjacent to the duchy, one permanently, the other temporarily. The

[1] *Rerum burgundicarum libri VI*, 218. This paragraph is based on Bergé, *IG* lx (1955), 316–408.

royal town of Mâcon, with its dependencies, was occupied and annexed in September 1417, and its integration into the Burgundian state was confirmed in 1424 and again by the treaty of Arras of 1435. On the other hand the county of Tonnerre and other lands wrested from Louis de Chalon by judicial and military action, which were ceded by John the Fearless to his son Philip, were returned by him some years after John's death to their former and rightful owner.[1]

John the Fearless's territorial acquisitions in the south were made at the expense of the French crown, and the same is true of the two significant and permanent additions which he made to his northern territories. The county of Boulogne was seized by force in 1416 from its rightful owner George de la Trémoille, and held in spite of his protests; and in August 1418, soon after he had re-entered Paris and regained control of the person of the king, John the Fearless arranged for the formal transference by Charles VI of the towns and castellanies of Péronne, Roye and Montdidier to his son Philip, count of Charolais. This high-handed action was justified on the pretext that these lands were transferred as a guarantee for the payment of what was still owing by the king of France for the dowry of his daughter Michelle of France, wife of Philip of Charolais. Needless to say, they were not returned to the French crown, and their transference to Burgundy, along with that of the county of Boulogne, was confirmed at Arras in 1435. A glance at the map on p. 5 demonstrates the significance of these acquisitions. The Boulonnais, added to the county of Artois, much increased its size, while the acquisition of Péronne, Roye and Montdidier extended John the Fearless's frontiers to the river Somme, and constituted an indispensable shield against a possible repetition of the 1414 French attack on Arras.

When Duke Anthony of Brabant was killed at the battle of Agincourt on 25 October 1415, the succession to his duchy became an open and crucial question. The interested parties were first, the people of Brabant, who were well organized politically and preferred their country to be as independent as possible; second, Duke Anthony's son John, aged thirteen; third, Duke John the Fearless; and fourth, the emperor-designate, King Sigismund. During the critical year that followed, John the Fearless made a determined attempt to add Brabant, even if only for a time, to the Burgundian

---

[1] For this paragraph, see above, pp. 13–14 and 184–6 (Besançon); pp. 181–3 (Mâcon); and pp. 10–11 and 177–81 (Tonnerre); and Faussemagne, *Apanage ducal*, 51–4. For the next paragraph, see Héliot and Benoit, *RN* xxiv (1938), 29–45 and de Beauvillé, *Montdidier*, i. 125–35 and 526–30.

238 JOHN THE FEARLESS

state, just as his father Philip the Bold had done before him. Like his father, he failed. The first reaction of the Brabanters to the death of their duke was to meet together in the three Estates early in November; to proclaim defiantly their united opposition to any prince who dared to infringe their privileges; and to install an elected Council of Regency to rule on behalf of Anthony's son John until he was old enough to take over the government. The first reaction of John the Fearless was to send an embassy in January 1416 to the three Estates of Brabant meeting at Brussels,[1] '. . . both to comfort and console them over the recent woeful death of our late very dear and beloved brother the duke of Brabant . . . at the lamentable discomfiture of the French at Agincourt, and to expound to the three Estates our rights to the guardianship and government of the persons of our nephews [John and Philip of Brabant] being minors, and of their lands and lordships.'

The answer of the three Estates of Brabant to John's emissaries was resolutely negative, and none of his subsequent efforts in the ensuing months met with any success. In February John visited Brussels in person; in March his deputies were in conference at Malines; in April they tried to win over Antwerp. John himself was back again in Brabant in May conferring with representatives of the prelates, nobles and towns, but in vain. The Brabanters were by no means prepared to see the government of their country transferred to John, for they had evidently surmised, probably correctly, that if they did this, Brabant would very soon be incorporated into the Burgundian state. An ultimatum, sent by John to Louvain on 1 June 1416, shows that the towns were the chief stumbling-block to his plans.

> In the town of Brussels, in our presence and in the presence of our . . .
> nephews John and Philip, children of our late . . . brother the duke of
> Brabant and Limbourg, being minors, we caused the right which we
> have and which belongs to us, to the guardianship and government of
> our said nephews and their lands and lordships, to be expounded to the
> clergy, nobles and deputies of the towns . . . of Brabant. . . . Since
> then we have written and sent on several occasions to your deputies and
> to the other deputies of the good towns [of Brabant], assembled at
> Brussels and elsewhere . . . but you have invariably proceeded with
> evasions, delays and procrastination. . . . We are absolutely amazed at

---

[1] Ducal letters of 7 March 1417 in ACO B11939, analysed in de Barante, *Histoire des ducs*, i. 608-9. The extract which follows this one is from Plancher, iii. no. 301.

this, especially because we desire and care for the welfare of our nephews and their lands, lordships and subjects. . . .

We therefore earnestly summon and require you, this time for once and all, to recognize our aforesaid right, as the clergy and nobles have done and are doing, by causing and allowing us to enjoy and possess it peacefully . . . and by notifying us sufficiently of your decision on this by means of the king [of arms] of Artois, our herald, bearer of these . . . before the tenth of this present month of June.

But this ultimatum was ignored, and the rich prize of Brabant, which John had done his utmost to obtain, was left for his son to add to the Burgundian state. This failure on John the Fearless's part is, however, not without interest, because of the light it throws on his own plans and aspirations. We see him throughout the year 1416, when he was poised to exploit Agincourt by engineering his return to power in Paris, haggling interminably with the Brabanters, and trying every possible expedient to acquire power there too. Clearly he appreciated that the Netherlands, like France, constituted an area of concern and consolidation for Burgundy. Certainly it was not for want of trying that John the Fearless failed to make territorial gains, or extend his power, in this area.

The family nexus

Philip the Bold had been the fortunate possessor of abundant material for the matrimonial game, which he played with skill, persistence and even vision. Six of his children survived to be married, and these had enabled him to lay down the foundations of a veritable family system of alliances and connections.[1] When John the Fearless took over from him in 1404–5 the pieces were deployed across Europe and the game was in full swing. As far as Philip the Bold's children were concerned, the state of play was as follows:

Margaret, John the Fearless's eldest sister, was married to William of Bavaria, count of Hainault-Holland. They had one daughter, Jacqueline.

Catherine was married to Leopold IV, duke of Austria, who had ceded her the county of Ferrette, but she had no children.

Mary, John's youngest sister, was married to Amadeus VIII, first duke of Savoy, who later became Pope Felix V.

[1] Vaughan, *P. the Bold*, 81–92.

Anthony, duke of Brabant, was married to Joan, daughter of Waléran de Luxembourg, count of St. Pol, but she died in 1407.

Philip, count of Nevers and of Rethel, was still unmarried.

John the Fearless's brothers and sisters were indeed brilliantly placed, by skill as well as good fortune, to extend his influence and protect his interests. The two principal powers of the Low Countries apart from his own county of Flanders, Brabant-Limbourg and Hainault-Holland, were bound to him by the closest possible ties, while in the south, Nevers, Ferrette and Savoy, likewise secured, seemed to lend protection and possibilities of expansion to the two Burgundies. What were the benefits which John the Fearless derived from this system set up by his father? And what was its significance for Burgundy?

It might be supposed that the kind of help afforded to John the Fearless by his neighbours and close relatives would be primarily military. But this was by no means the case. In fact, though Duke Anthony took contingents to Paris in 1405 and 1410, and though Amadeus VIII was always willing to permit John to raise mercenaries in Savoy, on the whole his relatives showed no enthusiasm to come to his aid. Indeed, during the major military crisis of John's reign, in 1414, they scarcely lifted a finger to help him with troops. In 1411, though Anthony was with John on his September campaign in Vermandois, he seems to have brought only a small contingent with him and, though Duchess Margaret of Hainault persuaded the citizens of Valenciennes to help her brother John, no other military aid came from Hainault-Holland. John's brother Philip, count of Nevers, rendered important military assistance by invading the county of Tonnerre on John's behalf in 1411, but he did nothing in 1414, except to encourage his brother's enemies by his abject surrender to the king. The fact is that Philip the Bold's family system was of limited military value. It seems likely that contingents of mercenaries from Savoy and Nevers would have fought in John's armies even if he had not been related to their rulers and, in any case, England and Picardy were probably as important, as Burgundian recruiting grounds, as Nevers or Savoy.[1]

---

[1] For this paragraph, see especially, above, p. 141; Quicke, *Mélanges . . .* Pirenne, 403; de Lichtervelde, *Grand commis*, 174–7; and *Cartulaire de Hainaut*, iii. no. 1033. For the next, see especially Cognasso, *Amedeo VIII*, ii.

If John the Fearless's relatives among neighbouring rulers were of little value as military allies, this is certainly not true of politics and diplomacy. Here Duke Anthony of Brabant, William of Bavaria and his wife Margaret of Burgundy and Amadeus of Savoy all made themselves invaluable to John on many occasions. After all, it was William of Bavaria who was largely responsible for the peace of Chartres in March 1409, and it was Anthony and Margaret who together helped to extricate John from the critical military situation of summer 1414 by persuading the dauphin and others to sign the peace of Arras. At this time and afterwards, the recovery of John's position in France seems to have united the entire family in a common resolve which survived the death of Anthony at Agincourt to take the form, in 1416, of a concerted move to restore John the Fearless to Paris on the pretext of installing there the new dauphin, John of Touraine, son-in-law of Duke William of Bavaria. Thus, in 1415–17, the Burgundian family system concentrated on a single political purpose on John the Fearless's behalf. As to Amadeus of Savoy, he intervened diplomatically in France in the interests of peace and of John the Fearless in 1410, 1412 and in 1418–19. In the affairs of France then, the matrimonial alliances contrived for John's brothers and sisters by Philip the Bold were of considerable diplomatic and political value to him. The real importance of the system, however, lay in the Empire rather than in France; in fact, in the Low Countries.

As count of Flanders, John the Fearless was one of the three principal rulers of the Netherlands, but his position there was immeasurably enhanced by the fact that both the other rulers in this area whose power approached his own were closely related to him. Because of this relationship, Brabant under Anthony and Hainault-Holland under William of Bavaria came within the Burgundian orbit or sphere of influence; and, with the second of these, came Liège, under William's brother, John of Bavaria. These rulers tended to pursue common policies of mutual self-interest; policies which were specifically Burgundian and often inspired or exploited by John the Fearless. It was this family system, just as much as his position as count of Flanders, senior member of the Burgundian house and, at times, master of France, which gave John the Fearless his dominating position in the Low Countries.

From the beginning of John the Fearless's ducal reign it became clear that he, William and Anthony planned to act in concert and to support each other. On 21 July 1405 they signed the treaty of Le

Quesnoy, which defined their relationships and policies during the decade which followed.[1]

John, duke of Burgundy, count of Flanders, of Artois and of Burgundy, palatine, lord of Salins and of Malines; William, count palatine of the Rhine, duke of Bavaria, count of Hainault, Holland and Zeeland, lord of Frisia; and Anthony of Burgundy, duke of Limbourg, count of Rethel and governor of Brabant, greetings to all those who see these presents.

May it please everyone to know that we, considering the ties of lineage and alliances of marriage which have existed and do exist between our predecessors and ourselves; the great love and friendship which has always been and we trust will always remain and increase between us . . .; and the very great honour and advantage which will accrue to us, our successors and our lands, have promised and covenanted in the name of good, firm and lasting alliances, and we do now promise and covenant . . . that we shall loyally guard and defend . . . each other; that we shall . . . help each other with all our power to obviate, remedy and resist any dishonour, evil or damage done to any one of us; that we shall loyally pursue each other's welfare and honour in all our affairs; and, to accomplish this, we shall help one another with all our power against everyone except my lord the king, his eldest son, our children. . . . Furthermore, it is our wish that disputes and questions arising between us because of our lands and lordships, or otherwise, shall be settled by the deputies whom we shall appoint to deal with [such] complaints. . . .

In witness and authentic confirmation of all this, we John, William and Anthony have caused these presents to be sealed with our privy seals and signed with our sign manuals. This was done and given at Le Quesnoy, 21 July 1405.

Jehan   Guillaume   Antoine

This verbal programme was followed by deeds. The three rulers jointly undertook a successful intervention in France in autumn 1405, and in 1408 they acted together militarily to put down the popular revolt in Liège and replace John of Bavaria on the episcopal throne, or at least in power, there. In 1409 the attention of the allies was again occupied in France, and they met together in Paris in March and December of that year; but John the Fearless's influence in the Netherlands, acting with and through his relatives, was clearly demonstrated in August 1409, in 1411 and in 1413, when he summoned them and the other rulers of the Low Countries to conferences pre-

[1] Plancher, iii. no. 247.

sided over by himself.[1] The assembly at Lille in August 1409 was the
first and grandest of these Burgundian Low Countries conferences
under John the Fearless. An intricate territorial and financial quarrel
between Anthony of Brabant and William of Bavaria was amicably
settled there by John the Fearless, all three rulers being present in
person, along with Margaret of Burgundy, William's wife and John's
sister, John of Bavaria, William's brother, and the count of Namur.
At the same time, John and William issued a revised version of their
sentence against the defeated Liègeois. This conference was followed,
in 1411, by a similar gathering held at Tournai, then a French enclave in the heart of the Burgundian Netherlands which, in spite of
its Burgundian bishop, Jehan de Thoisy, did its best to keep itself
outside the Burgundian sphere of influence. Witness the defiant
resolution of its magistrates on 28 July 1411, when John the Fearless
sent to ask them for the loan of eight or ten tents for his forthcoming
campaign: 'Resolved to excuse the town and, if he insists, to offer to
lend him two tents.' Here at Tournai, on 8 February 1411, John and
the other Burgundian princes of the Netherlands met together. But
the only trace of the agenda which has survived is an entry in the
Burgundian accounts which reads as follows:

> To my lord [the duke of Burgundy], in cash paid to him on 8 February
> 1411, to amuse himself and play at dice at Tournai with the dukes of
> Brabant and of Holland, the bishop of Liège and the count of Namur
> ... 67 francs and ten shillings tournois.

Another conference was held at Antwerp in December 1413,
present John the Fearless, Anthony, Philip of Charolais and his wife,
William of Bavaria, John of Bavaria and the counts of Cleves and St.
Pol. This time there is little difficulty in identifying the 'weighty and
important matters which they had to speak of and discuss together',
as the entry in the accounts has it.[2] Two things in particular occupied
the meeting: the settlement of a long-standing dispute between
Antwerp and Malines, and therefore between Anthony and John; and

[1] For this and what follows on the movements of the two brothers, see *Itin-
éraires* and Quicke, *Mélanges . . . Pirenne*, 391–409. The extracts are from
Extraits analytiques, 84 and ACO B1562, f. 18b. For the 1409 assembly, see
Monstrelet, *Chronique*, ii. 35; de Dynter, *Chronique des ducs de Brabant*, iii.
187–8; and *Cartulaire de Hainaut*, iii. 376–407.
[2] ADN B1903, f. 63b. See, too, de Lichtervelde, *Grand commis*, 210 and
Monstrelet, *Chronique*, ii. 419, where the printed text has Amiens in error for
Antwerp. For the next paragraph, see *Algemene geschiedenis*, iii. 230–6.

the affairs of France, where an all-out attack on John was being meditated and planned.

After the death, in 1415–17, of both Anthony of Brabant and William of Bavaria, the affairs of the Netherlands dissolved into turmoil and civil war. John of Bavaria, William's brother, never actually consecrated bishop nor fully committed to the episcopal throne of Liège, resolved to abandon it and to dispute with Jacqueline of Hainault the succession to his brother her father's territories of Hainault, Holland and Zeeland. Meanwhile she had married the youthful John IV, Anthony's son and successor as duke of Brabant. The war which now ensued over the succession to Hainault-Holland-Zeeland, between John IV of Brabant, acting for his wife, and John of Bavaria, was brought to an end with a compromise settlement, the treaty of Woudrichem, of 2 February 1419—a settlement which was authorized by John the Fearless and actually achieved by his son Philip, count of Charolais. Thus, right to the end of his reign, John the Fearless was able to dominate the complex history of the Netherlands. Already, the Low Countries were essentially Burgundian.

This growing Burgundian influence in the Low Countries, based on John the Fearless's use of Philip the Bold's family system, was by no means limited to diplomatic or political affairs. It was evident too, in administration. Indeed it is here, more than anywhere else, that we see the beginnings, or perhaps even the foundations, of the work of Philip the Good, in uniting the Low Countries under himself. This is most apparent in the duchy of Brabant, where Anthony, even before he became duke, had begun to reorganize the administration on Burgundian lines, with the help of Burgundian officials like Pierre de le Zippe and Jehan Chousat, lent him by his mother Margaret of Male.[1] Already in 1404 a *chambre des comptes* had been set up at Brussels by one of the Lille *maîtres des comptes*, David Bousse, who continued to visit Brussels and direct operations there, doubtless on Burgundian lines, in subsequent years. Moreover, two of Philip the Bold's most experienced Flemish councillors and officials, Simon de Fourmelles and Jaques de Lichtervelde, were transferred to Brabant in 1404 to serve for a time under Anthony; and in 1405–6, and again in 1409, Jehan Despoullettes, Philip the Bold's receiver-general of all finances in 1397–1401 and John the Fearless's treasurer and governor-general of finances in 1411–12, held office in Brabant as

---

[1] *IADNB* vii. 221 and Pocquet, *MSHDB* iv (1937), 53. For what follows, see above, p. 127; de Lichtervelde, *Grand commis*, 117–20; and ACO B1543, f. 62b.

combined treasurer and receiver-general of Duke Anthony's finances. Besides the Brussels *chambre des comptes*, Anthony tried to establish a council at Vilvorde on the lines of the council of Flanders; in 1407 he reorganized his household on Franco-Burgundian lines; and in 1408 he appointed a Burgundian-type chancellor, Pierre de Camdonck.[1] All this was not done merely on Anthony's initiative; he was encouraged and positively helped, first by his mother, and then by his elder brother John the Fearless, to improve and develop the government of Brabant in this way. Thus, under the aegis of John the Fearless, extensive administrative preparations were made for the subsequent integration of Brabant into the Burgundian state, preparations which were perhaps more important, though less spectacular, than John's determined efforts to get hold of Brabant in 1416.

So far, only those marriage alliances which Philip the Bold made for his own children have been mentioned here. But what of John the Fearless's children? They were employed and exploited in the traditional manner, for political ends. Six girls and a boy lived long enough to make some mark on history, and the matrimonial arrangements made for them during John the Fearless's lifetime were as follows:

Margaret, 1393–1442. Betrothed to Charles, dauphin of France, who died in 1401. Married Louis, dauphin of France, died 1415.

Mary, 1394–1463. Married Adolf, count and first duke of Cleves.

Philip the Good, 1396–1467. Married Michelle of France.

Catherine, 1399–1414. Married Louis d'Anjou, count of Guise.

Isabel, 1400–1412. Married Olivier de Blois, count of Penthièvre.

Anne, 1404–1432.

Agnes, 1407 (?)–1476. Betrothed to Charles de Bourbon.

It would be wrong to suppose that John the Fearless pursued a different marriage policy from Philip the Bold. In fact, both dukes used their children in a similar way, to extend the influence and, if possible, territories of Burgundy, especially in the Low Countries, and to strengthen her position inside France. It so happened, however, that most of Philip's children made alliances on the eastern frontiers of Burgundy, while most of John's married in France.

[1] Uyttebrouck, *RBPH* xxxvi (1958), 1135–72; Kauch, *RBPH* xxiv (1945), 180–201; and Renoz, *Chancellerie de Brabant*, 21.

Philip the Bold himself had arranged a fourfold Franco-Burgundian marriage alliance shortly before his death. This was his plan:[1]

Projected Franco-Burgundian marriage alliance of 1403

1. Margaret, John the Fearless's eldest daughter, to marry the dauphin Louis.

2. Philip, son of John the Fearless, to marry Michelle of France.

3. Another daughter of John the Fearless, unnamed, to marry John, duke of Touraine, younger brother of the dauphin Louis.

4. Jacqueline of Bavaria, daughter of William of Bavaria and Margaret of Burgundy, to marry Charles, youngest son of Charles VI, who later became Charles VII.

This elaborate scheme of 1403, which entailed the marriage of no less than four of Charles VI's children to four of Philip the Bold's grandchildren, had to be modified and somewhat truncated. What was actually achieved was a triple alliance, as follows:

Actual Franco-Burgundian marriage alliance of 1404–06

1. Margaret married the dauphin Louis, duke of Guienne.

2. Philip married Michelle of France.

3. Jacqueline of Bavaria married John, duke of Touraine.

The first two of these weddings took place in Paris at the end of August 1404, but the husbands of Margaret and Michelle, aged seven and eight respectively, had to wait until June 1409, according to the knowing chronicler Juvenel des Ursins, before they were permitted, or able, to consummate their marriages. Michelle brought with her the promise of a handsome dowry of 120,000 francs, non-payment of which was later exploited by John the Fearless to obtain the valuable territorial concessions on the river Somme mentioned earlier in this chapter (p. 237). Of Margaret's promised dowry of 200,000 francs we hear nothing more. The third of these marriages, which John tried to exploit in 1416–17, after the death of the dauphin Louis, was celebrated, with appropriate festivities, at Compiègne in July 1406. John the Fearless and his sister Margaret managed to persuade the reluctant queen to permit the bridegroom John, duke of Touraine, to leave her care and go to live in Hainault with his parents-in-law. Thus was the royal house of France entwined in the

---

[1] Vaughan, *P. the Bold*, 91 and n. 2.

tentacles of Burgundian matrimonial policy, and only the early and fortuitous deaths of two successive dauphins provided France with a king whose wife was not a Burgundian princess, in the shape of Charles VII.[1]

John the Fearless's matrimonial policy in France was by no means limited to members of the royal family. He also tried, though equally without eventual success, to use his daughters to cement alliances or win friendships among the other French princes. The most successful of these matches was that between his six-year-old daughter Isabel, substituted at the last moment for John's daughter Joan, who died shortly before the wedding, and Olivier, count of Penthièvre, one of the most powerful of the Breton lords, whose house had disputed the duchy of Brittany with the house of Montfort. The wedding ceremony was in July 1406, but this alliance was brought to a sudden end by the death of Isabel in 1412, when she was only twelve. Its principal political result had been to increase John the Fearless's influence over Duke John V of Brittany; an influence which, successfully maintained after 1412, kept the duke out of the Armagnac camp.[2]

John the Fearless's other marriage alliances with the princely houses of France were likewise short-lived or unsuccessful. In 1409, at the time of the peace of Chartres, a marriage was projected between one of John's daughters and Philippe d'Orléans, count of Vertus, but it came to nothing. In March 1410 the eleven-year-old Catherine travelled to Gien on the Loire to marry Louis d'Anjou, count of Guise, son of Duke Louis II, soi-disant king of Sicily, who needed the dowry money, not to mention the royal finance which John promptly made available to him, for his expedition to Italy. This marriage, which had actually been agreed to in October 1407, was broken off by the duke of Anjou in the late summer of 1413, and John the Fearless had to suffer the insulting effrontery of the return

[1] A fourth Franco-Burgundian marriage, between this Charles, then count of Ponthieu, and Agnes of Burgundy, is mentioned in a letter of 22 June 1406 as about to take place (above, p. 114). Can this have been the Agnes supposed to have been born in 1407, or was this perhaps an earlier Agnes who died in 1406–7? For this paragraph, see Relig. de St. Denys, iii. 212–14 and Plancher, iii. 215–16; Juv. des Ursins, *Hist. de Charles VI*, 444; Plancher, iii. no. 214; and *Cartulaire de Hainaut*, iii. nos. 908–12.

[2] Pocquet, *RCC* xxxvi (1) (1934–5), 53–67 and 164–71. For the next paragraph, see Plancher, iii. 270, 285 and 582–3; ACO B1560, f. 228b; de Boüard, *France et Italie*, 370; Coville, *Vie intellectuelle*, 31–2 and Lecoy, *Roi Renée*, i. 27–30.

of his daughter, whose marriage, one must suppose, had not yet been consummated, though Catherine herself was now fourteen and her husband about seventeen, and she had been living for three years at the Angevin court. Henceforth the house of Anjou was firmly Armagnac.

One other French princely house was persuaded to enter into a marriage alliance with Burgundy, that of Bourbon. A treaty was drawn up in August 1412 providing for the marriage of Charles de Bourbon, son of Duke John I, and Agnes of Burgundy, but the wedding was deferred. Although the project was revived in 1418, and although Charles was described in 1419, when he lived for a time at the Burgundian court, as John the Fearless's son-in-law, no wedding followed, and the whole affair was put off once more.[1]

The matrimonial ambitions which John the Fearless cherished for his children were not at all limited to France. In 1411 he offered his youngest daughter Agnes to the prince of Wales who, after he had ascended the English throne as Henry V, was given the choice, in 1414, of either Catherine or Anne. These advances, however, were perhaps not very serious; it was in the Low Countries that John the Fearless concentrated his remaining energies and material for dynastic expansion. As far as his own children were concerned, only one alliance was made, that between Mary of Burgundy and Adolf, count of Cleves. The treaty was signed in 1405, but the actual wedding was delayed until October 1406, and payment of the dowry and pension or fief-rent which John had promised to Adolf was delayed even longer. Indeed it is doubtful if Adolf obtained anything from John in either respect until 1410, and then he was compelled to accept the lands and castle of Wynendale in Flanders instead of a large part of the dowry. Finally Mary herself, who had been living all this time at the Burgundian court, was handed over to Adolf at Dijon in March 1415.[2]

The county of Cleves, erected into a duchy in 1417, was the only principality in the Low Countries which was brought significantly further into the Burgundian sphere of influence by means of a mar-

---

[1] Leguai, *Ducs de Bourbon*, 116–17; Plancher, iii. no. 286; and ACO B1601, f. 31a–b. For what follows, see O. van Dixmude, *Merkwaerdige geb.*, 67, and above, p. 206.

[2] Besides Hövelmann, *AHVN* clxi (1959), 232–43 and the works referred to there, I have used Plancher, iii. no. 251 and pp. 431–2; Laenen, *Archives de Vienne*, no. 214; Gachard, *BCRH* (4) ix (1881), 290; and a group of documents in ACO B295.

riage alliance with one of John the Fearless's children. But two other marriages, in both of which John the Fearless was closely concerned, marked important extensions of Burgundian influence in this area. The first was Duke Anthony of Brabant's marriage in July 1409 to Elizabeth of Görlitz, niece of King Wenzel. As a result of this marriage and the accompanying treaty, for the negotiation of both of which John the Fearless seems to have been mainly responsible, his brother Anthony was enabled to acquire the duchy of Luxembourg, and, though Anthony's death at Agincourt cut short this Burgundian triumph, it helped to lay the basis for Philip the Good's subsequent acquisition of the duchy.[1]

The other marriage alliance in the Low Countries with which John the Fearless was concerned was Jacqueline of Bavaria's second marriage. Her first husband, who had been found for her by John the Fearless, was the French prince who became dauphin in 1415, John, duke of Touraine. Her second husband, whom she married in 1418, was also selected, or at least approved, by John the Fearless. He was the youthful Duke John IV of Brabant, son and successor of Anthony. Amid the political turmoil of the Low Countries at this time the stately vision, implicit in this match, of the unification of Brabant with Hainault-Holland under a junior branch of the Burgundian dynasty, must surely have inspired its instigators. In fact these territories remained divided until Philip the Good united them under himself fifteen years later, but, in Hainault-Holland as in Luxembourg, John the Fearless had helped to lay the foundations on which his successor could build or, at the very least, provided a pretext on which he could act.

European diplomacy

It is not intended here to review, systematically, John the Fearless's relations with the other European powers, for these have already been partly touched on in the preceding pages and in earlier chapters. For instance, much has already been said about Franco-Burgundian relations under John the Fearless. Their intricate nature is illustrated by the fact that, while John hastened willingly to do homage to the

---

[1] See especially Richter, *WZ* v (1889), 3–8; van Werveke, *Erwerbung des Luxemburger Landes*; Pot, *R. Pot*, 116–17 and 122–4; Quicke, *PSHIL* lxiv (1930), 317–468; Wymans, *ASRAB* l (1956–61), 297–303; and Mirot, *AB* iii (1931), 319 n. 3. For the next paragraph, see de Dynter, *Chronique des ducs de Brabant*, iii. 342–4; *Algemene geschiedenis*, iii. 230–5; and David, *Du nouveau sur Jean sans Peur*, 66–7.

king of France for his French possessions, he made and signed treaties with other powers, and even with France herself, as if he were completely independent.[1] I have tried to show that his aim in France was to dominate, control, or actually obtain the government, not in order to usurp the throne, but in order to exploit France for the benefit of himself and his house. Again, John's relations with England have already been discussed, and it will suffice to note here that these were twofold. Negotiations took place almost every year, on the one hand for a political alliance between England and Burgundy which was never achieved, and on the other for a trade truce between England and Flanders which was successfully maintained throughout John's ducal reign.

If, then, the momentous subjects of Anglo-Burgundian and Franco-Burgundian relations, not to mention the matrimonial developments already discussed in this chapter, are omitted here, there still remain certain interrelated aspects of Burgundian diplomacy which, though perhaps not of such central importance to the emergence of Burgundy as a European power, are nevertheless worthy of consideration. I refer in particular to John the Fearless's relations with the Empire and to his scattered contacts with other powers. These are the subject of the remaining pages of this chapter.

The Empire, in the early fifteenth century, was a loose federation of practically autonomous political units, which equalled or excelled in number and variety those to be found in the whole of the rest of Europe put together. This Empire comprised a kingdom, Bohemia; duchies, counties and margravates; archbishoprics the size of any ordinary country; and well over fifty imperial cities; not to mention such curiosities as the state of the Teutonic Knights in Prussia, and federations like the Hanseatic League and the Swiss Confederation. The dominions of John the Fearless and his brothers and relatives were scattered along the western borders of this sprawling political oddity. It provided neither an army nor revenues, nor any significant means of power, for its rulers who, in John the Fearless's time, were not even crowned emperors. These rulers, in fact, were so weak and ineffectual in their own so-called Empire that rival organizations for keeping the peace arose spontaneously there in defiance of their authority, which was indeed completely disregarded with impunity by all concerned. The antics of Rupert, of Wenzel and of Sigismund, on the European stage, whether in journeying to Italy to try to obtain the imperial crown or to Constance to open a Council of the Church,

[1] Faussemagne, *Apanage ducal*, 94-5 and 231.

scarcely impinged on the realities of secular politics, where the rulers who enjoyed any real power, like those of the western kingdoms, of Burgundy, of some of the imperial principalities and of the Italian city-states continued, regardless of higher authority, to employ the time-honoured means of war, intrigue and territorial expansion in order to increase their power and further their own particular or dynastic interests. This was the general predicament of Europe in those days, and this explains why John the Fearless's relations with the Empire were of little practical significance in the development of Burgundy.

The formation of the Burgundian state had been made possible, in the first place, by means of large areas of French territory, notably the duchy of Burgundy and the county of Flanders. But henceforth, all along the eastern borders of France, from the Alps to the North Sea, Burgundian territorial ambitions were directed towards the Empire, and almost every further development of the Burgundian state impinged on imperial territories and infringed imperial rights. Thus John the Fearless found himself constantly involved with the rulers of the Empire: Wenzel, who, though deposed in 1400, still enjoyed and claimed a measure of imperial authority until 1411; his rival Rupert, who died in May 1410; and Wenzel's brother Sigismund, who became undisputed ruler, though with the title of king of the Romans only, in 1411.

Of the many points at issue between Burgundy and the Empire only the most important can be mentioned here. It must be emphasized that the attitude, or reaction, of the imperial rulers to Burgundian expansion at the expense of their Empire was more often diplomatic than political, and never military. Often there was no reaction at all. The imperial county of Cleves, for instance, was brought into the Burgundian orbit through the marriage alliance of 1405 without a murmur from either of the rival imperial rulers at that time, and it was erected by Sigismund into a duchy in 1417 for the benefit of Adolf II, John the Fearless's son-in-law. In the early years of his reign, John the Fearless was able to obtain almost anything he wanted from Wenzel, by agreeing not to support Wenzel's rival Rupert, or by promising or pretending that he would attack him. While King Rupert was threatening in 1407 to try to recover the imperial duchy of Brabant from John's brother Anthony, King Wenzel was persuaded to confirm Anthony's possession of it by a formal cession. Indeed, he went much further than this, for the treaty of 20 July 1408, between Wenzel, Anthony and John, had the effect of handing the duchy of Luxembourg over to Anthony as well, in exchange for an insincere and hypocritical promise of Burgundian military assistance for Wenzel against Rupert—as if the two rivals were powerful enough to wage war against each other![1] At the same time, when John the Fearless's acquisitive ambitions began to embrace the imperial city of Besançon, Wenzel was pleased, in February 1408, to cede him sovereignty over it without demur. Even more demonstrative, perhaps, of the weakness of the Empire while it was divided between Rupert and Wenzel, was the impunity with which John the Fearless intervened militarily and decisively in the affairs of Liège in 1408, without consulting either ruler.

John the Fearless maintained connections in 1409–10 with both Rupert and Wenzel, and with other imperial princes, but we can only guess at his attitude and influence during the interregnum after Rupert's death in 1410.[2] After 1411, however, when King Sigismund emerged as sole ruler of the Empire, the situation changed. The fact is that Sigismund was desperately anxious to restore the decaying splendours, the erstwhile prestige, and even the political power, of his Empire. To achieve this without an army or revenues was not easy, but he nevertheless resolved and embarked on a vigorous reaction against Burgundian encroachments in the Empire, which were personified in John's brother Anthony. Sigismund refused to recognize Anthony's possession of Brabant and he did all he could to encourage resistance to Anthony in turbulent Luxembourg, where Burgundian rule was only established as a result of three military expeditions. The opposition to the Burgundian annexation of Luxembourg was partly inspired by Charles, duke of Orleans, who, having inherited his father's claims there, now stirred the local nobility to hostile action against Anthony. For Sigismund, looking for a stick to beat the Burgundians with, it was a short step from his initial alliance with Charles of Orleans in September 1413, aimed mainly at Anthony, to a full-blooded alliance with the Armagnacs in June 1414, when they seemed

---

[1] Text of the treaty in *Regesta Ruperti regis*, 185. See, on this paragraph, Minder, *BSVAH* xli (1954), 163–4; van Werveke, *Erwerbung des Luxemburger Landes*; and above, pp. 184–5 (Besançon) and pp. 49–66 (Liège).

[2] See Leuschner, *DAEM* xi (1955), 541–4. For what follows, see especially Schoenstedt, *WG* xiv (1954), 150–63 and Crowder, *Historical Studies*, iv (1962), 93–110 and the works referred to by them. See, too, *Geschiedenis van Vlaanderen*, iii. 93–6; Hanssens, *Mélanges . . . Cauwenbergh*, 285–95; Quicke, *PSHIL* lxiv (1930), 317–468; and van Werveke, *Erwerbung des Luxemburger Landes*. Some of the most important documents are printed in *Acta concilii Constanciensis*, i and *Urkunden Kaiser Sigmunds*, i.

on the point of completing a victorious offensive against John the Fearless's northern territories.[1]

King Sigismund's intervention in 1414 on behalf of the Armagnacs was made futile by the peace of Arras, which Anthony, impelled perhaps more by his own interests than brotherly love, had helped to negotiate. This intervention was in any case limited to the realms of theory, though, like others of Sigismund's projects, it had a certain grandiose character. It entailed nothing less than the partition of Burgundy between the Empire, France and England. This formidable though politically naïve plan was committed to writing in a projected Anglo-imperial alliance dating from August 1414, when King Charles VI was still besieging John's city of Arras. The text, pruned of some of the imperial verbiage, runs as follows.[2]

The wishes of the most serene prince lord Sigismund, king of the Romans, etc. . . . are inclined towards undertaking what is written below, jointly with the most serene prince lord Henry, king of England and of France.

First . . . the king of the Romans ardently desires . . . that the kings of the Romans, of the French and of England, since they, among the catholic kings and princes of the world, are reputed to be and actually are, as it were, the three heads of christendom . . . should unite together . . . for the general good. . . .

Also, the said king of the Romans has thought of apt ways and means of bringing this about, in particular, a marriage alliance between the kings of France and of England. . . .

That most serene prince the king of the French has described repeatedly in his letters how John, so-called duke of Burgundy, raving with the fury of envy and ambition, has been constantly trying to disturb the peace and prosperity . . . of the kingdom of France. He caused the former duke of Orleans, Louis, [the king's] only and much-loved brother, to be wickedly assassinated . . . so that he might usurp all his power, authority and government . . . in the kingdom of France. Having become a parricide, he did not shirk from adding crimes to crimes and, relying for the most part on riots, and with the help of the ignoble and ignominious mob, especially of impious butchers (for noble and honourable citizens were and are always against him), he persecuted the princes of the blood as if they were deadly enemies, and drove them from the royal court, so that he could govern France according to his malign and tyrannical wishes. . . .

---

[1] Treaties of 12 September 1413 and 25 June 1414, printed in *Documents luxembourgeois à Paris*, no. 292 and *Corps universel diplomatique*, ii (2), 14–15.   [2] *Acta concilii Constanciensis*, i. 377–9.

Oh horrible crime and execrable deed! Sinful outrage so wickedly committed and inhumanly perpetrated which, in flouting both God and men, horrifies those hearing [about it] . . . and demands the severity of vengeance! Who does not abhor as a detestable deed the murder without cause of this innocent prince! Who does not deplore [the fact that] a guiltless man should be so cruelly slain as a result of blind greed! . . . Who would not freely exercise the rigour of revenge in punishing the perpetrators of such a crime . . .? The voice [of the dead prince] sounds in our ears, appeals to us, invokes us to judgement and provokes us to revenge.

From this it emerges clearly that the king of the French had and has good reason to proceed against, prosecute and condemn the so-called duke of Burgundy since he, because of the unparalleled enormity of this crime, has made himself hateful to all princes and, his own wickedness rendering him unfit, he has forfeited forthwith all his belongings, unworthy, and destitute of honour and fame. Moreover, as a vassal of the Holy [Roman] Empire, he loses those of his fiefs which form part of the Empire . . . and these lawfully return to us. . . .

Furthermore, Anthony of Burgundy his brother, who is endeavouring to usurp Luxembourg under the pretence and title of a dowry, claims to be duke of Brabant, though he has no reasonable right whatsoever to the said duchy of Brabant, which belongs to the Holy [Roman] Empire. . . .

It is to be concluded then, that the . . . aforesaid kings, allied together, should proceed against these perverse brothers of Burgundy, both on account of the crime committed and because of their [other] indiscretions. . . . Furthermore the king of the Romans, provided that the king of England helps him in the recuperation and acquisition of the imperial goods and rights which the above mentioned brothers of Burgundy hold . . . is prepared to confer and donate to him in fief those imperial goods and rights in Flanders which are held by the duke of Burgundy. . . .

As a matter of fact, the French and Burgundians were negotiating at the very moment when these proposals were drawn up, while at the same time Henry V was trying to persuade John the Fearless into an alliance with England. With such duplicity on all sides, it is scarcely surprising that nothing came of these diplomatic posturings of 1414, the futility of which was underlined in the following year, when all hopes of an Anglo-French alliance evaporated with the English invasion of France, and any prospect of a dismemberment of Burgundy disappeared with John the Fearless's political and military recovery. One event, however, suddenly diminished the Burgundian threat to Sigismund and the Empire: the death of Anthony of Brabant on the field of Agincourt in October 1415. It was this, as much as the failure of the 1414 project, which led Sigismund to a rapprochement with John the Fearless in 1416, and to a treaty in 1417.

Some historians like to invest Sigismund with aims they consider noble and elevated, though they comprised the destruction of heresy by burning, and the banishment of war from the West simply in order to carry it more effectively to the East. They like to think of Sigismund acting almost as an altruistic idealist in convening the Council of Constance and attempting to pacify the kingdoms of the West. In fact, he was an interfering busybody who, deprived by history of political authority in his own dominions, proceeded to practise self-aggrandizement in the only way left open to him, that is, by intervening, egotistically rather than altruistically, in the affairs of other countries. It was in 1416 that these interventions in the West reached their culmination, with Sigismund's famous though utterly ineffective visit to the rulers of France, England and Burgundy. To raise funds for his travelling expenses, he first sold the title of duke to John's son-in-law the count of Savoy. In Paris his diplomacy achieved nothing whatsoever, though he caused some annoyance in legal circles by taking the king's place in the *Parlement* of Paris and by intervening in a law-suit to knight on the spot a defendant who was alleged not to be a knight. In London he abandoned all thoughts of arbitration or pacification and went so far as to sign the treaty of Canterbury with 'our brother Henry of England, king of France', in which he actually made the absurd promise to help Henry V make war on France! Finally, at Calais on his return in October 1416, John the Fearless met him and did homage to him for his imperial possessions.

John's investment by Sigismund with his imperial fiefs was the prelude to, or part of, a long series of negotiations which led to a treaty between John and Sigismund in April 1417 in which Sigismund promised military aid to John against France, and to another personal meeting of the two rulers at Montbéliard in May 1418. The issues at stake between them were complicated and numerous, and there was no question of a genuine reconciliation or permanent settlement, for none of their tortuous diplomacy seems to have been in the least bit sincere. If John hoped that Sigismund would prove a useful ally against Armagnac France, he was soon disillusioned. The declaration of war against France, promised in the treaty of Canterbury for 22 March 1417, never came. Instead, on 1 September 1417, Sigismund despatched a letter of defiance to the count of Armagnac only, while notifying Henry V that unavoidable delays had caused the deferment of his planned invasion of France till 1 May 1418. If

John hoped that Sigismund would use his influence at the Council of Constance to obtain a judgement favourable to Jehan Petit, he was disappointed. It is unlikely, however, that John the Fearless cherished any illusions about Sigismund's generosity or utility to him on either of these scores. There were two other matters in 1416–17 which concerned both rulers: Burgundian claims in Alsace, and the succession to Brabant. Here too, it seems that John had no illusions about Sigismund's attitude.[1]

In Alsace John the Fearless's sister Catherine had acquired, together with her husband Leopold of Austria, a lordship in Upper Alsace based on the county of Ferrette. This she at first continued to rule after her husband's death in 1411, but Leopold's brother Frederick intervened in that year, and by 1414 he had occupied all Catherine's territories except Belfort and Rosemont. John the Fearless supported and helped his sister consistently throughout his reign, lending her military aid in the war against Frederick which followed these events; and in November 1415 he strengthened the remnants of Burgundian rule in Alsace by appointing Jehan de Neufchastel governor of Belfort and Rosemont. But all his efforts to negotiate with Sigismund the return of Ensisheim and the other lands and places which had been wrested from Catherine by Duke Frederick proved fruitless. Early in May 1418 Sigismund guaranteed these territories to Frederick, but, when he met John the Fearless later in the same month at Montbéliard, he was profuse with promises of help in restoring them to Catherine. Thus Burgundian encroachments in Alsace, made by Catherine and encouraged by John the Fearless, were successfully resisted by Duke Frederick of Austria, encouraged by Sigismund.

The question of the succession to Brabant was thrown wide open by Anthony's death in October 1415. While John the Fearless and Sigismund put in their claims and made and repeated their representations in due diplomatic form, the three Estates of Brabant organized a Council of Regency on behalf of the youthful ruler who was acceptable to them, Duke John IV, Anthony's son. There was however an important difference between the attitudes of John and Sigismund: the former soon accepted the succession and the rule of his nephew John IV, while Sigismund did not, so that the question

---

[1] For this paragraph and what follows, see, besides the works cited above, p. 252 n. 2, Quicke, *BCRH* xc (1926), 193–241; *Aus der Kanzlei Kaiser Sigmunds*; Stouff, *Catherine de Bourgogne*; Wackernagel, *Geschichte der Stadt Basel*, i; and Bazin, *MSHA Beaune* (1897), 103–4.

of Sigismund's recognition of John IV became yet another subject of negotiation between him and John the Fearless in 1416–17. After William of Bavaria's death in May 1417 the marriage of his daughter and heiress Jacqueline to Duke John IV of Brabant, mentioned above, which was engineered by John the Fearless, was resisted by Sigismund, who adopted William's brother, John of Bavaria, late bishop-elect of Liège, as his own candidate for the succession to Holland-Hainault. The confused events that followed have more to do with the subsequent unification of the Low Countries under Philip the Good than with the history of Burgundy under John the Fearless. Let it suffice to say here that, in the Low Countries in the years 1417–19, neither the complicated diplomatic manœuvres of Sigismund nor his protégé John of Bavaria's military efforts made any significant difference to the general situation of growing Burgundian predominance.

John the Fearless's relations with the Empire were not confined to diplomatic contacts with its rulers, for his need of military allies or quasi-feudal clients caused him to make treaties with a number of imperial vassals. Who were these clients and allies of John the Fearless inside the Empire? Some of course have been mentioned already: relatives of John like John of Bavaria, Amadeus of Savoy, Adolf of Cleves. Others may be mentioned here, first and foremost among them the duke of Lorraine, Charles II, whose extensive territories lay between Luxembourg and the county of Burgundy, wholly within the Empire. In return for an annual 'pension' from John the Fearless of 2,000 francs, Duke Charles swore, early in 1408, to serve Duke John in arms whenever he was requested to do so, the wages of himself and his troops to be paid by John the Fearless. Not only did Charles earn henceforth the reputation of being a 'perfect Burgundian',[1] he also became so anti-French that in 1409 he forbade his daughter to marry a French prince. On several occasions, notably at the siege of Rougemont in 1411; at the siege of Bourges in 1412; and in 1415, when John marched on Paris after Agincourt, he and his men performed the promised military service for John the Fearless.

The treaty of John the Fearless with the duke of Lorraine took the form of the creation of a fief-rent for Charles. That is to say, in return for the oath to perform military service and of fealty in general, John

[1] Dex, *Metzer Chronik*, 458. See, too, Calmet, *Hist. de Lorraine*, iii. cols. 517–23, etc.; Parisot, *Hist. de Lorraine*, i. 326 and 336; Monstrelet, *Chronique*, iii. 127, and, for the treaty between John and Charles, see John's letter of 6 April 1408 in *Documents luxembourgeois à Paris*, no. 267 = Plancher, iii, no. 255. In general, on John's military allies, see above, pp. 141–2.

gave Charles a money-fief or annual grant. Most of John's other imperial clients were attached to the Burgundian interest in a similar way. Count Eberhard IV of Württemberg, for instance, is said to have done homage to John in 1404–5, and his son Eberhard V was asked to perform military service for John in 1418. Eberhard IV, who had already served John in Paris in 1405 and possibly in Picardy in 1411, and who had sent him a bear as a gift in 1410, did homage, apparently for a second time, at Lille on 13 March 1416, along with two minor lords of the Rhine area. In 1405 a group of four German lords, led by Duke Stephen II of Bavaria, were negotiating with John the Fearless for alliances of some kind, which probably took the form of fief-rents.[1]

On the other hand, a few of the more powerful of John the Fearless's military allies in Germany were bound to him by means of a treaty as between two equals. Such an alliance was made on 24 August 1416 with Duke Frederick of Austria, the contracting parties promising to come to each other's aid against an aggressor with at least 200 men-at-arms. Provisions for the extradition of undesirables and the arbitration of disputes were also included in this treaty. A very similar mutual defence pact was proposed and probably made at about the same time with Dietrich von Mörs, archbishop of Cologne. Again, provision was made for the arbitration of disputes, and in this treaty military liabilities were defined geographically, as well as being limited to defence against aggression. There is no evidence, incidentally, that either of these treaties was actually invoked, and we can only guess at the number of similar alliances which John may have made with other imperial vassals. Their principal significance for history is the way they point, like so much else in John the Fearless's reign, forwards to the policies and projects of his successors. They, and the fief-rents mentioned above, represent part of a growing involvement with the Empire, of an eastward orientation of Burgundian policies and ambitions, which some historians, misled or mesmerized by John the Fearless's rôle in France, have chosen to ignore or, rather, to disregard until Philip the Good's reign.

Unfortunately, our knowledge of John the Fearless's diplomatic contacts with the various European countries is limited by the brevity of the entries in the accounts, which seldom state the cause

<hr/>

[1] *DRA* vi. 257–8; ACO B1594, f. 108b; Juv. des Ursins, *Hist. de Charles VI*, 424; Plancher, iii. 342; Coville, *Les Cabochiens*, 31, n. 1; ADN B1601, f. 118; and ADN B501/15424. See, too, above, p. 142. For what follows in the next paragraph, see *IADNB* i (1), 222–3 = ADN B290/15328, ADN B291/15405 and 14586.

or result of an ambassador's journey, but only the cost and destination. With Portugal, for instance, John the Fearless had contacts, but we can only guess at their significance. Between 1411 and 1418 a Portuguese squire served at the Burgundian court as ducal chamberlain. In 1412 the ducal painter, Jehan Malouel, was instructed to execute a portrait of John the Fearless for despatch to King John I of Portugal. Why, we do not know. Nor can we now ascertain what it was that brought a Portuguese ambassador to John the Fearless's court in September 1418, though the accounts record that he was given 300 francs to buy plate for himself 'so that he will always have a better recollection of my lord [the duke of Burgundy] and be more favourably disposed towards him and his affairs'.[1] These and similar questions will only be resolved by detailed researches in the archives of the Portuguese crown at Lisbon.

The friendly relations and periodic contacts between Burgundy and Aragon which had been cemented by a fraternal alliance or confraternity between Philip the Bold and Martin I, continued under John the Fearless, at least till Martin's death in 1410. Pons de Perellos, the Aragonese knight who had settled in France as councillor and chamberlain of the duke of Burgundy, acted as a go-between and almost as a permanent ambassador of Martin, whose councillor he also was, at the Burgundian court. John the Fearless gave him a handsome travel allowance of 500 francs when he permitted him to visit Aragon on temporary leave of absence in 1408 or 1409. At this time the confraternity between king of Aragon and duke of Burgundy was renewed, and in 1409 we find the two rulers exchanging embassies on the subject of the papal schism. With Castile, too, letters and embassies were exchanged, though little seems to have emerged from the embassy of King Henry III to John the Fearless in 1405, asking specifically for an alliance. John was too busy at that time, he explained in his reply to Henry, even to send an embassy, though he would have liked an alliance.

Burgundian relations with the kingdom of Scotland in John the Fearless's ducal reign were frequent though essentially trivial. While

[1] ACO B1594, f. 140. For this paragraph, see Monget, *Chartreuse de Dijon*, ii. 22–3; *Cartulaire de l'Estaple de Bruges*, i. no. 589; Pocquet, *France gouv. par J. sans Peur*, 49; and de Laborde, *Ducs de Bourgogne*, i. 68 and 142. For the next paragraph see Vaughan, *P. the Bold*, 109; Calmette, *RB* xviii (3–4) (1908), 139–96; ACO B1558, f. 70b; ACO B1560, f. 209; *Procesos de las antiguas cortes de Cataluña*, i. nos. 41 and 43; Vieilliard and Mirot, *BEC* ciii (1942), 99–150; and *Analectes historiques* (11), *BCRH* (3) vii (1865), 15–17.

Scottish pirates preyed on shipping in the North Sea, the privileges of Scottish merchants visiting Flanders were confirmed by John in 1407, as a result of an embassy from the regent of Scotland, the duke of Albany. In 1408 a Scottish knight was given a Burgundian pension, and another, the earl of Mar, who happened to be in Flanders at the time, fought in the Burgundian army at Othée. Scottish mercenaries, described in the accounts as 'wild Scots',[1] were actually recruited in Scotland for use with the Burgundian army in 1411. Early in 1413 Archibald, earl of Douglas, set out on a trip to Paris. Arrested soon after his landing at Sluis on the complaint of some citizens of Malines, who claimed that he had seized one of their wool ships while on his way, and sold it and its cargo for his own profit, he only managed to bail himself out of prison in Bruges by leaving two of his knights behind as hostages. While the earl of Douglas was in Paris, John signed a treaty of alliance with him on 11 April 1413, according to the terms of which the earl promised to bring 4,000 men to the assistance of the duke in Flanders or Artois whenever the duke needed them. John, for his part, made the palpably insincere promise to sail to Scotland in person with 300 men as soon as his help was needed there by the earl of Douglas. Besides these contacts, embassies with Scotland were exchanged on several occasions and gifts were sent by John to the duke of Albany, who lent him some money in 1418.[2]

Other powers with which John the Fearless maintained contact were the Hanseatic League and the Order of Teutonic Knights in Prussia. Relations with the Hanse were of course primarily commercial, and concerned Flanders rather than Burgundy as a whole or even John the Fearless himself. In 1405, however, and again in 1407, John tried to persuade the Hanse and the Grand Master of the Teutonic Knights to make war on England in alliance with him. These requests had no more effect than the Grand Master's appeal to John the Fearless and others, in 1411, for military aid against Poland. With the Italian states, John the Fearless's contacts were mostly ephemeral. In 1406 the Burgundian flag was unfurled on the walls of Pisa, which for a brief period then accepted the joint

---

[1] That is Highlanders, as opposed to 'tame' or Lowland Scots.
[2] For this paragraph, see *Hanserecesse*, v. no. 641 and vi. no. 605; *IAB* iv. 334–5; *Cartulaire de l'Estaple de Bruges*, i. no. 543; Pocquet, *MSHDB* viii (1942), 147; above, p. 55; *IADNB* iv. 61; Kervyn, *Flandre*, iv. 178–9; Plancher, iii. 373 = ACO B11937; quittance of 23 March 1418 in ACO B11926; ACO B1570, f. 77a–b; de Laborde, *Ducs de Bourgogne*, i. 96–7; Newhall, *English conquest of Normandy*, 106; and, in general, du Fresne de Beaucourt, *Hist. de Charles VII*, i. 305–20.

suzerainty of John the Fearless and Louis, duke of Orleans. In April 1413 John contrived to have himself appointed governor and lieutenant-general of Genoa for the king of France, but this was of much less real significance than his charter of privileges for the Genoese merchants in Flanders, issued on 1 October 1414.[1]

With Venice, John the Fearless found himself involved in a complex series of negotiations concerning a rent of 7,000 ducats per annum which had been paid or promised by Venice to King Sigismund. When that ruler, as king of Hungary, had offered 100,000 ducats towards the ransom of John the Fearless and his companions after the crusade of Nicopolis in 1396, but had been unable to find the cash, this rent had been accepted by the duke of Burgundy's financier Dino Rapondi, and, in exchange for it, Dino had paid Sigismund 100,000 ducats for him to give to John the Fearless towards his ransom. Subsequently, the duke of Burgundy reimbursed Dino his 100,000 ducats and took over the rent himself. But the Venetians refused to pay this rent of 7,000 ducats to the duke of Burgundy, maintaining that they were bound to pay it only to Sigismund. In any case they had only agreed to pay it to him in return for his promise to protect their shipping in the Adriatic, and, since Sigismund was not in a position to do this, the Venetians claimed that they were excused from paying the rent. John the Fearless sent several embassies to Venice, particularly in 1405–6 and again in 1410, to try to persuade the Venetians, since they were unwilling to pay this annual rent, to pay instead the capital sum of 100,000 ducats, or at least a large part of it. But the Venetians remained adamant and John, unwilling to undertake reprisals against Venetian merchants in Flanders because of the economic susceptibilities and political power of his Flemish subjects, let the matter drop. It was not finally settled until after his death.

Although it would be a mistake to attach special significance to John the Fearless's diplomatic contacts with other European countries, the general conclusion of this chapter must surely be that, under

[1] Finot, *Flandre et Gênes*, p.j. no. 4 and *Cartulaire de l'Estaple de Bruges*, i. no. 610. For this paragraph, see *Hansisches Urkundenbuch*, v; *Hanserecesse*, v, vi and viii; Beuken, *Hanze en Vlaanderen*; Daenell, *Blütezeit der Hanse*, i; above, p. 23; Voigt, *Geschichte Preussens*, vii. 151 and n.; and Stein, *Inventaire analytique*, no. 267. For the next paragraph, see Vaughan, *P. the Bold*, 74; Delaville le Roulx, *France en Orient*, i. 324–33; *Commerce et expéditions*, no. 24; and ACO B1543, f. 86b and 1560, fos. 204b–5 and 217b.

him, Burgundy was a major European power. Moreover, can we not discern, in John the Fearless's support of his sister Catherine; in his close relations with Savoy; in his contacts with Germany; and in his growing influence in the Netherlands, the ramifications of a deliberate policy of extending Burgundian power wherever possible? Would it be going too far to assert that in Alsace, in Luxembourg, in Brabant, in Hainault-Holland, John the Fearless was making careful preparations for the distant but possible annexation of these areas to the Burgundian state?

CHAPTER TEN

The Bridge of Montereau

Ever since his precipitate flight from Paris in August 1413, John the Fearless had been trying to regain power in France. In November 1417 he persuaded the queen to join him in setting up a government of their own; in May 1418 his troops seized Paris and, along with the capital, he obtained control of the person of the king and of the entire administrative and financial organization of the French crown. But, even though from June 1418 on John the Fearless enjoyed possession of ample funds and exercised unlimited theoretical power through his ability to issue letters and *ordonnances* in the king's name, nevertheless two men who had appeared on the French political scene in 1417 made this newly-won authority uncertain, restricted and even illusory. They were the fifteen-year-old dauphin Charles, who arrogated to himself the title regent of France and, before the end of the year 1418, had installed his own *Parlement* at Poitiers and his own *chambre des comptes* at Bourges; and King Henry V of England who, claiming to be king of France as well, had set about the systematic reduction of that country, starting with the conquest and military occupation of Normandy in 1417–18. Thus, in 1418–19, three rivals disputed political and military power in France: Duke John of Burgundy, acting through and with the king and queen, Charles VI and Isabel; their son Charles, the dauphin; and King Henry V of England.[1]

It is not intended here to trace in all their intricacy the military and political events which followed the Burgundian seizure of Paris in

[1] For this chapter I have used d'Avout, *Armagnacs et Bourguignons*; du Fresne de Beaucourt, *Hist. de Charles VII*; Jacob, *Henry V* and *Fifteenth century*; Pocquet, *France gouv. par J. sans Peur*; Wylie and Waugh, *Henry V*, iii; also the chroniclers, principally *Chronique des Cordeliers*; de Fauquembergue's *Journal*; Juvenel des Ursins, Monstrelet and the Religieux de St. Denys.

May 1418 and led to the assassination of John the Fearless in September 1419. Though the duke of Burgundy played a prominent part in them, they concern French rather than Burgundian history. There was much negotiation in 1418–19 between the three parties, but little fighting. The siege and conquest of Rouen by Henry V was the only major military operation, and this had no effect whatsoever on the general political situation, which was one of stalemate. The attitudes of the three contestants for power and the geographical areas they controlled scarcely changed at all during these fifteen months.

A map showing accurately the geographical division of France at this time between the Burgundians, the Armagnacs or Dauphinists,

7. The division of France between English, Dauphinists and Burgundians in 1418–19

and the English, would require a great deal of detailed research, for this division was in fact exceedingly complex. The English, besides their existing possessions of Calais and a large part of south-western France centred on Bordeaux, now held Normandy by force of arms, while the duke of Brittany, John V, seems to have been in Henry V's pocket. Having at last conquered Rouen in January 1419, Henry turned up the Seine valley, but his progress towards Paris in 1419 was slow: Pontoise did not fall until July.

The area held in 1418-19 by the Burgundians stretched from Flanders and Artois in the north, down the eastern side of France through Mâcon, to Nîmes in the extreme south. But this area by no means formed a continuous strip of territory. In the south, the obstinately Dauphinist city of Lyons formed a link between the Dauphiné itself, which was of course the dauphin's own apanage, in the extreme south-east of the country, and the rest of Dauphinist France. In the north, the princely houses of Anjou and of Orleans, supporters of the dauphin, possessed extensive domains in the valleys of the Aisne and Oise, including for instance the county of Guise, possession of which enabled them to capture such places as Soissons and Compiègne, and made it dangerous for the Burgundians to travel between Troyes and St. Quentin. Moreover the Dauphinists based on Meaux and Melun exercised something approaching a strategic stranglehold on Paris which, especially after the English conquest of Pontoise, became a beleaguered city. Indeed, John the Fearless was compelled to withdraw from it in January 1419, and set up his headquarters thereafter in the Dominican friary at Provins.[1] Strategically his position in Paris, and even in parts of Champagne and Picardy, was basically unsound.

It was the Dauphinists, as we must now call the Armagnacs since their titular leader Count Bernard VII had been murdered in Paris in June 1418, who enjoyed possession of the greater, and the most central, part of France. In Anjou, Berry, Blois, Orleans, Poitou, Bourbon and Auvergne they were supreme, and remained unchallenged, and they held or reconquered in this area important towns like Tours,[2] Poitiers and Bourges. Further south, in Languedoc, a local struggle in 1418-19 between the Dauphinist John, count of Foix, and the Burgundian Louis de Chalon, prince of Orange, resulted in the expulsion of the Burgundians from the whole area save for Nîmes and Pont St. Esprit.[3]

[1] ACO B1601, f. 132.   [2] See Delaville le Roulx, *CH* xxiii (1877), 161-231.
[3] Dognon, *AM* i (1889), 452-80.

On the whole, the respective attitudes of the three rivals in France seem to have been as fixed and unchangeable as their geographical situations. Here too, an impasse was reached which is perhaps hardly surprising when we appreciate that, during nearly the whole of this period, between May 1418 and September 1419, all three were fighting and negotiating with each other at the same time.

The attitude of Henry V to the affairs of France need not detain us long. It was mainly acquisitive. He had conquered Normandy, but he could not afford to pay indefinitely for the expensive army of occupation which was necessary to retain it. After this striking military success, which culminated in the taking of Rouen, some kind of political settlement was essential for him. He was prepared to listen to the offers of both the French parties but, during John the Fearless's lifetime, he accepted those of neither. Both parties were prepared to give him the hand of Catherine of France in marriage, but neither the dauphin nor John the Fearless could accept his absurdly extensive territorial demands, which included either Flanders, in return for an alliance with the dauphin against John; or Guienne, in return for helping John the Fearless against the dauphin.[1]

In June 1418 the fifteen-year-old dauphin Charles took over leadership of the Armagnac party and assumed the government of France on behalf of his father Charles VI, whose lieutenant-general he was. His attitude, or that of his advisers, is well expressed in the letter he sent at that time to Lyons and other towns loyal to him.

> To our dearest and well-loved, the consuls, burgesses and inhabitants of the town of Lyons, from the dauphin of Viennois, duke of Berry, of Touraine, count of Poitou and lieutenant-general of my lord [the king] in his kingdom.
>
> Dearest and well-loved . . . you have been sufficiently well-informed, by our own letters indeed, of the recent outrageous happenings at Paris. How, by treason, riot and popular sedition, certain rebels, disobedient to the king, entered the said town by night . . . on the very day when we had resolved to confirm the treaty of peace of this kingdom, which had been discussed for a long time by the ambassadors of both sides. . . .
>
> In Paris they seized the person of my lord the king, whom they have detained and are now detaining. They committed all sorts of cruelties,

---

[1] For the attitude of Henry V and the English council to the French parties, see *Procs. and Ords. of the P.C.*, ii. 350–8. The dauphin's letter which follows is printed by du Fresne de Beaucourt, *Hist. de Charles VII*, i. 98–101.

pillages, murders and inhumanities and, while crying peace!, with swords drawn and bloody they murdered or imprisoned, pillaged robbed and in general despoiled, all the good and loyal servants of the king and ourselves on whom they could lay their hands. . . . While this was going on . . . we withdrew to the Bastille St. Antoine to escape the fury. Then . . . we went to Melun, and thence to our town of Bourges. . . .

Since these events . . . the rebels . . ., not content with the perpetration of the above-mentioned . . . crimes and cruelties, have been round to all the prisons in Paris like people ignorant of God and without any human pity, furiously and in disorder, and have there inhumanly and cruelly murdered and cut to pieces the king's constable and chancellor, various bishops and prelates, knights and squires, royal officers and others . . . to the number of two or three thousand persons who were prisoners there. . . . These, cut into pieces like beasts, they have thrown and scattered on the streets of Paris . . ., reducing the town, which is the capital of this kingdom . . . to ruin and desolation. . . .

We let you know these things, dearest and well-beloved, in order to keep you truthfully informed and, what is more important, to keep you always in your good loyalty . . . and also so that, as true and loyal subjects, you will be [ready] in love and unity together to serve, succour and aid my lord the king with us and in our aid . . . without obeying anyone else except us, [acting] on behalf of the king. For we are his only son, heir and the successor to his crown, to whom, by reason and natural right, belongs the responsibility for governing and administering [this kingdom] while my lord the king is thus detained and kept in custody. . . .

Because the aforesaid rebels . . . have murdered the chancellor and seized our great seal and the king's, which they can abuse at their will, we forbid you to obey any letters or writs sent to you whatsoever, except our own, sealed with our privy seal and signed with our own hand, until the great seals are remade. . . .

We shall shortly be sending you some of our people to explain our news and plans more fully, and to give you aid and comfort in all things. . . . Dearest and well-beloved, may Our Lord be your guard. Written in our town of Aubigny, 29 June.

Charles   Alain

In July 1418 some of the dauphin's advisers and supporters encouraged him to seek a negotiated settlement with John the Fearless. The resulting conferences, in which the duke of Brittany played a prominent and somewhat partisan rôle, ended on 19 September with the triumphant publication in Paris and elsewhere of the treaty of St. Maur-des-Fossés between John the Fearless and the dauphin Charles. But the terms of this treaty were totally unacceptable to Charles, for their execution, by installing him with his parents at the

French court, would have placed him firmly in the hands of John the Fearless. He therefore repudiated it and, almost at once, made contact with the English with a view to seeking an alliance with them against John the Fearless.

The terms of the treaty of St. Maur illustrate the aim of John the Fearless, which was to undermine and disperse the Dauphinist party by gaining control of the dauphin's youthful person. Of course he used the royal seals in exactly the manner predicted by the dauphin, and royal letters putting forward his point of view reached and doubtless encouraged the towns loyal to him, just as the dauphin's letters were sent to the Dauphinist towns. The Burgundian interpretation of events in the second half of 1418 is set out in the following royal letter to Rheims.[1]

> To our dear and well-loved clerics, aldermen, burgesses and inhabitants of the town of Rheims.
>
> Dear and well-loved, we feel sure that there is no earthly thing more pleasant, desirable or agreeable to you than to hear good news of the health of our person, and to be informed of our situation and our affairs at the moment. We are writing to you now, as our good, true, loyal and obedient subjects, to tell you about these very matters; also to inform you fully and accurately about events in our kingdom during some time past; and to expose the monstrous disloyalty of certain people of mean condition, disturbers of the peace who, being in the entourage of our dearest and well-loved son the dauphin of Viennois, and keeping him in their power and under their influence . . . caused letters from our aforesaid son to be sent to several cities and good towns of our kingdom. . . . By this means they hoped to seduce and entice you and our other good and loyal subjects . . . from the loyalty and obedience which you have always had for us . . . who are your true king and sovereign lord. [This] under colour of the authority which, against God, reason, justice and all law, and against our wishes and pleasure, they granted and outrageously attributed without fear of God to our aforesaid son, in calling him and causing him to be named regent of our kingdom . . ., apparently wishing to expel and throw us out of our kingdom and usurp our crown, sceptre and royal majesty. . . .
>
> To come to the events since last July. Presumably you remember how our . . . cousin the duke of Burgundy at that time restored to us our dearest and well-loved consort the queen, whom the aforesaid disturbers of the peace had separated and taken away from us some time before, taking her, a prisoner in a miserable state, to Blois and thence to Tours. . . . You must also know of the considerable trouble we have gone to to

---

[1] *Lettres closes*, 27–34.

establish peace and union in our kingdom. . . . To this end our aforesaid cousin of Burgundy on the one side, and our son-in-law of Brittany
on the other, assembled at St. Maur-des-Fossés by our commandment,
together with several councillors of ours and of our aforesaid son . . .
and they agreed together to draw up a certain treaty of peace, to which
they swore, and which we approved and caused to be published in our
kingdom. And, to obtain similar ratification from our son the dauphin
and others of our blood and lineage, as well as to facilitate, through union
and concord, resistance to our ancient enemies and adversaries of England, who have occupied and still occupy a large part of Normandy . . .,
our said son-in-law of Brittany [and our other ambassadors] returned
to the dauphin . . . to try to induce him to [sign the] said treaty, but in
vain, because the above-mentioned disturbers of the peace . . . would
not allow our ambassadors to speak to him. . . . Indeed . . . they caused
our son [-in-law] of Brittany to be disavowed and all the points he had
undertaken and negotiated on our behalf to be annulled.

'The king' goes on to blame his failure to muster the French army
in the autumn of 1418 to raise the siege of Rouen on these same 'disturbers of the peace', whose military activities and direct prohibition
had hindered the royal vassals from obeying the summons to Beauvais
for 15 October.

Yesterday we arrived in good health . . . in this our town of Provins,
with our consort, our dearest and well-loved daughter Catherine, and
our cousin of Burgundy, and we intend to stay here for some time, since
it is a convenient place, well-suited for summoning and assembling our
vassals, subjects, friends and supporters of various countries, lands and
regions, so that we can, in the near future, make war on . . . our enemies
and adversaries of England. . . . At the same time we shall and do daily
devote ourselves to the task of procuring peace, love and concord in our
kingdom. . . .

We pray you as earnestly as we can, dear and good friends, and we
request you by the faith and loyalty which you owe us and which you
have always retained for us, to persevere more and more virtuously in
your good resolution, true loyalty and just intention, without giving
faith or credence to any adverse reports made to you about us and our
rule. In this you will be doing your duty, and you will earn merit with
God. . . . If it please Our Lord, witness of our conscience and guardian
of our right, we shall see very soon to all your affairs. . . .
Given at Provins, 23 January.

Charles   Tinel

While the people of Rouen sustained the English siege from 30 July
1418 until their surrender from starvation on 19 January 1419, the

people of Paris were little better off. Indeed the whole of north-east France, in the autumn of 1418, experienced chaos, turmoil and deprivation. Those contending for power concentrated their energies on fighting, negotiating, or raising support for themselves, and the civil administration of the country, good government and justice were neglected or abandoned. The Burgundian *maître des comptes* Toussains Bajart wrote from Paris to his colleagues at Lille on 19 October 1418:[1]

> As to news from here, pestilences of death and of war grieve us. Famine approaches unless God provides. Merchandise ceases by land and water, labour is scarce. . . . Treasons and seditions reign, brother against brother, neighbour against neighbour, the son against the father. Justice is moribund. Those in authority prefer their private advantage to the public welfare or the ruler's profit. At Rouen they are eating horseflesh. I do not know when the king and my lord [the duke of Burgundy] will depart. . . . Everything is going to perdition.

In the spring of 1419 both John the Fearless and the dauphin were negotiating with the English, but it was John the Fearless who was successful in arranging a personal meeting between himself and Henry V. Indeed a whole series of meetings were staged at Meulan between 30 May and 30 June, but these elaborate conferences were broken off without any agreement being reached, much to the annoyance of Henry V, if we are to believe Monstrelet, who had hoped to persuade John the Fearless to accept his territorial demands. The Dauphinist chronicler Juvenel des Ursins gives a curious and detailed account, embellished with the customary fictitious oratory, of this diplomacy and its picturesque trappings.[2]

> On the Tuesday following, which was 30 May 1419, the king fell sick and so he stayed at Pontoise. The queen and Madame Catherine, in a richly decorated litter with their ladies-in-waiting and maids of honour, arrived in the company of the duke of Burgundy at the tents near Meulan where the trumpeters and musicians were playing on their instruments, at about 2.0 p.m. About an hour before, the king of England had arrived at his tents for, though there was to be a single tent only in the centre of the field where the actual conference was to take place, nevertheless there were tents on either side [for each party] to retire into. Soon after the queen had withdrawn into her tent, the earl of Warwick came to see

---

[1] ADN B17624. Bajart, named among the Cabochiens in royal letters of 18 September 1413 (*Foedera*, iv (2), 46–8), was appointed *m. des comptes* at Lille in 1417, Lannoy, *Oeuvres*, 480.
[2] *Hist. de Charles VI*, 551–4.

her, with other English nobles, on behalf of the king of England, and it
was agreed that the queen and the king of England should leave their
tents at the same time and in like manner, and that they should walk
slowly as far as the centre of the field, where a stake was fixed. . . .
Only sixty nobles and sixteen councillors from either side were to enter
[the central tent with them], and these were to be summoned individually
by name.

The queen left her tent at about 3.0 p.m., the councillors preceding
her, two by two. When she and the king of England reached the above-
mentioned stake, the king of England took the queen's hand and kissed
it, and likewise Madame Catherine's. Similarly the king's two brothers
kissed them, almost kneeling on the ground while they did so. Then the
king of England took the queen by the hand and together they went to
the tent where the meeting was to be held. There the king and the
queen seated themselves in the thrones which were already prepared
[for them] in similar fashion, with cloth of gold and canopies over them.
. . . After this, the earl of Warwick knelt down and addressed the
queen of France, expounding briefly the purpose of their assembly.
But nothing was concluded, except for a prolongation of the truces for
eight days . . . and that the parties would gather again in the same place
and in like manner on the following Thursday. This conference
lasted from 3.0 p.m. until 7.0 p.m.

Now the meeting-place was arranged in the following manner. Near
the gate of Meulan on the Pontoise side there was a meadow, bordered
by the river Seine on one side and a pond on the other, through the
middle of which was a public right of way. This meadow was divided
into three. In one part, nearest the town, were the numerous tents of
the king and queen [of France], and the duke of Burgundy. The king of
England's tents were on the far side, along the river and, in the third and
central part of the meadow, between the tents of the kings of France and
England, there was an enclosure, fortified with ditches and a palisade,
which had only three entrances, each defended by excellent barriers and
fifty well-armed and well-prepared men. Besides this, the king and
queen's part [of the meadow] . . . was encircled with posts set together so
that it was like a fortified town, which no one could attack either with
lances or missiles. These posts went right to the bank of the river Seine,
and posts were also fixed across the river at this point . . ., so that neither
party could approach the other save through the central enclosure. The
English camp was likewise entrenched and palisaded, but not so strongly.

Now the stake where the queen and the king of England had met,
which was only about a foot high, was in the middle of the central
enclosure. . . . The pavilion in which they conferred . . . was set up
here, and two other pavilions were attached to it, one at each end,
into which the queen and the king of England could individually retire
when they chose. . . .

The parties assembled on several occasions, but various difficulties arose . . . and some people urged [the duke of Burgundy] that it would be better to treat with my lord the dauphin regent than to cede to the king of England's demands and grant his requests. . . . Sir Tanguy du Chastel, the lord of Barbazan, and others, visited Pontoise [on the dauphin's behalf] for this reason, to treat of the form and manner of peace, which they were very desirous of, affirming that my lord the dauphin regent, their master, and all his councillors, were of the same mind. . . .

[The duke of Burgundy] resolved that this matter should be debated, that is, whether or not it was desirable to negotiate and make peace with the English, accepting their conditions. Two well-known clerics were ordered to do this, one, Master Nicolas Rolin, the other, Master Jehan Rapiout. Rolin claimed that it was better to treat with the English . . . and that the king could well alienate some of his domain and give away part of his kingdom, in exchange for so great a benefit as peace. He maintained . . . that the power of the English made it necessary for them to make peace with the king of England . . .; that the dauphin was trying to come to an agreement with the English . . . ; that [unless they made peace] the city of Paris and other cities of the kingdom, seeing no hope of succour, would do as Rouen had done; and that, even if they were united with the dauphin in a peace settlement, it would still be necessary to treat with the king of England. . . .

Master Jehan Rapiout on the contrary tried to show . . . that the king could not and ought not to treat with the English, since this would amount to alienation, and he had sworn at his coronation not to alienate anything . . .; that . . . the king of England had no right to the French throne nor, because of the murder perpetrated by his father against the person of Richard II, had he any right to the English throne either . . .; and that if somebody else with a right to it seized the English throne, any treaty which they had negotiated would become null and void. . . .

At Meulan Henry V was cheated of the fair Catherine of France and of the territorial settlement favourable to himself which he had hoped to obtain from the duke of Burgundy. Uncertainty reigned, in July, among the English lodged at Mantes, who were well aware of the negotiations between John the Fearless and the dauphin mentioned in the foregoing extract. The following letter, giving news of their situation and prospects, was sent home to England from Mantes by one R. Priour on 14 July 1419:[1]

And, whanne [the treaty between us and the French] was broughte to the Point for to have ben Engrossed, and fullyth to be maad an Ende

---

[1] *Foedera*, iv (3), 126–7.

of, The saide Frenssh Partie hath comen with diverses Demandes and Questions, in Lettying and Taryyng of that Matere, so ferforthe that, now at this Tyme, it is nat knowen whethir we shall have Werre or Pees.

But, withynne six Dayes after the Date of this Lettre, y suppose that ther wole be redy Word of Pees or of Werre; Whethir that it be as soone, as that Tyme cometh, y shall certifie You in all haste.

Moreover, Worshipful Master, duryng al this Tyme of Convention between our Souvereyn Lord and the Frenssh Partie, the Daulphin and the Duc of Burgoine han had here Place of Convention and Metyng togeder beside Parys; and thaire Counseil han laboured on other Partie, that they have sette hem Tweyne in Reste and in Accorde; and Proclamed in Parys, that noon an so hardy to make noon Querel on eynes other, because of the Name of Burgoignon or Armaignac, *nec e converso.* For which Accord, it is y supposed in the Kynges Host rather Werre than Pees.

The rapprochement of the dauphin and John the Fearless had begun before the conferences at Meulan, for the royal proclamation of a three-month truce between the two parties was actually ratified by the dauphin on 20 May, and by John on 23 May.[1] During the first half of July three personal meetings took place between the dauphin and the duke of Burgundy: on 8 and 11 July, at Pouilly-le-Fort; and on 13 July, at Corbeil. From these conferences a peace of sorts emerged in the form of the treaty of Pouilly-le-Fort, dated 11 July, according to the terms of which the forty-eight-year-old duke of Burgundy and the sixteen-year-old dauphin promised to be friends, to govern France jointly, and to attack the English together. These terms were far too vague to be effective, and indeed neither party appears to have had any intention of carrying them out. John the Fearless maintained diplomatic contacts with the English during the second half of July and Charles, acting presumably on the advice of his councillors and supporters, refused to join his parents at the French court or make any move towards co-operation with John the Fearless.

The capture of Pontoise by the English, who surprised the town soon after dawn on 31 July, when the watch had left their posts after an all-night vigil, caused something approaching panic in Paris, and led John the Fearless to withdraw with the king and queen to Champagne. Soon afterwards, he broke off his negotiations with the English

---

[1] Documents printed in *Mémoires*, i. 251–4. The treaty of Pouilly and associated documents are also printed in *Mémoires*, i. 255–70.

and, in the first half of August, he was not only summoning troops from the two Burgundies in order to attack them, but was also again negotiating with the dauphin. Evidently he hoped to make a further attempt to gain control of, or at least influence over, the dauphin's person, by means of a negotiated peace. But it was only after much hesitation that John the Fearless agreed to another personal conference between himself and Charles, to take place on Sunday, 10 September, on the bridge of Montereau-Faut-Yonne, at the confluence of the Seine and Yonne some forty-five miles south-east of Paris as the crow flies.

Abundant and often detailed evidence has survived concerning John the Fearless's assassination on the bridge of Montereau and, in view of the disagreement of historians about the very nature of this event, it seems desirable to examine this evidence here. No attempt will be made to reconstruct the drama and tension of the final scenes of John's turbulent life and their aftermath; nor shall we on this occasion permit contemporaries, often confused or purposely misleading, to speak for themselves. Instead, it is proposed to analyse the available evidence in an attempt to answer the simple question: what actually happened?

Leaving aside everything of doubtful significance, the evidence now at the disposal of an investigation into the death of John the Fearless may be classified and summarized as follows:

1. *Archæological and topographical.* The supposed skull of John the Fearless, examined by kings and queens in the sixteenth and seventeenth and by panels of doctors in the nineteenth and twentieth centuries. Full details in Monget, d'Arbaumont, *et al.*, *MCACO* xiv (1901–5), 157–251. The skull is figured in van Swygenhoven, *BARB* x (2) (1843), 229–39. The drawing of the bridge of Montereau, now destroyed, made in 1611.

2. *Letters.* On the Burgundian side:
    (a) Anonymous letter to Philip the Good. The writer interviewed people at Montereau. No date. Printed, *Mémoires*, i. 286–7.
    (b) The duchess of Burgundy to the *maîtres des comptes* at Dijon, 18 November 1419. Summarized, *Mémoires*, i. 289–91.
    (c) Henry de Monstroeul to Tournai, written in Paris, 13 September 1419. Summarized, *Extraits analytiques de Tournai*, 180–1.

On the Dauphinist side:

(*a*) The dauphin to the French towns, 11 September 1419. Printed Plancher, iii. no. 309 and *Mémoires*, i. 298–9.

(*b*) The dauphin to Philip the Good, 15 September 1419. Printed du Fresne de Beaucourt, *RQH* v (1868), 220–2.

(*c*) Letter of Tanguy du Chastel, 16 July 1425, exculpating the dauphin's chancellor from complicity in the murder. Printed, du Fresne de Beaucourt, *Hist. de Charles VII*, ii. 654.

3. *Burgundian reports or quasi-official accounts.*

(*a*) Report by Philippe de Morvillers to Tournai, 2 October 1419. Summarized, *Extraits analytiques*, 184–7.

(*b*) Report by the duchess of Burgundy, sent to the duchess of Bourbon. Not dated. Printed, *Mémoires*, i. 287–9.

(*c*) Two accounts published by Kervyn de Lettenhove from two different MSS., in *BCRH* (3) viii (1866), 91–6 and (4) i (1873), 197–202.

(*d*) Report received by the magistrates of Mons, 20 September 1419. Printed, *Cartulaire de Hainaut*, iv. 206–8.

4. *Depositions and legal declarations.*

(*a*) Depositions made by four Burgundian knights and the ducal secretary Jehan Seguinat, all of whom were present with their duke when the murder was committed. Printed, *Mémoires*, i. 271–86.

(*b*) Sworn statement made by Jehan de Poitiers, bishop of Valence, exculpating the dauphin's chancellor, Robert le Maçon, from complicity in the murder. Printed, du Fresne de Beaucourt, *Hist. de Charles VII*, ii. 635–8.

5. *Chroniclers.* Those who have substantial accounts are Monstrelet, *Chronique*, iii. 338–46; Juvenel des Ursins, *Histoire de Charles VI*, 556–7; and Religieux de St. Denys, vi. 372–4. Le Févre, *Chronique*, i. 37–9 and *Chronique des Cordeliers*, 279–80, are dependent on the same material as Monstrelet. There are scraps of information of doubtful value in de Fenin, *Mémoires*, 111–17; Cousinot, *Geste des nobles françois*, 177; and de Fauquembergue, *Journal*, i. 317–18.

This, then, is the evidence at our disposal. Although the different accounts of what happened at Montereau vary a great deal, a certain body of undisputed fact emerges, which is supported by the bulk of the evidence from both sides. There is no doubt that John the Fearless went unwillingly, or at least hesitantly, to meet the dauphin at Montereau, having been persuaded to go by Charles's ambassadors,

as well as by some of his own people. No one disputes that it was the
dauphin or his advisers who took the initiative in making the arrangements for the meeting. It was the dauphin who made over the castle
of Montereau to John the Fearless and his people; who supervised
the construction of the palisades on the bridge between the castle
and the town where the meeting was intended to take place. It was
the dauphin who insisted that only ten men on either side should be
present at the meeting. All accounts agree, too, that John the Fearless
arrived from Bray-sur-Seine with some hundred men; left the bulk
of them in or near the castle at the confluence of the rivers Seine and
Yonne; and advanced onto the bridge over the Yonne and into the
palisaded enclosure constructed on it, to meet the dauphin. It was on
the bridge, inside this wooden enclosure, that he was struck down
and killed. Our evidence disagrees about the exact manner of his
death, but there is no dispute about what happened next: all the Burgundians who had entered the enclosure with their duke were taken
prisoner. Many of John the Fearless's other people fled precipitately
at this point; but some remained in the castle overnight, surrendering
the next day. The dead duke was buried in Montereau.

We come now to a question of central importance which historians
have answered in very different ways. Was the killing of John the
Fearless a premeditated crime? The Burgundians answered affirma-
tively, but the Dauphinists, right from the start, insisted that there
was no premeditation whatsoever. They put forward the story or
theory of a sudden scuffle, during which John the Fearless was more
or less inadvertently done to death, or killed in self-defence. It was
the dauphin himself who was responsible for this version of events,
which completely exonerated both him and his councillors. He even
went further, and suggested that John the Fearless was hoping and
planning to get hold of his person. When they met on the bridge,
John remonstrated with him, an argument broke out, and Archambaud de Foix, lord of Noailles, one of the Burgundian knights with
John the Fearless, drew his sword. A fracas ensued during which
John was killed. This theory of a sudden mêlée on the bridge, due
primarily to an argument between Charles and John which caused
tempers to rise, has been accepted by some historians, notably du
Fresne de Beaucourt, Kleinclausz, d'Avout and Calmette,[1] but no one
has taken seriously the suggestion that John the Fearless planned or
attempted to seize the dauphin.

[1] *Hist. de Charles VII*, i. 163–78; *Hist. de Bourgogne*, 146–7; *Armagnacs et
Bourguignons*, 296–300; and *Grands ducs*, 170–1.

The only contemporary or near-contemporary evidence for the fracas theory are two letters of the dauphin describing what happened on the bridge, both of them written in September 1419, and the account in the pages of Juvenel des Ursins, which may be derived from them. If anyone knew exactly what did happen on the bridge of Montereau, it was the dauphin; yet his story of events changes in a surprising way between his two letters. In the first, written to the French towns on the day after the assassination, no mention is made of Archambaud de Foix. Charles simply states that John the Fearless tried to draw his sword in an attempt to seize his person. But in the second letter, written to Philip the Good on 15 September, *after the death of Archambaud de Foix* from wounds he received on the bridge, the dauphin introduces him into the story and makes him draw his sword and hence cause the fracas. In neither letter does Charles give any further details of what happened. As a matter of fact, a somewhat sinister silence hangs over the whole event on his side: not a word has survived from any of his attendants and supporters on that day attesting to his version of events. This version is unsupported by other evidence; it was produced by an interested party; and it contains inconsistencies within itself. Moreover, the way in which Archambaud de Foix was introduced as the principal culprit only after his death, inevitably arouses our suspicions as to the veracity of the whole account. I conclude that we cannot attach credence to this story of a spontaneous scuffle or fracas, still less to the dauphin's suggestion of a Burgundian plot against his person.

Those modern historians who have insisted on the innocence of the dauphin Charles, and on the absence of all premeditation, have had to rely largely, for their reconstruction of the tragedy of Montereau, on the chronicler Juvenel des Ursins. There is no reason to believe that his account derives from strictly contemporary material but, even supposing that it does, it can be shown to be riddled with errors. For instance, Juvenel asserts that nobody accused the dauphin of complicity in the murder. Yet the duchess of Burgundy, in her letter of 18 November to the Dijon *maîtres des comptes*, states that the dauphin disloyally and treacherously caused her late husband to be killed. And, as early as 20 September 1419, the magistrates of Mons had been told that Charles gave the signal for the murder, and that some accused him of delivering the first blow. Again, Juvenel claims that the dauphin's chancellor, Robert le Maçon, was on the bridge with him; yet we have the sworn statement of the bishop of Valence, that Robert was in the town of Montereau at the time, and not on the bridge. Juvenel's account verges on absurdity when he makes only four of the dauphin's knights (the rest having withdrawn with the dauphin) overpower seven or eight Burgundians. The fact is that Juvenel wrote his version some time afterwards and that it is a hotchpotch of hearsay and miscellaneous information of no contemporary or original value. It, too, must be disregarded. It is only fair to mention that Juvenel does provide a summary of the Burgundian version of events, as well as elaborating on the dauphin's account. He also claims, rightly in some instances, as will shortly emerge, that it all happened so quickly that even those actually present did not see what occurred.

So far, then, we must conclude that the theory of a sudden mêlée on the bridge, leading to the unplanned and almost inadvertent killing of John the Fearless, is not borne out by contemporary evidence. On the other hand, all the significant contemporary material points to a premeditated crime—the carefully planned conspiracy which has been accepted by the Burgundian scholars d'Arbaumont and Oursel; by the Belgian historian Bonenfant; by Jacob in this country but not, so far as I know, by any French—as opposed to Burgundian—writer.[1]

By far the most important body of evidence for the death of John the Fearless is the group of depositions made soon afterwards by eye-witnesses on the Burgundian side. These may be summarized as follows:

1. *Deposition of John the Fearless's secretary Jehan Seguinat, made on 10 April 1421*

Jehan Seguinat describes how, though he was not one of the ten Burgundian knights chosen to accompany their duke onto the bridge, yet he entered the enclosure with them. Apparently thinking that he was one of the ten, Tanguy du Chastel hurriedly pulled his sleeve to get him in quickly, in order to close the gate behind the duke and his party. According to Seguinat, John the Fearless knelt on one knee before the dauphin, who was on the bridge near the town gate. The dauphin then took his hand and asked him to stand, and at this moment Seguinat saw one of the dauphin's attendants, Jehan Louvet, whisper to him. A moment later Louvet and the dauphin 'made a signal with their eyes' at Tanguy de Chastel, who thereupon struck

[1] For d'Arbaumont and Oursel, see *MCACO* xiv (1901–5), 237–48. See, too, Bonenfant, *Meutre de Montereau*, 15–16 and nn., and Jacob, *Fifteenth century*, 181.

John the Fearless with an axe he was carrying. While the dauphin's people cried Kill! Kill!, a man armed with a sword struck John on the face and badly wounded both his face and the arm he raised to ward off the blow. It was, however, a third blow, delivered by Tanguy with his axe, which caused the duke to fall to the ground.

Seguinat saw Jehan de Vergy, lord of Autrey, and the lord of Noailles rush forward to try to protect their duke but, when the shout of Kill! went up, the Dauphinists seized and overpowered the Burgundian knights in the enclosure—all except Jehan de Neufchastel, who escaped. Seguinat then describes how someone knelt over John the Fearless and plunged a sword into him as he lay on the ground.

2. *Deposition of two members of the household of Archambaud de Foix, lord of Noailles, made at Dijon on 14 September 1419*

They describe how they returned to Montereau on 13 September to find their master dying of a head-wound he had received on the bridge. He told them how John the Fearless met the dauphin on the far side of a barrier fixed across the bridge, near the gate leading from the bridge into the town. According to Archambaud, John was kneeling before the dauphin when Tanguy tried to strike him on the head with his axe. But he, Archambaud, managed to intervene and stop him. When the viscount of Narbonne, also of the dauphin's party, saw this, he lifted his axe threateningly, saying 'If any of you move, you'll die immediately!' While Archambaud grabbed the viscount of Narbonne's axe, the cry Kill! Kill! went up, and Tanguy struck Duke John on the head with an axe. The next thing that happened was that Archambaud himself was struck on the head by Tanguy, and atrociously wounded.

3. *Three other depositions, not dated, but evidently all made at the same time, probably early in 1421*

Guillaume de Vienne, lord of St. Georges and Ste. Croix, describes how the doorway into the enclosure was locked as soon as the Burgundians had entered it, and how John the Fearless doffed his hat and knelt down in the dauphin's presence. When the dauphin took him by the hand and raised him to his feet, they seemed to be talking in a friendly manner. Guillaume, however, was very sick at the time and withdrew to one side to rest. He turned round when he heard the cry Kill! Kill! and noticed a crowd of armed men entering the enclosure on the dauphin's side. He saw nothing of the actual deed.

Antoine de Vergy, lord of Champlitte and Rigney, made a deposition in similar terms and often in the same words, as Guillaume de Vienne. He did not see who struck John the Fearless. He heard the cry Kill! Kill! and saw armed Dauphinists rushing into the enclosure immediately afterwards.

Guy de Pontailler, lord of Talmay, adds some other details in his statement. He noticed that the doorway in the dauphin's side of the enclosure was open, and that Robert de Lairé held John the Fearless from behind by the sleeves of his robe while Tanguy struck him on the head with his axe.

These depositions ring true. They are surely authentic, otherwise the failure of both Guillaume de Vienne and Antoine de Vergy to see the actual crime is inexplicable. After all, the object of these depositions was to ascertain who the culprits were and to establish their guilt. Furthermore, the very variations between these statements, especially the last three, speak for their veracity. Certainly, these three knights did not just 'sign on the dotted line'. But even supposing that the last three depositions are collusive, which they almost certainly are not, the first two represent quite independent traditions, or versions, of what happened, each deriving from a different eye-witness. Taken together, these statements surely amount to conclusive proof of the premeditation of the crime. The following vital points are vouchsafed by at least two of them:

1. The entrance to the enclosure through which John the Fearless and his companions passed was locked behind them as soon as they had entered.
2. There was no argument leading to a scuffle. The first thing de Vergy, who was looking the other way, heard was the cry of Kill!
3. Tanguy du Chastel struck, or tried to strike, John the Fearless on the head with his axe, and this was the first violent move.

By far the most convincing argument for premeditation, as opposed to an unexpected scuffle, is the undisputed fact that, while three of those with John were wounded, and all, except possibly Jehan de Neufchastel, were taken prisoner, on the dauphin's side no one was hurt. This is only explicable if we accept what the eye-witnesses make clear: that the Burgundians were taken completely unawares, and that far more than ten persons entered the enclosure on the dauphin's side. Evidently, John the Fearless's companions were overpowered and disarmed by a carefully organized combination of surprise and superior numbers.

Other evidence shows that these preparations were not limited to what happened within the enclosure. In the anonymous letter written to Philip the Good, the writer describes how he went to Montereau and interviewed various people there. His mission was to discover the names of the culprits so that they could be punished. One of these was a certain Regnaudin le Normand, who had been responsible for constructing the wooden enclosure on the bridge. It was he who had closed the door behind the Burgundians. The writer adds that he and others were 'inside the mill in ambush'. These last words are significant. Evidently, there was a mill on the bridge containing concealed Dauphinist men-at-arms. This is confirmed by the duchess of Burgundy's report to the duchess of Bourbon, in which she states that 'there were men-at-arms and bowmen in the tower which was on the bridge, and they began firing cannon and bombards' immediately after the murder, to ensure that no help came from the direction of the castle for those trapped within the enclosure. A glance at Plate 8 makes it at least possible that the mill and the tower were one and the same building—the structure which is clearly visible, in the drawing made in 1611, between what looks like an islet with houses on it and the entrance to the town. The enclosure, which the eye-witnesses describe as being at the far end of the bridge from the castle, near the town-gate, would have been between this building and the town, so that John and his ten companions would have been effectively cut off from all assistance by troops stationed in it. The crime was not merely premeditated, it was minutely planned.

Although several accounts mention that one of the ten Burgundian knights who had entered the enclosure with John the Fearless, Jehan de Neufchastel, lord of Montagu, escaped and gave the alarm, it seems more likely that the second of the accounts of the murder printed by Kervyn de Lettenhove is correct when it states that in fact Jehan de Neufchastel was left behind—the door was shut so hurriedly behind the Burgundian party that he was left outside. This is borne out by the deposition of Jehan Seguinat, who was inadvertently *included* among the ten by this same hurried closing of the door. In any case, there must certainly have been some Burgundians left immediately outside the entrance to the enclosure after it was closed by the Dauphinists, even if Jehan de Neufchastel was not among them. We also know, from the duchess of Burgundy's letters of 18 November and from her report to the duchess of Bourbon, that a considerable body of Dauphinist troops had been stationed on the far side of the river Seine in the Faubourg St. Nicolas.

Let us try now to envisage the scene outside the enclosure immediately after the murder of John the Fearless. As soon as the alarm was given by the Burgundians on the bridge but not within the enclosure these people, reinforced by those who came rushing out of the castle, desperately tried to rescue their duke and his comrades by breaking through the closed door into the enclosure. But while they were hotly engaged by the Dauphinists who had entered the enclosure in large numbers from the far side, they were subjected to point-blank fire from those concealed in ambush in the building on the bridge. They were also attacked from the rear by the forces just mentioned, who now crossed over the Seine from the Faubourg St. Nicolas. Clearly, the complete success of the conspiracy was due to this careful and strategic disposition of troops, as well as to the detailed arrangements made for the meeting itself. All this explains the helter-skelter flight of John the Fearless's people from Montereau back to Bray-sur-Seine, except for those who sought refuge in the castle. It explains why John's confidential papers were left behind in the castle (though they were destroyed before it surrendered), and why the clerk of the receiver-general of the duchy and county of Burgundy lost his supply of cash, his letters and everything he had with him. Lastly, it explains something which would otherwise be rather puzzling, that is, the capture at Montereau by the Dauphinists of people like Jehan Coq, one of John the Fearless's household servants, who certainly did not enter the enclosure with him.[1]

An analysis of the surviving evidence, then, leads to certain inescapable conclusions. At Montereau, the Dauphinists successfully executed a carefully planned plot to kill John the Fearless. They persuaded him to enter an enclosure which was on their side of the bridge, with only ten companions. They made sure that they could overpower and capture these ten by locking the door behind them and by posting a body of reinforcements at the entrance to the town who could rush into the enclosure on the dauphin's side. Finally, they posted troops in a building on the bridge and on the far side of the river Seine, and these troops succeeded in scattering the remaining Burgundians in precipitate flight, or driving them into the castle. The conspiracy was so carefully contrived that it was only with difficulty, and after some delay, that the Burgundians discovered the fate of their duke, whom they had at first believed to be only a prisoner.

[1] ADN B1920, f. 77. See, too, *IACOB* i. 151.

Who was responsible for this carefully organized conspiracy to kill John the Fearless? Contemporary documents leave little doubt that the dauphin, who later became King Charles VII of France, was one of the murderers, and that several of his closest advisers, notably Jehan Louvet and Tanguy du Chastel, were his accomplices. Suppose John had been murdered more or less inadvertently. In these circumstances, perhaps, Charles VII would have done his best to protect the supposed assassins from opprobrium or punishment. But in what conceivable circumstances can he be imagined heaping them with rewards and favours, unless they were his accomplices in a premeditated crime? Yet this is exactly what he did. Tanguy du Chastel lived happily ever after in the royal service, enjoying a royal pension of 2,000 francs per annum, and Jehan Louvet, who was given a group of castles and lands in Dauphiné on 29 September 1419 by the dauphin, received a royal pension of 3,000 florins per annum for the rest of his life. Could there be anything more sinister, or more revealing, than these annual payments?[1]

In the first volume of his history of Charles VII, du Fresne de Beaucourt included an account of the death of John the Fearless, in which he tried to substantiate the theory of a sudden, spontaneous fracas, unforeseen by all concerned. A year later, in the second volume of this history, du Fresne published as an appendix a group of documents which had come to light since his first volume was written. These documents, contained in a single *vidimus* of 30 July 1426, are statements by Charles VII, Tanguy du Chastel, Jehan Louvet and Jehan de Poitiers, bishop of Valence, attesting to the innocence, in the death of John the Fearless, of Robert le Maçon, who was at that time the dauphin's chancellor. In the last of these documents, Jehan de Poitiers describes how he was present at an interview in Montereau between Charles VII and Robert le Maçon immediately before the meeting on the bridge.[2]

> After the oaths had been made [by the ten knights chosen on either side to enter the enclosure] the king, then regent, being about to leave for the meeting, called the lord of Trèves [Robert le Maçon], and spoke briefly to him on one side, asking him to accompany him. We noticed, from the behaviour of the said lord of Trèves, that he wanted to detain the king and to speak with him more at length and, as it seemed to us, he was contradicting what the king said. Then the king left him abruptly,

---

[1] Du Fresne de Beaucourt, *Hist. de Charles VII*, i. 208 and Mirot, A., *AB* xiv (1942), 197–210, especially 201–3.
[2] Du Fresne de Beaucourt, *Hist. de Charles VII*, ii. 656–7.

and had the said lord of Trèves summoned two or three times to follow him. But he would not go, and remained in the room with us and several others whose names I forget. As soon as the king, then regent, had left, we saw the lord of Trèves flop onto a bed, so we went up to him and asked him what was the matter. He replied in these words:

'Monseigneur of Valence, I wish to God I was in Jerusalem without money or belongings, and that I'd never met this lord here, for I'm very much afraid that he's been wickedly advised and that he'll do something today which will be very damaging both to him and to his kingdom.'

Is not this conclusive proof that the dauphin was party to a preconceived crime? About what else, in the circumstances, could his chancellor have been remonstrating with him? Another of these documents, the letter of Tanguy du Chastel, asserts that Jehan Louvet had wanted to 'take and execute' John the Fearless the second time he came to meet the dauphin in July, at Pouilly-le-Fort, between Melun and Corbeil. Indeed, according to Tanguy, he would have carried out this plan then and there, had he and Robert le Maçon not dissuaded him. Tanguy goes on to say that 'at the time when the council was held about the above-mentioned matter' the said Robert was absent. From the context the conclusion is inescapable, that this council was presided over by the dauphin. Here again, then, we have evidence of his complicity.[1]

On the Burgundian side, scapegoats for the death of John the Fearless were soon found. Two people in particular, both of whom fell into the hands of the Dauphinists at Montereau and thereafter joined the dauphin's party, came in for obloquy. They were accused of treachery and high treason, and have ever since been under suspicion of complicity in the crime. I refer to the lady of Giac and Philippe Jossequin.

Who was the lady of Giac, later reputed to have been the mistress of John the Fearless? Petit suggested Catherine, the wife of a ducal chamberlain, Pierre de Giac, who was related by marriage to the count of Tonnerre, enemy of John the Fearless.[2] But contemporary documents make it plain that the lady of Giac in question, who cer-

---

[1] On this paragraph, see Bonenfant, *Meutre de Montereau*, 15–16 and notes.
[2] Petit, *BSY* xlv (1891), 313. In fact, Pierre de Giac did not marry Catherine until some time after John the Fearless's death. A quittance of 6 April 1419 in ACO B310 mentions 'Jehanne du Peschin, dame de Giac'; see, too, Plancher, iii. 506 for both Jehanne and Pierre, and see letters of 1 December 1418 in ACO B11210. For Jehanne's marriage to Louis, see d'Avout, *Armagnacs et Bourguignons*, 291, n. 33.

tainly was a favourite of John the Fearless and recipient of many generous gifts from him, was Jehanne du Peschin, the mother, not the wife, of Pierre de Giac. Whether she was also the recipient of John's amatory advances seems doubtful, in view of the fact that she must have been at least fifty at the time, having married Louis de Giac in 1376. All accounts agree that Jehanne du Peschin had urged John the Fearless to go to Montereau, assured him of Charles's pacific intentions, and done all she could to achieve a rapprochement between the two. The reason for this behaviour was simple enough: her son Pierre was a chamberlain and knight of John the Fearless, while her brother, Jaques du Peschin, was a councillor of the dauphin. There is no evidence whatsoever that either Jehanne or her son Pierre were traitors. At Montereau, Pierre was one of those with Duke John in the enclosure, and his mother was in the castle. They changed sides after their capture by the Dauphinists because, as the chronicler le Bouvier explained, they feared unpopularity or even persecution among the Burgundians owing to their share in the efforts to bring about a personal meeting between Charles and John. It was this change of sides, immediately after the murder, which led to the rumour that they were accomplices in it.[1]

The case of Philippe Jossequin, *dit* le Musnier, whose father, from Brussels, had been armourer to Philip the Bold, was similar. He, too, was innocent of murder and treason. He had devoted his life to John the Fearless, and was a great favourite of the duke. He had been imprisoned with John by the Turks after the crusade of Nicopolis, and had served him thereafter as *valet de chambre* and keeper of his jewels. Favours were heaped upon him; he was given lucrative offices, gifts of all kinds and, in 1413, money to buy himself a house in Dijon, where he had found a wife in the shape of a daughter of the ducal financial official Estienne de Sens. In 1419, at Montereau, he was given special charge by the duke of the lady of Giac, and this explains why he, too, found himself in the castle there on that fateful day. His reason for remaining behind was, however, different from hers. If we

<hr>

[1] Le Bouvier, *Chron. de Charles VI*, 438, and *Chronique des Cordeliers*, 280. On what follows, concerning Philippe Jossequin, see *Chronique des Cordeliers*, 280; Monstrelet, *Chronique*, iii. 350-1; Simonnet, *Docs. inédits*, 70-1, 70, n. 3, and 74; d'Arbaumont, *Armorial*, 121; Plancher, iii. 330, 374 and 428-9; and Pocquet, *France gouv. par J. sans Peur*, 60-1, no. 3, n. 5. Monetary gifts to him are recorded in the accounts as follows: ACO B1554, f. 71b (200 francs); B1558, f. 94 (300 francs); B1576, f. 122 (1,000 francs); B1588, f. 181 (100 francs); and B1598, f. 165 (600 francs). Jossequin was also given two *sergenteries* in Flanders, ADN B1600, f. 141 and 1602, f. 37b.

may believe the chronicler, his intimate personal relationship with John the Fearless had aroused the envy or hatred of various people at court, including the mother and the son of the dead duke. It was for this reason that Philippe Jossequin found it expedient or politic to remain with the dauphin after the tragedy of Montereau.

Such, then, seems to be all we can now ascertain about the fatal conference on the bridge at Montereau on that September Sunday in 1419. John the Fearless was lured into a trap which had been carefully set for him by the dauphin and his councillors. He was murdered in Charles's presence according to a prearranged plan. The motives for the killing? Partly, private vengeance. Several of those concerned, notably Tanguy du Chastel, had been in the service of Louis of Orleans, and for them the crime of Montereau was revenge for the assassination of their master by John the Fearless in 1407. But partly, it was surely a matter of *raison d'état*. There must have been some who advised the murder of John the Fearless as a way out of the impasse which seemed to have gripped France. Others there may have been in Charles's entourage who feared that, if John were not done away with, he would somehow manage to gain control of the dauphin, and they would lose their influence and power, and possibly even their lives. As to the sixteen-year-old dauphin, it must surely have been fear which induced him to agree to a crime which, in any case, was not particularly out of the ordinary by the standards of those times. After all, everyone in France knew (or thought they knew) how Henry IV had got rid of Richard II.

Conclusion

The word state has been used in this book for want of a better one, not because fifteenth-century polities were similar to twentieth-century ones. No European power in those days was independent in the modern sense; none was homogeneous in any significant way. Nevertheless the polities of fifteenth-century Europe were distinct entities which in most cases comprised something more than the ruler and his family. After all, he needed administrative and representative institutions, revenues, an army and a court, in order to promote the interests of himself and his house.

During all too brief visits to the archives of Lille, Dijon and Brussels I have worked through some of the voluminous governmental records of Duke John the Fearless. From these papers, among them more than fifty signed by the duke himself, I have formed an impression of purpose, of deliberate governmental action. The duke and his advisers seem to have known what they were after; they did not do things inadvertently or by mistake. I do not perceive the 'involuntary and unconscious developments' of some historians. I find, reflected in these documents, policy, order, deliberation, even purpose. For me at any rate, John the Fearless pursued the same aims as his father, which were, broadly speaking, the aims of all the rulers of those days—self-aggrandizement. And, in the case of Burgundy, this self-aggrandizement took the deliberate, purposeful, form of exploitation of the weaknesses of both France and the Empire, in order to further the interests and enhance the power, of Burgundy. In this respect, as in others, John the Fearless followed in his father's footsteps. There is, in fact, an impressive element of continuity and common purpose between the two rulers. Of course, it would be ludicrous to envisage them as founders of anything like a modern state. But they did help to create for themselves, and rule, one of fifteenth-century Europe's most powerful political entities. Burgundy

288 JOHN THE FEARLESS

did not just come together by chance under Philip the Bold; nor was it mere accident which caused its power to increase under John the Fearless.

The sharp distinctions of the map of Europe in the first half of the twentieth century have made it difficult for the historian not to think in terms of France, Germany and the rest, even though these terms will probably soon become as inappropriate as they would be if applied in a political sense to the fifteenth century. The Council of Constance displayed the whole anatomy of fifteenth-century nationalism for what it was worth. To say that John the Fearless was a French prince is only true in the sense that he belonged to the French-speaking area of Europe. Politically, there were no French princes at that time, except the king of France, for the petty rulers on the periphery of royal France, dukes of Brittany, Savoy and Lorraine, all of them minor versions of the duke of Burgundy, were certainly not French in any political sense—they were just princes who spoke French.[1] In the south-west of France the counts of Foix and Armagnac struggled for dominance regardless of the French monarchy, to which they supposedly owed allegiance. Indeed, the fourteenth-century count of Foix, Gaston Fébus, has been credited, and rightly too, with the creation of a more or less independent and homogeneous state for himself along the northern side of the Pyrenees. There ought to be no controversy as to whether John the Fearless was a French or a Low Countries prince. He was both, and yet neither: he was Burgundian.

Yet John the Fearless, because of his violent and tragic rôle in French history, has always been treated as a French prince. In any history of France he finds an inevitable place and, along with him, the murder, the faction and the duplicity with which, in French history, he is associated. Indeed, du Fresne de Beaucourt and other French historians have done better than this for, by insisting that John the Fearless was a French prince, they have been able to condemn him as a traitor, disloyal to the French crown. To clinch the matter, attempts have been made to prove that he was associated in some way with Henry V. These attempts began with the interrogation of the ducal secretary Jehan Seguinat, captured by the Dauphinists at Montereau, and they have been continued in modern times with Calmette's theory of an 'infernal' Anglo-Burgundian pact in 1416–17. But these efforts, and these epithets, are really beside the point. To

[1] See Knowlson, *Jean V et l'Angleterre*, on Brittany, and, for what follows, Tucoo-Chala, *Vicomté de Béarn* and *Gaston Fébus*.

call John a French prince and a traitor may be true in some sense, but it is misleading. It is better to recognize him for what he was: the ruler of a complex of territories and rights which belonged to him and to his house. A ruler whose policies, whose unscrupulous methods, whose tortuous diplomacy, were all aimed at maintaining and if possible increasing his own and his family's power. Whatever he may have been to France, he was a loyal Burgundian.

Bibliography

Full titles of works referred to in the notes

Acta concilii Constanciensis. Ed. H. Finke. 4 vols. Münster, 1896–1928.

Actes concernant les rapports entre les Pays-Bas et la Grande-Bretagne de 1293 à 1468 conservés au château de Mariemont. Ed. P. Bonenfant. *BCRH* cix (1944), 53–125.

Algemene geschiedenis der Nederlanden. Ed. J. A. van Houtte *et al.* 13 vols. Utrecht, 1949–58.

Analectes belgiques, i. Ed. L. P. Gachard. Brussels, 1830.

Analectes historiques. Ed. L. P. Gachard, in seventeen parts, *BCRH* 1856–1872. Full list and references in *BCRH* (3) xiv (1872), 9, n. 1.

Andt, E. *La chambre des comptes de Dijon à l'époque des ducs Valois,* i. Paris, 1924.

Annales Ricardi secundi et Henrici quarti. Ed. H. T. Riley. RS. *Johannis de Trokelowe* . . ., 153–420. London, 1866.

Arbaumont, J. d'. *Armorial de la chambre des comptes de Dijon.* Dijon, 1881.

Aus der Kanzlei Kaiser Sigismunds. Urkundliche Beiträge zur Geschichte des Constanzer Concils. Ed. J. Caro. *AOG* lix (1880), 1–175.

Avout, J. d'. *La querelle des Armagnacs et des Bourguignons.* Paris, 1943.

Barante, A. de. *Histoire des ducs de Bourgogne de la Maison de Valois.* Ed. L. P. Gachard. 2 vols. Brussels, 1838.

Bartier, J. *Légistes et gens de finances au xve siècle. Les conseillers des ducs de Bourgogne.* MARBL l (2). Brussels, 1952.

Basin, T. *Histoire de Charles VII.* Ed. and transl. C. Samaran. Classiques de l'histoire de France au moyen âge. 2 vols. Paris, 1933, 1944.

Bauyn, P. 'Extraits des Mémoires sur l'histoire de Bourgogne.' *BSHF* (1847–8), 219–32 and 242–4.

Baye, N. de. *Journal.* Ed. A. Tuetey. SHF. 2 vols. Paris, 1885, 1888.

Bayot, A. 'Un traité inconnu sur le grand schisme dans la bibliothèque des ducs de Bourgogne.' *RHE* ix (1908), 728–35.

Bazin, J. L. 'La Bourgogne de la mort du duc Philippe le Hardi au traité d'Arras, 1404–35.' *MSHA Beaune* (1897), 51–269. Reprinted separately, Beaune, 1898.

Beauvillé, V. de. *Histoire de la ville de Montdidier.* 2nd edn. 3 vols. Paris, 1857.

Bergé, M. 'Les bâtards de la Maison de Bourgogne.' *IG* lx (1955), 316–408.

Bertin, J. 'Le siège du château de Vellexon en 1409.' *BSASH* (3) xxxi (1900), 1–190. Reprinted separately, Vesoul, 1901.

Bertucat, C. 'La juridiction municipale de Dijon.' *RB* xxi (2) (1911), 87–235.

Bess, B. *Zur Geschichte des Konstanzer Konzils. Studien, i. Frankreichs Kirchenpolitik und der Process des Jean Petit über die Lehre vom Tyrannenmord bis zur Reise König Sigismunds.* Marburg, 1891.

——. 'Die Lehre vom Tyrannenmord auf dem Konstanzer Konzil.' *ZK* xxxvi (1916), 1–61.

Beuken, J. H. A. *De Hanze en Vlaanderen.* Maastricht, 1950.

Bigwood, G. *Le régime juridique et économique du commerce de l'argent dans la Belgique au moyen âge.* MARBL xiv (1). Brussels, 1921.

Billioud, J. *Les États de Bourgogne aux xive et xve siècles.* MAD (5) iv (1922), extra number.

Blommaert, P. 'Inhuldiging van Jan zonder Vrees te Gent in het jaer 1405.' *Belgisch museum*, i (1837), 83–98.

Blondeau, G. 'Essai de transfert du Parlement de Dole à Besançon au xve siècle.' *MSEJ* (11) iv (1926), 185–203.

——. 'Guy Armenier, chef du conseil ducal, président des Parlements des comté et duché de Bourgogne.' *MSED* (10) viii (1938), 56–76 and (10) x (1940–42), 38–66.

Boitel, J. 'Les appels à l'Angleterre des partis français en lutte, 1411–18.' *PTSEC* (1942), 15–20.

Bonenfant, P. *Du meutre de Montereau au traité de Troyes.* MARBL lii. Brussels, 1958.

Bossuat, A. *Perrinet Gressart et François de Surienne.* Paris, 1936.

——. 'Étude sur les emprunts royaux au début du xve siècle. La politique financière du connétable Bernard d'Armagnac, 1416–18.' *RHDFE* (4) xxviii (1950), 351–71.

——. 'Une scandaleuse affaire au xve siècle. Richard de Chancey et la succession d'Hugues Moreau.' *CHCLG* vii (1962), 301–17.

Boüard, M. de. *Les origines des guerres d'Italie. La France et l'Italie au temps du Grand Schisme d'Occident.* BEFAR cxxxix. Paris, 1936.

Bouault, J. 'Les bailliages du duché de Bourgogne aux xive et xve siècles.' *AB* ii (1930), 7–22.

Boutaric, E. 'Rapport sur une mission en Belgique à l'effet de rechercher les documents inédits relatifs à l'histoire de France au moyen âge.' *AMSL* (2) ii (1865), 231–319.

Boutiot, T. *Histoire de la ville de Troyes.* 5 vols. Troyes, 1870–80.

Bowles, E. A. 'Instruments at the court of Burgundy.' *GSJ* vi (1953), 41–51.

Brabantsche Yeesten of Rymkronyk van Braband. Ed. J. F. Willems and J. H. Bormans. CRH. 3 vols. Brussels, 1839–69.

Budt, A. de. *Chronicon Flandriae.* Ed. J. de Smet. CRH. *Corpus chronicorum Flandriae,* i. 259–367. Brussels, 1837.

Buntinx, J. *De audientie van de graven van Vlaanderen.* VKVAL x. Brussels, 1949.

Caillet, L. 'Le traité d'Arras de 1414 d'après un nouveau texte des archives de Lyon.' *MAA* (2) xxxix (1908), 220–35.

——. *Étude sur les relations de la commune de Lyon avec Charles VII et Louis XI, 1417–83. AUL* (2) xxi (1909).

Calendar of the Close Rolls. Henry IV. iii, *1405–9.* London, 1931.

Calendar of letter-books of the City of London. I, 1400–22. Ed. R. R. Sharpe. London, 1909.

Calmet, A. *Histoire de Lorraine.* 6 vols. Nancy, 1745–57.

Calmette, J. 'Contribution à l'histoire des relations de la cour de Bourgogne avec la cour d'Aragon au xve siècle.' *RB* xviii (3–4) (1908), 139–96.

——. *Les grands ducs de Bourgogne.* 2nd edn. Paris, 1956.

——. and E. Déprez. *La France et l'Angleterre en conflit.* G. Glotz, *Histoire générale. Moyen âge,* vii (1). Paris, 1937.

Camp, P. *Histoire d'Auxonne au moyen âge.* Dijon, 1961.

Canat de Chizy, N. 'Étude sur le service des travaux publics, et spécialement sur la charge de maître des œuvres, en Bourgogne.' *BM* lxiii (1898), 245–72, 341–57 and 439–73.

Cartellieri, O. 'Beiträge zur Geschichte der Herzöge von Burgund.' *SHAWP* iii (1912), no. 11 and iv (1913), nos. 2 and 9.

——. *The court of Burgundy.* London, 1929. English transl. of *Am Hofe der Herzöge von Burgund,* 1926.

Cartulaire de l'ancienne Estaple de Bruges. Ed. L. Gilliodts van Severen. 4 vols. Bruges, 1904–6.

Cartulaire de Saint-Pierre de Lille. Ed. E. Hautcœur. 2 vols. Lille, Paris, 1894.

Cartulaire des comtes de Hainaut. Ed. L. Devillers. CRH. 6 vols. Brussels, 1881–96.

Catalogue des actes de Jean de Bavière. Ed. E. Bacha. *Bulletin de la Société d'art et d'histoire du diocèse de Liége,* xii (1900), 31–85.

Celier, L. 'Le meutre du duc Louis d'Orléans dans la chronique du Héraut Berry.' *Mélanges d'histoire du moyen âge dédiés à Louis Halphen,* 119–23. Paris, 1951.

Champion, P. *La vie de Charles d'Orléans, 1394–1465.* Paris, 1908.

——. 'Document inédit sur l'insurrection parisienne de 1413.' *BSHP* xxxvii (1910), 36–9.

——. and P. de Thoisy. *Bourgogne–France–Angleterre au traité de Troyes. Jean de Thoisy, évêque de Tournai.* Paris, 1943.

Chartes de communes et d'affranchissements en Bourgogne. Ed. J. Garnier. 3 vols. Dijon, 1867–77.

Chastellain, G. *Oeuvres.* Ed. Kervyn de Lettenhove. Académie royale de Belgique. 8 vols. Brussels, 1863–6.

Choix de pièces inédites relatives au règne de Charles VI. Ed. L. Douët d'Arcq. SHF. 2 vols. Paris, 1863, 1864.

Chronicon comitum Flandrensium. Ed. J. J. de Smet. CRH. *Corpus chronicorum Flandriae,* i. 34–257. Brussels, 1837.

Chronijk van Maastricht en omstreken. Ed. J. Habets. Publications de la Société d'archéologie dans le duché de Limbourg, i (1) (1864), 70–93.

Chroniken der deutschen Städte. Cöln. 3 vols. Leipzig, 1875–7.

Chronique des Cordeliers. Ed. L. Douët d'Arcq. SHF. E. de Monstrelet, *Chronique,* vi. 191–327. Paris, 1862.

Chronique des Pays-Bas, de France, d'Angleterre et de Tournai. Ed. J. J. de Smet. CRH. *Corpus chronicorum Flandriae,* iii. 115–569. Brussels, 1856.

Chronique du règne de Jean de Bavière, 1387–1423. Ed. S. Balau. CRH. *Chroniques liégeoises,* i. 145–214. Brussels, 1913.

Chronographia regum Francorum. Ed. H. Moranvillé. SHF. 3 vols. Paris, 1891–7.

Clerc, E. *Essai sur l'histoire de la Franche-Comté.* 2nd edn. 2 vols. Besançon, 1870.

Cognasso, F. *Amedeo VIII, 1383–1451.* Collezione storica sabauda. 2 vols. Turin, 1934.

Collas, E. *Valentine de Milan, duchesse d'Orléans.* 2nd edn. Paris, 1911.

Commerce et expéditions militaires de la France et Venise au moyen âge. Ed. L. de Mas Latrie. CDIHF. Mélanges historiques, choix de documents, iii. 1–240. Paris, 1880.

Corps universel diplomatique. Ed. J. Dumont. 8 vols. Amsterdam and the Hague, 1726–31.

Correspondance de la mairie de Dijon. Ed. J. Garnier. 3 vols. Dijon, 1868–70.

Cousinot, G. *Geste des nobles.* Ed. Vallet de Viriville. *Chronique de la Pucelle,* 87–204. Paris, 1864.

Coussemaker, F. de. 'Thierry Gherbode.' *ACFF* xxvi (1901–2), 175–385. Reprinted separately, Lille, 1902.

Coutumes des pays et comté de Flandre. Coutume de la ville de Gand, i. Ed. A. E. Gheldolf. Brussels, 1868.

Coutumes des pays et comté de Flandre. Coutume du Franc de Bruges, ii. Ed. L. Gilliodts van Severen. Brussels, 1879.

Coville, A. *Les Cabochiens et l'Ordonnance de 1413.* Paris, 1888.

——. 'Les vins de Bourgogne au concile de Constance.' *MA* xii (1899), 326–30.

——. *Les premiers Valois et la Guerre de Cent Ans, 1328–1422.* E. Lavisse, *Histoire de France,* iv (1). Paris, 1902.

——. 'Le véritable texte de la justification du duc de Bourgogne par Jean Petit.' *BEC* lxxii (1911), 57–91.

——. *Jean Petit. La question du tyrannicide au commencement du xve siècle.* Paris, 1932.

——. *La vie intellectuelle dans les domaines d'Anjou-Provence de 1380 à 1435.* Paris, 1941.

Crowder, C. M. D. 'Henry V, Sigismund and the council of Constance: a re-examination.' *Historical studies,* iv. Papers read before the fifth conference of Irish historians. London 1962.

Daenell, E. *Die Blütezeit der deutschen Hanse.* 2 vols. Berlin, 1905, 1906.

Daris, J. *Histoire du diocèse et de la principauté de Liége pendant le xve siècle.* Liège, 1887.

David, H. *Du nouveau sur Jean sans Peur.* Cahiers non périodiques du Centre d'Études Bourguignonnes, ix. Dijon, 1959.

Delaville le Roulx, J. 'La domination bourguignonne à Tours et le siège de cette ville, 1417–18.' *CH* xxiii (1877), 161–231.

——. *La France en Orient au xive siècle.* BEFAR xliv and xlv. Paris, 1886.

Demandes faites par le roi Charles VI . . . avec les responses de Pierre Salmon, Les. Ed. G. A. Crapelet. Paris, 1833.

Déniau, J. *La commune de Lyon et la guerre bourguignonne, 1417–35.* Lyon, 1934.

Deschamps de Pas, L. 'Essai sur l'histoire monétaire des comtes de Flandre de la Maison de Bourgogne, ii. Jean sans Peur.' *RN* (n.s.) vi (1861), 211–37 and ibid. (n.s.) xi (1866), 181–94.

Deutsche Reichstagsakten. Ed. J. Weizsäcker *et al.* 16 vols. Munich and Gotha, 1867–1928.

Devic, C. and J. Vaissette. *Histoire générale de Languedoc.* 15 vols. Toulouse, 1872–92.

Dex, J. *Die Metzer Chronik.* Ed. G. Wolfram. Quellen zur lothringischen Geschichte, iv. Metz, 1906.

Dimier, L. 'Les primitifs français, ii.' *GBA* (6) xvi (1936) (2), 205–32.

Dixmude, O. van. *Merkwaerdige gebeurtenissen vooral in Vlaenderen en Brabant van 1377 tot 1443.* Ed. J. J. Lambin. Ypres, 1835.

Documents luxembourgeois à Paris concernant le gouvernement du duc Louis d'Orléans. Ed. A. de Circourt and N. van Werveke. PSHIL xl. 53–148. Luxembourg, 1889.

Documents pour servir à l'histoire de la Maison de Bourgogne en Brabant et en Limbourg. Ed. H. Laurent and F. Quicke. BCRH xcvii (1933), 39–188.

Documents pour servir à l'histoire des relations entre l'Angleterre et la Flandre. Le Cotton MS. Galba B 1. Ed. E. Scott and L. Gilliodts van Severen. CRH. Brussels, 1896.

Dognon, P. 'Les Armagnacs et les Bourguignons ... en Languedoc.' *AM* i (1889), 433–509.

Douët d'Arcq, L. 'Document inédit sur l'assassinat de Louis, duc d'Orléans.' *ABSHF* (1864) (2), 6–26.

Doutrepont, G. *La littérature française à la cour des ducs de Bourgogne.* Bibliothèque du xve siècle, viii. Paris, 1909.

Duchesne, A. *Histoire généalogique de la Maison de Vergy.* Paris, 1625.

Du Fresne de Beaucourt, G. 'Le meutre de Montereau.' *RQH* v (1868), 189–237.

——. *Histoire de Charles VII.* 6 vols. Paris, 1881–91.

Dumas-Dubourg, F. 'À propos de l'atelier royal de Dijon.' *AB* xxxiv (1962), 5–45.

Durrieu, P. 'Jean sans Peur, duc de Bourgogne, lieutenant et procureur général du diable ès parties d'occident.' *ABSHF* xxiv (1887), 193–224.

——. 'MSS. de luxe exécutés pour des princes et des grands seigneurs français, iv, v.' *Le Manuscrit,* ii (1895), 82–7, etc. and 162–8, etc.

——. 'Acte original de la Ligue de Gien.' *MSAF* liv (1895), 167–204.

Durrieu, P. 'Découverte de deux importants manuscrits de la "librairie" des ducs de Bourgogne.' *BEC* lxxi (1910), 58–71.

Dynter, E. de. *Chronique des ducs de Brabant.* Ed. P. de Ram. CRH. 3 vols. Brussels, 1854–7.

Eulogium historiarum sive temporis. Ed. F. S. Haydon. RS. 3 vols. London, 1858–63.

Extraits analytiques des anciens registres des consaux de la ville de Tournai, 1385–1422. Ed. H. Vandenbroek. Tournai, 1861.

Fauquembergue, C. de. *Journal, 1417–35.* Ed. A. Tuetey. SHF. 3 vols. Paris, 1903–15.

Faussemagne, J. *L'apanage ducal de Bourgogne dans ses rapports avec la monarchie française, 1363–1477.* Lyons, 1937.

Fenin, P. de. *Mémoires.* Ed. L. M. E. Dupont. SHF. Paris, 1837.

Finot, J. *La paix d'Arras, 1414–15.* Annales de l'Est et du Nord (1906). Reprinted separately, Nancy, 1906.

———. *Étude historique sur les relations commerciales entre la Flandre et la république de Gênes au moyen âge. ACFF* xxviii (1906–7), xxv–384. Reprinted separately, Paris, 1906.

Foedera, conventiones etc. Ed. T. Rymer. 3rd edn. 10 vols. The Hague, 1739–45.

Fremaux, H. 'Anoblissements et légitimations donnés par les rois de France . . . en Flandre, Artois et Tournaisis, 1315–1525.' *BCHDN* xxviii (1911), 117–54.

Fris, V. 'Het Brugsch Calfvel van 1407–11.' *BAAB* (1911), 183–274.

———. 'Le meutre de Gilles van Brecht, pensionnaire de Gand, en juillet 1414.' *BSHAG* xix (1911), 295–321.

Gachard, L. P. *Rapport . . . sur les archives de Dijon.* Brussels, 1843.

———. *La Bibliothèque nationale à Paris. Notices et extraits des MSS. qui concernent l'histoire de Belgique.* 2 vols. Brussels, 1875, 1877.

———. 'Les archives royales de Düsseldorf. Notice des documents qui concernent l'histoire de Belgique.' *BCRH* (4) ix (1881), 267–366.

Garnier, J. 'Documents relatifs à la surprise de Paris par les Bourguignons en mai 1418.' *BSHP* iv (1877), 47–53.

———. *L'artillerie des ducs de Bourgogne.* Paris, 1895.

Gelder, H. E. van. 'Aantekeningen bij de Vlaamse muntslag, 1384–1434.' *RBN* cvii (1961), 137–56.

Geschiedenis van Vlaanderen. Ed. R. van Roosbroeck *et al.* 6 vols. Amsterdam, 1936–49.

Gesta Henrici quinti regis Anglie. Ed. B. Williams. RHS. London, 1850.

Geste des ducs Philippe et Jehan de Bourgogne, La. Ed. Kervyn de Letten-hove. CRH. *Chroniques relatives à l'histoire de la Belgique sous la domina-tion des ducs de Bourgogne. Textes français*, 259–572. Brussels, 1873.

Handelingen van de Leden en van de Staten van Vlaanderen, 1384–1405. Ed. W. Prevenier. CRH. Brussels, 1959.

Hanserecesse. Die Recesse und andere Akten der Hansetage von 1256–1430. Ed. K. Koppmann. 8 vols. Leipzig, 1870–97.

Hansisches Urkundenbuch. Ed. K. Höhlbaum *et al.* 11 vols. Halle, Leipzig, etc., 1876–1916.

Hanssens, S. 'Oorkonden betreffende het gezantschap van Anton van Bourgondie naar Konstanz, 1415.' *Scrinium lovaniense. Mélanges historiques. Étienne van Cauwenbergh*, 285–94. Université de Louvain. Recueil de travaux d'histoire et de philologie (4), xxiv. Louvain, 1961.

Hautcœur, E. *Histoire de l'église collégiale et du chapitre de Saint-Pierre de Lille.* 3 vols. Lille, Paris, 1896–9.

Heimpel, H. 'Burgund, Macht und Kultur.' *GWU* iv (1953), 257–72.

Héliot, P. and Benoit, A. 'Georges de la Trémoille et la mainmise du duc de Bourgogne sur le Boulonnais.' *RN* xxiv (1938), 29–45 and 182–6.

Héricourt, A. d'. *Les sièges d'Arras.* Arras, 1844.

Heuterus, P. *Rerum burgundicarum libri VI.* The Hague, 1639.

Houtart, M. *Les Tournaisiens et le roi de Bourges.* Annales de la Société historique et archéologique de Tournai (n.s.) xii (1908). Tournai, 1908.

Hövelmann, G. 'Die Anfänge der Beziehungen zwischen Kleve und den Herzögen von Burgund.' *AHVN* clxi (1959), 232–43.

Huguet, A. *Aspects de la Guerre de Cent Ans en Picardie maritime, 1400–50.* Mémoires de la Société des antiquaires de Picardie, xlviii and l. Amiens, 1941, 1944.

Humbert, F. *Les finances municipales de Dijon du milieu du xive siècle à 1477.* Dijon, 1961.

IAB. L. Gilliodts van Severen. *Inventaire des archives de la ville de Bruges, 13e–16e siècle.* 7 vols. Bruges, 1871–8.

IAC. C. Mussely. *Inventaire des archives de la ville de Courtrai.* 2 vols. Courtrai, 1854–8.

IACOB. C. Rossignol *et al. Inventaire sommaire des archives départe-mentales de la Côte-d'Or. Série B.* 6 vols. Paris and Dijon, 1863–94.

IADB. J. Gauthier. *Inventaire sommaire des archives départementales du Doubs. Série B.* 3 vols. Besançon, 1883–95.

IADNB. A. le Glay *et al. Inventaire sommaire des archives départementales du Nord. Série B.* 10 vols. Lille, 1863–1906.

IADNB Rép. num. M. Bruchet. *Archives départementales du Nord. Répertoire numérique. Série B.* 2 vols. Lille, 1921.

IAEB. E. Vanden Busshe. *Inventaire des archives de l'État à Bruges. Section 1ᵉ. Franc de Bruges.* 2 vols. Bruges, 1881, 1884.

IAEG, C. Wyffels. *Inventaris van de oorkonden der graven van Vlaanderen.* Ghent, n.d.

IAGRCC. L. P. Gachard *et al. Inventaire des archives des chambres des comptes.* 6 vols. Brussels, 1837–1931.

IAM. P. J. van Doren. *Inventaire des archives de la ville de Malines.* 8 vols. Malines, 1859–94.

IAY. I. L. A. Diegerick. *Inventaire analytique et chronologique des chartes et documents appartenant aux archives de la ville de Ypres.* 7 vols. Bruges, 1853–68.

Inventaire de la 'librairie' de Philippe le Bon, 1420. Ed. G. Doutrepont. CRH. Brussels, 1906.

Inventaires mobiliers et extraits des comptes des ducs de Bourgogne de la Maison de Valois, 1363–1477. Ed. B. and H. Prost. 2 vols. Paris, 1902–1913.

Itinéraires de Philippe le Hardi et de Jean sans Peur, ducs de Bourgogne. Ed. E. Petit. CDIHF. Paris, 1888.

Jacob, E. F. 'The collapse of France in 1419.' *BJR* xxvi (1942), 307–26.

——. *Henry V and the invasion of France.* London, 1947.

——. *The fifteenth century, 1399–1485.* Oxford, 1961.

Jarry, E. *La vie politique de Louis de France, duc d'Orléans, 1372–1407.* Paris, 1889.

——. 'Un enlèvement d'ambassadeurs au xvᵉ siècle.' *RHD* vi (1892), 173–93.

Journal d'un bourgeois de Paris, 1405–49. Ed. A. Tuetey. Paris, 1881.

Juvenel des Ursins, J. *Histoire de Charles VI.* Ed. J. A. C. Buchon. *Choix de chroniques et mémoires. . . . Anonyme chronique de du Guesclin etc.,* 323–573. Paris, 1875.

Kauch, P. 'L'organisation et le contrôle financier de l'hôtel d'Antoine de Bourgogne, duc de Brabant.' *RBPH* xxiv (1945), 180–201.

Kervyn de Lettenhove. *Histoire de Flandre.* 6 vols. Brussels, 1847–50.

——. 'Relation inédite de la mort de Jean sans Peur.' *BCRH* (3) viii (1866), 91–6.

——. 'Une nouvelle relation inédite de la mort de Jean sans Peur à Montereau.' *BCRH* (4) i (1873), 197–202.

Kirby, J. L. 'Calais sous les Anglais, 1399–1413.' *RN* xxxvii (1955), 19–30.

Kleinclausz, A. 'Les peintres des ducs de Bourgogne.' *RAAM* xx (1906), 161–76 and 253–68.

——. *Histoire de Bourgogne*. Paris, 1909.

Knowlson, G. A. *Jean V, duc de Bretagne, et l'Angleterre, 1399–1442*. Archives historiques de Bretagne, ii. Cambridge and Rennes, 1964.

Kuhnast, G. *La guerre de course en Flandres, Artois et Picardie maritime*. Unpublished thesis, University of Lille, 1956.

Kurth, G. *La cité de Liège au moyen âge*. 3 vols. Brussels, 1910.

Laborde, L. de. *Les ducs de Bourgogne*. 3 vols. Paris, 1849–52.

La Chauvelays, J. de. *Les armées des trois premiers ducs de Bourgogne de la Maison de Valois*. *MAD* (3) vi (1880), 19–335.

Laenen, J. *Les archives de l'État à Vienne au point de vue de l'histoire de Belgique*. Brussels, 1924.

Lallemand, A. *La lutte des États de Liège contre la Maison de Bourgogne, 1390–1492*. Brussels, n.d.

La Marche, O. de. *Mémoires*. Ed. H. Beaune and J. d'Arbaumont. SHF. 4 vols. Paris, 1883–8.

Lameere, E. *Le grand conseil des ducs de Bourgogne de la Maison de Valois*. Brussels, 1900.

Lannoy, B. de. *Hugues de Lannoy*. Brussels, 1957.

Lannoy, G. de. *Oeuvres*. Ed. C. Potvin. Louvain, 1878.

La Roncière, C. de. 'La domination française à Pise, 1404–06.' *MAH* xv (1895), 231–44.

——. *Histoire de la marine française*. 6 vols. Paris, 1899–1932.

Le Bouvier, G., dit le Héraut Berry. *Chronique du règne de Charles VI*. Ed. D. Godefroy. *Histoire de Charles VI*, 411–44. Paris, 1653.

Lecoy de la Marche, A. *Le roi René*. 2 vols. Paris, 1875.

Le Févre, J., lord of St. Rémy. *Chronique*. Ed. F. Morand. SHF. 2 vols. Paris, 1876, 1881.

Leguai, A. *Les ducs de Bourbon pendant la crise monarchique du xvᵉ siècle*. Paris, 1962.

Leroquais, V. *Un Livre d'Heures de Jean sans Peur*. Paris, 1939.

Le Roux de Lincy. *Chants historiques et populaires du temps de Charles VII et de Louis XI*. Paris, 1857.

——. and L. M. Tisserand. *Paris et ses historiens au xivᵉ et au xvᵉ siècle*. Paris, 1867.

Lettres closes de Charles VI conservées aux archives de Reims et de Tournai. Ed. L. Mirot. *MA* xxix (1918), 309–38 and xxx (1919), 1–44. Reprinted separately, Paris, n.d.

300 BIBLIOGRAPHY

Lettres de rois . . . et autres personnages. . . . Ed. J. Champollion-Figeac. CDIHF. 2 vols. Paris, 1839, 1847.

Leuschner, J. 'Zur Wahlpolitik im Jahre 1410.' *DAEM* xi (1955), 506–53.

Lichtervelde, P. de. *Un grand commis des ducs de Bourgogne, Jacques de Lichtervelde.* Brussels, 1943.

Livre des trahisons de France, Le. Ed. Kervyn de Lettenhove. CRH. *Chroniques relatives à l'histoire de la Belgique sous la domination des ducs de Bourgogne. Textes français,* 1–258. Brussels, 1873.

Lobry, M. R. 'Les relations entre la cour de Bourgogne et les milieux d'affaires parisiens sous Jean sans Peur.' Unpublished thesis, University of Lille, 1958.

Longnon, A. 'Entrée de la reine Isabeau et du duc de Bourgogne à Paris, 14 juillet 1418.' *BSHP* ii (1875), 104–9.

Marc, J. 'L'avènement du chancelier Rolin, décembre, 1422.' *MSBGH* xxi (1905), 323–78.

Mémoires pour servir à l'histoire de France et de Bourgogne. 2 parts. Paris, 1729.

Memorieboek der stad Ghent. Ed. P. J. van der Meersch. Maetschappy der Vlaemsche bibliophilen (2) xv. 4 vols. Ghent, 1852–64.

Merlet, L. 'Biographie de Jean de Montagu, 1350–1409.' *BEC* xiii (1852), 248–84.

Michelant, M. 'Inventaire des joyaux etc. de Charles Quint.' *BCRH* (3) xiii (1872), 199–368.

Minder, A. 'La rivalité Orléans–Bourgogne dans la principauté de Liège et l'assassinat du duc d'Orléans par ordre de Jean sans Peur.' *BSVAH* xli (1954), 121–90.

Mirot, A. 'Charles VII et ses conseillers assassins présumés de Jean sans Peur.' *AB* xiv (1942), 197–210.

Mirot, L. 'Raoul d'Anquetonville et le prix de l'assassinat du duc d'Orléans.' *BEC* lxxii (1911), 445–58.

——. 'Les préliminaires de la prise d'armes de 1411.' *Mélanges d'histoire offerts à M. Charles Bémont.* Paris, 1913.

——. *Les d'Orgemont.* Bibliothèque du xvᵉ siècle, xviii. Paris, 1913.

——. 'Autour de la paix d'Arras, 1414–15.' *BEC* lxxv (1914), 253–327.

——. 'L'enlèvement du dauphin et le premier conflit entre Jean sans Peur et Louis d'Orléans, juillet-octobre, 1405.' *RQH* xcv (1914), 329–55 and xcvi (1914), 47–68 and 369–419.

——. 'Études lucquoises, iii. La Société des Raponde. Dino Raponde.' *BEC* lxxxix (1928), 299–389. Reprinted in *Études lucquoises.* Nogent-le-Rotrou, 1930.

Mirot, L. 'Autour de la paix de Chartres, 9 mars 1409.' *AB* iii (1931), 305–42.

——. 'Un conflit diplomatique au xvᵉ siècle. L'arrestation des ambassadeurs florentins en France, 1406–08.' *BEC* xcv (1934), 74–115.

——. 'Jean sans Peur de 1398 à 1405, d'après les comptes de sa chambre aux deniers.' *ABSHF* (1938), 129–245. Reprinted separately, Paris, 1939.

——. 'Le licenciement des serviteurs de Philippe le Hardi, juin 1404.' *AB* xi (1939), 132–5.

——. 'Le Livre d'Heures de Jean sans Peur.' *BEC* ci (1940), 225–9.

——. 'L'État bourguignon-flamand au xvᵉ siècle.' *JS* (1942), 66–81.

Mollat, M. 'Recherches sur les finances des ducs Valois de Bourgogne.' *RH* ccxix (1958), 285–321.

Monget, C. *La Chartreuse de Dijon*. 3 vols. Montreuil-sur-Mer and Tournai, 1898–1905.

——. and J. d'Arbaumont *et al.* 'Les restes des ducs et princesses de Bourgogne à Saint-Bénigne de Dijon.' *MCACO* xiv (1901–05), 157–251.

Monstrelet, E. de. *Chronique*. Ed. L. Douët d'Arcq. SHF. 6 vols. Paris, 1857–62.

Morosini, A. *Chronique. Extraits relatifs à l'histoire de France*. Ed. G. Lefèvre-Pontalis and L. Dorez. SHF. 4 vols. Paris, 1898–9.

Newhall, R. A. *The English conquest of Normandy, 1416–24*. Newhaven, 1924.

Nieuwenhuysen, A. van. *La recette générale de Philippe le Hardi*. Unpublished thesis, University of Brussels, 1955.

Nordberg, M. *Les ducs et la royauté*. Studia historica upsaliensia, xii. Uppsala, 1964.

Ordonnance Cabochienne, L'. Ed. A Coville. Paris, 1891.

Ordonnances des ducs de Bourgogne sur l'administration de la justice du duché. Ed. E. Champeaux. *RB* xvii (2, 3) (1907).

Ordonnances des rois de France de la troisième race. Ed. D. F. Secousse *et al.* 21 vols. Paris, 1723–1849.

Ordonnances franc-comtoises sur l'administration de la justice, 1343–1477. Ed. E. Champeaux. *RB* xxii (1, 2) (1912).

Otterbourne, T. *Chronica regum Angliae*. Ed. T. Hearne. Oxford, 1732.

Owen, L. V. D. *The connection between England and Burgundy during the first half of the fifteenth century*. Oxford, 1909.

——. 'England and the Low Countries.' *EHR* xxviii (1913), 13–33.

Panofsky, E. *Early Netherlandish painting*. Cambridge, Mass., 1953.

Parisot, R. *Histoire de Lorraine*. 3 vols. Paris, 1919–24.

Perrault-Dabot, A. *L'hôtel de Bourgogne et la tour de Jean sans Peur à Paris*. Paris, 1902.

Petit cartulaire de Gand. Ed. F. de Potter. Ghent, 1885.

Petit, E. 'Le Tonnerrois sous Charles VI et la Bourgogne sous Jean sans Peur.' *BSY* xlv (1891), 247–315. Reprinted separately, Auxerre, 1892.

——. *Ducs de Bourgogne de la Maison de Valois, i. Philippe le Hardi, i. 1363–1380*. Paris, 1909.

Piquard, M. 'Étude sur la situation politique des archevêques de Besançon de 1290 à 1435.' *PTSEC* (1929), 193–200.

——. 'Thiébaud de Rougement, archevêque de Besançon, 1405–29.' *MSED* (10) i (1931), 86–101.

Pirenne, H. *Histoire de Belgique*, ii. 4th edn. Brussels, 1947.

Pisan, C. de. *The 'Livre de la paix'*. Ed. C. C. Willard. The Hague, 1958.

Placcaerten van Vlaanderen. Ordonnancien, statuten, edicten ende placcaerten ... van Vlaendren. 3 books. Ghent, 1639.

Plancher, U. *Histoire générale et particulière de Bourgogne*. 4 vols. Dijon, 1739–81.

Pocquet du Haut-Jussé, B.A. 'Deux féodaux: Bourgogne et Bretagne, 1363–1491, iii, iv. Jean sans Peur et Jean V, 1404–19.' *RCC* xxxvi (1) (1934–5), 53–67 and 164–71. Reprinted separately, Paris, 1935.

——. 'Le compte de Pierre Gorremont, receveur général du royaume, 1418–20.' *BEC* xcviii (1937), 66–98 and 234–82.

——. 'Les chefs des finances ducales de Bourgogne.' *MSHDB* iv (1937), 5–77.

——. 'Les dons du roi aux ducs de Bourgogne Philippe le Hardi et Jean sans Peur, 1363–1419.' 'Le don des aides.' *AB* x (1938), 261–89. 'Les dons ordinaires.' *MSHDB* vi (1939), 113–44. 'Les dons extraordinaires.' *MSHDB* vii (1940–1), 95–129.

——. 'Jean sans Peur. Son but et sa méthode.' *AB* xiv (1942), 181–96.

——. 'Les pensionnaires fieffés des ducs de Bourgogne de 1352 à 1419.' *MSHDB* viii (1942), 127–50.

——. 'Jean sans Peur. Programme, moyens et résultats.' *RUB* vii (1954–1955), 385–404.

——. *La France gouvernée par Jean sans Peur*. Mémoires et documents publiés par la Société de l'École des chartes, xiii. Paris, 1959.

——. 'La renaissance littéraire autour de Henri V, roi d'Angleterre.' *RH* cciv (1960), 329–38.

Pot, J. *Histoire de Regnier Pot*. Paris, 1929.

Potvin, C. 'Hugues de Lannoy, 1384–1456.' *BCRH* (4) vi (1879), 117–38.

Précis analytique des documents que renferme le dépôt des archives de la Flandre-Occidentale à Bruges. Ed. O. Delepierre and F. Priem. 1ʳᵉ série, 3 vols. Bruges, 1840–2. 2ᵉ série 9 vols. Bruges, 1845–58.

Prevenier, W. *De Leden en de Staten van Vlaanderen, 1384–1405*. VKVAL, xliii. Brussels, 1961.

Prims, F. *Geschiedenis van Antwerpen*. 11 vols. Brussels and Antwerp, 1927–49.

Proceedings and Ordinances of the Privy Council of England. Ed. H. Nicholas. 7 vols. London, 1834–7.

Procesos de las antiguas cortes y parlamentos de Cataluña, Aragon y Valencia. Ed. P. de Bofarull y Mascaró. Coleccion de documentos inéditos del archivo general de la corona de Aragon, i–viii. Barcelona, 1847–51.

Proost, G. *De financiele hoofdambtenaren van de Burgondische hertogen voor de regering van Karel de Stoute*. Unpublished thesis, University of Ghent, 1959.

Prost, B. 'Quelques acquisitions de manuscrits par les ducs de Bourgogne Philippe le Hardi et Jean sans Peur.' *AHAL* ii (1890–1), 337–53.

Quelques pièces relatives à Louis I, duc d'Orléans. Ed. F. M. Graves. Bibliothèque du xvᵉ siècle, xix. Paris, 1913.

Quelques textes pour servir à l'histoire politique des Parisiens au xvᵉ siècle. Ed. P. Viollet, *MSHP* iv (1877), 155–82.

Quicke, F. 'Rectifications et compléments à l'itinéraire d'Antoine de Bourgogne.' *Mélanges d'histoire offerts à Henri Pirenne*, 391–409. Brussels, 1926.

——. 'Les relations diplomatiques entre le roi des Romains Sigismond et la Maison de Bourgogne, fin 1416–début 1417.' *BCRH* xc (1926), 193–241.

——. 'L'intérêt, du point de vue de l'histoire politique, économique et financière du troisième compte des expéditions militaires d'Antoine de Bourgogne . . . dans le duché de Luxembourg, 1413–14.' *PSHIL* lxiv (1930), 317–468.

Raymond, P. 'Enquête du prévôt de Paris sur l'assassinat de Louis, duc d'Orléans, 1407.' *BEC* xxvi (1865), 215–49.

Recueil de diverses pièces servant à l'histoire du roy Charles VI. Ed. G. Besse. Paris, 1660.

Regesta chronologico-diplomatica Ruperti regis Romanorum. Ed. J. Chmel. Frankfurt, 1834.

Régestes de la cité de Liège. Ed. E. Fairon. 4 vols. Liège, 1933–40.

Religieux de St. Denys. *Chronique.* Ed. L. Bellaguet. CDIHF. 6 vols. Paris, 1839–52.

Renoz, P. *La chancellerie de Brabant sous Philippe le Bon, 1430–67.* CRH. Brussels, 1955.

Richard, J. 'Le gouverneur de Bourgogne au temps des ducs Valois.' *MSHDB* xix (1957), 101–12.

——. 'Trois lettres concernant l'occupation de Mâcon par les Bourguignons, 1417.' *AB* xxxiii (1961), 88–98.

Richter, F. 'Der Luxemburger Erbfolgestreit in den Jahren 1438–43.' *WZ* Extra vol. v (1889), 1–73.

Rössler, H. 'Habsburgs burgundisches Erbe.' *OW* v (1958), 113–51.

Royal and historical letters during the reign of Henry IV, i. Ed. F. C. Hingeston. RS. London, 1860.

Roye, G. de. *Chronique, 1415–30.* Ed. Kervyn de Lettenhove. CRH. *Chroniques relatives à l'histoire de la Belgique sous la domination des ducs de Bourgogne. Textes latines*, 167–210. Brussels, 1870.

Schneider, F. *Herzog Johann von Baiern. Erwählter Bischof von Lüttich und Graf von Holland, 1373–1425. Historische Studien*, civ. Berlin, 1913.

Schoenstedt, F. *Der Tyrannenmord im Spätmittelalter. Neue deutsche Forschungen*, cxcviii (1938).

——. 'König Siegmund und die Westmächte, 1414–15.' *WG* xiv (1954), 149–64.

Schoorman, R. 'Notice biographique concernant Jean de la Kethulle, 1351–1433.' *ASHAG* xii (1913), 109–74.

Schoos, J. *Der Machtkampf zwischen Burgund und Orleans.* PSHIL lxxv. Luxembourg, 1956.

Sellier, C. *Le quartier Barbette.* Paris, 1899.

Seur, J. de. *La Flandre illustrée par l'institution de la chambre du roi à Lille.* Lille, 1713.

Simonnet, J. *Documents inédits pour servir à l'histoire des institutions et de la vie privée en Bourgogne.* Dijon, 1867.

Slecht, R. *Die Forsetzung der Flores Temporum.* Ed. R. Fester. *Zeitschrift für die Geschichte des Oberrheins*, ix (1894), 79–145.

Stasino, N. *Bijdrage tot de kennis van de Standenvertegenwoordiging in Vlaanderen en van haar verhouding tot de vorst, 1410–27.* Unpublished thesis, University of Ghent, 1957.

Stavelot, J. de. *Chronique.* Ed. A. Borgnet. CRH. Brussels, 1861.

Stein, F. A. H. *Inventaire analytique des ordonnances enregistrées au Parlement de Paris.* Paris, 1908.

Steinbach, F. 'Gibt es einen lotharingischen Raum?' *RV* ix (1939), 52–66.

Stouff, L. *Catherine de Bourgogne et la féodalité de l'Alsace autrichienne.* *RB* xxiii (2, 3, 4) (1913). Reprinted separately, Paris, 1913.

Swygenhoven, C. van. 'Quelques considérations sur les ossements et particulièrement sur le crâne de Jean sans Peur.' *BARB* x (2) (1843), 229–39.

Tardif, J. Ed. *Monuments historiques. Inventaires et documents publiés par ordre de l'Empereur.* Paris, 1866.

Thomas, P. 'Le texte authentique de la paix d'Arras, 4 septembre 1414.' *RN* v (1914–19), 193–215.

——. 'Lettres de Thierry Gherbode.' *RH* cxviii (1915), 305–14.

Tits-Dieuaide, M. J. 'Une lettre de Jean sans Peur relative à ses visées sur Pise.' *BIHBR* xxx (1957), 97–112.

Tourneur, M. 'Antoine de Bourgogne, duc de Brabant, la papauté, et Liège, lors du schisme de Thierry de Perwez.' *BIHBR* xxvii (1952), 293–316.

Tucoo-Chala, P. *Gaston Fébus et la vicomté de Béarn.* Bordeaux, 1959.

——. *La vicomté de Béarn et le problème de sa souveraineté.* Bordeaux, 1961.

Urkunden Kaiser Sigmunds, 1410–37, Die. Ed. W. Altmann. *Regesta imperii*, xi. 2 vols. Innsbruck, 1896–1900.

Uyttebrouck, A. 'Les origines du Conseil de Brabant. La chambre du conseil du duc Jean IV.' *RBPH* xxxvi (1958), 1135–72.

Valat, G. 'Nicolas Rolin, chancelier de Bourgogne'. *MSE* (n.s.) xl (1912), 73–145; xli (1913), 1–73; and xlii (1914), 53–148.

Valois, N. *Le conseil du roi au xiv*ᵉ, *xv*ᵉ, *et xvi*ᵉ *siècles.* Paris, 1888.

——. *La France et le Grand Schisme d'Occident.* 4 vols. Paris, 1896–1902.

Van der Meersch, D. J. ''s Graven raedkamer van Vlaenderen.' *Belgisch museum*, ii (1838), 31–47 and 267–304.

Varenbergh, E. *Histoire des relations diplomatiques entre le comté de Flandre et l'Angleterre au moyen âge.* Brussels, 1874. Reprinted from *Messager des sciences historiques* (1869–73).

Vaughan, R. *Philip the Bold.* London, 1962.

Verbruggen, J. F. 'Un plan de bataille du duc de Bourgogne (14 septembre 1417) et la tactique de l'époque.' *RIHM* xx (1959), 443–51.

*Verzameling van XXIV origineele charters, priviligien en keuren van de provincie van Vlaenderen van de xiii*ᵉ, *xiv*ᵉ *en xvi*ᵉ *eeuw.* Ghent, 1787–88.

Vidler, L. A. *A new history of Rye.* Hove, 1934.

Vielliard, J. 'Les journées parisiennes de mai-juin 1418 d'après des documents des Archives de la Couronne d'Aragon.' *ABSHF* (1940), 124–53.

——. and L. Mirot. 'Inventaire des lettres des rois d'Aragon à Charles VI et à la cour de France conservées aux Archives de la Couronne d'Aragon à Barcelone.' *BEC* ciii (1942), 99–150.

Vignier, F. 'Jehan de Foissy, bailli de la Montagne, 1337–1411.' *MSHDB* xix (1957), 111–21.

Voigt, J. *Geschichte Preussens.* 9 vols. Königsberg, 1827–39.

Wackernagel, R. *Geschichte der Stadt Basel.* 3 vols. Basel, 1907–24.

Werveke, N. van. *Die Erwerbung des Luxemburger Landes durch Anton von Burgund 1409–15.* Athénée royal grand-ducal à Luxembourg. Programme, 1889–90. Luxembourg, 1890. Reprinted separately, Luxembourg, 1891.

Wille, E. *Die Schlacht von Othée.* Berlin, 1908.

Wylie, J. H. *History of England under Henry IV.* 4 vols. London, 1884–98.

——. and W. T. Waugh. *The reign of Henry V.* 3 vols. Cambridge, 1914–1929.

Wymans, G. 'La conclusion du contrat de mariage d'Antoine, duc de Brabant, et d'Élisabeth de Görlitz.' *ASRAB* i (1956–61), 297–303.

Zuylen van Nyevelt, A. van. 'Cés de loi du Franc de Bruges au xvᵉ siècle. Refus de rendre la justice par le magistrat.' *ASEB* lxvi (1923), 114–46.

——. *Épisodes de la vie des ducs de Bourgogne à Bruges.* Bruges, 1937.

Index